SYNTAX-SEMANTICS INTERFACE

EVA **HAJIČOVÁ**

KAROLINUM PRESS
PRAGUE 2017

KAROLINUM PRESS
Karolinum Press is a publishing department of Charles University
Ovocný trh 560/5, 116 36 Prague 1, Czech Republic
www.karolinum.cz
© Karolinum Press, 2017
© Eva Hajičová, 2017
Layout by Jan Šerých
Set and printed in the Czech Republic by Karolinum Press
First English edition

A catalogue record for this book is available from the National Library of the Czech Republic.

Reviewed by Prof. Libuše Dušková, Charles University, Faculty of Arts, Department
of English Language and ELT Methodology, and Prof. František Čermák,
Charles University, Faculty of Arts, Institute of the Czech National Corpus.

ISBN 978-80-246-3714-3
ISBN 978-80-246-3739-6 (pdf)

CONTENTS

To my teachers, who have shaped my way to understanding language structure. And to my past and present colleagues from ÚFAL, who have friendly accompanied me and supported me on this way.

FOREWORD

The present volume is a selected collection of papers published during my professional career. The theoretical framework I subscribe to is the Functionl Generative Description (FGD) as proposed by Petr Sgall in the early sixties and developed further by him and his pupils since then. This framework was conceived of as an alternative to the original Chomskyan transformational generative grammar and in a way can be characterized as an predecessor of those alternative frameworks that take into account semantics and start the generative process from that level. The FGD is deeply rooted in the structural and functional tenets of the Prague School Linguistics in its conception of language description proceeding from function to form, which is reflected in a multilevel design of the framework, in a duly respect paid to the communicative function of language and in the recognition of the distinction between (linguistic) meaning and (extralinguistic) content.

Thematically, the present volume covers issues ranging from the verb-argument structure of the sentence and its information structure through the capturing of the underlying structure in an annotated corpus to issue going beyond the sentence structure, adding finally some contributions comparing the point of departure of the treatment proposed in our papers with other approaches. In a way, the structure of the volume (except for the last Part) follows the development of my research interests in time: starting, in the late sixties and early seventies, with the core of the underlying sentence structure (Part 1 of this volume) my attention was then focused on those aspects of language that are not covered by the underlying predicate-argument core but still belong to it as they are semantically relevant, namely the topic-focus articulation (information structure of the sentence) and related issues such as negation and presupposition (Part 2). The possibility to validate the consistence of the theoretical findings on large language material offered by the technical availability of large electronic (computerized) corpora of texts have quite naturally led to my participation at the process of the design of a scheme of corpus annotation which would cover the issues studied and thus serve as a good test-bed for the formulated theory (Part 3). The transition from these aspects to phenomena beyond the sentence boundary was then quite natural (Part 4). Papers included in Part 5 compare our approach to the information structure of the sentence with the treatments within some other linguistic theories such as Chomskyan transformational grammar, the so-called optimality theory and Meľchuk's Meaning-Text model.

Each Part of the volume is accompanied by a Foreword briefly outlining the main issues under discussion and putting them into the overall context of investigations.

In the present volume, only papers where I was the only author are included, with the exception of two papers in the Appendix. One of them, co-authored by Jarmila Panevová, documents the very start of the use of "machines" in linguistic analysis, the core of the other one, co-authored by Petr Sgall, lies in the formulation of the formal background of the theoretical framework of FGD.

In order to make each selected paper a self-contained whole and to make it possible for the reader to follow the original argumentation, I could not avoid a reduplication of the general introductions or summarizations of the starting points in two or more papers. If I have decided to leave out a part of the text, I mark the deletions by brackets [...] and in some cases, I add a note indicating what is left out. In principle, however, the texts are left as they were in their original form, only evident misprints have been corrected.

A major adaptation concerns bibliographical references. In the original versions of the papers included in this volume, different ways of bibliographical reference were used: some were included in the texts themselves, some in the footnotes, in some of them there were separate lists of references at the end of the paper. I have decided to collect the references in a single list of Bibliography, which has allowed me to unify the references throughout the volume in the way described in the introductory note attached to the Bibliography.

My most sincere thanks go to Anna Kotěšovcová for her devoted and time-consuming technical work connected with the preparation of the electronic versions of the papers, which in case of earlier contributions involved laborious scanning and transmission to an electronic form. I am also most grateful to Barbora Hladká, who has helped me by the formatting of the Bibliography, by carrying out the visualizations in Part 4 of the volume and also by commenting upon the Introductory sections.

BIBLIOGRAPHICAL NOTES

The studies included in this volume are reprinted from the following original sources:

1. UNDERLYING SYNTACTIC STRUCTURE

E. Hajičová (1979). "Agentive or Actor-Bearer?" *Theoretical Linguistics* 6: 173–190.

——. (1983). "Remarks on the Meaning of Cases." *Prague Studies in Mathematical Linguistics* 8: 149–157.

2. TOPIC-FOCUS ARTICULATION AND RELATED ISSUES

E. Hajičová (2012). "Vilém Mathesius and Functional Sentence Perspective and Beyond." In *A Centenary of English Studies at Charles University: From Mathesius to Present-Day Linguistics*, edited by M. Malá and P. Šaldová, 1–10. Prague: Filozofická fakulta UK v Praze.

——. (1973). "Negation and Topic vs. Comment." *Philologica Pragensia* 16: 81–93.

——. (1983/1984). "On Presupposition and Allegation." In *Contributions to Functional Syntax, Semantics and Language Comprehension*, edited by Petr Sgall, 99–122. Prague: Academia; Amsterdam: J. Benjamins, 1984. A revised and modified version of two papers: "Presupposition and Allegation Revisited." *Journal of Pragmatics* 8 (1984): 155–167, and "Presuppositions of Questions," in *Questions and Answers*, edited by F. Kiefer, 85–96. Dordrecht: D. Reidel, 1983.

——. (1998). "Questions on Sentence Prosody Linguists Have Always Wanted to Ask." *Prague Bulletin of Mathematical Linguistics* 70: 25–36.

——. (1995). "Surface and Underlying Word Order." In *Travaux de Cercle Linguistique de Prague, N.S.* 1, Amsterdam: John Benjamins, 113–124.

——. (1998). "The Ordering of Valency Slots from a Communicative Point of View." In *Productivity and Creativity*, edited by Mark Janse, 83–91, Berlin – New York: De Gruyter.

——. (2000). "How Many Topics / Foci?" In *Linguistics and Language Studies Exploring Language from Different Perspectives*, edited by I. Kovačič et al., 9–19. Ljubljana: Filosofska fakulteta Univerze v Ljubljani.

——. (2010). "Rhematizers Revisited." *Philologica Pragensia* 20 (2): 57–70.

3. THEORETICAL DESCRIPTION REFLECTED
IN CORPUS ANNOTATION

E. Hajičová (2002). "Theoretical Description of Language as a Basis of Corpus Annotation: The Case of Prague Dependency Treebank." In *Travaux de Cercle Linguistique de Prague, N.S.* 4, 111–127. Amsterdam: John Benjamins.

——. (2012). "What We Have Learned from Complex Annotation of Topic-Focus Articulation in a Large Czech Corpus." *Echo des études romanes* 8 (1): 51–64.

4. BEYOND THE SENTENCE BOUNDARY

E. Hajičová (1987). "Focussing – A Meeting Point of Linguistics and Artificial Intelligence." In *Artificial Intelligence II – Methodology, Systems, Application,* edited by P. Jorrand, and V. Sgurev, 311–322. Amsterdam: North Holland.

——. (2013). "Contextual Boundness and Discourse Patterns Revisited." *Discourse Studies* 15 (5): 535–550.

5. COMPARISON WITH OTHER APPROACHES

E. Hajičová (1972). "Aktuální členění větné a nejnovější vývoj transformační gramatiky" [Functional sentence perspective and the latest developments in transformational grammar]. *Slovo a slovesnost* 33: 229–239.

——. (1986). "A Note on the Order of Constituents in Relation to the Principles of GB Theory." In *Language and Discourse: Test and Protest,* edited by J. L. Mey, 313–323. Amsterdam: J. Benjamins.

——. (2001). "Possibilities and Limits of Optimality Theory in Topic-Focus Articulation." In *Current Issues in Formal Slavic Linguistics,* edited by G. Zybatow, U. Junghanns, G. Mehlhorn, L. Szucsich, 385–394. Frankfurt am Main: Peter Lang.

——. (2007). "The Position of TFA (Information Structure) in a Dependency Based Description of Language." In *Meaning – Text Theory. Wiener Slawistisches Almanach* 69, edited by K. Gerdes, T. Reuther, L. Wanner, 159–178. Munich – Vienna.

APPENDIX: A GLIMPSE BACK AT HISTORICAL SOURCES

Eva Hajičová, and Jarmila Panevová (1968). "Some Experience with the Use of Punched-Card Machines for Linguistic Analysis." In *Les machines dans la linguistique. Colloque international sur la mécanisation et l'automation des recherches linguistiques (Prague, June 7–10, 1966),* 109–115. Prague: Academia.

Eva Hajičová, and Petr Sgall (1970/1973). "A Functional Generative Description (Backgound and Framework)" (abbreviated). In *The Prague Bulletin of Mathematical Linguistics* 14 (1970): 3–38; reprinted in *Functional Generative Grammar in Prague,* edited by W. Klein, and A. von Stechow, 1–52. Kronberg – Taunus: Scriptor Verlag GmbH, 1973.

1. UNDERLYING SYNTACTIC STRUCTURE

FOREWORD

The theoretical framework of the Functional Generative Description (FGD) we sub-scribe to is based on dependency syntax both at the deep, underlying layer (called tec-togrammatical) and on the surface syntactic layer. Thus the issues of valency are of crucial importance for the formulation of this framework and the introduction of "case grammar" by Charles Fillmore was a stimulus for a detailed comparison of the tenets of the FGD with Fillmorean approach. Within FGD, the attention to the issues of valen-cy, esp. with regard to Czech syntax, was paid especially by Jarmila Panevová (see her papers 1974, 1978 quoted in Bibliography and the monograph by the same author from 1980, her 1976 joint paper with Petr Sgall and our joint paper from 1984 comparing valency frames as postulated by the FGD theory of a selected set of Czech and English verbs). J. Panevová also studied in detail the distinction between actants (arguments) and free modifications (adjuncts) and formulated a so-called dialogue test for the de-termination of semantic obligatoriness of the given type of valency slot. Our own con-cerns were some specific aspects of Fillmorean approach, namely his specification of the first argument discussed in our 1979 study *Agentive or Actor-Bearer?*; this issue is closely related to the necessity or redundancy of the introduction of a specific formal device of "crossed brackets" (see Hajičová 1981, not included in this volume). In a more general vein, we examined the issue of the status of Fillmorean cases in the overal description of language: distinguishing the layer of linguistic meaning and a layer of cognitive content, and in line with Petr Sgall's (1980) paper, we argue in *Remarks on the Meaning of Cases* (1983) that a distinction is to be made between the formal means such as morphological case and prepositions in prepositional groups, the valency slots in terms of linguistic meaning and the ontological categories. We come back to the study of valency slots with regard to their ordering in the underlying structure in the study of information structure, included in Part 2 of this volume.

AGENTIVE OR ACTOR/BEARER?

The plausibility of the hypotheses is examined whether a single tectogrammatical (deep structure) participant can be postulated, which would be regarded as the primary meaning of the surface subject. If operational criteria concerning possible combinations of syntactic units are used and the tectogrammatical representation is conceived of as differing from the surface structure only in case of clearly substantiated distinctions, then the hypothesis obtains strong support. It appears useful to assign all verbs having a single participant slot in their case frame only a single type of participant (cf. Tesnière's "first actant") on the level of language meaning. The difference between such units as Agentive, Experiencer Theme, Locative (if rendered by surface subject) belongs then to a layer of organization of factual knowledge ("scenarios") rather than to the language structure. Such a treatment allows for a more simple and economic formal description, avoiding the necessity of such devices as crossed and embedded brackets.

1. One of the most important issues in the description of the semantic structure of the sentence is that of the "frames" of the verb, i.e. the classification of the types of participants of the verbs and criteria of such a classification. In the framework of generative description, the pioneering investigations of Fillmore are based on and develop the European theories of the functions of cases and sentence parts (subject, direct and indirect object, adverbials). In his latest paper on this topic, Fillmore (1977) clearly distinguishes between the deep structure level and that of cognitive content and makes a distinction between units belonging to the former and those belonging to the latter level (cf. the discussion of this distinction in Sgall, in press, who in this connection proposes to use the terms "participant" for the level of deep structure, tectogrammatics or linguistic meaning, and "role" for the domain of cognitive content or factual knowledge).

In the framework of functional generative description[1], to which we subscribe, the problems of deep structure (tectogrammatical representation) as belonging to the do-

---

[1]   For the first formulations of the functional generative description, see Sgall (1964); the latest version (the mathematical formulation of which can be found in Hajičová, Koubek and Sgall, 1977) is applied for Czech (with respect to topic/focus articulation) in Sgall, Hajičová and Buráňová (in print).

main of linguistic meaning were discussed in Sgall, Procházka and Hajičová (1977); in that framework, the "case" frames were analyzed in detail by Panevová (1977a; 1977b; Panevová and Sgall, 1976) who has formulated also an operational criterion distinguishing between semantically obligatory and optional participants.

If we understand well, both approaches coincide in the point that deep subject (actor, the "first actant' of Tesnière) may be considered to underlie the syntactic subject in the primary case – with some secondary deviations that should be specified. Our objective in the present paper will be to examine on a sample of English verbs the plausibility of a hypothesis that a single (deep structure, tectogrammatical) participant "actor/bearer" can be postulated, rendering the primary function of the syntactic subject; in the sequel, we do not use this well established term actor/bearer only because it is a two-word combination and we use instead the term "Actor" even though we are aware of the possible misunderstanding following from the fact that the term itself may imply a much narrower case relation. The distinction between the functions of participants identified by the actor/bearer is considered here not to belong to the linguistically structured meaning; it can be often regarded as determined by the specific (lexical) meanings of the given verb form.[2] These distinctions belong to a layer of organization of factual knowledge ("scenarios") rather than to the language structure. Our arguments corroborate the view that such a treatment leads to a more simple and economic description, avoiding the necessity of such notational devices as crossed and embedded brackets of Fillmore's case grammar.

2. Semantic considerations such as that concerning the identification of the case markers of the subject phrase in (2) with the object phrase in (1) (in both sentences "there is a semantically relevant relation between the door and open that is the same in the two sentences," Fillmore, 1966, p. 363) led Fillmore to distinguish different case relations of the subject NP's in such examples as the following:

(1) The janitor will open the door. (Agentive)
(2) The door will open. (Objective)
(3) The key will open the door. (Instrument)
(4) The smoke rose. (Objective)
(5) The mist ascends from the valley. (Objective)
(6) I know him. (Dative)
(7) Howard died. (Dative)
(8) Fire killed the rats. (Instrument)
(9) The wind broke the window. (Instrument)
(10) John broke the window. (Agentive)
(11) The window broke. (Objective)

---

2   As for a similar hypothesis stated for the NP's in the object position (with such examples as *build a table, ruin a table, see a table, sing a song*) see Sgall (1972a), esp. p. 204, our use of "NP" in the sequel covers also the prepositional phrases (the preposition being considered a mere surface phenomenon).

However sound a base of such a differentiation may be, the specification of the cases as found in Fillmore's studies differs from one writing to another and does not offer more than rather vague characterizations in terms of semantic (cognitive) notions. In addition, to be able to provide for a (single) case frame of such verbs as *break, crack, fold, bend*, Fillmore has to propose a feature of "conditional obligatoriness" (represented in his notation by "embedded brackets"): the case frame postulated for this group of verbs is O (I(A)), which means that if Agentive is present in the deep structure of the given sentence, Instrument must be present, too. In (10) above, it is understood that John broke the window with something (even if with his own body, when he butted into it), while in (9) no Agentive is present at all. A still different device is necessary to account for such verbs as *kill* with the case frame O(I͓A), where the crossed brackets indicate that at least one of the two adjacent cases must be chosen to provide for the possibility of (8) as well as of *Mother killed the rats with fire* and for the impossibility of * *The rats killed* (as contrasted with the verb *wake up*, where besides *My daughter woke me up with an explosion* one can say both *An explosion woke me up* and *I woke up*; the suggested case frame for *wake up* is O(I)(A), with both Instrument and Agentive being optional). However ellegant this proposal may seem, one is faced with serious obstacles when formulating explicit rules for the inclusion of such a treatment into some sort of generative grammar.[3]

Considerations of a similar kind underlie another, more or less simultaneously formulated treatment of semantic relations of the verbs and their participants, the system of the so-called thematic relations as proposed by Gruber (1965, 1967). Among several thematic relations, there is one that is present in every sentence, namely the Theme; again, no explicit criteria or definitions are given for the individual relations, which are specified by means of vague characterizations and often in different terms for different classes of verbs: thus Theme is specified as the NP understood as undergoing the motion with the verbs of motion, and as the NP whose location is being asserted with the verbs of location. The relation Agent is specified as attributing to the NP a will or volition toward the action expressed by the sentence (hence the Agent is always animate, as with Fillmore). Agent – if present – is generally the subject, but the subject can bear simultaneously also other thematic relations. (The thematic relations given in the brackets are those assigned to the subject NP's in the given sentences).

(12) The rock rolled down the hill. (Theme)
(13) John rolled down the hill. (Agent + Theme)
(14) Max owns the book. (Location)
(15) Max knows the answer. (Location)
(16) Bill inherited a million. (Goal)
(17) Charlie bought the lamp from Mary. (Agent + Goal)
(18) Harry gave the book away. (Agent + Source)

---

3   For a discussion of these difficulties and of a possibility of a different approach, see Panevová (1977 b).

(19) The rock stood in the corner. (Location)
(20) The book belongs to Herman. (Location)
(21) The dot is contained in the circle. (Theme)

Once again, as with Fillmore's case frames, several questions suggest themselves: if the difference in the assignment of thematic relations to the subject NP's in (12) and (13) is given only by the fact that John is animate while the rock is not, why to postulate a different thematic relation assignment rather than to capture this fact by a difference in the semantic features of the NP? Is there any reason other than the cognitive distinction between rolling down under one's own volition and rolling down not being aware of one's motion (e.g. when asleep) to distinguish these two "meanings" of (13) by means of assignment of both the Agent and the Theme relation to John for the former and only the relation of Theme for the latter reading (as done by Jackendoff, 1972, p. 34 following Gruber)?[4] If one is to assume that in every sentence there is one NP which bears the relation of Theme to the verb, which NP's bear this relation in (19) and (20)? If one assigns the NP *in the circle* the relation of Location (saying that the preposition *in* is an unmistakable mark of a Location phrase) in (21) – and, by way of analogy, also the NP *circle* in *The circle contains the dot* is considered to be a Location – are there two Locations in (19)? And compare *It was raining in Prague* (Location without Theme, or Theme and Location both represented by the *in*-phrase?) with *There was a thunderstorm in Prague* (where the *in*-phrase scarcely could be assigned another relation), and *Last Sunday it rained* (with Time and Theme combined?) with *Last Sunday it rained in Prague* (Time and Location, of course – but what criterion tells us which of them is combined with Theme?).

The list of such Objections probably would increase if further verbs were taken into consideration; there seems to be no reason to doubt that many of the distinctions regarded as different thematic relations are due to the specific lexical content of the given verbs not directly grammatically relevant, while others can be treated as well by means of a reference to the semantic features of the respective NP's.

Fillmore and Gruber meet in several respects with Halliday's treatment of participant roles. Halliday's (1967–8) distinction between three participant roles (actor, initiator and goal) and three functions of subject (labelled ergative, nominative, accusative) determined by the transitivity systems can be illustrated on the following examples:

(22) She washed the clothes. (actor + initiator; ergative)
(23) He marched the prisoners. (initiator; ergative)
(24) The prisoners marched. (initiator + actor; nominative)

---

4   And what about a situation, when a speaker comments upon a state of affairs looking at a child rolling down a hill, saying "He is rolling down the hill"? Does the speaker know, which type of participant he used in the sentence he uttered? Cf. also the objection Poldauf (1970, p. 120) has against distinguishing *John (intentionally) broke the window* and *John (falling from the roof) broke the window*.

(25) The prisoners were marched. (actor; accusative)
(26) She washed herself. (actor + goal + initiator; nominative)
(27) (a) The clothes were washed. (goal; accusative)
      (b) The clothes washed (easily).

As Poldauf (1970, p. 123) duly remarks, some of Halliday's distinctions are due to a certain "over-semantization" (e.g. the introduction of two participants – actor and initiator – in place of one in (22) and (24)), or based on the interpretation of the verbal idea (*he* in (23) is regarded as an initiator, because it was the prisoners who were the actors of marching, while in (24) *the prisoners* is both the actor and the initiator).

A "more abstract" view of cases is also the starting point of Anderson's (1971) compact study of the grammar of case in English. He opposes strongly against the attempts to characterize the subject – verb relation in terms like "actor action" and offers a great variety of case functions to be assigned to the subject NP's, according to the nature of their participation "in the "process" or "state" represented in the sentence" (p. 10):

(28) The rose smells nice. (Ablative)
(29) He smells the rose. (Locative)
(30) Egbert left. (Nominative + Ablative)
(31) The statue stood on the square. (Nominative)
(32) Mary obtained the book from John. (Locative + Ergative)
(33) John moved. (Nominative + Ergative)
(34) John moved the couch. (Ergative)
(35) John is cold. (Nominative + Locative)

When two functions are assigned to a single NP, one of them is called "case", the other "a feature on a case," the reasons for such a differentiation remaining unclear. The unclear status of the assignment of different cases to the NP's is illustrated by several apparent hesitations of the author himself: thus *Egbert* in (30) is assigned Nominative + Ablative in one place, but Nominative + Ergative in another (along with the subjects of such verbs as *work, remain, reach, walk*). Anderson's analysis is evidently influenced by the object language studied[5] – this may be the explanation why the morphemic sameness of the verb *smell* in English leads to the recognition of a single meaning unit both in (28) and (29) assigning the case Ablative to the NP *rose* in both of them – even though the function of the adverb makes it clear that the semantic relation between *smell* and *rose* is different *(This rose smells nicely* – *He smells the rose nicely);* in this respect, this verb differs from the famous Fillmorean example with the verb *open.* Let us note that in Czech, similarly as in many other languages, there are two lexical units correspondings to the single English form *smell,* one for its meaning as exemplified by (28): *vonět,* and one for (29): *čichat.*

---

5   The specificity of some of Anderson's observations for English as well as some other inappropriate conclusions
     arrived at Anderson's study has also been noted by Bauer and Boagey (1977).

3. After this short survey of some treatments of the differentiation of the "first actant", let us now test on a sample of English verbs[6] the plausibility of the idea of identification of the typical functions of the subject as a single deep structure participant called here "Actor".

The sample falls into the following groups:

3.1 Intransitive verbs without any morphemically identical transitive counterparts:

Even though the only participant of these verbs is classified under different headings, there is no reason why to differentiate between the various functions ascribed to this single surface sentence part in terms of deep structure participants. The difference of syntactic properties (unacceptability of imperatives or the impossibility of formation of the progressive forms with some of these verbs) can be easily provided for by means of subclassification of the verbs themselves and has no closer connection with the participant functions.[7]

3.2 Transitive verbs without any morphemically identical intransitive counterpart:

Semantic considerations based on examination of the degree of active participation, volition or will on the side of the "first actant" result in an assignment of different cases or "thematic" relations to the subject NP in (6) with the verb *know* (Dative with Fillmore, Location with Gruber) as well as in (14) with the verb *own* (Location), in (16) Goal with the verb *inherit*, in (17) Agent and Goal in Gruber's account of the verb *buy* and in (18) Agent and Source with the verb *give*. The double assignment of "thematic" relations in the last two examples might be compared with the above mentioned distinction (well known from European structural linguistics) between semantic patterning inside the language system and the language independent domain of cognitive content or factual knowledge (in connection with the structure of human memory); it would then be possible to distinguish the deep structure participant of "Actor" or "first actant" (as a matter of linguistically structured meaning) and the "role" of Source or Goal belonging to the layer of organization of factual knowledge (scenario structures with Kay, 1975, roles with Fillmore 1971, 1977) rather than to the language structure itself.

3.3 Verbs with which the subject position can be occupied by an NP that with the same form of the verb may occupy also a position of some other syntactic function (the semantic relation, as understood by Fillmore, being the same):

3.3.1 "Direct object" shifted into the position of subject:

---

6   The data used in our analysis were gathered by M. Turbová. For the purpose of the present paper we have analyzed the first 200 verbs out of her excerption of more than 1,000 verbs based on Hornby (1963) and comprising (i) intransitive and transitive verbs with inanimate subjects and (ii) such verb forms that may be used both transitively and intransitively, to which we added (iii) verbs quoted in linguistic writings as examples of different case frames.

7   We assume that such distinctions as that between Agentive, Experiencer, Theme or Dative etc. (in a position primarily corresponding to that of surface subject) belong to the domain of cognitive content (scenarios); the criteria concerning the existence of progressive forms with the given verb, of the difference between *do* and *happen* in a corresponding question, etc. appear not to characterize the class of consciously active Agentives; such a series as *Jim goes, Jim sits, Jim lies, the book lies*, corroborates the view that the linguistic patterning is the same.

This is the most numerous group, the most typical example being the often quoted verb *open*. It is necessary, however, to distinguish two different types of oppositions:

(36) (a) Mary opens the door with a key.
  (b) The door opens with a key.
(37) The door opens (and George is standing behind it).

In (36), the verb *open* is used in the meaning in which it clearly has an Actor in its case frame, which in (36)(b) is "general" and deleted in the surface structure;[8] in both (a) and (b) sentences, the NP *the door* is assumed to function as Patient (Objective) in the approach of functional generative description. The (b) sentence is thus understood as synonymous with the passive construction with a deleted *by*-phrase.

Similar examples are the verbs *bake, adjourn.*

(38) (a) The president adjourned the meeting at 5 o'clock.
  (b) The meeting adjourned at 5 o'clock.
    (= The meeting was adjourned at 5 o'clock.)
(39) (a) Mother bakes bread in the oven.
  (b) Bread bakes in the oven.
    (= Bread is baked in the oven.)

A different situation is faced in (37): here, no agent is involved in the action (not even a "general" agent), and the verb *open* can be treated as an intransitive verb with a single participant, which can be then understood as the "first actant", i.e. Actor (in the broader, non-literal sense, as above with the group 3.1).

In his analysis of the intransitive counterparts of transitive verbs (without an overt derivational morph) Poldauf (1969) argues convincingly that with similar verbs (e.g. in *the test applies to every supposition*) the intransitive meaning constitutes a new lexical unit; therefore we prefer not to work with such commonly used terms as "middle voice", which point rather to a grammatical distinction and might conceal the distinction between grammatical voice and productive formation of derived intransitive verbs.

The proposed analysis results in a distinction to be made between two verbs, *open$_1$* (transitive) and *open$_2$* (intransitive).[9] The relation between the two verbs may be described as being analogous to that between the "basic" form and a derived verb in pairs such as *lie – lay, fall – fell*; one may speak about a "zero morpheme" for the derivation of transitive verbs, or about a process of "zero modification" in English word formation.[10]

---

8   Similarly as in *One opens the door with a key*, under the assumption that (36)(b) either is synonymous with the latter sentence or with, say, *One can open the door with a key*. For a detailed discussion of "general" Actor, see Panevová (1973).

9   We leave here aside still another meaning of the verb *open*, namely that in *The door opens into the garden* (i.e. leads).

10   For the latter term, see Lyons (1968, p. 360).

The Czech counterparts of the intransitive verbs of this kind are often derived by the reflective particle *se:* cf. the Czech translation of (37):

(40) Dveře se otvírají (a Jiří stojí za nimi).

The Czech construction verb + *se* is ambiguous in a similar way as the English verbs of the type *open:* either an Actor is present and the construction has the function of the passive of a transitive verb as with (36)(b) above, or the verb denotes some change of state or unprompted "activity" of the first actant (as in (37) above); it is with the latter interpretation that the verb is classed along with the intransitive verbs (with its case frame including only Actor), as contrasted with the morphemically identical verb with a transitive case frame with Actor.[11]

In the sample analyzed, some verbs provide a similar pattern of grammatical and/or lexical oppositions as the verb *open.* Thus the verb *deflect* can be used in the following sentences, with different tectogrammatical structures being suggested by the intrasentential context: *The wind deflected the bullet from its course* (transitive active) – *The bullet deflected by the strentgth of the wind* (passive) – *The bullet deflected from its course* (intransitive); similarly, all the three possibilities can be found with the verbs *depreciate, collect, calefy, chip, blend, alternate.*

With other verbs it appears that only the transitive active and intransitive meanings seem to be present:[12] *He soon accumulated a library* (H) – *Dust soon accumulates if we don't sweep our rooms* (H); similarly *darken, crumple, crumble, crock, colour, clog, chape, bolt.*

With some verbs it is even more evident that a zero derivational morpheme is concerned (cf. the discussion about the verb *smell* above); compare the pairs of German equivalents of a single English verb form:

(41) (a) When the ship sailed the storm abated. (H)
     (b) We must abate the smoke nuisance in our big cities. (H)
         abate: nachlassen (intr.) – abschaffen (trans.)
(42) (a) The trees arched over the river. (H)
     (b) The cat arched its back when it saw the dog. (H)
         arch: sich wölben (intr.) – krümmen (trans.) – cf. Note 11 above
(43) (a) If you cut your finger it will bleed. (H)
     (b) Doctors used to bleed people when they were ill. (H)
         bleed: bluten – zur Ader lassen
(44) (a) A rubber ball bounces well. (H)
     (b) She was bouncing a ball. (H)
         bounce: springen – schlagen

---

11   See Králíková (diss.); German is partly similar to English here (cf. *öffnen*), and partly to the Slavonic languages, e. g, *(sich) verbreiten.*
12   In the sequel, we denote examples taken over from Hornby (1963) by (H). – All these English (pairs of) verbs have as their Czech counterparts a simple transitive verb on the one hand, and a verb "derived" by means of *se* (semantically distinct from the reflexive passive) on the other.

(45) (a) His pockets were bulging with apples. (H)
    (b) He bulged his pockets with apples. (H)
        bulge: anschwellen – ausbauchen
(46) (a) The crowds cheered as the Queen rode past. (H)
    (b) Everyone cheered the news that the war was over. (H)
        cheer: fröhlich sein – begrüssen
(47) (a) False news circulate quickly.
    (b) People who circulate false news are to be blamed. (H)
        circulate: umlaufen – verbreiten

Similar examples are the verbs *decline* (abnehmen – beugen), *corner* (um e. Ecke biegen – in die E. treiben), *appreciate* (im Werte steigen – abschätzen, hochschätzen), *accord* (harmonieren – anpassen), blink (blinken vermeiden).

Often the intransitive verb can be used with a specific modal meaning (especially in negative potential, cf. Halliday, 1967–8, p. 47, about *won't, don't*) – this is the well known type *The book reads well, The dress washes easily.* Similar examples are the verbs *construe* (*This sentence won't construe* – H), burnish (*material that burnishes well* – H), button (*My collar won't button* – H). This modal meaning may perhaps be taken as one of the meanings of the zero suffix. An interesting example of ambiguity in such cases is adduced by Halliday (1967–8, p. 49):

(48) Children don't wash easily.

with the meanings (i) themselves (the NP *children* is of the subject type of nominative), (ii) something (the subject functions as ergative), (iii) = it is difficult to wash children (the subject functions as accusative). We see a boundary line between (i) and (ii) on the one side, and (iii) on the other: in (iii) we are faced with an intransitive verb (with a modal meaning), in (i) and (ii) with a transitive one, with deleted Patient *themselves* in the former, and with the deleted "general" Patient in the latter case.

It should be noticed that *The dress washes easily* is not synonymous with *It is easy to wash the dress*; not only the topic/focus articulation differs, but the latter sentence can also be used with such a continuation as … *since there is a good laundry service here.*

3.3.2 A participant from another position than that of the object is "shifted" into the position of subject – from the position primarily belonging to the modification of place in (49) and (50), to instrument in (51) to (56):

(49) (a) The bees swarm in the garden.
    (b) The garden swarms with bees.
(50) (a) Fish abound in the sea. (H)
    (b) The river abounds in fish. (H)
(51) (a) He accounts for his absence by his illness.
    (b) His illness accounts for his absence.

(52) (a) You will benefit by a holiday. (H)
    (b) A holiday will benefit you.
(53) (a) The boy amused George by a funny song.
    (b) A funny song amused George.
(54) (a) Employers compensate workers for injuries suffered at their work
        by a payment.
    (b) Nothing can compensate for the loss of one's health. (H)
(55) (a) John opened the front door with this key.
    (b) The front door opens with this key.
    (c) This key opens the front door.
    (d) The front door was opened with this key.
(56) (a) The murderer killed his victim with a knife.
    (b) The car killed him in a street accident.

Two ways of accounting for sentences (49) to (56) suggest themselves: either (i) the semantic (deep, tectogrammatical) relation between the verb and the participants in the subject position in one case and in some other position (adverbial of place, instrument etc.) in the other is the same; there is either no semantic difference between the two verbs, or the semantic difference must be connected with some phenomenon other than the type of participants; or (ii) the semantic relation of the verb and the participants in different surface positions is not the same: the difference is then connected with the difference in participants which is often accompanied by a difference in the lexical content of the (morphemically) identical verbs. The latter analysis seems appropriate for the verbs in (50) to (54). From the point of view of linguistic structure, an NP in the subject position and the same NP in some other syntactic position with the morphemically identical verb belong here to different participant types (Actor in the former case, Instrument or some other type of adverbial modification in the latter). In some cases, however, they may be understood as having the same "roles" from the point of view of cognitive relationship or scenarios.

When discussing sentences like (49), Fillmore (1966, p. 370) quotes several similar examples (given to him by J. B. Fraser): *Spray the wall with paint* against *Spray paint on the wall; Stuff cotton into the sack* vs. *Stuff the sack with cotton; Plant the garden with roses* vs. *Plant roses in the garden; Stack the table with dishes* vs. *Stack the dishes into the table.* Fraser – according to Fillmore – speaks about "alternate meanings" of the quoted verbs; in a later study, Fillmore (1968) notes a "focusing" difference, which may be accompanied with slighter or stronger differences in meaning (p. 48). Thus e.g. the sentence (49)(b) implies that the garden is full of bees, while (49)(a) does not have such an implication: the Actor in the (b) example is affected fully by the action. Similar considerations (with the Patient being affected fully by the action) hold about examples with spraying paint on the wall and spraying the wall with paint, planting roses in the garden and planting the garden with roses etc. Fillmore quotes among such examples also the pair *make out of- make into;* however, while in the former set semantically different units are concerned, *make into* and *make out of* can be taken as inverse forms of a single verb, which similarly as the distinction of active/passive constructions serve as the means for expressing the difference in the topic/focus articulation.[13]

The example (55) illustrates an even more complicated situation, where the surface position of subject can be occupied by the NP that in other sentences with the same surface verb is in the direct object position (*the front door* in (a) and (c) as compared with (b) and (d)) and by the NP that in other sentences may appear in the position of instrumental adverbial (cf. (c) as compared with the rest of the examples in (55)). We have analyzed the former situation above and have come to the conclusion that the NP *the front door* in sentences like (55)(b) and (d) has the function of Patient (with Actor being deleted in both cases); the active form of the verb in (b) has the same "passive" function as the passive in (d). In the (c) sentence, with the NP *this key* in the subject position, we assume that *this key* functions here as an Actor rather than an Instrument: one can easily imagine a special key with two different ends, one of which (the flat one) opens the front door. Then we can say (with the Actor and the Instrument clearly differentiated):

(55) (e) This key opens the front door with the flat end.

When discussing examples of a similar structure, Fillmore proposes to work with an underlying structure that can be paraphrased as "the flat end of this key opens the front door" since he assumes that examples like (55)(e) are possible only in the sense of "this key ... with its flat end." This is not necessarily the case: a car can kill someone with its front wheel, but also with a branch broken off a tree that has been cut down by the car. As for a possible objection that the key cannot be understood as Agentive since in the passive sentence (d) the preposition of the corresponding instrumental NP is *with* rather than *by*, it should be noticed that the use of a preposition cannot be specified so simply; also the rule of distribution of *by* and *with* as Instrument prepositions is not so clearcut as it might seem from Fillmore's writings (1966, p. 374), namely that when Agentive is present in the deep structure, the Instrument preposition is *with*, while when there is no Agentive, the Instrument preposition is *by*: in *The boys amused themselves by drawing portraits of their teacher* (H), the Agentive is clearly *the boys* and nevertheless the Instrument (in Fillmore's conception) preposition is *by*.[14]

Thus out examples have not brought any counter-evidence against the treatment denoted by (ii), namely that the semantic difference between the two verbs is connected with the difference in the type of participants in different syntactic positions, and it follows from our analysis that for the examples (49) to (56) the solution (i) is not needed. Thus the hypothesis stated in § 1 about the possibility of the postulation of

---

13   Cf. the discussion of examples of inverse and converse predicates in Sgall (1972b).

14   Fillmore (1966, p. 365) adduces as the criterion for the distinction between Agentive and Instrument the impossibility of coordinating the two participants (**John and a hammer broke the window*). It has been noticed by Poldauf (1970, p. 126) that this impossiblity "is due to the stylistic clash of purposive activity of animates and non-purposive activity of inanimates."

an actor/bearer participant in the deep (semantic, tectogrammatical) structure of the sentence seems to be plausible.

4. The distinction made between Agentive and Instrument, and, at the same time, the necessity of the presence of at least one of these participants in the case frame of such verbs as *kill (see* example (56) above) leads Fillmore to an introduction of the notion of relative obligatoriness into the case frames and to the use of the notational device of the crossed brackets. The arguments for the differentiation between Agentive and Instrument are again based on semantic considerations about the relationship between the verb and the corresponding participants; an important role is played by the distinction between animate and inanimate participants of the action. With the approach proposed here, viz. with the identification of the animate and inanimate uses into a single participant, such a device as the crossed brackets is not necessary and a much more economic description can be achieved; in our framework, *kill* has an obligatory Actor and an optional Instrument.

Our sample contains a long list of verbs that may have both an animate and inanimate NP in the subject position with no distinction of the semantic relation to the verb: *attract, attest, appear, appeal, admit, absorb, adhere, demand, defy, comfort, cling, cause, betray, baffle,* etc. etc. The character of the process certainly may be influenced if an animate or an inanimate Actor is concerned, but this is a matter of extralinguistic content rather than of linguistic meaning. [15]

The examples of verbs quoted above may serve as an evidence for the hypothesis from § 1 according to which a single participant is concerned; these examples corroborate the view that in English, too, the Actor is structured as the "first actant" even if inanimate.

As for the "embedded" brackets, all the examples adduced by Fillmore concern the pair of cases Agentive and Instrument *(break, crack, fold, bend):* if Agentive is present, Instrument must be present, too. The approach proposed above for the verb *open* leads us to distinguish between *break[1]* – intransitive *(The window broke as it fell down),* with Actor as the only obligatory case, and *break[2]* – transitive *(John broke the window with a hammer, The wind broke the window, The hammer broke the window); break[2]* is present also in one of the readings of *The window broke as John and Tom were playing football in the room,* where the NP *the window* is a Patient and the Actor is deleted on the surface level; this sentence is taken as synonymous with *The window was broken as John and Tom were playing football in the room.* With such a treatment, the embedded brackets are no longer necessary.

A consistent differentiation between linguistic meaning and cognitive content allows us to distinguish between a single actor/bearer participant as a matter of linguistic structure itself (similarly with other deep structure, tectogrammatical participants

---

15   For the arguments against the ± Animate sub-categorization as one of the underlying distinctions between cases, see Poldauf (1970, p. 126) who speaks about the extralinguistic nature of the difference between intentional agency and unintentional agency; as for the vagueness of the distinction itself (with institutions or higher types of machines as Agentives), cf. Zoeppritz (1971), Sgall (1972a). This view is corroborated e.g. by Quirk et al. (1972, p. 325), who illustrate it by the sentence *The area was ravaged by floods and guerilla forces.*

such as Patient, Addressee, or free modifications as Locative etc.) and its (several) cognitive, conceptual roles as a matter of the level of cognitive content (where such distinctions as those between agent, experiencer, location, affected vs. effected object are provided for). Among the relationships between a participant and its roles, there is one which may by considered as primary; deviations however are possible, and the repertoir of roles is much richer (see Kay, 1975).

5. The analysis of a sample of English verbs had led us to distinguish the following possible situations:

(i)   There is no need to distinguish between the Actor and some other participant function with a verb the frame of which contains a single case; the distinction, if any, is given either by the features of the concepts involved (e. g. animate vs. inanimate) or by the lexical content of the verb (activity vs. state etc.) and has nothing to do with the distinction in the functions of participants as linguistic units.

(ii) Two (morphemically identical but semantically distinct) verbs rather than a single verb are concerned with two different case frames; one with the Actor as the only participant, the other with Actor and Patient (and possibly others, as the case may be). One of the two verbs may be regarded as derived from the other by a zero derivational morpheme. The possible semantic relatedness of the Actor in the former case with the Patient in the latter is then not a matter of linguistic structure but of some part or aspect of the organization of factual knowledge, which has not yet been studied deeply enough to give a more definite account of such "scenarios" or "templates".

(iii) In some cases, the superficially "active" verb form in English functions as a variant of the passive form of the transitive verb; we may speak about a zero morpheme for passivization; in such cases, a "general" Actor is understood to be present in the underlying structure (cf. Note 8), being deleted on the surface (cf. the reflexive passives in Slavonic and other languages). The subject NP then has the same participant function as the object NP in the active construction of the given verb, namely the Patient.

Thus Anderson's (1971, p. 8) objection of surfacism does not apply: not only in the superficial passive sentences, but also in the above quoted examples of derivation of passives in English by means of a zero morpheme (and probably also in other, more or less exceptional cases, such as the verb *belong*, which seems to have as its underlying structure the possesive verb *have*, and perhaps other verbs such as *please* vs. *enjoy*) the subject is assigned a function other than the Actor. The intuitive idea that there should be one "case" present generally in the deep structure of all sentences (if their verb is accompanied by a participant at all, not only by a free adverbial) is, as a matter of fact, present in many treatments: with Anderson, such a universally present case is called Nominative, with Gruber, it is the Theme; in neither approach, however, any clear criterion could be traced that leads to the postulation of such a universally present case. Our standpoint, demonstrated in the present paper by the hypothesis of Actor underlying the syntactic subject in the primary case[16], is based on operational criteria, as we have attempted to show in this paper; these criteria were systematically investigated in the quoted studies by Panevová. The approach of functional generative description is led by an endeavour to postulate a semantic representation close enough to the linguistic form and differing from it only in case of clear, substantiated and explicitly specifiable cases.

---

16 In this connection, Skalička (1962) speaks about the anthropocentrism of syntax; similar formulation can be found more recently with Oosten (1977, p. 469), who goes even further and considers also the subject of *This wine drinks like it was water* as "acting as agent." With our approach (cf. example (36)(b) above), this sentence contains a suffixless passive form of the verb *to drink* (with deleted general Actor).

REMARKS ON THE MEANINGS OF CASES

0. The introduction of "case grammar" (Fillmore, 1966; 1968; 1971; 1977) into the transformational generative description of language met with reactions of two kinds: on the one hand, "case" theory was appreciated as a most valuable hint for transformational grammar to take into account also semantic considerations when describing the structure of the sentence, while on the other hand it evoked considerable reservations about the use of the term "case" for semantic (or underlying) rather than morphemic units. The latter objection is not merely a matter of terminology: the use of a term traditionally belonging to the domain of morphemics also brought about a lack of substantial differentiation between morphemic, semantic and even cognitive issues (cf. Sgall, 1980, for a discussion supporting the necessity of distinguishing between the latter two aspects of the "case" relations between verbs and their participants).

In the present paper we want to plead for a three-stage treatment of what is often subsumed in transformational writings under the notion of "case", namely *morphemic case* – the meaning (function) of case *(verbal valency)* – the *cognitive roles* of verbal participants, the main emphasis being laid on the second of the three layers.

1. The most suitable starting point for the study of case meanings is offered, in our opinion, by Kuryłowicz' (1949) distinction between the syntactic function and the (semantic) meaning of (morphemic) case. This distinction, elaborated further by Skalička (1950), is supported by the fact that in inflectional languages prepositionless case has primarily a syntactic function while prepositional case has primarily a semantic function. In this way, the prepositional case comes close to such categories as tense, number, etc., which also have primarily a semantic function, referring to aspects of the extralinguistic situation.

In the classical writings distinguishing these two functions of the morphemic category of case the notion of syntactic function lacks a clear specification. For such a specification it is necessary to work within an explicit framework of linguistic description.

One of the frameworks serving this aim is the functional generative description, including a semantic base. In Sgall (1967), an explicit distinction is made (on the level of meaning) between functors (i.e. syntactic functions, distinguishing agent, patient, addressee, nominative complement and "determination") and "grammatemes" (as semantic variations of the "determination" function; under determination Sgall subsumed all kinds of adverbial functions). This classification was checked in detailed studies on the description of Czech and of other languages as well (esp. English and Russian). In the course of these studies, which were always guided by efforts to apply operational criteria to any distinction to be made, it appeared necessary to distinguish several kinds of local, temporal, etc. modifications as syntactically different functions; see Sgall and Hajičová (1970); Panevová (1980, p. 71f., Sect. 3.2), where a distinction is made e.g. between P_{where} as a syntactic function and the semantic variations "where on", "where in", "where behind", "where beside", "close beside"; similarly with R_{when} distinguishing between "in (a certain point of time)", "before (a certain point of time)", "after (a certain point of time)"; as a matter of fact, such a subtle classification corresponds to Kuryłowicz' approach.

It is necessary, however, to bear in mind that not only the relation between the morphemic and the tectogrammatical (semantic) level is concerned, but that this relation is again a two-stage relation: intermediate between the two levels there is the surface sentence structure. Thus if we understand the relation of function as a relation between two adjacent levels of the language system (as with Sgall, 1964), then we speak about a function of nominative (case), which primarily is the subject (as a unit of the surface syntactic level) and about a function of subject, which primarily is the actor/bearer (as a unit of the semantic level). It is, of course, true that sometimes it may suffice to work with two levels only: thus, e.g., prepositional cases such as *v* + locative (*in*), *nad* + instrumental (*above*), *pod* + instrumental (*under*), *mezi* + instrumental (*between*) etc., all express location "where," and thus they are semantic variations inside a single syntactic function. The usefulness of three levels, however, is demonstrated by examples where some relation of transformation occurs, be it the relation between active and passive construction (where it is necessary to distinguish between a morphemic category, as nominative, a syntactic category, as subject, and a tectogrammatical category, as actor/bearer), or between nominalization and the respective underlying construction (in *shooting of the hunters* the morphemic unit – genitive case – renders the syntactic function of attribute, which in its turn serves as an expression for the actor/bearer, or for the patient).

2. The syntactic functions and the meanings of cases were widely discussed and relatively well established for Czech before the elaboration of formal systems, mainly thanks to Šmilauer's (1947) syntactic monograph, in which one can find a detailed characterization of individual semantic variations of syntactic functions. As for English, the situation is more complicated: present-day English has no morphemic category of case as we are used to using the term, but this does not mean that the meanings of cases are missing, since the functions of cases are taken over to a great extent by prepositions and by the word order positions.

Relatively close to a two-stage understanding of case stands the approach of Quirk et al. (1973), who work with six "syntactically defined elements of clause", namely subject, direct and indirect object, complement to subject and complement to object and adverbial. Besides these units the authors postulate eight functions of these surface syntactic units, which they undertake in combinations with other syntactic sentence units: actor, affected object, recipient, current and resulting attribute, locative, temporal modification, instrument and effective (pp. 348–350; see also pp. 358, Table 7.1, where these semantic functions are classified according to the syntactic functions and patterns). However, the authors present no substantiated classification of the syntactic functions and of the semantic variations within each of these categories. They do not work with any dichotomy that would correspond to Tesnière's distinction of "actants" and "circonstants".[1]

In the writings on English syntax this issue has often its parallel in the distinction between prepositionless constructions (in transformational terms, noun phrases) and prepositional constructions. The prepositionless constructions are frequently classified as objects, while the prepositional ones are classed as adverbials, together with clear examples of circumstantial modifications (of place, time, manner, etc.), which clearly have the character of free modifications ("circonstants").

We assume that the criterion of the presence of a preposition in the construction under examination is a matter of surface structure and is not immediately relevant to the investigation of the semantic or underlying (tectogrammatical) structure of the sentence (though it may serve as a certain guide). Only in the transduction to the surface do the rules specific for individual verbs determine whether the given modification of the verb is to be rendered by a prepositional or prepositionless construction; this is similar to the handling of case endings in languages other than English.

An interesting process of transgression from prepositional to prepositionless construction is exemplified by such examples as: *The rain was lashing (against) the windows; We walked (along, through) the streets; He swam (across) the river; He passes (by) the notice; The horse jumped (over) the fence;* (similar features are exhibited by the verbs *climb, cross, mount, leave, penetrate, reach, surround, turn*). Here, the preposition becomes an integral part of the verb. With some examples, the co-existence of a prepositional and prepositionless construction is accompanied by a slight difference in meaning and these constructions would be translated into Czech by two different verbs:[2] *He lamented the death of his friend = Oplakával smrt svého přítele* vs. *He lamented for a friend = Plakal pro přítele.*

Quirk et al. (1973, p. 355) argue that such complements of verbs should be considered as objects since the constructions can be passivized: *the windows were lashed (against) by the rain, the streets were walked (along), the fence was jumped (over) by the horse,* etc. Passivization is often used as a criterion for a distinction to be made between object complement and adverbial in English (cf. Halliday, 1967; Quirk et al., 1973, p. 356, Note b). This criterion, however useful it may be, is not reliable, esp. for En-

---

1   It is worth noting in this connection that Fillmore also discusses only some participants and leaves others aside, without giving clear reasons; this distinction is a consequence of the transformationalist treatment of temporal or local circumstantial modifications as embedded predications.

2   For the interrelationship between constructions of verb + preposition and prefixed verbs in Czech, see Bémová, 1979.

glish, where passivization is a rather frequent means, primarily serving the purpose of placing the contextually bound element of the sentence in the initial position in the surface word order (cf. Mathesius, 1929, about the function of subject in English). The unreliability of passivization if taken as a criterion to distinguish between object and adverbial was discussed by Bolinger (1975), who analyzes several English verbs and points to the complicated character of the conditions for the application of the passive transformation: these conditions are determined not only by the lexical shape of the given verb, but also by other factors given by the broader context: one cannot use as an independent sentence *The defendants were brought charges against, while in a parallel context this is possible: The defendants – the ones arrested and brought charges against yesterday – are all expected to plead innocent.

Some restrictions on passivization are given by extralinguistic factors, as can be clearly demonstrated by another example taken from Bolinger: the sentence My brother has lived in Chicago cannot have a passive counterpart, while it is quite acceptable to say The house has been lived in by several famous personages. The dog walked under the bridge cannot be passivized while there is an acceptable passive in This bridge has been walked under by generations of lovers. Bolinger assumes that with sentences expressing current activities (events), passivization is not possible while if an aimed, planned activity is rendered, passivization is possible. It seems that the relationship between passivization and object vs. adverbial distinction is reverse: if some sentence elements can become a subject of a passive sentence, then this element expresses an inner participant as opposed to free modification; however, such a relationship does not hold in the opposite direction. The verbs quoted by Bolinger as examples of variance (oscillation) belong to the transition layer between participants and free modifications; with them the possibility of passivization often seems to depend on such features as the "specificity" of the NP occupying the subject position of the passive, cf. Bach (1980, 332 f).[3] This feature seems to be closely connected with the fact that the subject of an English passive clause is primarily contextually bound (belongs to the topic).

3. Criteria should be sought for establishing a firm basis for classification of the complements of verbs. At the present stage in the development of functional generative description, five inner participants of verbs are postulated, namely Actor, Patient, Addressee, Origin and Result, and a number of free modifications (for a more detailed account and the criteria used, see esp. Panevová and Sgall, 1976; Panevová, 1977, 1980; Hajičová, 1979, 1981). These participants and free modifications constitute the syntactic functions of morphemic cases in inflectional languages. Semantic variations within the individual syntactic positions are rich only in some specific cases, e.g., with location-where (in, on, under, by, between, ...), and also in those cases where a binary relationship is possible (e.g., positive or negative accompaniment and regard). Typical

---

3   Bach's account of Passive, based on intensional semantics, brings many new insights and deserves deeper attention, though his understanding of, e.g., persuade to go or regard as my friend as "transitive phrases" is connected with the tacit (and perhaps not fully intuitive) assumption that the direct object of persuade or regard is connected with the verb less closely than the to- or as-phrase. It is not fully clear how the class of transitive VP's can be delimited, cf. John was seen by a telescope. The house was bought before it was finished. You were badly missed...

syntactic functions without semantic variation are inner actants. Even here, however, exceptions can be found: in older Czech semantic variation occurred even with the syntactic relation of object ("wholeness," expressed by Genitive: *pít vody* "to drink water"); in Modern Standard Czech in *napít se vody* "to have a drink of water" the Genitive is already a regular morphemic form of an object without a specific semantic function.

We tried to show in Hajičová (1979, 1981) that for the specification of units of the structure of the sentence it is necessary to work only with those criteria that concern linguistic structuring. It is not adequate to use such cognitive features as "own force" or "will", if these features are not syntactically relevant. It appears that Fillmore's distinction between Objective as a primary function of the second complement of the verb (*John wrote a letter*) and Dative (with *murder, kill*) or Locative (with *pinch, hit, slap, strike*) belongs to the domain of cognitive roles rather than to that of linguistic meaning; with *hit in John hit Mary* it is even difficult to decide whether *Mary* has the cognitive role of Locative or that of an (affected) Objective (cf. *John hit Mary on the face*); identifying the roles of the second complement of *kill* (*to kill a mouse*) and of *give, promise* (*He promised John ...*) under the same function (Dative) is also debatable. Anderson (1971), too, distinguishes several functions of the second complement: Ablative in *He smelled the rose*, Ablative + Nominative in *He marched the prisoners*, Locative in *The play pleased some of the audience* and in *A statue occupies the plinth*. Since Anderson accepts the Fillmorean thesis that a given "case" can be present only once in a sentence, he would face difficulties when analyzing *In Regent Park a statue occupies the plinth*. We see no reason for a distinction to be made between the function of the second complement of *smell, taste, feel* (Ablative) and of other intransitive verbs (Nominative); similarly, we regard the function of the second complement with *march* as Patient and we distinguish between intransitive *march1* (*He marched in the yard*) and transitive *march2* (*He marched the prisoners*). As for the verb *please*, one can perhaps treat *please* and *enjoy* as two surface realizations of a single underlying verb; the surface subject of *please* (*The play pleased some of the audience*) and the surface object of *enjoy* (*Some of the audience enjoyed the play*) would be then assigned the same function (Patient), similarly as the surface subject of *enjoy* (*Some of the audience enjoyed the play*) and the surface object of *please* (Actor).

From this it follows that also the localist approach is not the best solution: it is certainly justified to a certain extent to look for something "directional" with Accusative and "local" with Locative, but it cannot be stated that this is the basic meaning of these morphemic cases. It is also possible to assume that this was the situation in previous stages of the development of some languages (e.g. this tendency is stronger in Latin than in Czech), but the modern development of languages goes in a different direction, the primary functions of most prepositionless cases being of a syntactic rather than semantic character. The localist approach includes a hypostasis of "case meanings" as directly referring to extralinguistic objects, which seems to be based on a false analogy with the meanings of tense, number and other morphemic categories.

Coordination is also often quoted as a possible criterion for the classification of verbal complements. It is assumed that the types of complements that cannot be coordinated do not share the same case meaning: e.g. even though in both *číst knihu* "to read the book" and *číst celou noc* "to read the whole night," the accusative is used in Czech, it is necessary to distinguish between the two meanings, since it is not possible to coordinate the two constructions in a single one: *to read the book and the whole night*. However this criterion is reliable in one direction only: it is possible to conjoin different types of adverbials such as "where" and "when" *(here and now you should tell me, where you have been)*, or cause and aim, and nevertheless we cannot say that cause and aim are identical meanings.[4]

4. One of the open questions concerns the nature of the so-called "hypercases". Different approaches can be distinguished in the writings on this question: Fillmore (1971) seems to group case relations into a hypercase if there is no possibility of co-occurrence. Similarly Zoeppritz (1972) assumes that, e.g., "since when" and "how long" is a hypercase because the two are incompatible. Under such an approach, *where to* and *until when* would belong to a single hypercase, and *from where* and *since when* to another, because they allegedly cannot co-occur simultaneously with the same verb; the hypercase would then be interpreted either temporally, or locally, depending on the semantics of the given verb. This approach culminates with Uličný (1973), who proposes a certain extreme treatment of the basic categories, namely starting with the triad of notions *beginning - centre - end* and assigning them categories such as *agentive - instrument - object*, or *from where - where - where to*, or *since (from) when - when - till when*.

However, the triads "Agentive - Instrument - Object", "from where - where - to where" and "since when - when - till when" are not fully mutually exclusive: with such verbs as, e.g., *go, come, carry* the syntactic, the spatial and the temporal modifications all are possible, so that it is not adequate to work only with a single triad, handling each of its three elements as a hypercase, neutralizing the distinction between the three triads. On the other hand, if the hypercases are understood as syntactically identical units of the underlying structure the distinction between which is of a semantic character, then typical examples of hypercases would be those that have the position of a label of an edge of the dependency tree (type of modification: one of the participants or adverbial modifications}, e.g. "where" itself, the semantic distinctions inside this unit being those of the meanings of prepositions (or subordinating conjunctions), i.e. *in, at, on, under,* etc., similarly for "when" with the semantic variation of *before, after, in*. Thus we arrive at the distinction between the functors (kinds of dependency relation) and the grammatemes. To give another series of examples let us recall the meanings of such prepositional cases as *with - without*, constituting two semantic variants of a single hypercase, Accompaniment; also Regard has a positive and a negative variant, and it seems worth checking whether the same holds for Condition (real - unreal), Comparison (*as ... as* vs. *more ... than*), perhaps also about Cause vs. Aim.

5. The difference between functors and grammatemes is rendered explicit in the framework of functional generative description, by which our remarks were guided.

---

4   See Panevová, 1980, p. 72ff.

Thus, in accordance with the known fact that the meaning of a scientific notion is given only within some theoretical framework, we may state that the more explicit the framework is, the better are the possibilities it offers to check the appropriateness of the conclusions drawn. This applies also to the characterization of the notions "case", "meaning of case," and "valency" with respect to typologically different languages, such as Czech and English.

2. TOPIC-FOCUS ARTICULATION AND RELATED ISSUES

FOREWORD

The distinction between the formal and the "topical" articulation of the sentence dates back to Vilém Mathesius and his pioneering studies (1907; 1939), in which he criticized the psychologically oriented studies by H. Weil (1844) and by linguists around the "Zeitschrift für Völker Psychologie" (e.g. Georg von Gabelentz, Hermann Paul, Philip Wegener), claiming that the issues they discussed under the term psychological subject and psychological predicate relate to the factual situation the utterance reflects rather than to the state of mind. In Czech linguistics, Mathesius' pioneering writings on these issues gave rise to two approaches, closely related though different in some important aspects, namely the so-called *functional sentence perspective* (sometimes referred to as Brno School as the originator of that approach, Jan Firbas, was affiliated to Masaryk University in Brno) and the theory of *topic-focus articulation* (sometimes referred to as the Prague theory because it was developed by Petr Sgall and his collaborators affiliated to Charles University in Prague). In order to make the relationships between Mathesius' original thoughts and the two mentioned "schools" explicit, we start Part 2 of the present volume by the study *Vilém Mathesius and functional sentence perspective, and beyond* written at the occasion of the centenary of English Studies at Charles University and published in 2012.

One of the crucial issues in the study and description of topic-focus articulation (TFA) from the point of view of the relation of form and function is its position within the language system. An important argument in favour of its inclusion in the description of the underlying level of the structure sentence, the level of (linguistic) meaning, was the study of the semantic relevance of this articulation with regard to negation. The semantic relevance of TFA for the interpretation of negation is systematically analyzed in our paper *Negation and Topic vs. Comment* (1973) referring back to the observations of J.-M. Zemb (1968) for German and A. Kraak (1966) for Dutch. A detailed analysis of negation, namely the question "what is negated in a negative sentence" has led us to a deeper study of the notion of presupposition and to the specification of a third kind of entailment, called allegation, first introduced in our contribution delivered at the conference on computational linguistics COLING in Debrecen in 1971 (see Hajičová 1971) and then put under scrutiny in several other studies (Hajičová 1974,

1975, 1984), out of which the most comprehensive is the paper *On Presupposition and Allegation* included in this Part.

As mentioned in the first paper in this Part, one of the tenets of our approach to TFA is a strict differentiation between the semantically relevant function of TFA and the forms of its expression, which may be of morphological, syntactic or prosodic nature. Prosodic means of TFA are in the core of the 1998 paper *Questions on Sentence Prosody Linguists Have Always Wanted to Ask;* discussed there are the issues concerning mainly the position of the intonation centre in English sentences, a possible prosodic indication of the boundary between topic and focus and also issues connected with a possibility to mark contrast in the topic part of the sentence, which is illustrated also on examples taken from writings on German.

Another means of expression of topic and focus, and especially the degrees of communicative dynamism understood as a scale from the communicatively least important to the most important items in the sentence is the ordering of sentence elements, both in the surface shape of the sentence and in its underlying structure. The arguments for the necessity to distinguish these two orders are summarized in the 1995 paper *Surface and Underlying Word Order*, while the postulation of an underlying order of valency slots in the focus part of the sentence supported by psycholinguistic experiments is argued for in the 1998 paper *The Ordering of Valency Slots from a Communicative Point of View.*

Related to the investigation of the prosodic means of expressing TFA was the question whether it is enough to work with a binary distinction between topic and focus, or whether a more subtle differentiation is neccessary. In the theory of TFA, we work with a binary relation of aboutness (the "focus" says someting about the "topic") and with a scale of communicative dynamism (underlying word order) as specified above. However, there are approaches to the information structure of the sentence that work with a differentiation of more than a single topic or a single focus in a sentence; one of our arguments against such a differentiation in the paper *How Many Topics and Foci?* (2000) was based on examples containing so-called rhematizers (focalizers, focussing particles). Our study of these particles indicates a close relationship between the specification of the (semantic) scope of these particles and that of negation and dates back to our Czech paper (Hajičová 1995) and to the monograph co-authored by Barbara Partee and Petr Sgall (Hajičová et al. 1998); we returned to these issues in 2010 in the paper *Rhematizers Revisited,* included in this volume.

VILÉM MATHESIUS AND FUNCTIONAL SENTENCE PERSPECTIVE, AND BEYOND

> *"Terminological profusion and confusion, and underlying conceptual vagueness,*
> *plague the relevant literature to a point where little may be salvageable."*
> (Levinson, 1983: x, quoted from Lambrecht, 1994)

1. MOTIVATION AND THE AIM OF THE CHAPTER

The aim of the present contribution is to demonstrate that Levinson's harsh statement upon the address of the literature on theme-rheme or whatever terms are used is unjust, both from the historical as well as the present-day state-of-the-art point of view. In spite of the undisputable fact that there is a superficial terminological "mish-mash" in the field (one can find such terms or dichotomies as psychological subject and psychological predicate, "movement of ideas," Functional Sentence Perspective, Theme-Rheme, Topic-Comment, Topic-Focus, Topic-Focus Articulation, Presupposition and Focus, Permissible range of focus, Information Structure, Information-bearing Structure, Background-Focus, Rhematizers, Focalizers, Focusing particles, Association with Focus and several others), the basic idea underlying the relevant inquiries is quite sound and appropriate. In our contribution we want to reduce at least some of the seemingly "conceptual vagueness" by an attempt to compare the basic starting points and main contributions of four stages or directions: (i) psychologically oriented 19th century insights (Section 2), (ii) structurally oriented and systematic contribution of Vilém Mathesius (Section 3), (iii) the follow-up and development of the theory of functional sentence perspective (FSP) by Jan Firbas et al. (Section 4), and (iv) the theory of topic-focus articulation (TFA) as developed within theoretical and formal linguistics by Petr Sgall et al. (Section 5). The latter section presents a brief sketch of the possibilities offered by the current development of computational (and corpus-based) linguistics for testing the linguistic theories and for their further developments. Finally, in Section 6 we offer a schematic comparison of the three Czech approaches to information structure discussed in our contribution.

2. PIONEERING PSYCHOLOGICALLY ORIENTED STUDIES

One of the first – if not the very first – comprehensive studies in what may now be called information structure of the sentence was H. Weil's (1844; English translation 1887) monograph on the order of words. According to Weil, "[w]ords are the signs of ideas; to treat of the order of words is, then, in a measure, to treat of the order of ideas" (p. 11, quoted from the 1887 English translation). The author recognizes two types of the "movement of ideas": *marche parallèle* and *progression:* "If the initial notion is related to the united notion of the preceding sentence, the march of the two sentences is to some extent parallel; if it is related to the goal of the sentence which precedes, there is a progression in the march of the discourse" (p. 41). He also noticed a possibility of a reverse order called by him "pathetic": "When the imagination is vividly impressed, or when the sensibilities of the soul are deeply stirred, the speaker enters into the matter of his discourse at the goal" (p. 45). Weil's study was not left unnoticed by Vilém Mathesius (1907), who refers to him (though mistakenly by the date 1855), and to linguists around *Zeitschrift für Völkerpsychologie,* such as Georg von der Gabelentz (1868), Hermann Paul (1886), and especially Philip Wegener (1885), but criticizes this approach for the terms "psychological subject" and "psychological predicate". Mathesius himself prefers to characterize the relevant issues by their relation to the factual situation from which the utterance originates, using therefore the Czech (untranslatable) term "aktuální členění" (literally: "the topical articulation").

3. VILÉM MATHESIUS AND HIS APPROACH

In his criticism of the psychologically based studies, Mathesius (1939, but referring back to his 1907 study) differentiates between the formal and the "topical" articulation of the sentence: while the former structure concerns the composition of the sentence from grammatical elements (its basic elements being the grammatical subject and the grammatical predicate), the basic elements of the "topical" structure are the starting point (Cz. *východiště*) of the utterance (referred to by J. Firbas as the initial point, and by J. Vachek as the basis), i.e. what is in the given situation known or at least evident and from what the speaker starts, and the nucleus (Cz. *jádro*), that is what the speaker says about it or with respect to the starting point. The initial point of the utterance is often its theme, but not necessarily so. It should be noticed that these two aspects of the "initial" point are reflected in the distinction made by M.A.K. Halliday between the thematic structure (theme – rheme) and the information structure (given – new) of the sentence (see Halliday, 1970: 160ff; Halliday characterizes the theme as "the peg on which the message is hung" (p. 161); he further says that in English theme is put in the first position of the sentence).

In his criticism of different contemporary approaches to Czech word order, Mathesius prefers to speak about the basis and nucleus rather than about known and unknown information (Mathesius, 1941). As early as in this paper, Mathesius notices that the initial point of the utterance, its basis, may contain more than a single element; the centre of the theme is that element which is "the most topical" one and the rest of the thematic elements are "accompanying elements" (Cz. *jevy průvodní*) that lead from the centre to the nucleus. In Mathesius'views, the predicate is a part of the nucleus but on its edge rather than in its centre and represents a transition (*přechod*) between the two parts of the utterance. The first sentence of a text can be non-articulated, it may contain only the nucleus and accompanying elements.

From this point of view, according to Mathesius, the word order in Czech serves to distinguish various degrees of importance (*závažnost, důležitost*) of the elements of the same sentence. However, if the speaker is very much captured by the nucleus, s/he then does not pay respect to the natural ordering from known to unknown and s/he puts the nucleus in the first position of the sentence. Such ordering is then called by Mathesius a subjective order, in contrast to the "natural," objective one. Summarizing Mathesius' stimuli, the following points emerge as important for the future investigations:

(i)   *Mathesius procedes from functional needs to formal means that satisfy them.*
(ii) The *dichotomy* is based on the distinction between Basis – Nucleus (Theme – Rheme) rather than on the distinction between known and unknown.
(iii) *The notion of "aboutness" is introduced.*
(iv) The functional articulation of the sentence is seen as more articulated (the notions of *transition and accompanying elements)* rather than as a mere dichotomy.
(v)   *The first sentence of the text may be composed only of the nucleus together with the accompanying elements.*
(vi) *The objective* (natural) order is distinguished from the *subjective* one.

4. FUNCTIONAL SENTENCE PERSPECTIVE (JAN FIRBAS AND THE BRNO SCHOOL)

Since Mathesius' Czech term *aktuální členění větné* is not directly translatable into English, Jan Firbas, a direct follower of Mathesius in the study of this domain – on the advice of Josef Vachek (Firbas, 1992: xii) and apparently inspired by Mathesius' use of the German term *Satzperspektive* in his fundamental paper of 1929 – coins the term *functional sentence perspective* (FSP henceforth). Firbas abandons the idea of a strict dichotomy and works first with a triad "theme – transition – rheme". His introduction of the notion of *transition* is basically motivated by the function of the modal and temporal elements of the sentence (Firbas, 1965). Firbas then passes over to a more gradual view, namely to the concept of (a hierarchy of) *communicative dynamism* (CD henceforth). He writes: "By the degree or amount of CD carried by a linguistic element, I understand the extent to which the element contributes to the development of communication, to which, as it were, it 'pushes the communication forward'" (Firbas, 1971: 135–136). Based on this notion, *the theme* is viewed (p. 141; cf. already 1964: 272) as "constituted by an element or elements carrying the lowest degree(s) of CD within a sentence". It should be added that Firbas (1992: 93) corrects this definition – referring explicitly (p. 72) to Petr Sgall's objection (presented in 1976 at the conference in Sofia, viz. that such a specification would imply that every sentence has a theme, which is not necessarily so, especially with sentences opening a text) – in the sense that a theme need not be implemented, while in every sentence there must be a rheme proper and transition proper. In his survey of the Czech(oslovak) approaches to FSP, Firbas (1974) states that the basic distribution of CD would reflect what H. Weil called the "movement of the mind"; Svoboda (2007) suggests that the degrees of CD can be viewed as degrees of communicative importance ("*sdělná závažnost*") from the point of view of the intention of the speaker.

According to Jan Firbas and all his followers, there are *four factors of FSP* that work in interaction: (1) linear arrangement (surface word order), (2) semantics (in the sense of the semantic character of a linguistic element as well as the character of its semantic relations (Firbas, 1992: 41ff)), (3) context, and (4) prosody. A certain hierarchy is assumed (in the reverse order) for these factors, the highest position of which is occupied by the prosodic factor and the lowest by the linear arrangement. The weight of these factors may differ for different languages.

Another notion important for the FSP theory is the notion of *context dependence*: the criterion is based on "actual presence of an element in, or its absence from, the immediately relevant context" (Firbas, 1992: 37).

Two scales of dynamic *semantic functions* performed by context-independent elements are postulated: a presentation scale (Setting – Presentation of Phenomenon – Phenomenon presented) and a quality scale (Setting – Bearer of Quality – Quality – Specification and Further Specification). The semantic functions within these scales are arranged in accordance with a gradual rise in CD (Firbas, 1992: 67).

Closely related to Mathesius' notions of objective and subjective order, there are the *two instance* levels, namely the first instance and the second instance level. According to Firbas (1979, see also Firbas, 1992: 111ff), the first instance level can be divided into a basic instance level on which all carriers of CD are context independent, and an ordinary instance level, where one or more carriers of CD are dependent on the immediate relevant context.

This brief account of the FSP theory is meant just to introduce the basic notions employed and is far from being fully exhaustive. It should also be mentioned that Jan Firbas has found a large number of followers, who have made substantive contributions both to the overall conception and to several particular points. Its basic approach was also followed by František Daneš (1974) in his development of the idea of thematic progressions (akin to Weil's "progressions of ideas") and in his pioneering description of Czech intonation with respect to the theme-rheme structure. A prominent Czech Anglicist Libuše Dušková focused her attention in several of her syntactic writings (e.g. 1999) and also in her comprehensive contrastive grammar of English (2006 [1988]) on a comparison of the function and the means of expression of FSP in English and Czech. Several detailed studies of Czech word order with respect to FSP have been published by Ludmila Uhlířová (e.g. 1974; 1987).

Among Firbas' direct students, the main role was played by Aleš Svoboda (2007), who further elaborated the theory of FSP with respect to a more detailed hierarchization of the sentence elements within the so-called distributional fields (Svoboda, 1968) and by introducing the notion of a diatheme as a specific element standing between theme proper and transition in the CD hierarchy (Svoboda 1981). An important continuation of Firbas' insights concerning the relation between FSP and intonation is found in the work of Jana Chamonikolasová (2007) and also in her habilitation monograph (forthcoming), in which she gives – in the context of spoken English dialogue – a well-informed and deep comparison of FSP and TFA; in this monograph, as well as in her previous studies (2010), Chamonikolasová pays due respect to the communicative aspects of FSP.

5. TOPIC-FOCUS ARTICULATION (PETR SGALL AND THE PRAGUE SCHOOL)

Although there are several similar points between FSP and the theory of topic-focus articulation (TFA) as proposed in the sixties of the last century by Petr Sgall and then elaborated by him and his followers (Sgall, 1967; Sgall et al., 1973; 1980; 1986; Hajičová, Partee and Sgall, 1998), TFA is not a mere "translation" or "rephrasing" of the term FSP; a different term is used with the intention to indicate *certain differences* in the starting points, which can be summarized as follows:

(a) Firbas (1964) defined the *theme* as the element (or elements) carrying the lowest degree of communicative dynamism within the sentence; as already mentioned above, such a definition would imply that every sentence *has* an item with the lowest degree of communicative dynamism and would exclude the existence of sentences without a theme, the so-called topicless sentences. (But see above in Section 4 on Firbas' correction of the original definition.) Instead, the term *topic* of the sentence is used in TFA to refer to that part of the sentence that the sentence is *about*, which does not exclude "hot-news sentences", i.e. sentences which bring the addressee straight into the "deep water" of the news.

(b) In the same vein as in FSP, the TFA theory assumes that every item in the sentence carries a certain degree of *communicative dynamism*, but it is still the basic dichotomy between the topic of the sentence and its focus conveying information about its topic that plays an important role, especially with respect to the semantic interpretation of negation and its relation to presuppositions of the sentence (see examples supporting this argument below).

(c) The TFA supporters argue that there is an *important difference in the nature* of the four factors distinguished in FSP, namely that of linear arrangement, prosody, semantics and context. The first two belong to the means of expression of information structure and the other two to its functional layers.

(d) TFA is claimed to be a phenomenon belonging to the underlying, deep syntactic structure of sentences. The formal description of language the Prague group works with has a form of a multi-level language description, with the level of underlying syntactic structure called tectogrammatical as a representation of the linguistic meaning of the sentence (see below in this Section on the annotation scheme of the Czech corpus). As the differences of TFA are semantically relevant (see point (ii) below), the description of TFA is considered to be a part of this tectogrammatical level.

From the point of view of theoretical linguistics, it is of primary importance that the Praguian TFA theory is the first attempt to integrate the description of what was later more broadly referred to as the information structure of the sentence *into a formal description of language* (Sgall, 1967; 1979; from a more general viewpoint, cf. 2009). The basic tenets of the TFA are as follows:

(i) The dichotomy of the topic of the sentence and the focus of the sentence is specified as a bipartition of the sentence into *what the sentence is ABOUT* (its topic) and *what the sentence says about the topic* (its focus); in other words, the borderline lies between "what we are talking about" and "what we are saying about it". TFA is understood as linguistic rather than cognitive structuring; the bi-partition is based on the given-new strategy, but not identical to this cognitive dichotomy, as illustrated by the following examples (the assumed position of the intonation centre is denoted by capitals):

(1) John and Mary entered the DINING-ROOM. They looked from the WINDOW (and...).
(2) Mary called Jim a REPUBLICAN. Then he insulted HER.
(3) Mary called Jim a REPUBLICAN. Then he INSULTED her.

In the second sentence of (1), it is evident that the speaker means the window of the room, which can be characterized as an old piece of information; however, the reference to it is placed in the focus of the sentence: the speaker is telling about Jim and Mary what they did. In the second sentences of (2) and (3), both Jim and Mary are (cognitively) "known" since they are referred to in the first sentence, but only (3) is linguistically structured as being about both of them and the information in focus is the event of insulting. In (2), Mary is put into focus, as a target of Jim's insult. In addition, at least on the preferred reading, (2) implies that calling somebody a Republican is an insult. This interpretation is supported by the different intonation patterns of (2) and (3), as indicated by the capitals.

(ii) The semantic relevance of TFA can be best documented by the relationships between TFA and the *semantics of negation*. If in terms of the aboutness relation, the

Focus holds about the Topic, then in the prototypical case of negative sentences, the Focus does not hold about the Topic; in a secondary case, the negative sentence is about a negated topic and something is said about this topic.

(4) *John didn't come to watch TV.*

Prototypically, the sentence (4) is about John (topic) and it holds about John that he didn't come to watch TV (negated focus). However, there may be a secondary interpretation of a negative sentence, e.g. in a context of (5).

(5) *John didn't come, because he suddenly fell ill.*

One of the interpretations of (5) in terms of TFA is that the sentence is about John's not-coming (topic) and it says about this negated event that it happened because he suddenly fell ill (focus).

As Hajičová (e.g. 1973; 1984) documented, there is a close relation between TFA, negation and *presupposition* (see already the original analysis of presupposition as a specific kind of the entailment relation by Strawson, 1952):

(6) (a) John caused our VICTORY.
   (b) John didn't cause our VICTORY.
   (c) Though he played well as usual, the rest of the team was very weak (and nothing could have prevented our defeat).
(7) (a) Our victory was caused by JOHN.
   (b) Our victory was not caused by JOHN.

Both (6)(a) and (7)(a) imply that we won. However, it is only the negative counterpart of (7)(a), namely (7)(b), that implies that we won, while (6)(b) may appear in a context suggesting that we were defeated, see (6)(c). In terms of presuppositions, the statement that we won belongs to the presuppositions of (7) since it is entailed both by the positive as well as by the negative sentence, but not to the presuppositions of (6) as it is not entailed by the negative sentence.

Sgall and his colleagues present in their writings (with many references to examples quoted by other linguists) many convincing examples of pairs of sentences that differ only in their TFA which leads to different semantic interpretations; the outer forms of the members of these pairs may differ in word order, active or passive forms of the verb or intonation patterns, but the common denominator of these differences is their topic-focus articulation.

(iii) The notion of communicative dynamism is applied in TFA to refer to the underlying (deep) order of elements of the sentence rather than to the surface order of words; it is assumed that the deep order of elements in the topic part of the sentence is guided more or less by contextual criteria (the communicatively least important element comes first, the verb standing on the boundary between topic and focus) and a rather strong hypothesis is formulated concerning the deep order of elements in the focus part of the sentence called *systemic ordering:* "In the focus part of the sentence the complementations of the verb (be they arguments or adjuncts) follow a certain canonical order (not necessarily the same for all languages)". A tentative list showing the systemic ordering of modifications in Czech (Sgall et al., 1986: 198ff) suggests the following order of the main complementations: Actor – Condition – when – for how long – Cause – Regard – Aim – Manner – Accompaniment – Locative – Means – Addressee – Origin – Objective (Patient) – Directional – Effect.

This canonical order has been tested by a series of psycholinguistic experiments (with speakers of Czech, German and English, and more recently also on corpus material which offers richer and more consistent data). It is evident that different languages may differ in some specific points of this order (e.g. in English the assumed order of selected complementations is Temporal – Actor – Addressee – Objective (Patient) – Origin – Effect – Manner – Accompaniment – Directional) but in general, the hypothesis seems to be plausible and brings an interesting issue for further investigation.

A good test for the TFA theory is offered at present by the *annotated electronic corpus* of Czech called *Prague Dependency Treebank* (PDT, see Hajič, 1998; Hajič et al., 2006), which is an annotated collection of Czech texts with a mark-up on three layers: (i) morphemic, (ii) surface shape, and (iii) underlying (tectogrammatical). The current version of PDT (annotated on all three layers of annotation) includes 3,168 documents comprising the total of 49,442 sentences (833,357 occurrences of forms). The annotation on the tectogrammatical layer includes an indication of TFA values in terms of contextual boundness: three TFA values are distinguished, namely t – contextually bound non-contrastive, c – contextually bound contrastive, and f – contextually non-bound. On the basis of these values an algorithm was formulated and fully tested that performs the bipartition of the sentence into its topic and focus. The hitherto achieved results are encouraging and offer interesting observations: e.g. in 95 per cent of the cases, the hypothesis (present also in the FSP theory, see Firbas on the transitional character of the verb) that in Czech the boundary between topic and focus is in the prototypical case signalled by the position of the verb was confirmed. Also, a comparison of the results of the automatic procedure with human annotation has revealed that the most frequent differences, if any, concerned the difference in the assignment of the verb to topic or to focus. This again confirms the transitional character of the verb in Czech.

The existence of a parallel syntactically annotated corpus of English and Czech offers a further extension of the corpus-based study of TFA, with the multilingual material at hand.

6. A SCHEMATIC COMPARISON OF THE THREE CZECH APPROACHES TO INFORMATION STRUCTURE OF THE SENTENCE

To summarize our brief characterization of the three Czech approaches to the information structure of the sentence, given in the previous sections of our contribution, we present below an attempt at a comparison of their main tenets, starting – in the left column – with the original ideas formulated by Vilém Mathesius, and, on the same line in the two following columns, suggesting the counterparts of these ideas (or comments on them) as reflected in the FSP (Brno) and TFA (Prague) theories, respectively.

Mathesius	Brno FSP	Prague TFA
from function to form	factors – not clear	function and form clearly distinguished
basis x nucleus	yes: theme x rheme	yes, topic vs focus !semantic relevance
"aboutness"	observed	emphasized, basic
transition	explicit	implicit
accompanying elements	communicative dynamism	communicative dynamism in "deep" structure
	Svoboda: communicative importance	
"all-rheme"	basic instance level	recognized, "topicless"
subjective order	yes	yes
	dynamic semantic function	systemic ordering
	contextual boundness:	
	retrievability	basic, primitive notion

Figure 1 A comparison of the three Czech approaches to the information structure of the sentence

This comparison demonstrates that many ideas on what is now more generally called "information structure" are already *in nuce* in Mathesius' writings. His stimuli have been developed fruitfully in Brno, Prague, as well as by many scholars in Europe and the US (sometimes unknowingly re-inventing the wheel, but also often bringing in new aspects and viewpoints, not to speak about language data from typologically different languages). We also hope to have demonstrated that a serious examination of what Levinson calls "terminological profusion and confusion, and underlying conceptual vagueness" uncovers important issues and respectable results that have served and will also serve in the future for a deeper analysis of the communicative function of language. In the context of the centenary celebration for which this contribution has been prepared, it is also important to recall this fruitful resource offered by Prague English studies to the modern linguistic community.

ACKNOWLEDGEMENT

This chapter was written under the support of the grant of the Czech Republic Grant Agency P/406/12/0658; in its relevant parts, the author has been using language resources developed and/or stored and/or distributed by the LINDAT-CLARIN project of the Ministry of Education of the Czech Republic (project LM2010013).

NEGATION AND TOPIC VS. COMMENT

1. The treatments of negation in the transformational generative framework have not made clear so far whether such a framework provides for the fact that such sentences as (1) and (2) are not – at least in all their readings – paraphrases (the capital letters in the examples denote the placement of the intonation centre).

(1) He was not glad that they had COME.
   Cz. Nebyl nadšen tím, že PŘIJELI.
(2) That they had come didn't make him GLAD.
   Cz. Tím, že přijeli, nebyl NADŠEN.

While (2) can be used only if "they had come," (1) corresponds also to a situation when "they need not have come". Accounting for the difference in meaning between (1) and (2) is only possible under the assumption (advocated by Chomsky, Jackendoff and others) of the relevance of surface structure for the semantic interpretation. However, as has already been pointed out (cf. recently e.g. B. Hall Partee, 1971) there are good reasons for not abandoning the idea that transformations preserve meaning. In the present paper we shall try to show – after a brief account of recent studies on negation (1.) and a sketch of the functional generative description to which we subscribe (2.) – a possible approach to the description of negation in Functional Generative Description, using semantic representations in which the order of elements (interpreted as the scale of communicative dynamism) is semantically relevant (3.). Such an approach enables us to specify the (semantic) scope of negation (4.) and to show the necessity to distinguish between the means adequate for the logical negation and for the negation in a natural language (5.).

In the original conception of transformational grammar, which counted with kernel sentences and with transformations that change meaning, the relation between the positive sentence and its negative counterpart was understood as the relation of transformation (Chomsky, 1957, 109). On the other hand Klima (1964), whose study on negation can be taken as the most detailed analysis of negation in English within the framework of TG, postulates a single negative element, which can be derived by the phrase structure component in various places of the constituent structure of the sentence: according to which place it is generated, Klima distinguishes the so-called sentence and constituent negation.

Klima's work in a sense anticipates the further development of TG in that negative transformations, belonging originally to optional transformations, are made obligatory in most cases. This is why Katz and Postal (1964, 73–74, § 4.2.2) refer to his treatment when trying to justify their claim that all optional transformations that change meaning can be formulated as obligatory ones if the semantical relevant "signal" for their application has already been generated in the underlying phrase marker.

In the discussions that followed, concerning the character of transformations with regard to the meaning of the sentence, the problems of negation are in the centre of attention (together with the problems connected with other types of operators, e.g. quantifiers). Jackendoff (1969; 1971) is close to Klima's views: he insists on the differentiation between constituent and sentence negation and suggests to account for the difference of meaning between such sentences as *Many arrows didn't hit the target* and *Not many arrows hit the target* by considering not only the deep structure but also the surface structure, namely the placement of the negative particle in the surface structure of the sentence. According to Jackendoff the above sentences would have the same deep structure but would differ in the semantic scope of negation, determined by the position of *not* in the surface structure. Such an approach is supported by examples with passive constructions. The sentence *The target wasn't hit by many arrows* can be understood as coinciding partly with the meaning of the latter example above, in which the negative particle *not* also precedes the noun phrase including the quantifier *many*. Chomsky (1971; 1972) uses Jackendoff's analysis of negation as one piece of evidence for his extended standard theory; negation belongs among such phenomena for the correct semantic interpretation of which it is also important to take into account the surface structure of the sentence. He claims that it is necessary to provide for the semantically relevant articulation of the sentence into presupposition and focus and, from this point of view, the position of the negative particle *not* in the surface structure is important for determining what is presupposed by the sentence and what is asserted.

On the other hand Lakoff (1971) as well as McCawley (1970) conceive the negative element as a main verb and argue that sentence and constituent negation is conditioned by the fact how "high" the negative element is placed in the underlying phrase marker. In their approach the position of the negative particle in the underlying phrase marker uniquely determines the semantic scope of negation and the transformations do not change the meaning. To ensure that from one underlying phrase marker there are not derived two surface structures with different meanings, Lakoff employs the so-called global constraints (global rules).

An interesting observation is made by Bach (1968, 96 ff.), who points out that there is a relationship between what is negated and the stress: the sentence *The professors didn't sign a petition* can be pronounced either with the main stress on *DIDN'T*, or on *PROFESSORS*, or on *PETITION*, which is directly connected with the three possible interpretations of this negative sentence.

A stimulative attempt to describe negation in the framework of TG was made by Kraak (1966). As was rightly remarked by Seuren (1967, 348 ff) Kraak's approach is close to the conception of the articulation of the sentence into the theme and the rheme. Seuren, however, does not accept such an approach and regards such an articulation to be the matter of performance only, and not of competence. Kraak himself does not work with the notions of theme and rheme and he does not pursue the relation between negation and theme/rheme articulation any further. Seuren's (1969) general conception of deep structure is based on the distinction between operators and the nucleus of the sentence. Negation is one of the operators which in the deep structure precede the nucleus. Thus he can provide for the difference in meaning between such sentences as *Many smokers do not chew gum* and *Not many smokers chew gum* (differing in the mutual positions of the operators *neg* and *mult*) but he cannot provide for the difference between (1) and (2) or between such sentences as *That our building exploded wasn't caused by Harry* and *Harry didn't cause our building to explode* etc. (cf. below § 3.1).

The relationship between the placing of the negative particle *nicht* in the surface structure of German sentences and the articulation of the sentence into the theme and rheme is pointed out by Zemb (1968). He shows on sentences with negation that the traditional division of the sentence into subject and predicate is not suitable and that it is necessary to take into account the articulation of the sentence into the theme and the rheme (p. 40) and he connects the placing of the particle *nicht* with regard to the verbal complements (in sentences with sentences negation) with the boundary between theme and rheme (p. 50).

It is evident from this brief survey that the linguists who base their study on languages where the word order belongs to the means for expressing some semantic distinctions (as e.g. Kraak, 1966; Zemb, 1968; Bald, 1971; and Seuren, 196 1969) have also taken intonation into consideration, or even the communication situation, the distinction between "given" and "new" information, etc.[1] In our linguistic tradition such an approach is applied in many classical works on negation: for instance, Mathesius, 1937; Vachek, 1939; 1947; Poldauf, 1947; Daneš, 195; Křížková, 1968a; b; 1969, to mention but a few.[2] The aim of this paper is to show that such an approach is also fruitful within the framework of generative grammar and that it supplies an explanation to phenomena which otherwise are only recorded.

2. In the Functional Generative Description (FGD) as proposed by Sgall in early sixties and elaborated by his collaborators[3] in the Prague group of algebraic linguistics, the description of the sentence[4] is conceived of as a sequence of its representations

---

1   Cf. Bald's hypothesis (1971, 20) that the verbal complement which carries the intonation centre of the sentence belongs in the semantic scope of negation (but cf. 4 below); he remarks that this intonation centre, standing at the end of the sentence, brings new information.

2   Cf. the detailed analysis of several examples quoted by these authors, as given in our dissertation.

3   Cf. Sgall (1964; 1966a; b; 1967a, b); Sgall, Nebeský, Goralčíková, Hajičová (1969); Sgall, Hajičová (1970); Panevová, Benešová, Sgall (1972); Machová (1972).

4   The term "sentence" is used here for the phonetic shape of the sentence (as it is usual in algebraic linguistics); in terms of the approach of Dokulil and Daneš we would speak about an utterance event.

on several levels of the language system. These levels have a hiearchical order and we speak about "higher" (towards meaning) and "lower" levels (towards phonetic form). The representation of the sentence on the highest (semantic) level – called tectogrammatical in our system – is generated by a context-free phrase-structure grammar and is then transduced by means of the rules of transduction to the representations on lower levels, until the surface shape of the generated sentence it reached. It is then possible to say that the FGD anticipates the development of TG in that even the original form of FGD (formulated as early as in 1963–1964) counts with a sort of generative semantics.

2.1 The following assumptions held by FGD are relevant to the present discussion:[5]

(a) The representation of the sentence on the tectogrammatical level (henceforth the semantic representation, SR) has the form of a dependency graph, with the verb as its root. The nodes correspond to word forms and the edges (connecting the two members of a syntactic pair) to the relations of syntactic dependency. In the sequel we use the linearized form of SR's where parentheses are substituted for the edges, with the labels of the syntactic relations (e.g. *ag* for actor, *caus* for adverbial of cause etc.) as the subscripts.

(b) The use of dependency syntax makes it possible to interpret the left to right order of elements of SR's as a scale of communicative dynamism (CD),[6] with the element carrying the lowest degree of CD standing at the extreme left-hand side and that carrying the highest degree standing at the extreme right-hand side in the SR. It is assumed that, with each type of participant of the verb, it is possible to determine its position in the systemic arrangement of the participants according to their CD. In a given SR, however, any of the elements can be topicalized, i.e. placed to the left of the verb.

(c) In SR of each sentence it is marked which elements are contextually bound and which are contextually non-bound. Contextual boundness is understood rather broadly. Not only objects known either from the preceding context or from the situation are included among the contextually bound elements, but also relatively general determinations (modifications) having the character of Firbas' "local or temporal setting". It might seem that such a characteristics is superfluous since we work with a more subtle articulation according to the degrees of CD. However, as will be shown below in § 3 and 4, it is of great value to count with the characteristics of contextual boundness, in the analysis of negation.

We work here only with the verb and its participants as wholes without taking into account their internal structure, but we are aware that it should be investigated whether, for example, the boundary between the contextually bound and non-bound elements can be drawn only after or before a participant taken as a whole, or whether

5   For a detailed discussion of the questions of topic/comment articulation in the framework of the Functional Generative Description cf. Sgall (1967b; 1970; 1971a; 1972b); Sgall (in press); Procházka, Sgall (in press).

6   Cf. Firbas (1964), for the notion of CD. The cases of Bolinger's (1952) second instance are left aside for the purpose of our discussion here.

it would be also possible to draw this line for instance inside such a participant standing at the extreme right-hand side of SR.

As for the position of the verb in the SR, we assume that it always stands between its contextually bound and contextually non-bound participants; the verb is thus either the most dynamic contextually bound element, or the least dynamic contextually non-bound element. All elements before the verb are contextually bound; all elements after the verb are contextually non-bound.

Such a specification of the position of the verb in the semantic structure means that, at least in the description of functional sentence perspective in Czech, we count with a deep order of the type VSO. It remains to be investigated whether we can also work with such an order in the description of English, or whether the semantic structures of English and of Czech differ to such an extent that it would be better to count for English with actor in the first position in SR (without topicalization), as is done e.g. by Sgall (in press).

There are three questions which should be answered when deciding upon a method of incorporating the description of negation into the framework of the Functional Generative Description; namely (i) the status of the operator of negation (*Neg*) in SR, (ii) the restrictions concerning its position in SR, and (iii) the specification of the notion of "semantic scope of negation".

3.1 As for (i), two possibilities offer themselves in the proposed framework: the operator of negation can be either treated as a free modification of the verb, or can be represented by the means of a grammateme[7] (similarly to the grammatemes of tense, of mood, etc.). The latter solution is supported by the fact that there are certain restrictions which distinguish *Neg* from the usual types of free modification. As we shall show below, the placement of *Neg* in SR is restricted to some specific positions; it is also doubtful whether we can speak about a contextually bound and non-bound *Neg*, which is connected with the fact that *Neg* is not a lexical element. On the other hand, however, the treatment of *Neg* as a grammateme would lead to undesirable complications, if the so-called "constituent negation" – where the verb is outside the scope of negation – is to be taken into account (for a more detailed discussion, cf. Hajičová, 1972b), This is why we work here with *Neg* as a "free" participant, with some specific restrictions on its position and other properties (cf. 3.2 and 3.3 below).

3.2 Passing to the questions of the possible restrictions on the position of *Neg* in SR, let us consider examples (3) to (5).

(3) (a) John didn't come since his wife was ILL.
    (b) Since his wife was ill, John didn't COME.
    (c) Since his wife was ILL, John didn't come.

---

7   By a grammateme we mean such an element of the complex symbol representing a word form on the tectogrammatical level that corresponds to a "morphological meaning"; thus we speak about grammatemes of tense, aspect, number, etc.

(4) (a) Harry didn't cause our building to EXPLODE.
    (b) That our building exploded, wasn't caused by HARRY.
    (c) That our building EXPLODED, wasn't caused by Harry.
(5) (a) Harry didn't cause our DEFEAT.
    (b) Our defeat wasn't caused by HARRY.
    (c) Our DEFEAT wasn't caused by Harry.

Under the normal intonation, i.e. with the intonation centre on the last lexical item of the sentence, the sentences (a) and (b) in each set differ in that the units before the negated verb in examples (b) express facts that are not touched by negation. Thus, for example, the sentence (3)(b) can probably be used, under normal intonation, only in a situation when the speaker assumes that John's wife was ill. We think that the sentence (3)(a) can be used without such an assumption: it can be continued both by (i) *He had to go for a doctor to examine her thoroughly,* and (ii) ... *but because he was too busy yesterday; his wife is in the mountains with the children* (i.e. he does not come, but the reason lies elsewhere). Besides that, the sentence (3)(a) can be also used if it continues (iii) ... *but since he wanted to meet Harry* (i.e. he did come, but not because his wife was ill). Analogous interpretations can be assigned to the examples (4) and (5).

It should be noticed that for the sentence denoted as (c) in (3) to (5) the same considerations hold as for the sentences denoted as (a) in the respective sets. These observations suggest that that part of the sentence which in the hierarchy of CD stands to the left of the verb is out of the scope of negation; the verb itself may either be included in the scope (cf. interpretations (i) and (ii) for (3)(a) above), or excluded (cf. interpretation (iii)). To speak in terms of the position of the operator *Neg* in the semantic representation, we can say that *Neg* stands either immediately before the verb (to the left of the verb), or after the verb (to the right of the verb). To decide whether the position of *Neg* after the verb is restricted to certain positions or not, let us take example (6).

(6) Mother didn't scold her daughter because of her FATHER.

Although sentence (6) can be used in several contexts, only those in which the verb is outside the scope of negation (i.e. which are more or less synonymous with *mother scolded ... but ...*) are relevant for the present discussion. We suppose that both (6)(a) and (6)(b) can be regarded as continuations of (6):

(6) (a) ... (she scolded) but her son because of his bad marks at school.
    (b) ... (she scolded her daughter) but because of her bad marks at school.

(6) can be followed by (6)(a) only if the verb in (6) is contextually bound and the object the *daughter* is non-bound, i.e. if (6) is an answer to *Why did mother scold whom?* rather than *Why did mother scold her daughter?* On the other hand, if followed by (6)(b), the sentence (6) may be used as an answer to the latter question and not to the former, i.e. the verb and also the daughter are contextually bound. (Notice that the question

test is used here in the stronger sense, the question being supposed to include all the activated items of the stock of shared knowledge; for these notions, cf. Sgall, 1973.)

Also such examples as (7) and (8) corroborate the view that if the verb is outside the scope of negation, i.e. if *Neg* is placed after the verb in the hierarchy of CD, it always stands immediately before the first contextually non-bound verbal complement (participant).

(7) What have you promised to whom? – I haven't promised anybody any WIND MILLS ... but my wife a new dress.

(8) With whom did you talk about what? – I didn't talk about bombs with FOREIGN-ERS ... but about a new essay with a friend of mine.

To sum up, *Neg* can stand in SR of the sentence either immediately before the verb or also, in the case where the verb is a contextually bound element, immediately after the verb. Thus the sentence (6) would have the following SR's.[8]

(i) $[(\text{mother}^b{}_{ag} (Neg) \text{ scolded } (\text{her daughter}_{obj}) (\text{the father}_{caus})]$
(ii)   (a) $[(\text{mother}^b{}_{ag}) (Neg) \text{ scolded}^b (\text{her daughter}_{obj}) (\text{the father}_{caus})]$
       (b) $[(\text{mother}^b{}_{ag}) \text{ scolded}^b (Neg) (\text{her daughter}_{obj}) (\text{the father}_{caus})]$
(iii) $[(\text{mother}^b{}_{ag} (\text{her daughter}^b{}_{obj}) (Neg) \text{ scolded } (\text{the father}_{caus})]$
       (a) $[(\text{mother}^b{}_{ag}) (\text{her daughter}^b{}_{obj}) (Neg) \text{ scolded}^b (\text{the father}_{caus})]$
       (b) $[(\text{mother}^b{}_{ag}) (\text{her daughter}^b{}_{obj}) \text{ scolded}^b (Neg) (\text{the father}_{caus})]$

4. Let us pass over now to the specification of the notion "the semantic scope of negation". An assumption suggests itself to define the semantic scope of negation as that part of SR that stands to the right of *Neg*. However, the examples (3)(a) and (b) show that the situation is more complicated. The sentence (3)(a) may be understood at least in two ways:

(i)   he came, but not because his wife was ill
(ii)   = (3)(b) (if we disregard the hierarchy of CD)

In (ii) the end of the scope of negation is before the verbal complement (participant) which in (3)(b) stands at the beginning of the sentence, that is, in general we should count with the following form of semantic representation:

$A^b{}_1 ... A^b{}_k \, Neg \, V^{(b)} A_{k+1} ... A_m / A_{m+1} ... A_n$

where / denotes the end of the scope of negation,

$A^b{}_1 ... A^b{}_k$ are the complements which are contextually bound,

---

8   In our notation we use formulas linearizing dependency graphs, so that parentheses are substituted for edges, and subscripts are used to denote the labels of edges (*ag* stands for actor, *obj* for object, *caus* for adverbial of cause). The subscript *b* denotes that the element in question is contextually bound. In our simplified representations attributes are written together with the modified nouns.

$A_{k+1} ... A_m$ stand for the complements which are contextually non-bound and which are in the scope of negation, and

$A_{m+1} ... A_n$ stand for contextually non-bound complements which are outside the scope of negation.

To specify more precisely the right-hand boundary of the scope of negation, or the conditions under which this or that position of the boundary is possible, we must answer the following three questions:

(1) Are there cases where the distinction between the SR.

$A_1^b ... A_k^b \, Neg \, V^{(b)} A_{k+1} ... A_m \, / \, A_{m+1} ... A_n$

and the SR

$A_1^b ... A_k^b \, Neg \, V^{(b)} A_{k+1} ... A_m \, A_{m+1} ... A_n \, /$

(with the same lexical setting, the same structure, the same distribution of CD and the same placement of the boundary between the contextually bound and contextually non-bound part of the sentence) is semantically relevant?

If the answer to (1) is positive, then it is necessary to investigate

(2) whether there is some relation between the placing of the end of the scope of negation and the articulation of the sentence into its contextually bound and contextually non-bound parts;

(3) whether the two SR's quoted above are possible under all circumstances or whether they are possible only under some special conditions, i.e. with some specific types of verbal complements.

4.1 As an example let us take the sentence (9) and two situations (10) and (11) in which, in our opinion, the given sentence can be used.

(9) *She didn't come in time from the cinema because of her AUNT.*
$A_1^b \, Neg \, V^{(b)} A_2 A_3 A_4$

(10) *What has Joan done? (Why is her father angry with her?) She didn't come in time from the cinema (which was) because of her aunt.*

(11) *What is the matter with Joan today? She didn't come from the cinema in in time (not even) because of her aunt, and that's something.*

In both cases only the actor *(Joan)* is contextually bound, all other participants are non-bound. In the situation (10) a satisfactory answer could be *She didn't come from the cinema in time;* the reason of the event *(because of her aunt)* is mentioned in addition to the main (negative) statement, i.e. more or less parenthetically. The corresponding semantic representation could be (10'):

(10') $A_1^b \, Neg \, V \, A_2 A_3 \, / \, A_4$

In the situation (11) it is common that Joan comes from the cinema in time, at least because of her aunt; this time, however, she hasn't done so. For this interpretation, the corresponding semantic representation could be (11'):

(11') A^b_1 *Neg V* $A_2 A_3 A_4$ /

A similar reasoning can be applied to the example (12), where only the actor, or also the verb (cf. situation (15) below), are contextually bound.

(12) *He doesn't sleep because he is TIRED.*
A^b_1 *Neg* $V^{(b)} A_2$
(13) *I don't know how long Paul can endure such a busy life.*
He is in his office the whole day, he works over midnight at home, and then he doesn't sleep (which is) because he is tired.
(14) *What is the matter with him tonight? (Usually) be doesn't sleep because he is tired, only today he couldn't endure such a tension and be got asleep.*
(15) *Why hasn't Paul yet got asleep? He has been skating the whole afternoon and he doesn't sleep because he is tired.*

In the situations (13) and (14) similar considerations are valid as in (10) and (11); the corresponding semantic representations could be:

(13') A^b_1 *Neg V* / A_2
(14') A^b_1 *Neg V* A_2 /

The situation (15) differs from the preceding ones in that in the context preceding sentence (12) the fact that Paul doesn't sleep has already been mentioned. The negated verb is contextually bound and fatigue is quoted as the reason for the event. From the point of view of the scope of negation, this case is analogous to (13), the main difference being the contextual boundness of the verb. The corresponding semantic representation for (15) would be:

(15') A^b_1 *Neg* V^b / A_2

4.2 Thus we pass to the second question, i.e. what is the relationship between the positioning of the boundary of contextual boundness and the right-hand boundary of the scope of negation. In the semantic representation of sentence (12) in the situation (15) both boundaries coincide. The example (12) cannot give a clue to the question as to whether two different meanings of the sentence are concerned: in (12) only one participant is contextually non-bound, and this participant is outside the scope of negation both in (13) and (15). Thus, a more decisive example is to be found, where in the scope of negation (i.e. after the negated verb) there would be yet another participant which would show more clearly whether or not it is within the scope of negation. Let us take (16) with the corresponding situations as an example.

(16) *I don't know any poems by X.Y. because I don't read POETRY (very) much.*
A^b_1 *Neg* $V^{(b)} A_2 A_3$

(17) *It seems you know everything concerning Australian literature or is there something you don't know? – I don't know any poems by X.Y. because I don't read much poetry.*

(18) *Would you tell me something about the works of Australian writers? – They wrote first of all short stories and novels, some of them even poems. I don't know any poems by X.Y. because I don't read much poetry (. . . because he most probably didn't write any).*

We suppose that sentence (16) could not be used in the context (17) if the speaker didn't assume that X.Y. wrote poems, otherwise the whole situation would be shifted into the sphere of irony, mockery, joke. Thus, the speaker assumes the existence of poems written by X.Y. and states the reason for his ignorance. On the semantic level, in this interpretation, sentence (16) could have the following representation:

(17') $A^b_1 Neg\, V^b / A_2 A_3$

However, as the possible causative clauses used in (18) show, for this situation the assumption that X.Y. wrote poetry is not necessary. Whichever continuation of the main clause is chosen, it can be used in the context (18). The corresponding semantic representation could be (18'), with an additional specification of the reason synonymous with *which is because ...*

(18') $A^b_1 Neg\, VA_2 / A_3$

Thus we have come to the conclusion that there is a certain relationship between the placement of the boundary of the scope of negation and the placement of the boundary of the contextual boundness. If the verb is contextually bound and the negation is before the verb, then the end of the scope of negation is immediately after the verb, i.e. at the boundary between the contextually bound and the contextually non-bound part of the sentence (cf. (17')). If the verb is contextually bound and the negation is after the verb, then the end of the scope of negation is at end of the sentence. If the verb is contextually non-bound, the operator of negation is always before the verb and the end of the scope of negation is either at the end of the sentence or before some participant (cf. (13') and (18')).

4.3 It remains only to answer the third of the questions mentioned above, viz. whether the end of the scope of negation can be before any type of participants, whether it is possible to specify the conditions under which the end of the scope of negation need not coincide with the end of the sentence. The examples given below show that if the end of the scope of negation does not coincide with the end of the sentence (in the case of a contextually non-bound verb), then it is before participant with the highest degree of CD. An analysis of the examples of various types of participants in complex sentences in Czech quoted by Šmilauer (1966, 169–355) showed that the end of the scope of negation cannot be placed before so-called intentional (close, necessary) modification. As for the so-called free modifications, the end of the scope of negation can be placed before the adverb of cause in the broader sense of the term (cf. examples (25) and (22)), perhaps also before some adverbials of manner (cf. ex. (20) and ex. (21)) and the "predicative complement" ("doplněk," cf. ex. (19)), or, eventually before some other types as well (cf. ex. (23), (24)).[9]

(19) *(Co je s nimi?) Nevracejí se, otřeseni úlekem,*
(What's the matter with them?) They do not come back, shocked by fright.

(20) *(Jak to dopadne?) Nezkazíš to – tím, ze přijdeš včas.*
(How will it end?) You won't spoil it – by coming in time.

(21) *(Co se jí zase stalo?) Včera se nespálila – pokud vím.*
(What's again the matter with her?) Yesterday she didn't burn herself as far as I know.

(22) *(Jak se rozhodl velitel?) Velitel nepůjde bažinou, v souhlase s rozkazem.*
(How has the commander decided?) The commander will not go through the moorland, in accordance with the command.

(23) *(Co se vám na něm nelíbí?) Nepromluví ani slovo, kdykoli vstoupí místnosti někdo neznámý.*
(What don't you like about him?) He doesn't utter a word, whenever some stranger enters the room.

(24) *(Jak se máš?) Nebydlí se mi zrovna dobře, ve věžáku.*
(How are you?) I don't live very comfortably, in a skyscraper.

(25) *(Co je nového?) Děti nešly dva dny do školy na základě výnosu ministerstva školství.*
(What is the news?) The children didn't go to school for two days on the strength of a decree of the ministry of education.

All the examples quoted involve modifications loosely attached to the rest of the sentence, often as an additional, parenthetical restriction. In Czech, such modifications can be attached by means of an expression *a to* (which can be translated into English by *which is*), Šmilauer (1966, 257) comments upon such types of modifications that they represent a sort of intermediate type between subordination and coordination. In spoken language it is natural to make a short pause before such an additional adverbial.[10] Thus, as for their semantic structure, the sentences with such adverbial can be understood as complex sentences with a coordinate or appositive relation between two clauses. In the course of the transduction down to the morphemic struc-

---

9   Cf. Also Leech's (1969, 73) observation that in such sentences as *He doesn't listen on purpose. He didn't do it to annoy his daughter. He hasn't been staying here for a long time. I don't feel particularly upset of what he said*, the verbal complement (standing at the end of the sentence) is either in the scope of negation or outside this scope. He adds an interesting remark that, when placed before the subject of the sentence, such a verbal complement is always outside the scope of negation.

10 Cf. Seuren's (1967, 342–343) and Kraak's (1966) observation that in Dutch prepositional phrases of a certain (not yet precisely specified) type, if they are at the end of the sentence and if there is a pause before them in spoken language, may have a character of an additional modification, of a coordinate appendix, which can be often paraphrased by the means of "which is" or "namely": *He doesn't work – to my satisfaction* (meaning: either *his works doesn't satisfy me* or *he doesn't work, which is to my satisfaction*).

ture, the contextually bound part of the second (attached) clause is deleted and only the contextually non-bound adverbial is left.

(26) *I do not know any poems by X. Y. (which is) because I don't read much poetry.*
(27) *(I)[b] do not know any poems by X. Y. – (I do not know the poems)[b] because I do not read much poetry.*

Thus, we have arrived at the following specification of the right-hand boundary of the scope of negation:

In the scope of negation is everything standing to the right of the operator of negation up to the boundary between the contextually bound and non-bound parts of the sentence. If the operator of negation stands immediately on this boundary, then the end of the scope of negation coincides with the end of the sentence. (By the sentence we understand here a sentence governed by the verb to which the operator of negation is related, i.e. only one of the clauses in coordinate relation.)

To sum up, three factors have to be taken into consideration in deciding on the position of negation and its scope, namely the boundary of contextual boundness (denoted here by slash), the position of the verb and the position of the operator of negation relative to the verb. Theoretically, the following cases are possible:

(i)   V   Neg   /
(ii)   Neg   V   /
(iii) V   /   Neg
(iv)   Neg   /   V
(v)   /   V   Neg
(vi)   /   Neg   V

Cases (i) and (iv) can be excluded on the grounds that in the scope of negation there would not be any member of the sentence: in both (i) and (iv) the operator of negation immediately precedes the boundary of the contextually bound and non-bound parts of the sentence – and the end of the scope of negation coincides with this boundary. Our analysis has led us to the conclusion that, if the verb is outside the scope of negation and only some member standing after the verb is negated, then the verb is always contextually bound. If further empirical investigations show that such an assumption does not hold in full, even such cases as above can be described in the frame of our hypothesis on the scope of negation. Thus as indisputable examples there remain cases given as (ii), where to the negated topic as a contextually bound part of the sentence there is attached a positive focus in the sense of a contextually non-bound part of the sentence, (iii) in the sense of "constituent negation" and (vi) with negated focus.

5. Our considerations about the possible placing of the scope of negation show that, for the description of negation in a natural language, the means used by logicians are not the most suitable. In logic, the logical negation of a formula proposition is formed by means of the expression *It is not true that...* In natural language, however, the negation of a sentence e.g. *John sleeps because he is tired* is not synonymous with the sentence *It is not true that John sleeps because he is tired.* It seems more adequate to work with a performative construction *I say about X that Y* where *X* stands for the contextually bound part of the sentence.[11] Thus for the sentence (28) we may get among others the following paraphrases, which show the relevant interpretations of the negative sentence (28).

(28) *John doesn't sleep because he is TIRED.*
(a) *I say about John that it is not true that he sleeps because he is tired.*
(b) *I say about John's sleeping that it is not true that it is because he is tired.*
(c) *I say about John's not sleeping that (it is true that) it is because he is tired.*

What is before the expression *it is not true that* is not negated, so that in terms of logic, we cannot speak about the negation of the whole proposition, whereas in linguistics we must admit the presence of a sentence negation. The relation *I say about X that Y* can be interpreted in terms of the functional sentence perspective as the the articulation of the sentence into the contextually bound *(X)* and the contextually non-bound part of the sentence (Y). Within the framework of the Functional Generative Description sentence (28) would have the following semantic representations which would correspond to the paraphrases (a), (b), and (c), respectively:

(a') $[(John^b_{ag}) \, (Neg) \, sleeps \, (he \, is \, tired)_{caus}]$
(b') $[(John^b_{ag}) \, sleeps^b \, (Neg) \, (he \, is \, tired)_{caus}]$
(c') $[(John^b_{ag})(Neg) \, sleeps^b \, (he \, is \, tired)_{caus}]$

Such an approach leads to the following specification of the (semantic) sentence negation: If the contextually bound part of the sentence is called the topic of the sentence and the contextually non-bound part its focus, then we can say that what is negated is the relation between the topic and the focus,[12] what is identified by the topic, is presupposed (and as such is not touched by sentence negation, it is outside the scope of negation) and what is inside the focus is either presupposed ("existential presuppositions" in the broad sense of the term)[13] or it is the so-called allegation.[14] Moreover, the presupposed topic itself can be negated (cf. here (c)).

---

11 Cf. Ross and Sadock's hypothesis about the performative hypersentences (Ross, 1970; Sadock 1969a; b); for the possibility of employing such hypersentences in the description of the functional type, cf. Sgall (1970).
12 Cf. Sgall (1970).
13 For a tentative attempt at the classification of presuppositions cf. Hajičová (1972a); the term „existential" presuppositions is used by Dahl (1970) and Karttunen (1970) for presuppositions connected with definite noun phrases: in a sentence as *The man kissed the woman* the existence of both persons is presupposed. Here we apply the term in a somewhat broader sense, viz. also for presuppositions connected with factive and some similar types of verbs (cf. Kiparsky, 1970; Karttunen, 1970; 1971a; b; Poldauf, 1972a; b; in press) and verbal constructions.
14 As for the term allegation, cf. Hajičová (1972a); by this term we mean such a part of the sentence that, under negation , is neither negated nor asserted but it expresses a possibility of its content: in the sentence *Harry didn't cause our defeat* (if the end of the scope of negation coincides with the end of the sentence) the noun phrase *our defeat* is an allegation.

ON PRESSUPPOSITION AND ALLEGATION

Though the fashionable wave of using (and misusing) the notion of presupposition in linguistic writings had its climax at the beginning of the seventies, the notion still remains one of the widely discussed issues in present-day linguistic writings. In this paper I would like to return to my previous investigations which have led me (1) to introduce the trichotomy of "meaning proper," presupposition and allegation, (2) to re-examine the appropriateness of the notion of allegation form the point of view of some more recent writings on presupposition, and (3) to add some considerations concerning the presuppositions of interrogative sentences.

1. First, let me summarize briefly the conclusions I drew in my paper at the COLING conference in Debrecen (Hajičová, 1971). I proposed there to distinguish three kinds of entailment[1], which can be specified for declarative sentences in the following way:

(i)   meaning proper: A is a (part of the) meaning proper of B, if B entails A and not-B entails not-A[2];

(ii)   presupposition: A is a presupposition of B, if B entails A and not-B entails A;

(iii) allegation: A is an allegation of B if B entails A and not-B entails neither A nor not-A.

The three notions can be preliminarily exemplified by sentences (1)–(7)[3].

(1) Since John was ill, we won the MATCH.
(2) Since John was ill, we didn't win the MATCH
(3) Harry caused our VICTORY.
(4) Harry didn't cause our VICTORY.
(5) We won the MATCH.
(6) We didn't win the MATCH.

---

1   In our specifications we use the notion "entail" in the sense of logical entailment as defined by Keenan (1972): S logically entails A if A is true in all situations and possible worlds in which S is true. It may be more precise to speak about reference assignments instead of situations.

2   Our understanding of not-A and not-B is discussed in § 2. It is not identical with the logician's formulation "it is not true that...," since we are convinced that this formulation disguises the linguistic structuring of negative sentences, esp. the distinction between sentences with and without a topic (categorical and thetic judgements).

3   The capital letters in our examples denote the bearer of the intonation centre.

(7) John was ILL.

(8) ... He tried hard, but Johnny took all the initiative, was the best player on the team and helped most of all to get back the CUP.

(9) ... This time, unfortunately, we lost the game.

(5) is a part of the *meaning proper* of (1), since it is entailed by (1) and (6) is entailed by (2); (7) is a *presupposition* of (1), since it is entailed both by (1) and by (2); (5) is an *allegation* of (3), because it is entailed by (3) and neither entailed nor denied by (4), as the two possible continuations of (4) show, which we exemplify here by (8) and (9). This is to say, that in the case of allegation, there is a potential possibility under negation of what was entailed by the affirmative sentence.

A closer look at the examples analyzed reveals interesting relationships between entailment and topic/focus articulation; with the NP *our victory* being topicalized, (5) is a presupposition of (10), since it is entailed both by (10) and by (11); (11) can be followed by (8), not by (9).

(10) Our victory was caused by HARRY.

(11) Our victory wasn't caused by HARRY.

An explanation offered itself in terms of the scope of negation[4]: as our investigations in the framework of Functional Generative Description have shown (Hajičová, 1973), in the unmarked case, the scope of negation is identical with the focus of the sentence. Let us assume that in the underlying structure of sentences the scope of negation is determined on the left-hand side by the position of the operator of negation and on the right-hand side by the end of the semantic representation of the sentence, or by the boundary between topic and focus (if this boundary stands between the operator and the end of the sentence). Another hypothesis at which we arrived analyzing empirical data says that the operator of negation stands either immediately before, or after the verb; the latter possibility is present only if the verb belongs to the topic of the sentence. Primarily, the verb belongs to the focus of the sentence (it predicates something about the topic), and in this case the scope of negation always extends from the juncture between topic and focus to the end of the sentence (i). What is negated here, is the relation between the topic and the focus. In the secondary case, where the verb is in the topic, there are two possibilities, illustrated by (ii) and (iii), respectively: either the negation again concerns the focus, but then it does not touch the verb (as a part of the topic), cf. (ii), or the negation concerns only the verb (the scope of negation includes the verb alone, as an elementary constituent); in this case, the end of the scope of negation is the boundary between topic and focus (cf. (iii)).

---

4   Our understanding of "scope of negation" differs from the approach of Kempson (1977, p. 133f), who discussed the relationships between the component parts of a single lexical item; it is possible to agree with her that *It wasn't a woman that came to the door*, for example, is indistinct rather than ambiguous as concerns the negated part of the meaning of *woman*, but from this nothing follows for the scope of negation in the usual sense (with respect to the structure of the sentence).

(i) $A^t_1...A^t_k$ / Neg V $A_{k+1}... A_m$ %
(ii) $A^t_1... A^t_k$ V^t / Neg $A_{k+1}... A_m$ %
(iii) $A^t_1... A^t_k$ Neg V^t% / $A_{k+1}... A_m$

$A^t_1...$ A^t_k stand for the participants (cases and free adverbials) included in the topic of the sentence, V^t stands for the verb included in the topic, $A_{k+1}... A_m$, V stand for the participants and verb, respectively, included in the focus of the sentence, the slash denotes the juncture between topic and focus, and % denotes the end of the scope of negation.

The following examples (with paraphrases of their preferred readings) may illustrate the point:

(12) Harry didn't cause our VICTORY (but our defeat)
 – He *caused* something, but not our victory – (ii)
(13) He didn't come because his wife was ILL
 – The reason why he *didn 't come* is that his wife was ill – (iii)

With (i) it is predicated about the topic of the sentence that the focus (which includes the main verb) does not hold about it – see e.g. (11); with (ii) the situation is similar, only the verb is included in the topic: in the given reading of (12) it is predicated about the fact that Harry caused something that the thing he caused was not "our victory"; with (iii) the negated verb is a part of the topic, i.e. something is predicated about the fact that an action (state) did not take place; e.g. (13) is more or less equivalent to "The cause of his not having come was that his wife was ill."

It follows from our specification of presupposition and allegation and from the above specification of the scope of negation that the entailments connected with the elements in the topic (except for the verb in (iii)) belong to presuppositions (see (7) for (2), and (5) for (11)). As for the entailments connected with the elements in the focus in (i) and (ii), our discussion of several types of phenomena referred to as "presuppositions" in linguistic writings had led us to the conclusion that most of these entailments should be classed as allegations, except for the entailments connected with complements of factive verbs and definite NP's (as for the latter exception, we shall return to it below).

2. It has soon become evident that the current understanding of the notion of presupposition covers a heterogeneous collection of phenomena. Attempts to apply the test of negation consistently and to expose the examples of "obvious" presupposition-carrying structures to a detailed empirical analysis have led to serious doubts about the appropriateness of the introduction of presuppositions into linguistic (as well as logical) theory. Several ways-out have been suggested: from proposals for a recognition of a certain "gradience" in entailment (Bolinger, 1976) through broadening the notion of presupposition to cover all presupposition-like phenomena even if they do not fulfill the current definitions (Cooper, 1974), or, contrary to that, dividing this collection into categories at least one of which, namely a conventional implicature, can be well compared with the original strict account (Karttunen and Peters, 1977, 1979), up to refusing to include the concept of presupposition in the semantics of natural language and accounting for the phenomena in question within a Gricean pragmatic framework (Kempson, 1975). In his revealing review of Kempson (1975) Cresswell (1978) points out that the problem of presupposition can be transposed to that of the scope of negation. But this does not solve the whole problem: as Hausser (1976) duly pointed out, a Russellian analysis (assuming the ambiguity of *The present king of France is not bald* on the narrow scope and wide scope negation reading) is untenable for two reasons:

(1) the above sentence is intuitively unambiguous,

(2) the analysis cannot be extended to other instances of presuppositions.

As for (1), a topic/focus analysis of the sentence offers a suitable explanation: in its highly preferred reading this sentence is not "topicless" (since the subject position is occupied by a definite NP); as for (2), I believe that these other instances include e.g. factives.

We have followed a similar line of thinking when arguing for the necessity of the recognition of allegation; in addition, we attempted to specify the scope of negation in its close relation to topic/focus articulation as briefly outlined above. In our formulations, not-B refers to the negation of the sentence B in the sense of the negation of the relation between the topic of B and the focus of B, see types (i) and (ii) above. This can be compared with what is called by the logicians internal negation, negation over merely some part of the sentence. In terms of our understanding of the relation between topic and focus on the one hand and of the scope of negation on the other, external negation is the case of negation of topicless sentences; informally speaking, such sentences that may answer a very general question such as *What's the matter?*, *What has happened?*, *What's the news?* and that include no indexical or other lexical item referring broadly to the given situation (setting): *No RAIN is falling, A stranger fell DOWN* are topicless, while *Yesterday it RAINED* and *There was a STRANGER here* are not.

It is interesting to see that in many of the writings quoted in the preceding paragraphs several hints can be found pointing to the necessity of a recognition of some unit similar to that of allegation; in some of them, also the close connection between the kind of entailment and the articulation of the sentence into topic and focus is taken into account. Thus it has been revealed and is now widely accepted (and in this sense also our conclusions made in Hajičová, 1971, should be ammended) that with definite NP's, the failure of the "existential" (in our terms, referential) entailment carried by such a definite element leads to a meaningless statement ("presupposition failure") if this NP is in the topic part of the sentence (those who rely on English only and take it as a prototype of natural language speak mistakenly about the subject position of the NP, see e.g. Wilson, 1975), while if included in the focus, the falsity of such an entailment leads to the falsity of the whole statement (see e.g. Cooper's, 1974, example *He spent the morning interviewing the king of France* and his reference to Strawson, 1974, pp. 88–89; cf. also Lyons, 1977, p. 601; Sgall, 1979; Keenan, 1976). It seems that also the "ordered entailments" of Wilson and Sperber (1979) come rather close to our suggestion to study presupposition in close connection with the topic/focus articulation (especially with the hierarchy of communicative dynamism).

Keenan, to our knowledge, was one of the first to make a distinction between "logical" and "pragmatic" presuppositions; he understands the latter as being determined by culturally defined conditions on the context which have nothing to do with the speaker's beliefs of the truth or falsity of the entailed expression. Perhaps it was misleading to call them "presuppositions"; we are convinced – contrary to Stalnaker, 1974, who claims that "the semantic and pragmatic notions of presupposition provide two alternative accounts of the same linguistic phenomenon" – that two different though overlapping sets of phenomena are concerned, one having an immediate impact on linguistic meaning while the other has more in common with Gricean conversational principles and implicatures[5]. As Verschueren (1978) notes, there are pragmatic "presuppositions" that "disappear" under negation; cf. also Schwarz (1979). Hausser (1976, p. 258) offers a plausible explanation concerning this point; he argues that it is *sentences* that have presuppositions (we would only replace "sentence" by "sense of a sentence," i.e. their semantic representation plus the specification of reference); the speaker (and hearer) may have their assumptions, but the speaker must reckon with the semantic properties of the sentence (including its semantic presuppositions); if he wants to be sincere, he should take care that the semantic presuppositions of the sentence he uses are not in conflict with his assumptions.

Let us only note in this connection that probably every genuine presupposition (i.e. "logical" or "semantic") is connected also with pragmatic impact, its fulfillment being a necessary condition of linguistic performance without disturbances (cf. Verschueren, 1978, p. 109). The other class of phenomena, such as the distinction between *tu* and *vous* in French, also has a similar impact, but this impact itself belongs to the domain of conversational implicatures, felicity conditions and similar regularities of communicative competence rather than to linguistic competence itself.[6] The pragmatic aspects of "logical" or "semantic" presuppositions follow also from the just noted fact that it is the sense of a sentence (i.e. its meaning plus reference assignment) that is connected with a certain presupposition. In other words, it is necessary to know the reference assignment of the given occurrence of the sentence to be able to check whether its presuppositions are met.

Even if it can be shown that many of the examples of presuppositions can be explained either by means of the scope of negation (which does not include the topic of the sentence) or in terms of the Gricean pragmatic framework, there still will remain presuppositions carried by the complements of factive verbs (I *know that...*), which must be admitted to be connected with a kind of entailment different from that of "meaning proper" and allegation.

---

5   The former are defined in terms of van Fraassen's definition, the latter by means of conversational acceptability of the utterance P when the speaker of P assumes Q and believes his audience to assume Q as well (Stalnaker, 1974, pp. 222–223; cf. Schwarz, 1977, p. 247).

6   See Sgall's (1974) discussion of Keenan's pragmatic presuppositions.

Careful investigations of the so-called factive verbs and of the entailments connected with their complements in the position in the topic and in the focus of the sentence point out that the set of factive verbs is probably smaller than was formerly assumed; e.g. for *to regret, to be glad*, the test connected with the change of topic and focus shows that their object clauses are presupposed only when standing in the topic, while in the focus position they are connected with allegations.

(14) He regretted that his friends came to see him.
(15) He didn't regret that his friends came to see him.
(16) That his friends came to see him, he didn't regret.
(17) Oh no, you're mistaken, his friends didn't come.
(18) His bad humour was due to the fact that the weather didn't allow him to plan a skiing weekend this time. As for the friends, they all came to the party, and it was a nice party, you can believe me.
(19) His bad humour was due to the fact that the weather didn't allow him to plan a skiing weekend this time. As for the friends, they had to stay at home, since their child was ill.

If the "fact" that the friends came to see him were presupposed in (14) to (16), then the reaction (17) would point to a presupposition failure and (19) would be excluded. This is the case with (14) and (16); however, (15) can be coherently followed both by (18) as well as by (19). Creswell's (1978, p. 443) doubts about the possibility of subsuming the problem of factives under the analysis of the anaphorical use of the definite article are more than justified.

(20) John doesn't know (the fact) that he lost a pound.

It would be really difficult to show that the definite article in *the fact that* ... plays some anaphoric role, which is the key feature in Kempson's (1975) analysis of definite article. Rather, *the fact* refers to the following relative clause and this relative clause belongs primarily to the focus of such a sentence. The object of such verbs as *to know* belongs to the topic only in specific contexts, e.g. in *John lost a whole fortune, but he does not KNOW yet that his financial situation has become so bad.*

We hope that this gives support to the necessity of distinguishing the relation of presupposition as a specific type of entailment; as for the two remaining types, namely meaning proper and allegation, Kempson (similar to many other authors) does not feel the need to differentiate them; she speaks about entailment as such. However, even if we – for the sake of argument – accept the analysis of a sentence as a conjunction of propositions, we cannot overlook a different status of different elements of such a conjunction. Thus e.g. if we take (21) as a conjunction of several propositions, among others of (22) (a) and (b), the respective negative reactions (23)(a) and (b) differ from each other:

(21) John knows that Jane married Jim.
(22) (a) John knows the fact.
  (b) Jane married Jim.
(23) (a) No, he doesn't know it.
  (b) Oh no, you are mistaken, she did not.

Such reactions as (23)(b), or those starting with *Oh no, you see..., How could it be so?...* indicate that there is a certain discontinuation in the dialogue. The speaker makes clear by them (often, not always) that one of the tacit assumptions made by the other participant is not met in the given situation. It is, of course, also possible to say just *No, she did not,* but such a simple continuation is by far not so natural as (23)(a). It can be then suggested that such reactions as (23)(b) may be regarded as typical for presupposition failure, i.e. for cases where the conventional implicature is not met in the given point of discourse.

A similar consideration may hold for Kempson's (1975) example (24), with a reaction (24)(a), which is evidently different from a reaction (24)(b); only the latter entails the truth of the fact that Edward had been unfaithful to Margaret.

(24) Sue didn't realize that Edward had been unfaithful to Margaret.
  (a) You must have been mistaken. How could she have done! I know Edward has never been unfaithful to her!
  (b) Oh no, on the contrary, she did realize it!

The first reaction points to the "presupposition failure" case; the second to the falsity of the sentence (24), for which the reaction beginning with *On the contrary* may be taken as a good test. For sentences bringing partially true information, such as *The flag of France is red and blue,* such falsifying reactions as *Not only that* are typical.

The approach distinguishing presupposition from other kinds of entailment is thus corroborated by (i) distinguishing allegation from presupposition, and (ii) working in a systematic way with the topic/focus articulation. In this way it is possible to find out that the cases where the negative sentence is connected with the required entailment are restricted, and that there are other cases with genuine presuppositions. Besides factive verbs this concerns, as we have seen above, definite NP's in the topic of the sentence; it should be tested empirically if also the NP's connected with the delimiting feature Specific are connected with a presupposition, if belonging to the topic. Such examples as (25) seem to support this view:

(25) It was PAUL who saw a white crow yesterday.
(26) Paul saw a white CROW yesterday.

Contrary to (26), which contains the relevant NP in the focus, (25) mentions it as contextually bound, as given by the preceding co-text or situation, i.e. as one of the salient items of the stock of shared knowledge. We assume that reaction (27) is natural if it follows (25), while (28) is a smooth continuation of (26), but not vice versa. It follows then that the position in the topic is a condition on the presence of a presupposition also with at least some specific NP's, not only with definite ones.

(27) Oh no, you are mistaken, no one ever found a white crow.
(28) No, on the contrary, he saw only black ones.

Also the fact that such words as *even* or *also* are connected with genuine presuppositions (Karttunen and Peters, 1977) seems to be conditioned by the specific position of such words in the topic/focus articulation. In *They saw even JANE* or *They met also PAUL* these adverbs mark the following nouns as being the only item included in focus, the verbs and their subjects then belong to the topic, so that such sentences can be used appropriately only in such contexts where it belongs to the salient items that "they" saw (met) someone.

As for proper names, however, it seems that even if included in the focus they are connected with genuine referential presuppositions: both *John has (not) met MARILYN* and *John has not MET Marilyn* entail that there is a person (in the relevant part of the universe of discourse, not necessarily in the real world) that is referred to as Marilyn. Such a continuation as *I don't know who you mean by Marilyn* must be understood as an instance of presupposition failure.

These considerations lead us to maintain our original position and to distinguish between three types of (factual) entailment, namely meaning proper, presupposition and allegation, as specified in § 1. These notions are closely connected with the notions of topic and focus and with the specification of the scope of negation.

3.1 To specify what is a presupposition of a question (or, to be more precise, of an interrogative sentence) is even a more difficult problem because the test of negation cannot be used directly for this purpose. Let us first discuss from this point of view some aspects of wh-questions.

An integrated formal analysis taking into account both logical and linguistic aspects of wh-questions was given by Keenan and Hull (1973), who define presuppositions of questions as logical consequences of every pair consisting of the given question and one of its logical answers. According to their definition an L-sentence (i.e. roughly a logical form of a sentence) S "is a logical presupposition of a question Q just in case, for every answer A to Q, S is a logical consequence of the pair [Q, Y]," where A is the phrase which with other approaches would be considered the (non-omissible) focus of the answer.

With such a specification of a presupposition of a question based on the logical answer to a wh-question it is not quite clear whether a negative pronoun might be considered a logical answer to a wh-question: If one supposes that "nobody" is a possible answer to (29), then – using the above mentioned framework – we see that (30) is not presupposed by the given question, since (30) is not a logical consequence of the pair (*Who came? Nobody*); only if one assumes a priori that "nobody" does not belong to appropriate answers to the given question, then (30) is presupposed by the question.

(29) Who came?
(30) Somebody came.

The view that (30) is a presupposition of (29) is shared by many of those who discuss this problem (see Katz and Postal, 1964; Karttunen, 1978; Bolinger, 1978a, 1978b; Hintikka, 1978, but cf. below).

A more differentiated view is held by Kiefer (1977); he makes a distinction between a *presupposition* of a question (which must be shared by the answer) and a *background assumption* (which may but need not be shared by the answer). He exemplifies this distinction on (31) to (33).

(31) Who has studied water pollution?
(32) There is no water pollution.
(33) Nobody.

(32) is a negation of (one of) the presupposition(s) of (31) (one can speak here about "presupposition failure": the response might have started with the words "You're mistaken, there is no water pollution").[7] On the other hand, (33) only indicates that the hearer does not share the background assumption of the speaker ("somebody has studied water pollution").[8]

Joshi (in his lecture in Prague, 1979) proposed to make an interesting distinction between presuppositions and presumptions of a question: P is a presupposition of Q, if for all direct answers A_i of Q, $A_i \rightarrow P$ and $\sim A_i \rightarrow P$. P is a presumption of Q, if for all direct answers A_i except one, say A_j, $A_i \rightarrow P$, $\sim A_i \rightarrow P$, $i \neq j$. This is to say that in case P is a presupposition of Q, then one cannot answer Q by a negative pronoun (see (34) and (35)).

(34) When did John take CSE 110?
(35) John took CSE 110. (=presupposition)

If, on the other hand, P is just a presumption of Q, such an answer is possible (see (36) to (38)).

(36) Which faculty members teach CSE?
(37) Faculty members teach CSE. (=presumption)
(38) Noone.

In the latter case, Joshi adds, the questioner may add "if any", which admits the negative answer (38).

---

7   Sometimes this phenomenon is explained in terms of cohesion: the dialogue breaks down at the moment (see Kiefer, 1977).
8   When making a distinction between speaker's and hearer's assumptions one should bear in mind that the speaker always formulates his utterance according to his assumptions about the speaker's assumptions.

We tried to show (Hajičová, 1976) that the intuitive acceptability of a negative answer such as (41) to wh-questions depends on the way in which the question is pronounced: if the intonation centre is on the wh-element (as in (40)), then (41) is highly
inappropriate, and it more or less breaks down the dialogue (the speaker might have
added: "You're mistaken, noone came late"), while if the intonation centre is at the end
of the question (as in (39)), such an answer is quite acceptable.[9]

(39) Who came to the MEETING?
(40) WHO came to the meeting? = WHO was it who came to the meeting?
(41) Nobody.

With (40) one expects to be given a non-empty list of persons who attended the
meeting, which is not necessarily the case with (39).

If these intuitions are true, then again the presuppositions of questions must be
studied in close connection with the topic/focus articulation of questions. The intonation centre on the wh-element shows that the rest of the question belongs to the topic
part; if the intonation centre lies on the last element of the question, then (at least)
this element belongs to the focus (see Hajičová, 1976, for the topic/focus distinction in
questions).

It should be mentioned in this connection that Bolinger's (1978b) analysis of the
possibility and interpretation of the final position of the wh-element in wh-questions
is based on very similar considerations; if the wh-element is in the final position, then
only the wh-element is assumed to be in the comment (focus), the whole rest of the
question belonging to the topic (42)(a).

(42) (a) You gave the book to WHOM?
     (b) WHOM did you give the book to?

In this particular paper[10], Bolinger does not take into consideration the possibility
of the front position of the wh-word with a shift of the intonation centre on it, thus
marking it also as the comment (focus) (cf. (42)(b)).

When examining the way the distinction between presupposition and presumption (as defined by Joshi) is determined by the structure of the interrogative sentence,
one easily finds that the difference between the placement of the intonation centre on
the wh-element and on some other element of the question is only one of the relevant
factors: While this criterion is sufficient for such examples as (43) or (44) (where a
negative answer is acceptable only for the (a) variants, so that (c) is a presumption

---

9   Our approach seems to be corroborated by Stechow's (1980) account of the difference between *Who likes*
     HANS-ROBERT (p. 87, ex. 176A) and *WHO did call?* (p. 78, ex. 143). According to Stechow, his 176A can be appro-
     priately answered by *NOONE likes Hans-Robert* and it is not connected with an assumption that someone likes
     Hans-Robert, whereas his 143 has a topic "Someone called".
10   However, in other writings on this subject, Bolinger duly works with intonation as one of the most important
     factors determining the semantic structure of the sentence, see esp. Bolinger (1972).

of (a) and a presupposition of (b)), in other examples, such as (45), (c) belongs to the presuppositions of both (a) and (b).

(43) (a) Who came LATE?
     (b) WHO came late?
     (c) Someone came late.
(44) (a) What did you buy for him for a Christmas PRESENT?
     (b) WHAT did you buy for him for a Christmas present?
     (c) You bought him something for a Christmas present.
(45) (a) Why did you come LATE?
     (b) WHY did you come late?
     (c) I came late for some reason.

These considerations led us first to a preliminary hypothesis that this distinction is connected with that between inner participants (inner cases) and free (adverbial) modifications.[11] It soon turned out, however, that the facts are not so simple. There are examples in which an interrogative sentence with a wh-element in the syntactic position of a free modification is connected with the presupposition (c) only in its (b) variant; this is the case in Joshi's example (36) above, as well as in (46), and probably also (47). On the other hand, there are examples of interrogative sentences which include a wh-element in the position of an inner participant, but are connected with a respective presupposition in both variants (cf. (48), where (c) is a presupposition of both (a) and (b)).

(46) (a) How many people DIED?
     (b) HOW MANY people died?
     (c) Some people died.
(47) (a) When did you visit ITALY?
     (b) WHEN did you visit Italy?
     (c) You visited Italy at some time.
(48) (a) To whom did Mary give the BOOK?
     (b) To WHOM did Mary give the book?
     (c) Mary gave the book to someone.

Also (49) quoted by Bierwisch in the discussion at the conference on question-answering at Visegrad, May 1980, behaves similarly as (48) above, i.e. the answer *Nobody* is appropriate; it is connected with a presupposition failure.

(49) Who took my COFFEE?

---

11   For the distinction between inner participants and free modifications, see Panevová (1974; 1978a) and Hajičová and Panevová (1984).

The position of the intonation centre is connected (as we have already remarked) with the topic/focus articulation of the sentence; if the bearer of the intonation centre is the wh-element, all other elements of the interrogative sentence belong to the topic of the sentence. It is quite natural that, if the verb is included in the topic, the event (action) identified by such a verb is assumed to be "given" and the answer to the question by a negative pronoun renders a presupposition failure, as in (43)(b) above. However, even this is not a fully reliable criterion: compare (50), in which all elements except the attribute *French* belong to the topic, and yet a negative answer (b) is fully appropriate.

(50) (a) Where is there a FRENCH film on?
(b) I'm sorry, there is no French film on this week.

Also other examples have been found where the situation is not quite clear: as for *how many*, an explanation offers itself that in interrogative sentences standing close to mathematical formulations (see e.g. (51)) also the variant (b) may have the negative pronoun as an appropriate answer.

(51) (a) How many points with the mentioned properties lie inside the triangle as specified ABOVE?
(b) HOW MANY points with the mentioned properties lie inside the triangle as specified above?

The above discussion indicates that a further empirical investigation of some larger corpus is necessary because also some contextual features seem to be at stake here which have not yet been systematically studied.

Joshi made an analogy between his concept of a presumption (mentioned above) and the notion of allegation of a declarative sentence. I am convinced that his analogy is corroborated by the following argument:

If the interrogative sentence is understood as a request having the form of a declarative sentence, then e.g. (52) differs from (53) just in the topic/focus articulation; the question word is the only element of the focus of (53), so that "somebody's coming late" is included in the topic (it is not in the scope of the negation) and it belongs to the presuppositions of (53). In (52), "coming late" belongs to the focus of the question and is connected with an allegation: (54) may be followed by (55) as well as by (56).

(52) I request you to tell me who came LATE.
(53) I request you to tell me WHO came late. (=… WHO it was who came late)
(54) I don't request you to tell me who came LATE.
(55) I know all were there in time.
(56) I know that John did.

However, as we have remarked, why-questions (and perhaps others) seem never to allow for an answer with a negative pronoun, i.e. they are connected with presuppositions even if the "inducer" of the presupposition belongs to their focus: in this they behave similarly to sentences with factive verbs and (simple) proper nouns.

It should be emphasized that we do not claim that presuppositions and "inclusion in the topic" are the same phenomenon; the inclusion in the topic of the sentence is only one of the factors that lead to presuppositions, such as factive verbs with their complements, proper names, questioned modifications such as *why*, and perhaps others. Thus inside a topic, there may be elements with "multiple" or "strengthened" presuppositions, e.g. in (58):

(57) Why did John marry JOAN?
(58) Why did JOHN marry Joan? (Why was it JOHN who married Joan?)

In (57) the presupposition that Joan is married is based on the fact that (57) is a *why*-question, while in (58) the placement of the intonation centre on *John* (as well as the cleft construction in the equivalent structure) "strengthens" the said presupposition, since in (58) the fact of Joan being married is stated in the topic of the question (as "given" and recoverable information).

In this connection, Hintikka's (1978) modification of his original proposal for a formal treatment of questions is worth mentioning. He distinguished within a question two ingredients, namely the optative (or imperative) operator and the desideratum; the presupposition of a question then equals the desideratum of the question minus its initial epistemic operators. Thus (59) would entail that the speaker wants it to be made true that (60), which arguably implies (61). As Hintikka (1978, p. 286, ex. 25 to 27) says, this would lead to a mistaken implication: "part of the force of the question would be to try to marry Mary off". Therefore he modifies the optative operator and changes the original formula to (62).

(59) Who is Mary married to?
(60) (Ex) K_I Mary is married to x
(61) (Ex) Mary is married to x
(62) Assuming that (Ex) $F(x)$ bring it about that (Ex) K_I $F(x)$

The motivation of the change seems to be clear;[12] the consequences of its acceptance are somewhat dubious. What happens if the assumption (evidently of the questioner) is not fulfilled (i.e. there does not exist any x such that $F(x)$)? Tichý (1978) would say that such a question "does not arise," but it does arise, as is exemplified by (59).

3.2 Passing over to the yes/no-questions, we can take Kiefer's (1980) considerations as the point of departure. He uses again the notion of background assumptions (a proposition that is formed by substituting a Pro-element such as *somebody, sometime,* etc. for the focused element in the question) and for that purpose he distinguishes a

---

12   See our discussion of (43)(a) above.

focused part of the question (underlined in (63)). If there is such a focused part present in a question, then the speaker takes the background assumption for granted and asks, in fact, for a more specific modification.

(63) Is John leaving for Stockholm TOMORROW?
(64) WHEN is John leaving for Stockholm?

Thus (63) should be interpreted by the hearer as (64): if the hearer answers by a simple *NO*, then the answer is not complete from the point of view of the questioner.

On the other hand, if (in Kiefer's terms) there is no focused element in the question (as in (65)), then the speaker wants to know whether his assumption is right or wrong:

(65) IS John leaving for Stockholm tomorrow?

In this case, the answer *No* is a complete answer.

I want to add just two remarks. First, it is true that with a question such as (63) the negative answer *No* may mean that the speaker admits that John is leaving for Stockholm, but that it is not tomorrow, while in (65) – with the intonation centre on the verb – this need not be the case. In our approach to topic/focus articulation every sentence (including interrogative sentences) has a focus. In (63), the focus is the time adverbial *tomorrow*, in (65) only the verb belongs to the focus. In case the verb belongs to the topic, the action (event) identified by the verb is assumed as "given" and a negative answer to the question has in the scope of negation only the focused part of the sentence (he leaves for Stockholm, (but) not tomorrow). If the verb belongs to the focus of the question, as in (65), the action identified by the verb is negated by the negative answer (he does not leave for Stockholm).

Also other examples show that yes/no-questions are sensitive to topic/focus articulation in the same manner as declarative sentences are, and that in *yes/no*-questions the type of presuppositions connected with the inclusion of an element into the topic of the sentence is also present. If the speaker asks (66), then in one of the readings of the question only Stockholm belongs to the focus, i.e. (66) in this reading is connected with the presupposition that John is leaving tomorrow for some place.

(66) Is John leaving for STOCKHOLM tomorrow?

The hearer can state that this presupposition is not fulfilled (as e.g. in (27)).

(67) Oh, you are mistaken, John is not leaving tomorrow.

A mere *No* denies that it is Stockholm for which John is leaving tomorrow, and accepts that John is leaving somewhere tomorrow.

The "markedness" Kiefer ascribes to some of his examples is not surprising if we accept that there exists a systemic ordering of participants of verbs given by the character of the participants and observed in the focus part of the sentence; every sentence the participants in which are not ordered in accordance with this systemic ordering has some feature of markedness in Kiefer's sense. Thus (70) – his (37)(b) – has the order direction – means (manner), which is not in accordance with the systemic order of these participants (*I'm going by train to STOCKHOLM* rather than *I'm going to Stockholm by TRAIN* is a most natural answer to *What are you doing TOMORROW?*). In such a case the phrase *by train* is (as Kiefer says) almost exclusively determined as the focus of the question (*to Stockholm* belongs to the topic).

(70) Are you going to Stockholm by TRAIN?

The same holds true, when the intonation centre is placed on an element in some other position than the final one; this has the consequence that all modifications (participants) following the bearer of the intonation centre are in the topic. Our explanation of the "marked character" of (71) – Kiefer's example (38) – consists in the fact that the marked intonation of (71) is combined with a marked word order, differing from the systemic ordering.

(71) Are you going to STOCKHOLM by train?

The non-marked counterpart of (71) is (72), with the order means – direction.

(72) Are you going by train to STOCKHOLM?

Here, it is not quite clear where the boundary between topic and focus lies: not only the verb, but also the phrase *by train* can belong to the topic (if it is contextually bound, see Sgall and Hajičová, 1977) as well as to the focus (if it is non-bound). This ambiguity may be understood as one of the reasons for using the marked counterpart (71) instead of the non-marked one (72).

This example illustrates the interplay of word order, intonation, communicative dynamism and contextual boundness in yes/no-questions and suggests a possibility of accounting for this interplay by means of a framework which has been found to give valuable results for declarative sentences.

QUESTIONS ON SENTENCE PROSODY LINGUISTS HAVE ALWAYS WANTED TO ASK

1. INTRODUCTION

The requirements of modern phonetic-acoustic analysis include the need of a manysided description of language phenomena, both within and beyond the boundary of the sentence. Not only lexicon and grammar are concerned, but the whole of the process of communication, understood as consisting of discourse regularities and the patterning of texts of different kinds, the speakers' goals and strategies, different layers of their attitudes, their empathies, objects of their attention in various contexts, the states of their memories, (direct and indirect) speech acts, conversational implicatures, and so on. Moreover, if the primary object of description is seen in the dialogue, it is necessary to analyze all these aspects in view of the presence and the involvement (more or less active, intensive and attentive) of (a possibly large number of) the participants of a discourse.

All the mentioned aspects concern conditions that have to be mastered before the proper aim of the phonetic-acoustic analysis can be achieved. It certainly would be naive to believe that the rich set of complex tasks briefly characterized above can be seriously approached without the only and limited tool that has been developed up to now for the analysis of language, namely without the results gained in the study of grammar. The conceptual dichotomy of "langue" and "parole," or of linguistic competence and performance, certainly is too rough and simplifying to be able to serve as a basis of a systematic description of all the so-called suprasegmental features of speech in their relationship to semantic and pragmatic functions or conditions.

If one thinks of the possibilities offered by applications of grammatical analysis in the context of speech processing, one has to look for an appropriate framework, adapted to study language with regard to its interactive nature. In our opinion, such a framework should account for the topic-focus articulation of the sentence, as for one of the hierarchies of its underlying structure (which, as has been broadly recognized and will be briefly summarized below, is also semantically relevant). The notions of topic and focus (of the sentence), be they "narrow" or "wide" (i.e. including one or more sentence parts), of contextual boundness (as a grammatical counterpart of cognitive "givenness") and of communicative dynamism (i.e. the underlying word order) may be helpful in connecting the issues of sentence structure with those of the process of communication.

An indication of this prospect is the research in different kinds of sentential and phrasal stress as carried out along the lines of the work of J. Pierrehumbert, J. Hirschberg, and M. Beckmann, or, in a slightly different context, of E. Selkirk. Especially M. Steedman's recent studies support our view that the kinds of stress and other features of sentence prosody should be studied in their relationships to phenomena such as focus, topic (proper, old vs. "new," etc.) and contrast. These phenomena have been described as belonging to grammatical structures of individual languages, and it is important for the phonetic-acoustic analysis that grammatical frameworks have been elaborated that make it possible to work with strong hypotheses concerning the positions of this or that kind of stress in utterances embedded in discourse.

2. TOPIC-FOCUS ARTICULATION IN FUNCTIONAL GENERATIVE DESCRIPTION

2.1 MOTIVATION

2.1.1 One of the tenets of the theory of Topic-Focus Articulation (TFA) developed in Prague within the formal description of language (Functional Generative Description, FGD) is the claim that TFA is not only contextually, but also semantically relevant (in the narrow sense of "semantics," i.e. for truth conditions) and thus has to be integrated into the level representing the meaning of the sentence (the tectogrammatical representation, TR). This concerns examples with specific quantifiers, such as in (1), but also without them, see (2) and (3). (Capitals denote the bearer of the intonation centre, IC).

(1) (a) John talked to many girls about few PROBLEMS.
    (b) John talked about few problems to many GIRLS.
(2) (a) Staff behind the COUNTER.
    (b) STAFF behind the counter.
(3) (a) I do linguistics on SUNDAYS.
    (b) On Sundays I do LINGUISTICS.

Furthermore, the semantic opposition between the (a) and (b) examples cannot be accounted for just by referring to the dichotomy of "given" and "new" (which again certainly is beyond grammar). We are in a similar situation here as with grammatical tenses, the distribution of the morphemic means of which are not described in grammars with a direct reference to the time axis and time intervals; grammarians have found good reasons to speak about tenses (present, past, future, ...) and their meanings as mediating between morphemic items and issues of time. What is needed in the domain of TFA is exactly such a mediating (interface) level, or the respective items of this level – notions such as topic (T), focus (F), contextual boundness (CB) and communicative dynamism (CD, see Section 2. 2 below).

2.1.2 Along with accentuation, deletion itself is to be described in a grammar, and cannot be described without reference to TFA. Otherwise, a grammar could not state that the speaker may utter just (4")(a) instead of (4')(a), and (4")(b) instead of (4')(b), where the bracketting indicates the possible TFA's of (4') (for a possible prosodic differentiation of these two readings, see below in Section 3. 2. 6).

(4)   Jim was swimming in the POOL.
(4') (a) (Jim)^{topic} (was swimming in the POOL)^{focus}
        (b) (Jim was swimming)^{topic} (in the POOL)^{focus}
(4") (a) Swimming in the pool.
        (b) In the pool.

This is not to say that it is always possible to delete the whole topic part of a sentence (e.g. contrastive topic does not get deleted, and there may be some grammatical restrictions preventing the deletion of some parts of topic). On the other hand, it holds that if something can be deleted in the outer shape of a sentence, then it belongs to the topic (of the sentence or of a clause; more precisely: to the contextually bound elements), with strictly limited exceptions such as those concerning coordination deletion, cf. (5).

(5) We were offered red and white WINE.

2.1.3 To present another illustration of phenomena which require TFA to be taken into account in grammatical description, we recall certain specific issues of word order, especially in presence of such focus sensitive particles as *only*.

Example (6)(a) is at least three ways ambiguous, as for the focus of the particle (which, in our understanding, is here identical to the focus of the sentences; this is the prototypical case with such particles).

(6) (a) They only travelled from London to EDINBURGH.
      (b) They travelled only from London to EDINBURGH.
      (c) They travelled from London only to EDINBURGH.
      (d) They travelled only to EDINBURGH from London.
      (e) ??They travelled only to Edinburgh from LONDON.
      (f) They only travelled to Edinburgh from LONDON.

In one of the readings of (6)(a), the focus contains everything that follows the particle; in the second, it contains the two prepositional groups (this is also the reading of (b)); in the third, identical with that of (c) and of (d), only the *to*-group belongs to the focus. If the description is to mark (e) as odd, then reference is to be made to the fact that only the order of *from – to* (i.e. the order of Directional-from and Directional-to), rather than the reversed one, is acceptable if both the groups are included in the focus. This is what is predicted by the hypothesis of "systemic ordering" (see Sgall, Hajičová and Panevová 1986, Ch. 3; Hajičová and Sgall 1987): there is a certain ordering of the kinds of complementation that underlies the communicative dynamism (CD, deep word order); if A precedes B under this ordering, then the order A B is unmarked in the scale of CD (and, in prototypical cases, also in the surface word order). The marked order B A (with B less dynamic than A) can occur only if B is contextually bound (belongs to the topic). Thus (6)(a) and (6)(b) have *from London* in topic on some readings, in focus on others; (f) has *from London* in focus and *to Edinburgh* in topic on all readings.

2.1.4 Also a complete account of the distinction between active and passive in English requires to refer to TFA, since, as Mathesius (1924) already noted, passivization is often used to bring the surface word order into harmony with CD (in order to start the sentence with its topic even when this is the Objective), as in (7):

(7) (Jim wrote a new book.) The book was reviewed by HOPKINS.

In English, passivization compulsorily triggers the word order shift, but a comparison with German or Czech shows that without such a shift the truth conditions of the active sentence and of its passive counterpart coincide:

(7') (Jim hat ein neues Buch geschrieben.) Das Buch ist von HOPKINS rezensiert worden. = Das Buch hat HOPKINS rezensiert.

This is not to claim that there is (otherwise) a full synonymy of active and passive. Sentences with sentential adverbials such as *willingly, deliberately, with pleasure* show that in the general case the truth conditions of the two diatheses differ:

(8) (a) The cannibals willingly ate the MISSIONAIRES.
    (b) The missionaires were willingly eaten by the CANNIBALS.

This opposition concerns also languages such as German or Czech, in which active and passive can be characterized as quasisynonymous, in the sense that normally (in the absence of such a sentential adverbial) passivization does not change the truth conditions (not affecting TFA).

2.2 HOW TO REPRESENT TFA ON THE LEVEL OF UNDERLYING STRUCTURE

It seems that TFA can be accounted for by a relatively simple and empirically substantiated framework (see Sgall, Hajičová and Panevová 1986), which follows up a long-term discussion among Czech, German, Russian, Polish and other linguists and is based on the representation of the sentence in terms of a dependency tree. We work with the following two oppositions (we have tried to show in several of our previous publications that the dependency shape of the representation has many advantages but we are convinced that the two oppositions summarized here are not theory dependent):

(i) The (elementary) notions of contextually bound (CB) and non-bound (NB) nodes of the tree.

This opposition is the linguistic counterpart of the pragmatic notions of "given" and "new" information. The opposition, as systematically patterned in the structure of the language, does not precisely correspond to the etymology of the cognitive terms, but is determined rather by grammatical and prosodic properties. Thus, e.g., if a language distinguishes between "strong" and "weak" pronominal forms, the "weak" ones are always CB. In certain other cases, the word order or the intonation pattern of the sentence gives a clue.

In the prototypical case, a CB element occurs in the topic (T) of the sentence and an NB element occurs prototypically in F; however, there may be NB elements in T and CB elements in F, see the use of *younger* and *his* in (9), where the boundary between T and F is indicated by a slash and a possible preceding and following context is included in the brackets:

(9)   (Yesterday, I was visited by my aunt's family.)
      My^{cb} younger^{nb} cousin^{cb} / brought^{nb} his^{cb} camera^{nb} (and made some pictures).

The relevance of the distinction between CB and NB elements for anaphora resolution is discussed in more detail in Hajičová et al. (1995), where examples similar to those in (10) through (13) are adduced:

(10) You have been listening to our night programme. The piano concertos by Chopin were played by Richter. We will devote to him also our next programme.

(11) You have been listening to our night programme. The piano concertos by Chopin were played by (Mrs) Kramperová. We will devote to him also our next programme.

(12) You have been listening to our night programme. The piano concertos by Chopin were played by (Mrs) Kramperová. We will devote to her also our next programme.

(13) You have been listening to our night programme of the works of F. Chopin. Chopin's piano concertos were played by S. Richter. We will devote to him also our next programme.

The issue in question is the reference of the pronoun in the last sentence of each sequence. Two observations are worth mentioning: (12) seems to offer a smoother context for deciphering the reference in the last sentence than (11), which would point to a preferential assignment of pronominal reference to a (mental image of an) object occurring in F of the previous sentence. However, the comparison of these examples with (13), where *him* seems to preferential to refer to an item in T, indicates that a CB element in T (*Chopin*, in our case) establishes a preferential candidate for pronominal reference.

(ii) Communicative dynamism as the underlying word order.

Sentences in (14) and their Czech equivalents in (14') show that the order of the elements of the (underlying) syntactic structure has to be added as one of the primitive concepts (the items of interest here being the nouns in the non-focussed part).

(14) (a) It is JIM who does linguistics on Sundays.
     (b) It is JIM who on Sundays does linguistics.
(14') (a) Lingvistice se v neděli věnuje JIM.
     (b) V neděli se lingvistice věnuje JIM.

The order of elements in the relative clause in the English cleft-construction in (14)(a) and (b) corresponds to the order exhibited by (3)(a) and (b), respectively, and the semantic effect is the same, though in the former pair of examples both *linguistics* and *on Sundays* are in T (as indicated by the prosodic contour of the clefting structure) while in the latter pair of examples the two sentences differ as for the appurtenance of these elements to T and to F.

Within such a framework, the definition of T and F can be anchored in the concepts of contextual boundness and of CD. In Sgall et al. (1986, Ch. 3) this definition is based on characterizing the verb itself and any of its immediate dependents as belonging to T iff they are CB (with a specific proviso for cases where all these items are CB). The use of the terms "topic" and "focus" is then a matter of transparency of reference rather than a matter of an independent distinction.

The combination of the opposition of contextual boundness and the hierarchy of communicative dynamism seems to be sufficient to express all systematic oppositions concerning the information structure of the sentence, its TFA. More empirical investigations are needed to decide about the status of such issues as contrast, emphasis and some related phenomena; it has to be found out whether these phenomena (and the ways in which they are conveyed) go perhaps beyond the system of language or whether the above framework is to be enriched to account for them.

For the time being, a specific marker for a contrastive (part of) topic has been added to the two oppositions briefly characterized above as (i) and (ii), for reasons given in more detail in Hajičová, Partee and Sgall (1998) and will be referred to briefly in Sect. 3.2.3 below.

3. TFA AND PROSODY

3.1 INTRODUCTORY COMMENTS

The above characteristics of the TFA aspects of meaning naturally invites the question whether we can find their reflections in the outer, phonetic shape of the sentence.

The analysis of the relevant examples indicates that topic-focus articulation prototypically determines the location of sentence accents. The intonation centre (IC; for some remarks on the notion of IC, see Sect. 3.2.1 below) has its prototypical position at the end of the sentence; with its secondary position, the complementations of the verb standing to the right of the bearer of the intonation centre belong to the topic.

This assumption is in agreement with Bolinger's (1972, 644) statement that the distribution of sentence accents is determined by semantic and emotional highlighting rather than by syntactic structure. To support his claim, Bolinger (1972, 633) discusses e.g. the following examples:

(15) The end of the chapter is reserved for various problems to COMPUTERIZE.
(16) The end of the chapter is reserved for various PROBLEMS to solve.

Bolinger assigns the difference in the position of IC in (15) and (16) to the difference between a specific and a general meaning of the verbs (in the infinitive) and he speaks about "predictability". In the terms characterized in Section 2 above, we may say that the verb with the "general" meaning is contextually bound (and thus predictable), while that with a specific meaning is contextually non-bound (it conveys a non-predictable information). A similar explanation is offered for examples (17) and (18) (Bolinger 1972, 639): if somebody is strangled, then it is more or less "predictable" that this will result in his death, which is not the case with "hounding". With (19), with the figurative meaning, of course, the context of situation is not clear and according to Bolinger, there is a choice.

(17) They STRANGLED him to death.
(18) They hounded him to DEATH.
(19) They scared him to death.

Also the research based on the tradition of Czech linguistics and on recent results presented by J. Pierrehumbert, J. Hirschberg, and M. Beckmann, or, in a slightly different context, by E. Selkirk, C. Gussenhoven, and found in M. Steedman's recent studies, supports the view that the kinds of stress and other features of sentence prosody are directly relevant to phenomena such as focus, topic (proper, old vs. "new," etc.) and contrast. However, there still remain some open questions, which I will try to formulate below and which I hope some of the competent specialists in phonetics will help me to answer. For most of the issues involved, the framework of TFA sketched above would supply an appropriate representation; it remains to be shown which of the distinctions in meaning the framework is capable to capture are also realized (rendered) in the surface (phonetic) shape of the sentence.

Before passing over to these questions, one point deserves mentioning in the context of Bolinger's claim. The fact that the distribution of sentence accents is determined by semantic and emotional factors rather than by (a "traditional" sort of) syntactic structure can be reflected in a linguistic description in several ways. Thus even the claim that "any differences in the patterns of phrase, and sentence, stress between two languages should follow from their respective constituent structures, as determined by purely syntactic parameters such as the head-initial or head-final character of their phrases" (Cinque 1993) need not be contradictory to the Bolinger's belief if more than one procedure of stress assignment are distinguished; this is what Cinque (1993) does when postulating (a) the sentence grammar procedure, assigning the main stress of the phrases, which falls on the most deeply embedded constituent under his theory, and (b) the discourse grammar procedure, imposing the requirement that the main stress of the phrase in focus be made more prominent than the main stress of the "presupposition", in Chomskyan terms, or topic, in our terms, which may lead to destressing in case of marginalization of the "presupposed" constituent. Another way out from the discrepancy between the phrase structure and the impact of TFA on the prosodic structure of the sentence is to modify the syntactic structure in order to reconciliate it with the TFA requirements; this is the way Steedman (1991) follows when postulating the so-called floating constituents.

However, there is another possibility, namely to acknowledge that focus need not be a single constituent and to look for a formalism that would allow for representing focus irrespective of this fact; we believe that dependency grammar offers such a formalism. In addition, working with TFA on the underlying level and with the surface order of sentence elements as a string of morphemes (that can be interpreted phonetically or graphemically, as the case may be), we can account also for what Höhle (1982) called "discontinuous focus," see below.

3.2 QUESTIONS WAITING FOR AN ANSWER

When looking for which of the distinctions in meaning related to TFA are also rendered (be it obligatorily or optionally) in the surface (phonetic) shape of the sentence, the following issues come to my mind:

3.2.1 If a sentence has more than one pitch accent, is there some phonetically observable hierarchy among them? In other words, can we speak about the intonation center of the sentence?

A rather trivial case is that of sentence coordination: in such sentences, each of the compound clauses or coordinate constructions has its own topic-focus articulation, see (20) and (21):

(20) Jim read a BOOK and Mary prepared the DINNER.
(21) John slept WELL, and so did JIM.

A similar analysis can be offered for examples that involve sentence apposition (with a possible deletion of "thus", "which happened", "namely" etc.), as in (22):

(22) She cannot SLEEP (, (namely)) because of her DISEASE.

However, the approach to intonation contour based on the British tradition (best known perhaps from O'Connor and Arnold 1973), which recognizes the intonation contour associated with the stretch of speech known as "tone group" as an important unit of analysis, leads to a recognition of more than one tone groups (and thus more than one nucleus) also in such sentences as (23) and (24) quoted from Gussenhoven (1985a, p. 87, ex. 13 and p. 98, ex. 70; these sentences are taken from a spoken corpus):

(23) But one doesn't want one's / SON | mixing with / PEOPLE | who can't SPEAK properly.
(24) We have a \BRANCH | in Milton \ KEYNES you know.

The boundary of tone groups is denoted by |, the slashes / and \ denote the rising and falling intonation contour, respectively. The capitals denote the nuclear accent. The question then is whether all the nuclear accents have the same properties or whether one can single out one of them to be the IC of the sentence. Notice that the opposition of rise and fall might help to distinguish *speak* as the IC in (23) since the nuclear accent on *speak* is connected with a fall, which is typical for the IC standing at the end of the sentence, but this criterion does not help in (24), where both nuclear accents are connected with falls. Gussenhoven (pers. comm.) believes that all the pitches are of an equal character, and that one can distinguish an intonation center only by its position (as the last pitch accent in the sentence).

3.2.2 Are all pauses within a sentence given only rhythmically or are they (perhaps optionally) connected with the articulation of the sentence into T and F?

There has been a long discussion in linguistic writings whether the boundary between topic and focus is marked prosodically. Schmerling (1971), who worked with the notion of the scope of permissible focus (following Chomsky 1971), assumes that the boundary between Chomsky's "presupposition" (a very close notion to our notion of "topic") and "focus" is phonetically marked. Pierrehumbert and Hirschberg (1990, p. 309, note 4) are more careful: they remark that while the general association of accent with components of NP's seems fairly clear, constraints on the accenting of parts of a VP are much less understood.

3.2.3 Does the prosodic realization of contrastive topic differ from the phonetic realization of focus proper, and if yes, how?

In her detailed analysis of prosody of German sentences Féry (1992:36f; see also Féry 1993) claims that there is no prosodic distinction between a (contrastive) topic and a (non-proper) part of focus, cf. her example (19)ii and iii quoted here as (25). According to Féry, (25) (with the indicated intonation contour; the prosodic notation used follows that of Pierrehumbert 1980) is ambiguous with regard to the topic-focus structure: on one reading, "Gabi Müller" is included in the topic, while on the other interpretation both "Gabi Müller" and "Lena Sommers" are in the focus (with "Lena Somers" being the focus proper):

> (25) Gabi MÜLLER wohnt bei Lena SOMMER.
>   L*H   H*L

Note: Not being a specialist in the domain of prosody, I am relying here and in the sequel on the judgements of the authors assigning the particular prosodic contours to the quoted examples.

A similar case is Steedman's (1991:289) example (71) quoted here as (26):

> (26) (a) [FRED didn't eat the POTATOES. HARRY ate THEM(?).]
>   (It was the BEANS)(that FRED ate).
>   H*L   L+H* LH%
>   (b) [Fred didn't eat the POTATOES. He threw THEM(?) AWAY.]
>   (It was the BEANS)(that Fred ATE).
>   H*L   L+H*LH%

The context is included in square brackets; the bracketting in the example sentences denotes a certain "phrasing" which, in our terms, corresponds to their topic-focus articulation, with focus "fronted" in the surface structure (by means of the cleft construction) and topic following focus. Here, similarly as in (25), the contrastive topic (*Fred* in (a) and *ate* in (b)) carries the L*H accent, while the focus element *beans* carries the H*L accent.

In writings on formal semantics, the investigations of issues connected with TFA began by inquiries into the semantic properties of such particles as *only, even, also*. These particles were called focussing particles (focalizers, focus sensitive particles; cf. the notion of rhematizer in the Prague tradition); focalizers are characterized as those sentence elements that are "associated with" bearers of the pitch accent, i.e. with "focus". However, there exist also peripheral cases where a focalizer is present in the topic of the sentence. Such a situation has been observed in the analysis of negation by Hajičová (1973; 1984) and in that of many kinds of focalizers by Koktová (1986); cf. (27), if answering e.g. *Why doesn't Jim sleep?*, and (28) in the context indicated by the sentence in brackets.

> (27) Jim does not sleep / because of his ILLNESS.
> (28) (All of us were worried). If even Paul was worried, then the situation clearly was CRITICAL.

In the analysis of these cases, it is necessary to take into account the prosodic properties of the sentence (e.g. the kind of – phrasal? – stress on *Paul*, see below on Bartels' observations).

As (29) illustrates, a sentence may include two focalizers; it is then possible that one of the focalizers occurs in the prototypical position, i.e. "associates" with focus, and the other within T. At least some focalizers, like "even", may occur in T without being repeated from the preceding co-text (as in (28) above). However, these combinations of focalizers occur most often in echo sentences, closely bound to preceding co-text from which the latter focalizer is repeated, like in (29):

(29) (What did even PAUL realize?) Even Paul realized that Jim only admired MARY.

Although in (29) two focus-sensitive operators occur, the finding of Bartels (1995) convincingly confirms that the sentence does not contain two foci: there is a difference between the prosodic features of what we distinguish as the focus of the sentence and of what is the "focus" of a focus sensitive operator. This finding also supports our understanding of the noun groups bearing the (rising) phrasal stress in such sentences as contrastive topics, rather than as parts of focus, in which we differ from those researchers who tend to identify the two kinds of stress.

Under the above mentioned assumptions, also Jacobs' (1991, p. 5) example can be analyzed in a similar way as (29) above (the notation of the intonation center by capitals and of the stress within topic by italics is added by us):

(30) Sogar PETER kennt nur einen *Roman* von Goethe. [Even PETER knows only a *novel* by Goethe].

We assume that (30) may occur in such a context position as if preceded by (31) or (32):

(31) Nobody reads Goethe's poetry here.
(32) Nowadays manysided classical writers are known much more from their prose than from their poetry or theoretical writings.

Thus we can analyze (30) as having *even Peter* as F, whereas the rest is CB (reading Goethe's novels has been activated by the negative mention of other writings of his or of classical writers in general); the (phrasal – perhaps weaker and not falling?) accent on *novel* identifies this noun as the contrastive part of the topic.

A similar analysis can be provided for (33) (i.e. Rooth's 1992 example quoted by Krifka):

(33) Farmers that GROW rice often only EAT rice.

On the discussed reading, *only* accompanies the repeated occurrence of *rice*, and both the words are contained in the topic of the sentence. The verb *grow* can be understood as a contrastive topic (perhaps with Bolinger's B, rising accentuation rather than the falling one, typical of focus, see our note on ex. (30) above).

The same reading can be assigned to (33'), which, however, is not ambiguous as (33) is:

(33') Farmers that GROW rice often EAT only rice.

In languages in which a verb cannot freely intervene between a focalizer and its focus (such as Czech), there are equivalents of (33) and of (33') that are not ambiguous; thus, in Czech, (34) corresponds only to that reading of (33) in which *eat* is the focus of the focalizer (e.g. "... (they) only EAT rice, (they do not sell it)"), (34') corresponding to (33'):

(34) Zemědělci, kteří rýži pěstují, často rýži jenom JEDÍ.
     [farmers who rice grow often rice only eat]
(34') Zemědělci, kteří rýži pěstují, často jenom rýži JEDÍ.
     [farmers who rice grow often only rice eat]

3.2.4 If the focus proper is placed in the surface shape of the sentence in other position than the final one, is its prosodic realization different from the case when it is placed in its normal, i.e. final position?

To illustrate this issue, let us repeat here for convenience one minimal pair of sentences from example (6):

(6) (c) They travelled from London only to EDINBURGH.
   (d) They travelled only to EDINBURGH from London.

Is there a difference between the contour on EDINBURGH in (c) and (d)? Gussenhoven (pers.comm.) again does not see such a difference.

3.2.5 To what extent (and by what means) does the prosody of ambiguous sentences distinguish the different meanings?

There are interesting cases of ambiguity that can be ascribed to different "scopes" of the focalizer.

(35) (a) We are required to study only SYNTAX.
    (b) We are required to only study SYNTAX.

The sentence (35)(a) has been characterized as ambiguous, see Rooth's (1985) (5)(c) and (6)(c) on p. 90. Rooth's explanation is based on the assumption that "only" is a part of the NP headed by "syntax" and that this NP has the narrow scope on one reading (with which the sentence can be paraphrased by "We are required not to study any other subject than syntax") and the wide scope on the other reading, with which the main verb belongs to the scope and to the background of the focalizer.

It appears that the examples discussed by Rooth, quoting Taglicht, can be analyzed, in a dependency based framework, so that the focalizer depends on the verb "study" in such sentences as (35)(a), (35)(b), on their preferred readings, and its scope thus is the maximal projection of this verb. In the secondary reading of (35)(a), the focalizer may be understood to depend on the higher verb and thus has the wide scope, covering the whole sentence, similarly as in (35)(c).

(35) (c) We are required only to study SYNTAX.

It may be assumed that a focalizer can depend on a higher verb only if this verb is CB, in the topic of the given clause, perhaps under some not yet identified syntactic or lexical conditions, e.g. for a certain group of verbs. The combination of such a verb with the infinitive might then be handled as a specific cluster. (I owe this point to B. H. Partee, personal communication.)

This is one example of a situation where the framework we work with offers us a possibility to adequately represent the distinct meanings of an ambiguous sentence and we would like to know whether the phonetic (prosodic) realization of the distinct meanings would also differ.

A similar case, where a written shape of the sentence is ambiguous, are sentences that involve relative scopes of focalizers and quantifiers.

In our study of the semantics of negation, we have argued that there is a close relationship between the "(semantic) scope of negation" and the topic-focus articulation (see e.g. Hajičová 1973; 1984). Our treatment can be rather straightforwardly applied to Féry's prosodic analysis of German examples of sentences with an interplay of negation and quantification.

Let us first look at Féry's (1992:40f) examples (22) and (25) (see also Höhle 1991, 159) quoted here as (36) and (37).

(36) (a) BEIDE Theaterstücke sind NICHT gespielt worden.
　　　　 L*H　　　　　　　　　　H*L
　　 (b) BEIDE Theaterstücke sind nicht gespielt worden.
　　　　 H*L　　　　　　　　　　(H*L)
(37) (a) ALLE Politiker hat so mancher NICHT verstanden.
　　　　 L*H　　　　　　　　　　　　 H*L
　　 (b) ALLE Politiker hat so mancher nicht verstanden.
　　　　 H*L

The (preferred? only?) interpretation of (36)(a) implies that though it is not the case that both plays were not played, one of them might have been played. For such a reading, the only part of the focus would be the negative particle "nicht" (marked in the surface structure by the high-low contour), with the "scope" of negation covering the whole rest of the sentence. In (36)(b), the high-low accent on "beide" seems to indicate that this is the focus part of the sentence, with the rest in the topic; in such a case, the scope of negation is over the verb in the topic but is not going beyond the topic-focus boundary.

Similar considerations can be applied to (37)(a) and (b): the high-low contour on "nicht" in (a) indicates that this particle is in the focus; one possible interpretation of the low-high contour on "alle" is that of marking this member of the sentence as a (part of the) topic. The topic-focus structure and thus the assignment of the scope of (37)(a) would be similar to that of (36)(a). In the same vein, we can draw a parallel between the (b) sentences in (36) and (37): the high-low contour on "alle" in (37)(b) marks this element as the only part of the focus. In this case, the (preferred? only?) reading of (37)(a) is "as for not understanding the politicians by several people, this concerns all politicians".

To complete our attempt to integrate our analysis of negation with observations on sentence prosody, let us adduce one more example, again borrowed from Féry (1992:50f, her ex. (36) quoted here as (38)).

(38) (a) Ein JUNGE WEINT nicht.
       L*H   H*L
  (b) Ein JUNGE weint nicht.
       H*L

The "hat contour" of (38)(a) indicates that this sentence may have two interpretations: "ein Junge" either belongs to the (contrastive?) topic of the sentence and then the topic-focus structure would correspond to the paraphrase "as a boy" (topic), "(he) does not cry" (focus); the reading is generic and is perhaps the preferred reading of the (a) sentence; the scope of negation is over the focus, i.e. over the verb. Or, the whole sentence constitutes the focus (as is the case with thetic judgements), in which case the scope of negation would cover the whole sentence ("it is not the case that a boy cries"). The high-low contour on "Junge" in the (b) sentence marks this member as the focus of the sentence, the rest (standing in "the shade" of the intonation centre, as it were) being the topic. In such a case, when the negated verb is in the topic, the scope of negation includes the verb but does not extend beyond the boundary between topic and focus.

3.2.5 If the sentence is long and it is prosodically segmented, have the items at the end of the segments a similar prosodic contour as the bearers of the contrastive topic?

3.2.6 In our framework, we can distinguish a so-called "narrow" focus (i.e. the focus consists in a single subtree depending on the root of the tree, the verb) and "wide" focus (more than one such subtree or also the verb belong to the focus). Does this distinction find a different prosodic realization?

If we understand well the arguments of Selkirk (1984; 1995), the functional distinction between (39)(a) and (b) may be illustrated by questions which can be answered by the given sentences. The questions are understood here as representing each a class of contexts in which the sentence can be appropriately used (though in an actual dialogue this sentence - without a deletion or pronominalization - would constitute a redundant answer).

(39) (a) Jim was *swimming* in the POOL.
    (b) Jim was swimming in the POOL.
(39') (a) What was Jim doing?
    (b) Where was Jim swimming?

Selkirk claims that for (39)(a) to be an answer to (39')(a), the verb *swimming* has to carry a phrasal stress (indicated here by italics).

Gussenhoven (1984; 1998) supported by an experimental work of Byrd and Clifton (1995) has a slightly different judgement: he considers the minimal pair of sentences (40)(a) and (b) (Gussenhoven's 1998 (3)(a) and (b) and concludes that only the (a) sentence is appropriate for a full-focus context (i.e. broad focus in its extreme case, i.e. if the whole sentence is taken as focus) illustrated here by the question (41)(a); the sentence (b) does not have a full-focus reading. However, the question (41)(b) – implying a narrow focus on *feather* – can be answered both by (40)(a) and (b).

(40) (a) JOHNs tickling MARY with a FEATHER.
    (b) John's tickling Mary with a FEATHER.
(41) (a) What's going on?
    (b) What's John tickling Mary with?

This is to say that (40)(a) is ambiguous as for the readings with "broad" and "narrow" focus, while (40)(b) is not. Gussenhoven (1998) adds that possibly there is a phonetic distinction between obligatory and optional pre-nuclear stress, in our examples the stress on *John* and *Mary*, which in the narrow focus version may have reduced excursions.

3.2.7 There are some specific cases of sentences that may be called "second instance" or "corrections" (e.g. repetitions due to some misunderstanding, the so-called "echo-sentences", etc.). How does the prosodic contour of these sentences differ from that of the "first instance" (with narrow focus)?

One possible type of such cases are sentences with focus only on the polarity item, as in (42) taken from Selkirk (1995):

(42) A: Mary didn't buy a book about bats.
    B: Mary DID buy a book about bats.

Silkirk believes that (42) requires an interpretation with broad focus (all-sentence focus, which would result from her projection rules); I agree with Gussenhoven (1998) who opposes this view. He even assumes (pers. comm.) that the pitch accent on *did* is the same as if it were on any other item of the sentence (e.g. on *bats* in (43)). On the other hand, if (42) is compared with (44), where the polarity is also the single element of the focus, but the speaker does not correct a previous statement with a different polarity, one can ask whether the accents do differ only in their intensity rather than in some other characteristics.

(43) (What did Mary buy?)
    Mary bought a book about BATS.
(44) (Did Mary buy a book about bats?)
    (Yes,) Mary DID buy a book about bats.

4. CONCLUSION

Our remarks on the interpretation of prosodic contours concerned only such interpretations that were related to what we call "literal" (linguistic) meaning (for a detailed discussion of the distinction between (linguistic) meaning and (extralinguistic, cognitive) content, see Sgall, Hajičová and Panevová, 1986). This is not to mean that we are not aware of the wide range of other possible interpretations of prosodic contours. For example, Hirschberg and Ward (1992) discuss a variety of possible interpretations of a single intonation contour in English, exemplified here on the example (45) (their examples (1) and (2) on p. 243):

(45) ELEVEN in the morning.

Sentence (45) can be used (with the contour of "eleven" being $L^* + H$) either as an expression of the speaker's uncertainty (e.g. if preceded by the interlocutor's question "So, do you tend to come in pretty late then?," it may be used to show that the speaker wants to be sure what is meant by "pretty late"), or as an expression of the speaker's incredulity (for example as a reaction to "I'd like you here tomorrow morning at eleven", (45) would imply "I can't believe that you want me to come at eleven").

However, these issues, though very interesting and deserving a detailed investigation, go beyond the scope of the topic of our paper and will not be dealt with here.

The claims and observations argued for in the present paper can be summarized as follows:

(i)   Sentences with identical lexical setting, syntactic structure, and even word order but differing in the position of the intonation center have different (literal) meaning. This distinction in meaning is due to the different topic-focus articulation of the sentences under examination. Topic-focus articulation is also relevant for the scopes of operators and other cases.

(ii) The representation of topic-focus in the underlying (deep) level should include: (i) the distinction between contextually bound and non-bound nodes, (ii) deep word order, and (iii) a marker for a contrastive topic.

(iii) The sketched linguistic prerequisites can be taken as a possible starting point for an evaluation of the output of prosodic analysis. We have formulated and briefly discussed – adducing examples from linguistic literature – some questions that arise when confronting the descriptive possibilities the framework we subscribe to offers and the (rather non-systematic, at least to our knowledge) inquiries into the prosodic means exploited to render these subtle distinctions.

SURFACE AND UNDERLYING WORD ORDER

1. The myth of the classification of languages according to whether they exhibit "fixed" or "free" word order has necessarily led (a) to an underestimation of the possibility to ascribe to word order variations a semantic relevance and (b) to an overlooking of the differentiation of surface and underlying word order.

1.1 In modern trends of theoretical linguistics, such a position was fostered by the fact that in their early stages they were deeply (if not exclusively) influenced in their metalanguage by the native tongue of their proponents, namely English. In these approaches, the order of words was viewed upon as uninteresting, contributing only to the syntactic functions of words in the sentence (VP-external NP – to the left of the VP – being the subject of the sentence, VP-internal NP – to the right of the verb – being the object). Only gradually, in new stages of the "old" theories or in the theories formulated later, the order of elements becomes a matter of interest. Thus, e.g. Chomsky (1981: 31) asks: "What properties of the categorial component must be stipulated in a grammar? Perhaps such properties as order of major constituents, insofar as this is not determined by lexical properties and other principles of grammar." However, the base of the description still remains "English-oriented" and special kind of operations have to be designed (the so called adjunction, apparently violating one of the basic principles, namely the projection principle; in order to prevent this, the projection principle has to be formulated in a way that does not include non-subcategorized positions) to provide for constructions in languages without a grammatically fixed word order which allow for the switch – without any structural change – of the subject – verb order into that of verb – subject (see the Italian sentences *Molti studenti telefonano* versus *Telefonano molti studenti* in Sells 1985, p. 47).

1.2 In the standard conception of the Generalized Phrase Structure Grammar (GPSG), the phrase structure rules encoded two kinds of relations, those of immediate dominance and those of linear precedence (LP). One of the reasons was to solve some problems of those languages which have a high degree of free constituent order. LP statements are supposed to be important in the analysis of cross-linguistic variation, and they vary from language to language (for an analysis of German, see Uszkoreit 1984).

1.3 At the same time, the surface order of subject and object relative to verb served as a basis for typologizing languages (this tradition began with the work of Greenberg 1963; but see already Tesnière's 1959 "langues centripetales" and "langues centrifugales"). The idea of basic order has been re-emerging in various contexts and schools; recently, in Payne (1992) several contributions explore this idea with respect to most different languages.

2. After a closer examination we see that the notion of order has obtained divergent interpretations:

2.1 In the most generally known variant of the Chomskyan description a certain fixed, grammatically determined order is specified, on which movement rules are applied, finally resulting on the one hand in the order of the elements in the outer shape of the sentence, and on the other in the order of the elements of the logical form. Thus, a surface order is distinguished from an underlying one; more exactly, besides a surface order, two "underlying" orders are postulated. One of these two, namely that on the d-structure level, is an immediate result of the application of X-bar theory, which is supposed to constitute a part of Universal Grammar. Thus, the question arises whether this order is supposed to be identical in most different languages. The other "underlying" order, that on the level of logical form, is derived by movement rules, the parameters of which may be set according to the language concerned, although this level is understood as the input of semantic interpretation.

Let us examine the following example:

(1) An oak grew from every acorn.

According to Sells (1985:46), the s-structure of (1) is (2):

(2) [$_s$ an oak$_i$ INFL grow from *every acorn*$_j$]

In order to obtain the only interpretation of (1) that is acceptable for the world we live in, the quantifier raising of *every acorn* must be applied to get the logical form in (3):

(3) [$_s$ every acorn$_j$ [$_s$ an oak$_i$ INFL grow from e$_j$]]

However, it remains to explain what is the difference between (1), requiring this movement, and (4), which does not require it, although it seems to exhibit the same structure as (1).

(4) A boy ran around every playground.

If (1) is examined not just in its written shape, but as a spoken utterance, it can be claimed that it displays a marked prosodic contour, with the intonation center on *oak*.

(1′) An OAK grew from every acorn.

This secondary placement of the intonation center (the primary position of which is at the end of the sentence, which seems to be the natural pronunciation of (4)) has its grammatical (and semantic-pragmatic) relevance.[1] In the prototypical case, the bearer of the intonation center is included in the focus of the sentence (in the Prague School tradition this is one of the long established tenets since Mathesius; cf. also Chomsky 1971). This is in accordance with the fact that the focus prototypically follows the topic (for the non-prototypical case, the so-called subjective order, see below). As can be seen from (3) above, it is exactly this prototypical order which is the result of the application of quantifier raising. Thus, it appears to be appropriate to anchor the structural difference between (1) and (4) in the presence of the secondary placement of the intonation center in (1) and its absence in (4): in both cases, the position of the focus in the underlying word order is to the right from the topic.[2]

A similar effect can be obtained if the inversion form of the verb is used, as in (5), where the focus follows after the topic also on the surface.

(5) Every acorn developed into an oak.

2.2 GPSG, as well as its later offsprings, claims to basically differ from Chomsky's framework by its monostratal character and it was the surface order what adherents of GPSG had in mind when speaking of order or linear precedence. However, especially within the development of HPSG there appear proposals to distinguish between the order of the nodes in the syntactic tree and the surface word order.

2.3 Also with the Greenbergian tradition, mentioned in 1.3 above, the order referred to by such patterns as SVO, SOV, etc. can only be the surface order of sentence parts or smaller elements.

3. In the light of what has been said, the question may be raised whether the distinction made between surface and underlying word order (be this that of Chomsky's d-structure or logical form, or of another kind of underlying structure) is necessary. Technically, the underlying order of words and sentence parts can be understood as the order of nodes in a representation of the sentence structure (having the shape of a tree), whereas the surface order may be attributed to a morphemic representation (in the shape of a string of symbols).

One argument in favour of the distinction lies in the fact that it offers a uniform treatment of a semantic distinction that finds diversified means of expression (in different languages and within the same language).[3] The treatment in terms of an under-

---

1 In our examples we denote the bearer of the intonation center by capitals only in case it is in a marked position; if the bearer of the intonation centre is at the end of the sentence we do not use any special notation.

2 Cf. Sgall's (1972) analysis of Fillmore's (1970) examples with *develop into* and *develop out of*, where Sgall suggests (p. 286) that the sentence "An oak developed out of every acorn" (as a paraphrase of "Every acorn developed into an oak") should have the intonation center on "an oak" (in both shapes).

3 It has been shown elsewhere that the distinction of topic/focus articulation is a semantic one rather than a

lying order is closely related to the way in which the semantic distinctions related to the order of quantifiers are captured.

The concept of underlying order in this understanding is based on the notion of communicative dynamism, introduced by Firbas (1956; most recently 1992); for an explicit characterization of communicative dynamism, see Sect. 6 below.

4. The switch of topic and focus, i.e. the different shapes of the underlying order can have different realizations in the surface shape of the sentence.

4.1 The difference in the underlying order can be reflected in the surface order without an accompanying structural change, as the comparison of (6)(a) and (b) shows:

(6) (a) John talked to few girls about many problems.
    (b) John talked about many problems to few girls.

These sentences illustrate that even in English, i.e. a language supposed to exhibit a great degree of grammatically fixed word order, word order shifts can be used to express different semantic relations. Lakoff (1971) argues that the two sentences in (6) differ in their meanings: while in (a) a particular group of (few) girls is referred to with which each of the (many) problems is discussed, this is not the case in (b), where it is only said that the group of girls with whom John talked about many problems is small.

4.2 The difference in the underlying order can be reflected in the surface order accompanied by some other structural change, as in (7):

(7) (a) Everyone in the room knows at least two languages.
    (b) At least two languages are known by everyone in the room.

Chomsky (1965, p. 224, Note 9 to Chapter 3) sees the semantic difference between (a) and (b) in that only in (b) the same two languages can be referred to; he alludes to the surface distinction between active and passive as a possible source but is ready to accept also an explanation in terms of topicality.

4.3 Two different underlying orders can be realized on the surface by the same surface order, but the prosodic contour is different, as in (8):

(8) (a) Fred ate the beans.
    (b) FRED ate the beans.

The order present in (8)(b) was called (in connection with Czech examples) "subjective" order by Mathesius (1939). In English, the "subjective" (emphatic) character of this order is not that marked, since the surface word order often is not "free" enough

---

matter of pragmatic issues such as coherence etc. Therefore we do not discuss this matter here again, and it will be clear from our examples in Sect. 4 below that a true semantic distinction is involved.

to allow for a switch that would put it into correspondence with the underlying one; thus, such English sentences as (8)(b) more often are stylistically more neutral than their Czech counterparts.

With a contrastive topic, it is typical that both the subject and the predicate nouns bear pitch accents, one of which (exhibited by the focus) has the character of Bolinger's A accent (falling, denoted here by capitals), the other one (contrastive topic) having the shape of the B accent (rising, denoted by italics):

(8) (c) *Fred* ate the BEANS.
(d) FRED ate the *beans*.

These examples are taken over from Jackendoff (1972: 261f) who points out the different contexts in which either of these sentences can be used; this difference corresponds to the division of the sentence into "presupposition" and "focus" (these terms, introduced by Chomsky 1971, can well be compared to our "topic" and "focus," respectively).

These features of the sentence prosody have been further studied in relation with the information structure (topic-focus articulation) of the sentence (understood as an aspect of sentence syntax) by Steedman (1991), who takes over Pierrehumbert's (1980) classification of intonational contours (more recently see Pierrehumbert & Hirschberg 1990). In this notation, the A accent is denoted by H*L, the B one by L+H*, and also further phenomena from the domain of prosody (boundary tones, etc.) are analyzed; a compositional approach to tune interpretation is formulated on this basis, which is helpful for an inquiry into the relationships between prosody and information structure.

Féry (1993:130, ex. 23; cf. similar examples discussed by Höhle 1991) presents sentences such as those in (9) as a support for the view that differences in intonation contours have their impact on the semantic interpretation of the given sentences.

(9) (a) BEIDE Theaterstücke sind nicht gespielt worden
  H*L   (H*L)
(b) BEIDE Theaterstücke sind NICHT gespielt worden.
  L*H   H*L

If Féry's parentheses are understood as indicating that the pitch accent on *gespielt* in (9)(a) is essentially weaker than that on *beide* (as is confirmed by the contour in the corresponding figure, representing the recording), then (9)(a) and (b) illustrate very well how the semantic interpretation of negation is related to the topic/focus articulation. Our approach to these phenomena was originally presented in Hajičová (1973); for a more detailed formulation in Czech, see Hajičová (1975), in English, Hajičová (1984); the alleged ambiguity of negation is discussed in Hajičová (1989). The topic/focus articulation of the two examples in (9) can be schematically represented as (a') and (b'), where the subscript T stands for topic and F for focus:

(9) (a') (plays were not played)$_T$ (both)$_F$
    (b') (both plays played)$_T$ (not)$_F$

In (a'), the negation is included in the topic and the sentence (9)(a) asserts about the plays which were not played that this concerns the two of them. In (b'), the negative modality is the only part of the focus; the interpretation of the sentence (9)(b) is weaker in the sense that it just asserts about two plays that they were not played (although one of them might have been).

5. An interesting example illustrating the impact of topic/focus articulation on the semantic interpretation of sentences is the different interpretation of coordinated structure in topic and in focus (the examples are taken over from Lakoff 1970, who, of course, does not relate the difference to TFA).

(10) (a) John saw an explosion.
     (b) Max saw an explosion.

The coordination of (10)(a) and (b) results in the sentence (11), which has a reading on which different explosions can be referred to.

(11) John and Max saw an explosion.

This is not the case if "an explosion" is in the topic position of the simple sentences which are coordinated: (13) refers to the same explosion.

(12) (a) An explosion was seen by John.
     (b) An explosion was seen by Max.
(13) An explosion was seen by John and Max.

However, if the intonation centre is placed on "explosion," as in (14), the shift of intonation center reflects a change in TFA and influences the interpretation: the interpretation of (14) then equals the interpretation of (11). (I owe this observation to the late Professor Poldauf.)

(14) An EXPLOSION was seen by John and Max.

The sentence (14) exhibits a non-prototypical surface order of topic and focus, namely focus preceding topic (see above on Mathesius' "subjective order").

(15) (a) TÁTA přišel.
     (b) Přišel táta.
     (c) FATHER came.
     (d) It's FATHER who came.

As we have mentioned, the markedness of "subjective order" in Czech follows from the fact that there are no grammatical barriers there to place the bearer of intonation centre in the surface at the end of the sentence as in (b). The translation of (15)(a) and (b) can be realized in English either as (c), by the means of the placement of the intonation centre, or as (d), by means of a specific syntactic construction to mark the focus.[4] (15)(c) can hardly be understood as a marked case; the grammatically determined surface word order does not allow to construct sentences with intransitive verbs in an "objective order". Similar difficulties arise when the sentence includes a transitive verb but the actor of the action identified by the verb is general, as in (16).

(16) Several EXPERIMENTS were carried out and the hypothesis was confirmed.

Experiments as the most communicatively dynamic element of the first conjunct of (16) belong to the focus of this conjunct, the verb *carried out* being less dynamic. In the underlying order then *experiments* follow the verb while in the surface the order can only be subject – verb. Similar situation obtains also in other cases where the grammatically fixed order does not allow a rearrangement of lexical items in the surface, as in (17):

(17) My neighbour dug a HOLE with a hoe.

In a context where digging a hole with a hoe (rather than pruning the trees, or mowing the lawn etc.) is the information delivered about the neighbour, i.e. with the partition of the sentence into (my neighbour)$_T$ (dug with a hoe a hole)$_F$, the most dynamic element of the sentence is the Objective (see below in Section 8 for a substantiation of this claim). However, it cannot be placed at the end of the sentence, after the prepositional group rendering the Instrument. The result is the placement of the intonation centre at some other position in the sentence. The question to be studied is whether in such cases as (16) and (17) the position of the intonation centre is not neutralized in favour of the unmarked position at the end of the sentence.

6. An explicit specification of communicative dynamism (CD) as the "underlying" order was given by Sgall et al. (1986, pp. 185f). Working with a dependency based representation on the level of meaning and with a primary notion of contextual boundness, communicative dynamism can be specified as follows:

(i) a word is less dynamic than its governing word iff the dependent word is contextually bound,

(ii) the degrees of CD of the contextually non-bound nodes are determined by the systemic ordering (see below, Sect.8),

---

4   The two Czech sentences are synonymous, either of them having two readings: (i) without any topic (with the two parts both belonging to the focus), and (ii) with the verb in the topic (triggering a presupposition that someone came). In the English equivalents, (c) shares these properties of the Czech sentences, whereas (d) has only the interpretation (ii).

(iii) the degrees of CD of the contextually bound sister nodes are primarily distributed in such a way that a word corresponding to a more foregrounded (activated)
item in the stock of knowledge assumed by the speaker to be shared by him and
the hearer is less dynamic,

(iv) the verb stands on the boundary between its contextually bound and contextually
non-bound daughter nodes.

7. Further differences between the two layers of word order concern the "shallow"
movements, which have to be accounted for by specific means within any theoretical framework. With our approach, these differences can be handled as oppositions
between (i) the left-to-right order of the nodes of the syntactic tree (which can be
defined either as a linear ordering of all the nodes in the tree, or as determined by the
linear orderings of minimal subtrees – consisting each of a head and its dependents
– together with the directions of the edges of the tree) and (ii) the linear order of the
elements of the string representing the morphemic pattern of the sentence (as composed from the outer forms of autosemantic and function words).

At least the following kinds of differences between the syntactic (underlying) and
the morphemic (surface) layers of word order are to be distinguished:[5]

(a) the placement of the verb in different languages,

(b) the positions of different kinds of adjuncts of a noun,

(c) the placement of relative words and question words, prototypically at the beginning of their clauses ("wh-movement"), including long distance dependencies
such as *Who have you believed John planned to send to Paris?*,

(d) other cases of discontinuous constituents, or non-projective sentence parts,[6] such
as: *a larger town than Boston, I met a man yesterday, who told me...*;

(e) the shift of "heavy constituents" (especially in English) towards the end of the
clause,

(f) the relatively fixed position of clitics (primarily in "Wackernagel's position", e.g. in
Czech).

8. "Underlying" order as discussed in Sections 3. through 7. above is understood
as the order of elements in a structure corresponding to a particular sentence. Inquiries into the fundamental notions of topic/focus articulation have shown (see Sgall et
al. 1986; more recently Pfeiffer et al. 1994) that in addition to the "underlying" order
corresponding to the communicative dynamism as displayed by individual sentences,
an important hypothesis can be formulated concerning a basic order of complementations of the verb as given by the grammar of a given language. This ordering has

---

5 This does not mean that every theory needs all these kinds of movements; e.g., in our framework, those cases subsumed under (c) where the wh-word depends (immediately) on the main verb are described without a
movement: the wh-word as the least dynamic element of the sentence gets the leftmost position directly.

6 The condition of projectivity restricts the relationship between dependency and the left-to-right order of the
nodes of the tree so that for every two nodes connected by the relation of (immediate) dependency it holds
that every node occurring between them in the sense of the left-to-right order is subordinated to one of them
(where subordination is the transitive closure of dependency, i.e. being subordinated means to depend, immediately or not).

been called the systemic ordering and several psycholinguistic tests have been carried out in order to establish its scale for individual languages (first of all Czech, but also German and English). For English, the hypothesized systemic order of the main complementations of the verb is as follows:

Temporal – Actor – Addressee – Objective – Origin – Effect – Manner – Norm – "from where" – Accompaniment – "which way" – Benefit – Directional (see *Sgall et al. 1986, p. 201*).

The positions of Locative, Means, Extent, Difference and many other complementations have still to be investigated; it seems to be well substantiated, however, that Means (Instrument) follows the Objective. This is corroborated by the fact that (17) (repeated here for convenience) rather than (18) is an appropriate answer to the question (19):

(17) My neighbour dug a HOLE with a hoe.
(18) My neighbour dug a hole with a hoe.
(19) What did your neighbour do yesterday afternoon?

9. Conclusion: "Underlying" and "surface" word orders have to be distinguished though not necessarily accompanied by an opposition of "surface" and "deep" syntax: the outer shape of the word order can be accounted for on the morphemic level of the language description. On this level also the synsemantic (functional) words (such as prepositions, articles, conjunctions, auxiliaries etc.) can be represented as separate words (in contrast to the syntactic level where they are not represented as separate nodes) and their word order position can be then determined by a rule of the same kind as those handling the adjuncts of a noun, clitics, etc. (see Section 7). The treatment of surface word order as determined by communicative dynamism and by assignment of positions in the morphemic string makes it possible to describe topic/focus articulation as one of the aspects of the syntactic structure of the sentence.

THE ORDERING OF VALENCY SLOTS FROM A COMMUNICATIVE POINT OF VIEW

1. LINGUISTIC MEANING

European structural linguistics offers a suitable starting point for a systematic inquiry into the relationships between syntax and semantics, since it has never excluded the notion of meaning from linguistic investigations, and has found an appropriate way how to handle the relationship between human cognition and the patterning of meaning in individual languages.[1] The linguistic structuring of meaning, contrasted by de Saussure, Hjelmslev, Coseriu as well as by the Praguian scholars with the ontological or cognitive content and substantiated with a deep insight into the matters of linguistic meaning by Professor E. M. Uhlenbeck (see e.g. Uhlenbeck 1980), may be understood on the one hand as the underlying structure of the sentence (representing, to a certain degree, a counterpart both to Chomskyan D-structure and to Logical Form, LF), and on the other hand as one element of the series of explicata necessary for the presystemic notion of meaning. This member of the series belongs to the system of language, while the others (one of which combines the linguistic meaning with the specification of reference, others belonging to the layers of intension and extension) pertain to the interdisciplinary domain of semantic interpretation.

In the present contribution I would like to demonstrate on one specific issue, namely the way in which the information on valency slots can be enriched by adding information on their communicative weight, that the level of meaning conceived in the above mentioned way, should also capture those aspects of the communicative function of language that are encoded by the grammar of the given language.

---

1   This contribution is a modified version of the paper presented at the Annual Meeting of Societas linguistica Europaea, held in Gothenburg, Sweden, August 1997. Work on this paper was supported by grant VS-96-Í51.

2. VALENCY FRAMES AND THE ORDERING OF VALENCY SLOTS

It is a matter of more or less general agreement nowadays that some kind of information on the valency of individual lexical units is an inevitable component part of a lexical entry in the lexicon, be it in the traditional form of a (printed or CD-ROM) dictionary or in a modern electronic form of some sort of a database designed to serve various applicational purposes. In this contribution, I would like to concentrate on additional important information the valency frames can provide and encode, namely the so-called systemic ordering underlying a rather strong hypothesis about the (deep) ordering of the complementations of the verb in the focus part of the sentence (Section 3), to indicate and briefly summarize the psycholinguistic experiments used to determine this ordering (Section 4) and to point out the appropriateness and usefulness of such an information for a procedure generating sentences and identifying the topic-focus articulation of sentences (Section 5).

3. SYSTEMIC ORDERING OF COMPLEMENTATIONS

The concept of a fundamental ordering of the different kinds of complementations, i.e. of "arguments" and "adjuncts", is understood in our approach (for a more detailed discussion see Hajičová, Sgall 1987; Sgall, Hajičová, and Panevová 1986) as partly determining the underlying word order, or communicative dynamism (CD) in individual sentences; if a complementation A precedes another one, B, under the systemic ordering (SO), then the order A < B is unmarked in the hierarchy of CD (and, in prototypical cases, also in the surface word order). The marked order B < A (with B less dynamic than A) can occur only if B is contextually bound.

SO may be illustrated by the asymmetry in (la) and (lb) below. In (la) the *from*-group is in the topic on some readings, in the focus on others; on the other hand, in (lb) the *to*-group can only be in the topic. This asymmetry can be accounted for on the basis of SO, if (i) in English, SO determines the order *from* < *to*, rather than *to* < *from* as the unmarked order, and if (ii), in general, a departure from SO marks what is displaced to the left as part of the topic. This means that within the focus the scale of CD always is in accordance with SO.

(1) (a) *They flew from Chicago to Boston*
            A   < B
   (b) *They flew to Boston from Chicago*
            B   <   A

As examples (2)–(4) show, a similar relationship can be found with other pairs of complementations:

(2) (a) *They went by car to a river* [Means-Direction.2]

        A < B

  (b) *They went to a river by car*

        B < A

(3) (a) *Jim dug a ditch with a hoe* [Objective-Means]

        A < B

  (b) *Jim dug a DITCH with a hoe*

        A < B

(4) (a) *Ron cannot sleep quietly in a hotel* [Manner-Loc.]

        A < B

  (b) *In a hotel Ron cannot sleep quietly*

    B < A

Here again, each of the (a) examples is ambiguous in that in some of its readings the last-but-one complementation, marked by A in the examples, belongs to the focus and in others to the topic. The (b) examples are less ambiguous in that the B group has a lower degree of CD than the A group; since this relative CD differs from the SO, the B group must belong to the topic in all readings corresponding to the given intonation pattern. The capitals in (3b) denote the marked placement of the intonation center,[2] which plays a role similar to the marked word order of the other (b) examples.

Let us add that "free" word order, which is also present in English (see examples (1), (2), (4)), is not arbitrary, but is determined by the topic-focus articulation (TFA), or more precisely, by the hierarchy of CD. The limitations on freedom of surface word order in English are correlated with the fact that a secondary intonation center (as in (3b)) occurs relatively often in English. The experiments described below in Section 4 and other research have shown that SO differs from one language to the other. It appears that for some of the main complementations of English the scale of SO is as follows:[3]

complementation	*illustration*
Actor	subject of active verb
Addressee	indirect object
Objective	direct object

---

2   If there is no word in our examples denoted by capitals, then we assume the intonation centre to fall on the last lexical item of the sentence.

3   Our classification of complements comes close to Fillmore's deep cases in some points, but is more syntactically based with regard to subject and object (cf. Panevová 1978). Actor may be understood as "deep subject" and Objective as "deep object"; we believe that such differences like those between Agentive, Experiencer, Theme belong to a cognitive layer not directly structured by natural languages such as English, German, Czech or Latin. This viewpoint makes it possible to understand e.g. the opposition between Agentive and Experiencer as determined by context and inferencing: with a verb such as *build* or *hit* the Actor corresponds to the cognitive role of Agentive, with *meet* or *hear* to that of Experiencer, and with *break* a larger context is needed (and may be insufficient) to find out whether a deliberate action (with Agentive) or just an involuntary event (with Experiencer) is referred to.

Origin (Source)	*out of wood*
Effect	*make into a canoe*
Manner	*quietly*
Directional 1	*from Boston*
Means	*with a hoe*
Directional 2	*to Chicago*
Locative	*in a hotel*

Czech, and probably also German, differ from English in that the positions of Objective and Effect in these languages are more to the right, after most of the adverbial complementations. This may be conditioned typologically, since in English the participants expressed without a function morpheme could not be easily recognized if separated from the verb by a series of prepositional groups. In German, Means probably still precedes Objective under SO, so that (5a) is ambiguous with respect to the position of Means (in the topic or in the focus), whereas (5b) lacks this ambiguity (the Objective always belongs here to the topic):[4]

(5) (a) *Jim hat mit einer Hacke eine RINNE gegraben*
      Jim has with a hoe a ditch dug
   (b) *Jim hat eine Rinne mit einer HACKE gegraben*

4. PSYCHOLINGUISTIC EXPERIMENTS TO TEST SYSTEMIC ORDERING

4.1 DESCRIPTION OF THE EXPERIMENTS

The hypothesis stated briefly at the beginning of Section 3 has been tested by a series of psycholinguistic experiments, which were first formulated for Czech (Sgall et al. 1980) and then used for German (Sgall et al. 1995) and for English (Preinhaelterová 1997). The basic pattern of such experiments was as follows: the subjects (native speakers of the given languages, mostly grammar school students in the highest grade of their studies) were given:

(a) a pair of testbed (simple, indicative) sentences differing only in the order of the two complementations of the verb the SO of which is being tested;

---

4   Scholars differ in analyzing German as having the verb basically either in the rightmost position (with the direct object immediately preceding it in the prototypical case), or having the verb closer to the beginning of the sentence. The experiments reported in Sgall et al. (1995) support the view that German has much in common with Slavic languages in the positions of the complementations of the verb, although there are important differences, concerning (i) the "frame construction", and (ii) a gradual development of the SO in German towards the state present now in English.

(b) two to four *wh*-questions in which the *wh*-word stands for one or more of the complementations of the verb; the rest of the tested sentence is shared by the question;

(c) the subjects should mark which (if any) of the testbed sentences can serve (in a coherent dialogue) as an answer to the given questions.

The following instructions were given to the subjects:

(a) the sentences were presented in the written form, but the subjects were informed that they should understand them as "silently" read in a natural way, i.e. with stressing the last word of the sentence;

(b) the subjects were free to mark the sentences as an answer to one question, or (in some of the experiments) to more than one, or to none of them.

Let us illustrate these experiments on one example taken from the Czech testbed. The sentences in (6) were among those presented to the subjects:

(6) (a) *očkovací látku*   *vstříkneme*   *injekční stříkačkou*   *pokusnému zvířeti*
         vaccination substance (we) inject   (by) syringe   (to) experimental animal
    (b) *očkovací látku*   *vstříkneme*   *pokusnému zvířeti*   *injekční stříkačkou*
         vaccination substance (we) inject   (to) experimental animal   (by) syringe

The subjects were asked to mark by crosses to which questions which of the sentences can be an answer (we fill in the expected judgements):

		(a)	(b)
(i)	Komu vstříkneme očkovací látku injekční stříkačkou? Whom (we) inject with a vaccine (by means of a) syringe?		x
(ii)	Co vstříkneme pokusnému zvířeti injekční stříkačkou? What (we) inject (the) experimental animal (with) (by means of a) syringe?		
(iii)	Co uděláme s očkovací látkou? What (we) do with (the) vaccine?		x
(iv)	Čím vstříkneme očkovací látku pokusnému zvířeti? (By) what (means) (we) inject a vaccine (the) experimental animal?	x	

Out of this set of questions, the diagnostic question was question (iii); it "models" a context in which only *očkovací látku* "vaccination substance" belongs to the topic while the verb *vstříkneme* "(we) inject" and the two complementations of the verb the position of which in the SO we test (Means: *injekční stříkačkou* "with syringe" and Addressee: *pokusnému zvířeti* "(to) experimental animal") are "questioned", i.e. they will be in the focus in the answer. The order of these complementations in the answer would then indicate the SO of these complementations: in our illustrative example, the answer of the subject suggested the order Means < Addressee.

4.2 RESULTS OF THE EXPERIMENTS

The first series of experiments for Czech was conducted with 137 informants (mostly grammar school students in the highest classes, age 17–18). There were two thresholds set as measures of success: if the deviation was up at most 20 (i.e., if 117 or more answers agreed with the initial hypothesis for the given pair, 84% of success) we considered the hypothesis to be fully confirmed. This occurred in the following cases:

Means < Addressee (6)
Direction-*to* < Result (7)
Temporal-*when* < Direction-*from* (8)
Addressee < Patient (9)
Direction-*from* < Direction-*to* (10)

(7) *Přihlásil se*   *do nově zřizovaného útvaru*
(He) applied (himself)   in newly established body
za člena komise
for member (of) cultural committee

(8) *Honza učí*   *zítra*   *od čtyř hodin*
Honza teaches   tomorrow   from four o'clock

(9) *Když přišel*   *domů,*   *vypravoval*   *našemu Honzovi*
When (he) came   home   (he) told   our Honza
o zkoušce   *z historické mluvnice*
about exam   in historical grammar

(10) *Na Můstku*   *přestoupíte*   *z jedenáctky*   *na dvaadvacítku*
At Můstek (you)   change   from eleven   to twenty-two

We accepted as satisfactory also the rate of success below 84% but above 78%; this was the case with the following pairs of complementations:

Measure < Instrument (11)
Until-*when* < How often (12)
How often < Location-*where* (13)
Location-*where* < Manner (14)

(11) *Láhve naplnili*   *až po okraj*   *plnicím automatem*
Bottles (they) filled   to the brim   (by) filling machine

(12) *Jirka k nám*   *chodil*   *až do své nemoci*   *dvakrát za měsíc*
Jirka to us   used to come   until his illness   twice a month

(13) *Vlak*   *se zdržel*   *až dvě hodiny*   *na hraničním přechodu*
Train (itself)   delayed   up to two hours   at border-crossing

(14) *Po příjezdu*   *Karel*   *usnul*   *v nezvyklém prostředí*
After arrival   Karel   fell asleep   in unfamiliar environment
neklidným spánkem
(by) troubled sleep

The second series comprised four experiments and was carried out in the late eighties and early nineties with a total of 192 subjects, with new testbeds and for more pairs of complementations. We also introduced some minor changes: no "double" crosses were allowed and in some of the experiments, commutations rather than questions were used to model the context.

Based on the experience with the tests for Czech, a similar method has been applied to German (experiments with 231 subjects in Vienna and Cologne are reported in Sgall et al. 1995) and to English (Preinhaelterová 1997). The conclusions of all the tests can be summarized as follows;

(a) SO is one factor of the word order;

(b) the testbed sentences must be carefully chosen to eliminate "suggestiveness" of the particular lexical setting (collocations, semantic closeness, e.g. *to owe taxes*), the implied contextual boundness (*he moved there from a village*), background knowledge, etc.;

(c) there are differences between languages emerging during the development of languages; the continuous character of language change may have also led to differences in SO of individual verbs (or small groups of verbs).

5. CONCLUSIONS

It goes without saying that more extensive work along the above lines should be carried out in the study of individual languages. This is necessary not only for the achievement of a deeper empirical and theoretical insight into these questions, which would allow to arrive at a more profound description of word order and its interrelationships to topic-focus articulation, but the results are also needed for the application of these insights in systems of natural language processing: the information on SO included in the lexicon is appropriate and useful for a procedure generating sentences (see the proposal for a generative procedure in Hajičová – Panevová – Sgall 1990) and this information can be used with great profit for the formulation of a procedure identifying TFA (Hajičová – Skoumalová – Sgall 1995).

HOW MANY TOPICS/FOCI?

INFORMATION STRUCTURE OF THE SENTENCE – ONE DICHOTOMY OR MORE?

The issues of what is commonly called "the information structure of the sentence" is nowadays a frequently discussed phenomenon both in syntax and in semantics, though the terminology is highly misleading: one can find such terms and oppositions as theme-rheme, given-new, topic-focus, presupposition-focus, topic-comment, focus-background, tail-link-focus, and many other. It is then quite appropriate to ask whether one faces an abundance of terms or different dichotomies. In the present paper we would like to discuss some relevant issues connected with the above-mentioned differences and to argue for the position developed within the Praguian framework of Functional Generative Grammar as the theory of topic-focus articulation (TFA, see e.g. Sgall, Hajičová and Benešová 1973; Sgall, Hajičová and Panevová 1986; Hajičová, Sgall and Partee 1998), namely that it is sufficient as well as necessary to work with (i) one dichotomy based on the primary opposition of contextual boundness (context in broader sense), and with (ii) a hierarchy of underlying word order (communicative dynamism, CD).

In the European tradition, the main trend advocating more than one dichotomy is represented above all by Halliday (1967–68; 1985), who works with two series of notions: (i) the theme (and possibly rheme), which is closely connected with word order, and (ii) "given" (and "new").

It is, of course, possible to give the position as such a specific label ("theme" as the first meaningful word in the sentence), but the function it exhibits in the information structure of the sentence varies widely, especially in accordance with the placement of the intonation center, see e.g. the difference between the function (and prosodic features) of "women" in (1) and (2).

(1) Women are supposed to work as NURSES.
(2) WOMEN are supposed to work as nurses.

It is sometimes claimed that two notions of topic (T) are to be distinguished: (i) "given" in the sense that it was present in preceding co-text, and (ii) "what the sentence is about". However, natural languages (or, at least, the languages we know) display but one dichotomy: in some cases, T directly connects the given utterance with the preceding one, in others T is more oriented towards the situation of the discourse, in a narrower or broader sense.

Another distinction found in literature is that of "old topic" (present as T already in the preceding co-text) vs. "new topic" (only present in the focus, F, of one of the preceding utterances or made salient just by the situation). It is true that not all elements of T have the same degree of givenness; this is reflected in our framework by an assignment of different degrees of CD: a "new topic" generally corresponds to our T proper (the least dynamic item), while an "old topic" (and also the temporal or local setting) is more dynamic, although also contained in T.

Engdahl and Vallduvi's (1995) opposition of "link" and "tail" corresponds more or less exactly to the Praguian distinction between T proper and other parts of T. Topic proper is often contrastive, and it may bear a secondary pitch or phrasal accent (raising) indicated by italics in our examples. Carlson (1983, p. 200f) gives the example quoted here as (3) to illustrate that a contrast may lead to specific implications: if the defendant is asked what he hit the victim with and utters (3) (with *him* being a contrastive T and *bicycle chain* bearing the intonation center, i.e. the falling main stress, and being in F), it is understood that he must have hit also other victims.

(3) I hit *him* with a BICYCLE CHAIN.

A related question concerns the distinction of "broad focus" vs. "narrow (marked constituent) focus" (which is actually similar to the question whether one might distinguish between a broad and a narrow topic); this opposition can easily be accommodated in the Praguian framework working with degrees of CD. "Narrow" T (F) would then correspond to T (F) proper and the "broad" T (F) to the whole T and F parts of the sentence. For the time being, we leave unresolved the issue whether presentational (completive) F (as in (4') in reply to (4)) should be distinguished from contrastive F (as in the context of (4"))

(4) (What has John given to the man?)
(4') John gave him a BOOK.
(4") John gave him a BOOK. (He hasn't given him a JOURNAL!)

This distinction is apparently relevant for German scrambling phenomenon (see Choi 1998), as illustrated by the impossibility of using (5)(a) in case of presentational F, while it is quite acceptable in the context (5)(b) or (c), i.e. in the case of contrastive F.

(5) (a) *weil Hans ein BUCH dem Mann gegeben hat
    (b) weil Hans ein BUCH dem Mann gegeben hat, nicht eine ZEITUNG
    (c) weil Hans NUR ein BUCH dem Mann gegeben hat

It is not the purpose of the present contribution to resolve the question of how many topics/foci are to be distinguished in general, but to demonstrate on the example of the so-called focussing particles that an approach working with a single dichotomy together with the notion of deep word order has an important explanatory force.

FOCUSSING PARTICLES

In the tradition of TFA studies in continental linguistics (H. Weil, G. von der Gabelentz, Ph. Wegener, V. Mathesius, J. Firbas and many others), T and F (or in a different terminology, see above) have been understood as two parts of the sentence (or of its structure, of its syntactic representation), or, more precisely, of an utterance event. The focus sensitive particles (focalizers, rhematizers, i.e. negation, *only, even, also*, sentential adverbials) have been then treated as specific items, the position and interpretation of which is closely connected with the general phenomenon of TFA. On the other hand, the most recent theories accounting for F in formal semantics (J. Jacobs, M. Rooth, M. Krifka) start their analyses with such overt focalizers, sometimes adding one or more covert ones, such as e.g. ASSERT (assuming that if negation acts as a focalizer, it seems plausible to recognize a counterpart positive operator). We believe that these two approaches can be reconciled in the following way (for more details, see Hajičová, Partee and Sgall 1998):

A. Prototypically, a focalizer has F of the sentence as its focus (ff), as illustrated in (6):

(6) (a) John only / introduced / Bill / to SUE.
 (b) John only / introduced / BILL % to Sue.

The slashes indicate the possible positions of the boundary between T and F of the sentence, and, consequently, the position of the focalizer *only* in the underlying structures of (6). The sign "%" indicates that *Bill* is the last element of the underlying structure of (b) on all its readings (*to Sue* belongs to T of (6)(b) on all the readings).

Sentences in (7) document that F and ff need not be restricted to contain only the intonationally highlighted word:

(7) (a) He only said that Mary liked the DANCER.
 (b) He said that Mary only liked the DANCER.
 (c) He said that Mary liked only the DANCER.

Simplified underlying representations of (7) are given in (7') to point out the ambiguity of these sentences, which leads to different truth conditions; it should be noticed that the TFA of (c') equals that of (b').

$(7')$ (a') $(he)_{Actor}$ / (only) say $(_{Obj}$ $(Mary)_{Actor}$ like $(_{Obj}$ dancer))

$\quad$ (a'') $(he)_{Actor}$ say / (only) $(_{Obj}$ $(Mary)_{Actor}$ like $(_{Obj}$dancer))

$(7')$ (b') $(he)_{Actor}$ say $(_{Obj}$ $(Mary)_{Actor}$ / (only) like $(_{Obj}$dancer))

$\quad$ (b'') $(he)_{Actor}$ say $(_{Obj}$ $(Mary)_{Actor}$ like / (only) $(_{Obj}$dancer))

$(7')$ (c') $(he)_{Actor}$ say $(_{Obj}$ $(Mary)_{Actor}$ like / (only) $(_{Obj}$dancer))

B. In peripheral cases, when ff is not identical to F, the following situations may occur:

(a) ff is the local focus of an embedded finite verb clause with the prototypical position of the intonation center, as in (8):

(8) (What was his reaction concerning John's sister?) He insisted that John's sister only broke her CAR.

In complex sentences, TFA exhibits recursive properties: the embedded clauses there have their own foci and topics. In (8), F is constituted by the VP of the whole sentence and ff is more restricted, consisting of the local focus of the embedded clause (i.e. its VP).

(b) The focalizers may also occur in the T of the sentence. This situation relates directly to the issue of the recursivity of TFA: something like embedded TFA structure may be imported into the topic from preceding co-text:

(9) (a) Who criticized even Mother TERESA as a tool of the capitalists?

$\quad$ (b) JOHN criticized even Mother Teresa as a tool of the capitalists.

However, in contrast to (8), there are no multiple clauses with their own TFA in (9)(b). The analysis of negation by Hajičová (1973; 1984) and that of many kinds of focalizers by Koktová (1986; 1987) indicate that this situation can be accounted for in terms of relative CD rather than of literally recursive TFA: ff belonging to T would then consist of those parts of T that are more dynamic than the focalizer. Thus the underlying structure of (9)(b) can be (preliminarily, as we will see below) represented (with many simplifications again) as in (9)(c):

(9) (c) (tool $(_{Appurt}$capitalist)$)_{Manner}$criticize (even) $(_{Obj}$Mother Teresa) / $(_{Actor}$John)

Two important caveats are in place here:

(i) The structure (9)(c) violates a fundamental condition with which the Czech theory of TFA works since the first publications of J. Firbas (now see his 1992), and according to which the verb occupies a position on (or, in our terms, adjacent to) the boundary between T and F. This is to say that the verb *criticize* should be understood as more dynamic than the rest of T, i.e. also than *even Mother Teresa*.

(ii) Often (perhaps, prototypically) it is the topic proper what constitutes the ff occurring within T, see (10):

(10) (Is there a film only JIM liked?) Only Jim liked AMADEUS.

We believe that this position of ff in T typically coincides with the primary position of contrastive T. Since contrastive T is a grammatical opposition, it should be marked explicitly in the underlying representations; for this purpose we use the superscript c and the underlying representation of (9)(b) should then be modified as (9)(d):

(9) (d) (even) $(_{Obj}$ Mother Teresa^c) (tool $(_{Appurt}$ capitalist))$_{Manner}$ criticize / $(_{Actor}$John)

The postulation of a feature characterizing a contrastive T is corroborated by its specific phonetic realization in the sentence prosody; as convincingly documented by Bartels (1995), this realization is different from the prosodic features characterizing the F proper of the sentence. Bartels' observations offer an independent support for understanding the noun groups bearing the (rising) phrasal stress in such sentences as (12)(b) and (13) as contrastive T, rather than as a part of F (in contrast to those researchers who tend to identify the two kinds of stress).

Another independent support for the view that contrastive T should be marked in the underlying structure, is supplied by von Fintel's (1994, p. 22, quoting Tunstall) observation that *it* as the weakest English pronoun cannot occur as ff in the second occurrence (i.e. in T), but the pronoun *he* can; *he* differs from *it* in that the former can be stressed.

The number of occurrences of focalizers in T is not restricted to a single one, as illustrated by B in (10):

(10) (A: All of us have seen that Jim only eats vegetables.)
B: If even Paul realized that Jim only ate vegetables, we would choose another RESTAURANT.

On the primary reading, B can be paraphrased as follows: "If the fact that Jim ate nothing else than vegetables was realized by Paul (as well as by other, more attentive witnesses), then we would choose another restaurant". It should be noted that a contextually bound item can be ff even though the focalizer *only* appears with this second occurrence of the item in question; the contextual boundness of a focalizer in the T position may be understood as based on a kind of anchoring in the preceding utterance given by the factual relationships concerning the contextual boundness of the noun to which the focalizer is attached. Sentence (11) is an example of the situation when one focalizer occurs in T, one in F:

(11) (What did even PAUL realize?) Even Paul realized that Jim only admired MARY.

The analysis of such examples is analogous to the previous cases: the prototypical position (and thus a prototypical interpretation) is that of the focalizer *only*; the focalizer *even* occurs in T.

(c) In the dependency framework of FGD, a focalizer prototypically depends on the verb; it depends on a noun only if its ff is limited to an adjective (or to another adjunct) depending on the noun, as in (12) with the interpretation "she saw no other car than a yellow one":

(12) She saw only (or: only saw) a YELLOW car.

(d) In the secondary cases, a focalizer may carry the intonation center of the sentence, as in (13) or (14):

(13) Mary ALWAYS takes John to the movies.
(14) They ALSO were there.

In these sentences, the focalizers constitute the whole F of the sentences and the rest of the sentence belongs to T. We leave it open for further investigation (though we are inclined to accept the second alternative) whether such sentences are to be described with the focalizer itself constituting the (contrastive) ff of an implicit ASSERT operator (or equivalent), or whether the ff is determined by the structure being in a sense "inherited" from the licensing co-text.

To sum up: The above considerations lead us to suggest that the prototypical (unmarked) position of a focalizer is that of the least dynamic element of F; ff then consists of those elements of F which are more dynamic than the focalizer. If a focalizer occurs in T, its ff consists of those elements of T which in the underlying word order follow the focalizer and extends up to an item marked by the superscript c. If the focalizer is stressed (carries the intonation center), then it constitutes the whole F; its ff again is specifically marked (by the superscript c) in dependence on the preceding co-text.

RHEMATIZERS REVISITED

ABSTRACT

The specific function of certain particles from the point of view of the bipartition of the senten-ce was noted first by Jan Firbas (1957), who later called them "rhematizers". The same class of words was studied in detail in the context of formal semantics by Math Rooth (1985) in relati-on to the prosodic prominence of the words that followed them; he called this class "focalizers". Both terms refer to the apparent function of these particles, namely as being "associated" with the focus of the sentence. Since then, Rooth's approach has been followed by several specialists in formal semantics. However, the assumption of such an exclusive function of these particles has been found to be too simplistic, an analogy with a semantic analysis of negation was clai-med to be a more adequate approach (Hajičová, 1995) and a distinction has been made between "the (global) focus" of the sentence and "the focus" of the focalizer by Hajičová, Partee and Sgall (1998). Based on the observations of Kateřina Veselá, who has devoted considerable attention to the issue of the scope of focalizers as reflected in the richly annotated corpus of Czech (Prague Dependency Treebank) and a similarly based annotation of English in the so-called Prague En-glish Dependency Treebank, we single out in our contribution some complicated (and intricate) cases concerning first of all the occurrence of focalizers with a restricted freedom of position, with a distant placement of focalizers and their possible postposition, and the semantic scope of focalizers.

1. INTRODUCTION AND SOME HISTORICAL REFERENCES

The main aim of the present paper is to put under scrutiny a special class of particles known under different names such as "rhematizer" or "focalizer" or "focusing parti-cle". The terms used indicate that these particles have something to do with rheme/ focus of the sentence, and the question raised by our discussion is "What exactly?"

In Czech linguistics, the first observation of a specific rematizing function of the adverb *even* was mentioned by Firbas (1957); in his later paper (Firbas 1959, p. 53) he calls such particles "intensifying elements" and says that "(they) are,... as it were, su-perimposed on the sentence structure, considerably *changing* its FSP by rhematizing (frequently even turning into rheme proper) the element to which they are made to

refer". [1] The name "rhematizer" was first used by Firbas (1974, p. 20). Specific attention was paid to some of them in Czech by Daneš (see e.g. Daneš 1985, Sect. 6.1, 6.2.1
and 6.2.2), who distinguishes direct restrictors (*jen "only"*), indirect restrictors (*vyjma
"except for"*) and contextualizers (*také "also", a přece "and still"*). Following Firbas, the
function of certain particles from the point of view of the bipartition of the sentence
into theme and rheme is also discussed by Dušková (1988, pp. 527, 532). It should be
also mentioned at this point that a semantic impact of the position of several kinds of
adverbials and quantifiers was substantiated already by Sgall (1967), who exemplifies
the semantic relevance of topic/focus articulation on the English quantifier *mostly*.
Sgall's argumentation was followed by Koktová (1999, but also in her previous papers),
who distinguishes a specific class of adverbials called attitudinal.

The same class of words was studied later in the context of formal semantics by
Math Rooth (1985) in relation to the prosodic prominence to the words that followed
them; he called this class "focalizers." Both terms refer to the apparent function of
these particles, namely as being "associated" with the focus of the sentence; the position of the focalizer (and the accompanying placement of the intonation center) indicates which reading of the sentence is being chosen from the set of alternatives. Since
then, Rooth's approach has been followed by several specialists in formal semantics.
Rooth himself refers to Jackendoff (1972) and his analysis of examples such as *I only introduced BILL to Sue* in contrast to *I only introduced Bill to SUE* (the capitals denoting the
position of the intonation center) and also to D. Lewis's (1975) recognition of a class of
"adverbs of quantification" (*always, usually, frequently* etc.) exemplified by the semantic difference between *MARY always takes John to the movies* and *Mary always takes JOHN
to the movies* (expressed, in the surface shape of the sentence, by the difference in the
placement of the intonation center).

2. FOCALIZERS AND THE SCOPE OF NEGATION

2.1 It was already recognized by Vachek (1947) that in Czech there is a certain relation between the semantic scope of negation, quantifiers and topic/focus articulation.
Similar observations hold about negative particles in some other languages: Dutch
niet (Kraak 1966), German *nicht* (Zemb 1968), and even in languages outside the In-
doeuropean family such as Navajo (Eloise Jelinek, pers.comm.). We have studied these
relationships more systematically in Hajičová (1972; 1975) and have arrived at the
conclusion that an adequate explanation is that based on the relation of *aboutness*:
the speaker communicates something (the focus of the sentence) about something

---

1   In our understanding of topic-focus articulation (Firbas's FSP) as a matter of the underlying structure of the
     sentence one should not speak about a *change* of FSP but rather about a more or less explicit *indication* of FSP
     (in protypical cases, by the position of the focalizer, but see below our discussion of secondary positions).

(the topic of the sentence), i.e. F(T), the focus holds about the topic. In the case of negative sentences, the focus does not hold about the topic: ~F(T). In a secondary case, the focus holds about a negative topic: F(~T).

A supportive argument for the relationships between the semantic scope of negation and TFA can be traced in the discussions on the kinds of entailments starting with the fundamental contributions of Strawson. Strawson (1952, esp. p. 173ff.) distinguishes a formal logical relation of entailment and a formal logical relation of presupposition; this distinction – with certain simplifications – can be illustrated by (1) and (2):

(1) All Johns' children are asleep.
(2) John has children.

If John's children were not asleep, the sentence (1) would be false; however, if John did not have children, the sentence as well as its negation would not be false but meaningless. Thus (2) is a presupposition of (1) and as such it is not touched by the negation of (1).

Returning to the relation of aboutness, we can say that (1) is about John's children, and for (1) to be meaningful, there must be an entity John's children the speaker can refer to.

The close connection between the notion of presupposition and TFA can be documented by a more detailed inspection of the notion of presupposition, exemplified here by sentences (3) and (4).

(3) The King of France is (not) bald.
(4) The exhibition was (not) visited by the King of France.

It follows from the above mentioned discussions of presuppositions that Strawson's (1964) ex. (3) is about the King of France and the King's existence (referential availability) is presupposed, it is entailed also by its negative counterpart; otherwise (3) would have no truth value, it would be meaningless. On the other hand, there is no such presupposition for (4): the affirmative sentence is true if the King of France was among the visitors of the exhibition, while its negative counterpart is true if the King of France was not among the visitors. The truth/falsity of (4) does not depend on the referential availability of the entity "King of France". This specific kind of entailment was introduced in Hajičová (1972) and was called allegation: an allegation is an assertion A entailed by an assertion carried by a sentence S, with which the negative counterpart of S entails neither A nor its negation (see also Hajičová, 1984; 1993, and the discussion by Partee, 1996). Concerning the use of a definite noun group in English one can say that it often triggers a presupposition if it occurs in topic (see sentence (3)), but only an allegation if it belongs to focus (see sentence (4)).

Following these considerations, the scope of negation can be specified, in the prototypical case, as constituted by the focus, so that the meaning of a negative declarative sentence can be interpreted as its Focus (F) not holding of it, i.e. ~F(T). In this way it is possible to understand the semantic difference present in (3) and (4).

In a secondary case, the assertion holds about a negative topic: F(~T), see (5) on the reading when answering the question "Why didn't he come?".

(5) He did not come because he was afraid.

Here again, the scope of negation is dependent on TFA: it is restricted to the Topic part of the sentence. The assertion entailed (on this reading) by the *because*-clause in Focus is not touched by negation.

2.2 Going back to the studies quoted in Sect.1 that introduced the notion of "focusing particles", their motivation was clearly guided by considerations similar to those about the prototypical cases of the semantic scope of negation: the focalizer (by its word-order position and also with regard to the placement of the intonation center) *indicates* which element(s) of the sentence is(are) its focus. In other words, if the topic/focus of the sentence is understood (as it should be) as a part of the underlying structure of the sentence (its meaning), the position of the focalizer and the prosody of the sentence are the outer form (expression) of this function of focalizers (Hajičová, 1995; 2009).

Examples (6)(a) through (6)(d) illustrate this prototypical situation with the following interpretations: for (a), the only person John introduced Bill to, was Sue, for (b) the only person who was introduced by John to Sue was Bill, for (c) the only action John did as for Bill and Sue, was introducing, and (d) the only person who introduced Bill to Sue was John.

(6) (a) John introduced Bill only to SUE.
    (b) John introduced only BILL to Sue.
    (c) John only INTRODUCED Bill to Sue.
    (d) Only JOHN introduced Bill to Sue.

As has been observed by several grammarians of English (this observation can be traced back at least to Jespersen 1949)[2], it is possible in English to preserve the preverbal position of such particles as *only* and still to have several possibilities of the interpretation of the sentence according to the scope of this particle (see more on the scoping properties in Sect. 4 below), as indicated by the possible continuations of (7)(a) in (7)(b) through (d).

(7) (a) John only introduced Bill to SUE.

---

2   "Purists insist on placing *only* close to the word it qualifies, but as a matter of fact it is by most people placed between S and V, and stress and tone decide where it belongs." (Jespersen 1949, p. 95). The author refers to H. E .Palmer's *Grammar of Spoken English* (1924, par. 386) and to the difference between: *He did not listen; he only / talked* and *The others listened/ he only talked.*

(b) ... and not to MARY.
(c) ... and not Nick to MARY.
(d) ... and did not say hello to the HOSTESS.

It is, of course, also possible to keep the focalizer in the preverbal position and to mark the "scope" of this particle only by the position of the intonation center; sentences (8)(a) through (8)(d) correspond, in (one of) their interpretations, to (6)(a) through (d), respectively.

(8) (a) John only introduced Bill to SUE.
(b) John only introduced BILL to Sue.
(c) John only INTRODUCED Bill to Sue.
(d) JOHN only introduced Bill to Sue.

3. SECONDARY POSITIONS OF FOCALIZERS

Comparing the analysis of the semantic scope of negation and the analysis of the function of focalizers, it is necessary to consider also the possibility of having a secondary interpretation of the position of the focalizers, namely a situation similar to that with negation of a verb in the topic of the sentence. This issue was analyzed by Hajičová, Partee and Sgall (1998, Sect. 6.3) and it has been demonstrated on examples such as (9)(a) and (10)(a) that in secondary cases a focalizer need not be an indicator of focus.

(9) (a) JOHN criticized even Mother Teresa as a tool of the capitalists.
(b) Who criticized even MOTHER TERESA as a tool of the capitalists?
(10) (a) Only Jim liked AMADEUS.
(b) Is there a film only JIM liked?

The sentence (9)(a) may occur in a context illustrated by the question (9)(b): the predicate *criticized even Mother Teresa as a tool of the capitalists* of (9)(a) is repeated from the question and the only part of this sentence that stands in the focus is *John* (with a paraphrase "the person who critized even Mother Teresa as a tool of capitalists was John"). In a similar vein, (10)(a) can be interpreted as "the film only Jim liked is Amadeus", with *Amadeus* being the only element of the focus of the sentence and the focalizer *only* included in its topic. The authors suggest that the position of the focalizer in the topic part of the sentence indicates which element of the topic stands is contrast and introduce the notion of a distinction betweeen global focus (of the whole sentence) and the local focus (of a focalizer). They distinguish between a global focus (*JOHN* and *AMADEUS*, respectively, for examples (9)(a) and (10)(a)) and a focus of a focalizer (*even Mother Teresa* and *only Jim*, respectively). The focus of a focalizer can then be specified as the part of the sentence that follows the focalizer. Such an understanding would compare well with the sometimes indicated recursivity of topic/focus articulation.

A supportive argument for such a treatment is the use of strong (long) pronouns in Czech in such a position (cf. Koktová, 1999); the question-answer pair in (10) is a quite cohesive part of conversation corresponding to the English example (9)(b) followed by (9)(a), just replacing the proper name *Honza* with a pronoun *jemu* (Dative, singular, "long" form; the alternative short form is "mu", which is not possible in this position) preceded by the focalizer *jenom* ("only").

(11) (Znáš nějaký film, který by se líbil jenom Honzovi?) Jenom jemu se líbil AMA-DEUS.

Hajičová, Partee and Sgall (1998, Sect. 6.3) also present complex examples with two focalizers in the topic of the sentence reproduced here as (12)(b) in the context of (12)(a).

(12) (a) We all knew that John eats only vegetables.
(b) If even Paul knew that John eats only vegetables, we should have gone to another restaurant.

In (12)(b), the contrastive character of the element introduced by a focalizer in the topic part of the sentence is rather evident: Paul is one of all of us (i.e. he is referred to in the topic part of the sentence), but at the same time, he is contrastively singled out. The global focus of (12)(b) is *we should have gone to another restaurant*; in terms of the relation of "aboutness," this is what the sentence presents as an irretrievable, "new" information. Both *Paul* and *vegetables* are parts of the topic, the former being a local focus of the focalizer *even* and the latter being the local focus of the focalizer *only*. [3]

As the Czech example (13) (translated into English as (13'), with "just a" corresponding to the Czech focalizer "jenom" = "only") indicates, the two focalizers need not be in separate clauses (V. Petkevič, personal communication). It should be noted that similarly to (10) above, also here the long form of the pronoun is used ("jemu" = "him").

(13) (Kdo poslal i Honzovi jenom pohlednici?) I jemu poslala jen pohlednici MARIE.
(13') (Who has sent a single postcard even to John?) MARY has sent just a postcard even to him.

---

3   Some linguists introduce the notion of "second occurrence focus" or "double focus" (for a summarizing discussion, see Féry and Ishibara, in press). Investigations into prosodic realization of sentences with a contrastive topic, however, have demonstrated that the prosodic realizations of focus on the one hand and of contrastive topic on the other significantly differ (see e.e. Bartels; for Czech, this has been demonstrated by Veselá, Peterek and Hajičová, 2003).

4. SOME REMARKS ON THE SCOPE OF FOCALIZERS

In our discussions of the semantics of negation, we have argued that it is the articulation of the sentence into its topic and focus that determines the scope of negation rather than the position of the negative particle (or negative verb) in the surface shape of the sentence. In a similar vein, we believe that it is a misleading claim to say that the scope of a focalizer is indicated by its position in the surface shape of the sentence. To substantiate the claim let us look at (14).

(14) They were advised to learn only SPANISH.

Taglicht (1984), Rooth (1985) and König (1991) (as well as several other authors discussing these and similar sentences) understand this sentence as ambiguous; Rooth (1985, p. 90, ex. (5)(a) and (7)(c) and (d)) provides the readings "they were advised not to learn any other language" and "they were not advised to learn any other language," and he claims, following Taglicht (1984), that the scope ambiguity can be avoided by shifting *only* to a preverbal position, as in (15) and (16).

(15) They were advised to only learn SPANISH.
(16) They were only advised to learn SPANISH.

Two remarks are in place: first, sentence (16) itself is not unambiguous; in addition to the interpretation "no other language were they advised to learn" it may be paraphrased as "no other advice was given to them" (as in (17)) or "they were told nothing else than ..." (as in 18)).

(17) They were advised only to learn SPANISH.
(18) They only were advised to learn SPANISH.

Second, the ambiguity of (14) points to the fact that the position of the focalizer in the surface shape of the sentence is not relevant for the determination of the semantic scope of the focalizer; instead, what is important is its position in the underlying sentence structure taking in account the topic-focus articulation. On the interpretation which (14) shares with (15), the verb *advise* is in the topic of the sentence and thus outside the scope of *only*, while on the interepretation (14) shares with (16), the verb *advise* together with its complementation expressed by the infinitival construction are both in the focus of the sentence and the scope of *only* extends over the focus.[4]

And third, the situation is made clearer if the focalizer *only* is replaced by negation, as in (19).

---

4 Hajičová, Partee and Sgall (1998, p. 139f.) discuss the possibility to capture this scope ambiguity within a dependency account of the syntactic structure of the sentence but the issue of grammar formalisms is out of the scope of this contribution and therefore we do not analyze the arguments here.

(19) They were not advised to learn SPANISH.

Schematically, the underlying structure respecting the possibilities of the topic-focus articulation of this sentence in relation to the position of the negative element is indicated in (20)(a) through (c), where the negative element is placed on the boundary between topic and focus. In the brackets after each scheme we suggest a possible continuation (see Chomsky, 1968 on natural responses as a test for his "range of permissible focus"). As a matter of course, we consider the sentence (19) with the placement of the intonation center on the last word, i.e. SPANISH; if the placement of the intonation center is changed, the interpretations of the sentence(s) (and their topic-focus articulation) would be different.

(20) (a) they / NEG were advised to learn Spanish (... but they taught them to drive a car)
     (b) they were advised / NEG to learn Spanish (... but to dress modestly)
     (c) they were advised to learn / NEG Spanish (... but English)

There is a fourth possibility illustrated here by (21), namely that the negative particle and the verb is in the topic of the sentence, and the scope of the negative particle does not reach beyond the boundary between topic and focus. Sentence (19) is then understood as being about the fact that they were not advised (to do something).

(21) they were NEG advised / to learn Spanish

Another misleading claim found in the literature is the statement that if the focalizer is placed before the subject of the sentence, only the subject is in the focus. This is how Koenig (1991, p. 21, ex. (38)(a) and (b) quoted here as (22) and (23), respectively) explains the impossibility of (22), with the focalizers before the subject and the intonation center on the last element of the sentence, i.e. on an element other than the subject.

(22) Even/only FRED gave a present to Mary.
(23) *Even/only Fred gave a present to MARY.

First of all, our examples (10)(a) and (12)(b) above have indicated that a focalizer before a subject that is not a bearer of the intonation center can occur in the topic of the sentence. Second, evident counterexamples to Taglicht's claim are sentences in passives such as (24) in the interpretation "only a single question (out of many) was answered by both Joan and Susan" (e.g. used in the context "... while two questions were answered by ... and all questions by the rest of the class").

(24) Only one question was answered by both JOAN and SUSAN.

5. SOME REMARKS ON EMPIRICAL INVESTIGATIONS: CZECH AND ENGLISH

5.1 The richly annotated corpus of Czech (Prague Dependency Treebank, about 50 000 sentences from continuous pieces of texts annotated – in addition to the morphemic and analytic surface layer – with respect to their underlying, tectogrammatical structure including topic-focus articulation) and a similarly based annotation of English in the so-called Prague English Dependency Treebank (henceforth PEDT, much smaller at the time of writing of this paper) has allowed for a more detailed contrastive analysis of sentence structures in which particles of the above-mentioned class occur. Based on the observations of Kateřina Veselá, who has devoted considerable attention to the issue of the scope of focalizers as reflected in the two above mentioned treebanks, some general though tentative conclusions can be attested.

5.2 While in Czech a typical position of a focalizer in the surface shape of the sentence is immediately before the sentence element the focalizer is "associated with," in English this need not be the case, as illustrated above by the example (7)(a) and its interpreations repeated here for the sake of convenience as (25) with possible continutations in (25').

(25) John only introduced Bill to SUE.
(25') (a) ... and not to MARY.
    (b) ... and not Nick to MARY.
    (c) ... and did not say hello to the HOSTESS/and he LEFT.

In Czech, we have to distinguish the readings of (25) by placing the focalizer immediately before the focused element (or group of elements, i.e. before the focus of the sentence) even in the surface shape; this is illustrated by the Czech equivalents of (25) in its three possible interpretations (where (26)(a) through (c) corresponds to (25')(a) through (c), respectively)

(26) (a) Honza představil Billa jenom ZUZANĚ (... a ne MARII).
    (b) Honza představil jenom Billa ZUZANĚ (... a ne Nicka MARII).
    (c) Honza jenom představil Billa ZUZANĚ (... a nepozdravil HOSTITELKU/ODEŠEL).

It is interesting to notice that contrary to the general characteristics of Czech as a language with a relatively "free" word order (i.e. without grammatical word-order restrictions), in the placement of the focalizer *only* English is more flexible than Czech is: this particle can be placed either immediately before the element it is "associated with" or between the subject and the verb.

5.3 Another difference between English and Czech concerns the fact that a focalizer may have a "backward" scope more frequently in English than in Czech. For example, the intonation center in the sentence (27) from the PEDT, if pronounced, would be placed on the word *inflation* (as indicated here by capitals); the postposited focalizer *only* having its scope to the left. In the Czech translation of (27), given here as (28), the focalizer *jenom* has to be placed in front of the focused element.

(27) Scenario 1, known as the "Constant Dollar Freeze", reimburses the Pentagon for INFLATION only.

(28) Scénář 1, známý jako "konstantní zmrazení dolaru", nahrazuje Pentagonu výdaje jen kvůli INFLACI.

Typical examples of a "backward" scope in English are sentences with a postponed focalizer *too*, and similarly with *also*, see sentences (29) and (30) from the PEDT; the preceding contexts, in which these sentences occur in the treebank, are quoted in brackets.

(29) (European community employers fear that the EC Commission's plans for a "charter of fundamental social rights" is a danger to industrial competitiveness.) The British government also strongly opposes the charter in its current form.

(30) (Norman Young, a "mud-logger" at the Sniper well, has worked all but about nine days of this year.) Butch McCarty, who sells oil-field equipment for Davis Tool Co., is also busy.

As the context in (29) indicates, the focus of the focalizer *also* (which in this case equals the global focus of the sentence) is the British government; the part of the sentence after the focalizer belongs to the topic (the sentence is "about" strong oppositions to the current form of the charter). Similarly, for (30), the focus of the focalizer (again, equal to the global focus) is the subject of the sentence, its topic being *is busy* (the sentence is "about" hard intensive work).

In Czech, backward scope of focalizers is not that frequent as in English, but it is also possible. Example (31) is quoted from Daneš (1957, pp. 84ff.)

(31) Psal TAKÉ česky
Lit. (He) wrote ALSO in Czech.

Daneš considers (31) as ambiguous between "besides writing in other languages, he wrote also in Czech" (in our terms, with a (typical) "forward scope," in which reading the sentence is synonymous with (32)), and as an answer to the question "Did he write also in CZECH?," with the scope over the whole predicate in the topic.

(32) Psal také ČESKY.
Lit. (He) wrote also in CZECH.

It should be noted that in their spoken form, Czech sentences with *také* are not necessarily ambiguous, see (33) and (34), where the surface placement of the focalizer is the same but the sentences differ in their topic-focus articulation, which is indicated by the different placements of the intonation center.

(33) (Karel má kočku.) Karel má taky PSA.
    Lit. (Charles has a cat). Charles has also a DOG.
(34) (Já mám psa.) Karel má TAKY psa.
    Lit. (I have a dog.) Charles has ALSO a dog.

In (33), it is asserted that besides having a cat, Charles has (also) a dog, while in (34) it is asserted that besides me, a dog is owned (also) by Charles.

5.4 The manual annotation of large corpora has also confirmed that the class of focalizers is larger than originally (and usually) assumed; propertiers similar to those of "prototypical" focalizers *only, even, also* are evident also with *alone, as well, at least, especially, either, exactly, in addition, in particular, just, merely, let alone, likewise, so much as, solely, still/much less, purely,* and several others. Even more importantly, our Czech material provides an evidence that according to the contexts in which they are used, these elements may acquire functions other than that of a focalizer (as in (35)): they may have a function of a discourse connective as in (36) meaning "among other things, mentioned previously, ...", or a typically adverbial function as in (37) or an attitudinal function as in (38).

(35) Nezapomeň hlavně NA MNE.
    Lit. Don't forget especially ME.Hlavně na mne NEZAPOMEŇ.
    Lit. In the main, do not FORGET me.
(36) Hlavně na mne NEZAPOMEŇ.
    Lit. In the main, do not FORGET me.
(37) Tohle je zvlášť VELIKÉ.
    Lit. This is especially LARGE.
(38) Jenom se opovaž lhát!
    Lit. Just try to lie!

ACKNOWLEDGEMENT

Thanks are due to Kateřina Veselá for supplying relevant material from the PDT and PEDT and for insightful discussions on the matter under investigation. The work presented in this contribution was funded by the Companions project (www.companions-project.org) sponsored by the European Commission as part of the Information Society Technologies (IST) programme under EC grant number IST-FP6–034434 and it was supported also by the grant of the Ministry of Education of the Czech Republic MSM 0021620838.

3. THEORETICAL DESCRIPTION REFLECTED IN CORPUS ANNOTATION

FOREWORD

Papers included in the previous Parts of this volume tackled two main topics of our interest, namely the description of valency and the representation of topic-focus articulation (in more recent terms the information structure of the sentence) on the underlying level of language description and the means of its expression, and its importance for some other aspects of the meaning of the sentence such as negation and presupposition. The empirical resources for these studies were rather traditional, or, in the case of the ordering of elements in the underlying structure, experimental. The availability of electronic corpora and of the tools for their compilation, processing and search has made it possible to expand the empirical basis on the one hand, and to test the formulated hypothesese on this material on the other. For Czech, the efforts to this purpose started about the end of the nineties of the last century (see Hajič 1998) by the formulation of a multi-level linguistic annotation scheme based on the theoretical tenets of the Functional Generative Grammar, which was applied to a part of the Czech National Corpus (CNC); the annotated collection is called the Prague Dependency Treebank (PDT). After an overall description of the reflection of the FGD principles in the PDT, which we presented in our 2002 paper *Theoretical Description of Language as a Basis of Corpus Annotation: The case of Prague Dependency Treebank,* we focus our attention on several hypotheses and assumptions we work with in the domain of topic-focus articulation (discussed in some detail in the papers in Part 2 of this volume) and document on the PDT material the possibilities the annotated corpus offers for their testing, in which points the theoretical frame is supported by the material and in which points and in which way it can be modified (*What We Have Learned from Complex Annotation of Topic-Focus Articulation in a Large Czech Corpus,* 2012). It goes without saying that the PDT annotation scheme is not a frozen scenario and it undergoes revisions and modifications, which are then realized in upgraded versions of PDT (for the most actual state, see Bejček et al. 2013).

THEORETICAL DESCRIPTION OF LANGUAGE AS A BASIS OF CORPUS ANNOTATION: THE CASE OF PRAGUE DEPENDENCY TREEBANK

1. INTRODUCTION

The raised interest in corpus linguistics in the last two decades of the past century has opened new horizons for linguistic (and not only linguistic) research, but also brought along several fundamental issues for discussion. One of them is that of designing annotation (tagging) scenarios. This issue is topical esp. at the present stage when no problems of principle are connected with a mere compilation of very large corpora of texts (not that much of speech, though, which is still a serious problem, mostly of a technical and organizational nature). In the present contribution we would like (i) to argue that such scenarios should include an underlying level of syntactic annotation and (ii) to demonstrate on the example of the Prague Dependency Treebank (using a part of the texts gathered in the Czech National Corpus) that a design of such a scenario if based on a sound explicit linguistic theory is a feasible task.

We present first a brief account of such a theory, viz. the Functional Generative Description (FGD, Section 2), followed by a sketch of the overall tagging scenario of the Prague Dependency Treebank (PDT, Section 3). The core of the paper is Section 4, in which the theoretical assumptions of FGD concerning the tectogrammatical (underlying) syntactic level are confronted with the properties of the tagging scheme (the tectogrammatical tree structures, TGTSs). Some conclusions are drawn in Section 5.

2. FUNCTIONAL GENERATIVE DESCRIPTION

2.1 GENERAL OVERVIEW

The annotation scheme on the deep structure level (TGTSs) is based on the theoretical framework of the Functional Generative Description (FGD), namely on its level of the tectogrammatical representations (for motivating discussions and for more details, see e.g. Sgall 1967 and 1992; Sgall *et al.* 1986; a formalization can be found in Petkevič 1987 and 1995). It has been shown in which way the class of these representations can be specified on the basis of a small number of general principles accounting for the core of grammar and by specific rules for peripheral patterns. The two features of FGD distinguishing it from most of other theoretical frameworks are the dependency-based syntax and the systematic incorporation into the description of an account of information structure of the sentence (its topic-focus articulation, TFA).

2.2 TECTOGRAMMATICAL LEVEL

2.2.1 A GENERAL CHARACTERIZATION OF THE TECTOGRAMMATICAL LEVEL OF FGD

The tectogrammatical level can be characterized as the level of linguistic (literal) meaning, i.e. as the structuring of the cognitive content proper to a particular language. On this level, the irregularities of the outer shape of sentences are absent (including synonymy and at least the prototypical cases of ambiguity) and it can thus serve as a useful interface between linguistics in the narrow sense (as the theory of language systems) on one side and, on the other, as a background for such interdisciplinary domains as that of semantic interpretation (logical analysis of language, reference assignment based on inferencing using contextual and other knowledge, further metaphorical and other figurative meanings), that of discourse analysis or text linguistics, and so on.

A tectogrammatical representation (TR) of the sentence basically has the shape of a dependency tree. The edges of the tree denote the dependency relations and the nodes carry complex labels indicating their lexical and morphological values. No nonterminals and no nodes corresponding to function words (auxiliaries, prepositions, conjunctions, articles) are present in the tree. Counterparts of function words (and function morphemes) are parts of the complex symbols of the nodes. Instead of using the notion of phrase, we work with subtrees (i.e. the governor and its dependents, or all its subordinate nodes, where "subordinate" is the transitive closure of "dependent," so that "*b* is subordinated to *c*" means "*b* immediately or through mediation of other nodes depends on *c*"). The left-to-right order of the nodes of the dependency tree corresponds to the topic-focus articulation of the sentence.

TRs meet the strongly restrictive condition of projectivity: a dependency tree is projective if for every three-element set of nodes *a*, *b*, *c* present in the tree, it holds that if *a* depends on *c*, and *b* is placed between *a* and *c* in the left-to-right order, then *b* is subordinated to *c*. The cases of non-projective constructions in the surface structure (which are strongly limited as for their types, though not as for their frequency) can be described by means of movement rules concerning morphemics (see Sgall 1997b; Hajičová 1998a and the writings quoted there). The orientation of the dependency relation (i.e. the determination of which of the pair of the nodes connected by an edge is the governor and which is the dependent) can be specified on the basis of the following operational criterion: the dependent node is that member of the pair that is syntactically omissible, if not in a lexically specified pair of words (as is the case with the endocentric syntagms), then at the level of word classes. Thus e.g. in *((very) slow) progress* the syntactic potential of the heads prototypically is identical to that of the whole groups. In *Jim met Sally* nothing can be deleted, but we know from other cases that the verb is never deletable (without a specific context), whereas object can be absent e.g. with *read*, and subject (or, more precisely, its prototypical tectogrammatical counterpart, the Actor or Actor/Bearer) is absent e.g. with *rain* (the E. pronoun *it* is just a morphemic filler, having no semantic relevance, since no other option is present), and in the so-called pro-drop languages such as Czech or Latin (no subject pronoun is present).

As mentioned above, function words do not occupy specific positions in the syntactic structure of the sentence as represented by the TRs. This is substantiated by the fact that articles and prepositions are, as a rule, connected with nouns, auxiliary verbs and conjunctions with verbs, and they cannot be freely modified by other elements of the sentence. Thus it appears not to be appropriate to assign them the same status as to proper (autosemantic) lexical units. Their underlying counterparts thus should be differentiated from those of the autosemantic words and denoted by more economical means than separate nodes. Thus e.g. an embedded clause such as *(We knew) that Jim arrived* is represented by a subtree the head of which is labeled by the lemma of its verb with the functor PAT corresponding to the function of the conjunction "that" in this sentence: arrive.ANT(erior).INDIC.PAT.

The labels of the nodes of the TR are complex symbols consisting of three parts: (i) a lexical part, (ii) a combination of symbols (called grammatemes) for values of grammatical categories such as number, tense, modality, etc., and (iii) symbols (called functors) denoting the kinds of syntactic dependency (the valency positions). The functors can equivalently be written as labels of edges (or, in a linear notation, as indices of parentheses). The TR of a sentence thus can be rendered by a string of complex symbols corresponding to lexical occurrences (of the autosemantic words), with every dependent included in a pair of parentheses. Along with dependency, the TRs include a specification of several further relations. One of these is the topic-focus articulation (TFA), expressed in the surface structure mainly by an interplay of word order and sentence prosody (esp. the position of intonation centre); in the TRs, TFA is represented by the left-to-right order of the nodes (denoting the so-called communicative dynamism, i.e. the underlying word order) and by an index attached to the verb to denote whether it is contextually bound or non-bound; the nodes to the left of their governor are contextually bound, those to the right are contextually non-bound (for a definition of topic and focus as based on these primitive notions, see Sgall *et al.* 1986).

Other kinds of syntactic relations are those of coordination (conjunction, disjunction and others) and of apposition. Their interplay with dependency cannot be accounted for with full adequacy by trees if we do not want to neglect the difference between the binary dependency relations and the coordinated (and appositional) constructions, some of which may have an indefinite number of members. However, even a network with a greater number of dimensions, which in this sense can serve as the shape of a TR, can be formally described in the form of its one-to-one linearization (see Petkevič 1995; Sgall 1997a), namely by a string of complex symbols with which a pair of parentheses surrounds every dependent item. The kinds of dependency relations are written as indices of parentheses (attached to the parenthesis that is placed on the side of the head). Also the kinds of coordination are indicated by such indices (on the righthand parenthesis).

2.2.2 VALENCY AS THE CORE NOTION OF TRS

The core of syntax in FGD lies in the notion of valency, i.e. of sets of kinds of dependents (see esp. Panevová 1974 and 1980; Hajičová and Panevová 1984). Within the dependents, arguments or inner participants are differentiated from free modifications (circumstantials, adjuncts) on the basis of the following criteria:

   a) inner participants are bound to certain groups of verbs only;
   b) they occur at most once as dependent on a single verb token.

Five types of inner participants of verbs are distinguished: Actor/Bearer (**Jim** *runs, sits, sleeps...,* **the brook** *runs*), Objective (*to build* **a house***; to destroy* **a house***; to see* **a house***; to address* **someone***; to elect* **the chairman***; to choose* **a spokesman**), Addressee (*to give* **Mary** *a book*), Effect (*to do sth. as* **chairman***; to elect somebody* **the chairman***; to choose him as* **chairman**), Origin (*to make a canoe* **out of a log**). Valency is not restricted to verbs; among the inner participants of nouns there is e.g. Material (*Partitive,* **two baskets of sth.**) and Identity (*the river Danube, the notion of operator*).

There is a rich repertoire of free modifications: mostly for verbs, there are several types of Temporal circumstantials (when, how many times, since when, till when, how long, for how long), Manner, Regard, Extent (*he spent his money to the last penny*), Norm (*in accordance with*), Criterion (*according to*), Substitution (*instead of*), Accompaniment (*with someone*), Means (Instrument), Difference (*two inches taller*), Benefit (*for someone*), Comparison (*as bright as something; brighter than sth.*), Locative, three types of Directional-1. from where, 2. which way, 3. where to, Condition, Cause, Aim (*in order to, for the sake of*), Concession (*although*), Result (*so that*); dependent mainly on nouns, there are e.g. Appurtenance (*my table, Jim's brother, Mary's car*), Restrictive (*rich man*), Descriptive (*the Swedes, who are a Scandinavian nation*).

A participant or a free modification can be either obligatory or optional with a given head: participants are prototypically obligatory (e.g. Actor and Objective with the verb *meet: Jim met Eve.*), but they can also be optional (e.g. the Addressee with the verb *to read: to read a book (to somebody))*. Free modifications are prototypically optional, e.g. *to be sitting (somewhere) (for a reason) (for some time)*, but they can also be obligatory (as e.g. Manner with the verb *to behave: to behave badly*, or Temporal, how_long with the verb *to last: to last for a week*, or Direction-to where with the verb *to arrive: to arrive at Prague*).

To decide whether a complementation of the verb is obligatory (i.e. present in the underlying structure), although deletable in the surface structure, the so-called "dialogue test" was formulated by Panevová (1974, 1980; see also Sgall *et al.* 1986). It is based on an assumption that the speaker is obliged to be able to add the information he deleted in his utterance (assuming that it is an information known to the hearer), if he is asked for it. Thus the dialogue in (1) is not coherent, since the speaker A should be able to answer the question posed by the hearer B.

(1) A: Jerry arrives tomorrow.
   B: Where to?
   A: I don't know.

The dialogue test exemplified in (1) indicates that with the verb *arrive* the free modification of Direction-3. where_to ("predictable" for the hearer, i.e. known by the speaker and deleted in the surface shape of the sentence precisely because A believes it to be easily recoverable by B) is obligatory. On the contrary, the dialogue in (2) is coherent, which indicates that with the verb *arrive* the free modification of Cause is not obligatory.

(2) A: Jerry arrives tomorrow.
   B: Why?
   A: I don't know.

Along with the information on the valency requirements of each lexical entry, there is also other grammatical information included in the valency frames, such as surface deletability (e.g. Directional-3 with *to arrive* is deletable, Objective with *to meet* is not: *We met there* is a case of reciprocity, rather than of deletion), markers denoting an optional or an obligatory controller (e. g. Actor is an obligatory controller with *to try*, an optional one with *to decide*; Addressee is an optional controller with *to advise, to forbid*), and the dependent's ability to occupy certain syntactic positions (e.g. of Subject with Passivization, of a *wh*-element) or to constitute barriers for movement, and subcategorization conditions.

2.2.3 TOPIC-FOCUS ARTICULATION IN TRS

TFA is characterized on the basis of two concepts (discussed in detail in Sgall *et al.* 1986; Hajičová 1993; Hajičová, Partee and Sgall 1998; and the writings quoted there):

a) Contextual boundness: Contextually bound (cb) items are the primary grammatical counterparts of expressions carrying so-called given information, and contextually non-bound (nb) items refer in prototypical cases to "new" information; primarily, nb items belong to the focus of the sentence and cb items constitute the topic of the sentence.

b) Communicative dynamism (CD): In prototypical cases the scale of CD corresponds to the surface word order, but there are secondary cases, e.g. with the most dynamic item (focus proper, which carries the intonation center of the sentence, often a falling stress) occurring elsewhere than at the end of the sentence, or the verb occupying the second position in the uppermost subtree according to language specific rules (which are more or less obligatory in German, optional in Czech).

It should be emphasized that for a proper interpretation of the given occurrence of the sentence in a given discourse it is necessary to take into consideration the sentence prosody and other specific aspects.

In the TR's, CD is indicated by the left-to-right order of the nodes of the tree, in which every cb dependent is placed to the left of its head and every nb item is placed to the right of its head. The values f, t, c of the grammateme TFA indicate whether the given item is nb (in the focus), or cb (in the topic), or a contrastive topic, respectively, as indicated in the examples (3) through (5) below; the questions in brackets indicate the context for that reading of the sentence which is considered in these examples.

    (3)   Father came home.
         (What about your father?)
    (3') father.t come.f home.f
    (4)   (It is) father (who) came home.
         (Who came home?)
    (4') home.t come.t father.f
    (5)   Mary went home and Fred stayed at school.
         (What about Mary and Fred?)
    (5') Mary.c went.f home.f and Fred.c stayed.f at school.f

3. THE SCENARIO OF THE PRAGUE DEPENDENCY TREEBANK

The annotation scheme of the PDT consists of the following three layers of tagging:

1. The morphemic layer, arrived at by an automatic procedure of POS tagging and by disambiguation of the rich inflectional system of Czech, contains disambiguated values of morphemic categories (see Hajič and Hladká 1997, 1998; problems of this step are not discussed in the present paper).

2. Syntactic tags on the analytic layer (analytic tree structures, ATSs), encoding functions of individual word forms (including also e.g. punctuation marks) as they are

rendered in the surface shape of the sentence (see Hajič 1998; a manual has been prepared for the human annotators, see Bémová *et al.* 1997, and translated into English); at the present time, about 100 000 sentences from CNC are tagged on this layer. The layer of analytic syntax does not immediately correspond to a level substantiated by linguistic theory, although in some aspects it may be viewed as coming close to the level of "surface syntax" as present in the earlier stages of FGD (see Sgall 1992 as for reasons to abandon this level). The main difference between "surface" and the analytic layer is that every function word and punctuation mark gets a node of its own in the syntactic network. We have been led to the inclusion of the analytic layer into the tagging procedure by two reasons: (a) it makes it possible to work with a relatively large set of syntactically tagged sentences without much delay, (b) it is a useful intermediate step in the transduction of the surface shape of the sentence (as a string of words) into its underlying structure (as a dependency tree structure), and (c) it allows for a comparison of the results with the outputs of several tagging and parsing procedures which have been implemented for other languages in different research centres.

3. Syntactic tags on the tectogrammatical layer (TGTSs) capture the deep (underlying, tectogrammatical) structure of the given sentence, i.e. its dependency based syntactic structure proper (see Hajičová 2000).

A significant part of the annotation procedure of both 2. and 3. is carried out automatically. The annotators involved in the intellectual part of the procedure have a software tool at their disposal that enables them to work with the graphic representation of the trees on both these layers, modifying the trees in several respects, esp. in what concerns adding or changing the complex labels of the nodes, or adding and suppressing nodes.

4. TAGGING ON THE TECTOGRAMMATICAL LAYER

4.1 TECTOGRAMMATICAL TREE STRUCTURES (*TGTSs*)

A node of the TGTS represents an occurrence of an autosemantic (lexical, meaningful) word; the contribution of the synsemantic (auxiliary, functional) words to the tectogrammatical structure of the sentence is reflected in the indices to the autosemantic words to which the function words "belong" (i.e. auxiliary verbs and subordinating conjunctions to the verbs, prepositions to nouns, etc.); coordinating conjunctions remain as nodes of their own (similarly as in the ATSs).

In cases of deletions in the surface shapes of sentences nodes for the deleted autosemantic words are added to the tree structure.

Not only the direction of the dependency relation (dependent from the right – dependent from the left), but also the ordering of the sister nodes is specified in the TGTSs (in accordance with CD, see Section 2. 3. 3. (b) above).

Each TGTS has thus the form of a projective dependency tree with the verb of the main clause as its root (to be more precise, the root of the TGTS is a special node identifying the sentence of which the given structure is the TGTS, and the node of the main verb is the only node incident to this identifier). In case of nominal "sentences" (i.e. of constructions without a finite verb), three possibilities obtain: (i) the governing verb is added (in case of surface deletions, which is relatively rare), or (ii) a symbol for "empty verb" ("EV") is added as the governor (e.g. *Od našeho washingtonského zpravodaje* "From our correspondent from Washington", with the node for "correspondent" depending on "EV"), or (iii) the governing nominal node acts as the governor (e.g. with author names).

4.2 CHARACTERIZATION OF THE LABELS OF THE TGTS NODES

Each label of a node in a TGTS consists in the following parts:
1. the lexical value proper of the word (represented in a preliminary way just with the usual graphemic form of the word, the "lemma");
2. the values of the morphological grammatemes (corresponding primarily to the values of morphological categories such as modality, tense, aspect with verbs, gender and number with nouns, degree of comparison with adjectives);
3. the values of the attribute "functor," corresponding to (underlying) syntactic functions (Actor, Objective, Means, Locative, etc.; in our examples, we write the values of functors in upper case letters); as a matter of fact, in case of doubts, the annotators have the possibility to indicate two different values for every functor;
4. the values of the attribute "syntactic grammateme", corresponding to secondary aspects of syntactic functions and combined with some of the functors, leading thus to a more subtle (semantic) subcategorization of these syntactic relations that is rendered on the surface first of all by prepositions and cases of nouns; this concerns the functors with the meaning of location LOC, DIR-1, DIR-2 and DIR-3 (corresponding to the questions "where?", "from where?," "through which place?" and "where to?," respectively); thus e.g. LOC (expressed in Czech by several prepositions combined either with the locative (Loc) or with the instrumental (Instr) case of the noun) is subcategorized into *na*+Loc ("on": *na stole* "on the table"), *v*+Loc ("in"), *u*+LOC ("by"), *nad*+Instr ("above"), *pod*+Instr ("under"), *před*+Instr ("in front of"), *za*+Instr ("behind"), *mezi*+Instr ("among"), *mezi*+Instr ("between"), etc.; as for functors having a temporal meaning, a similar subcategorization is established with the functor TWHEN (with the grammatemes AFT "after," BEF "before," ON "on Monday," "next year"); a positive or negative grammateme is attached to ACMP ("with" vs. "without"), REG ("with regard" vs. "without regard") and BEN ("for" vs. "against"), etc.;
5. the values of a special grammateme capture the basic information about the topic-focus articulation (TFA) of the sentence.

At the present stage, the tentative and preliminary inventory of the tectogrammatical labels for Czech comprises 10 attributes for morphological grammatemes (e.g. number, tense, aspect, degrees of comparison) and 47 values for the attributes of "functor" and "syntactic grammateme" (functor: Actor, Patient, Addressee, Locative, Means, etc.; syntactic grammateme: see point 4. above). In addition, there are specific attributes for the relations of coordination, apposition, for marking "restored nodes" (i.e. such nodes that have been deleted in the surface shape of the sentence and restored in its tectogrammatical structure), and three attributes to account for the basic features of coreference (both intra- and intersentential).

4.3 AN ILLUSTRATION

The (preferred) ATS of sentence (6) is given in Fig. 1, its TGTS (on the reading "(I tell you about) Mary (that she) is carrying books to the library") in Fig. 2 (with many simplifications):

(6) Marie nese knihy do knihovny
    Mary is-carrying books to (a) library

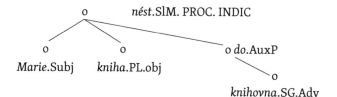

Figure 1   *A simplified ATS of sentence (1), where "nést" is the infinitive of "nese", AuxP is the syntactic label for a preposition, and the other abbreviations correspond to morphological values (tense: simultaneous, aspect: processual, etc.) and to types of dependency on the level of "analytic" syntax.*

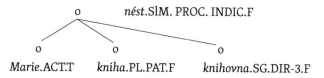

Figure 2   *A simplified TGTS of sentence (1), with abbreviated symbols corresponding to the values of grammatemes and functors. The indices T and F stand for the values of the TFA attribute, namely "contextually bound" and "non-bound," respectively.*

4.4 CONFRONTATION OF TR's AND TGTS's

4.4.1 MOTIVATION OF DIFFERENCES

As has been stated above, TGTSs are based on the theoretical conception of TRs; this does not mean that the resulting tagged structures are "deteriorated" by being biased to a specific theoretical framework. On the contrary: TGTSs have a theoretically sound and empirically tested basis with a perspicuous structure and other properties favourable for the possibility of comparison with other frameworks; this might be taken as an advantage, since it makes it possible to specify the properties of TGTSs in a precise and explicit way. Thus these structures will be a useful source of information also for those who work in other frameworks.

However, there are some points in which TGTSs differ from the TRs; the differences have been motivated by an effort, first, to encode peripheral relations (other than pure dependency) in a straightforward way (see below 4. 4. 2) and, second, to preserve also those pieces of information from the surface shape of the sentence that might be of interest for future (mostly linguistic) research (Section 4. 4. 3).

4.4.2 COORDINATION AND APPOSITION

To specify TGTSs as two-dimensional trees, coordination and apposition are treated in a way that differs from their treatment in FGD: although coordinating conjunctions belong to function words, they retain their status as nodes (labeled as CONJ, DISJ, etc., with the lexical value of the conjunction) in the TGTSs; the same holds for the expressions denoting an apposition. In addition, the nodes for the words standing in the coordination (apposition) relation get a special index. Compare the bracketted shapes of the TGTSs (disregarding other than structural relations) for (7): in (7a), the interpretation is "(old men) and (women)"), while (7b) stands for the interpretation "(old men) and (old women)," with an added node (marked by ELID) corresponding to the restrictive adjunct "old," which has been deleted in the surface shape of the sentence.

> (7) *staří muži a ženy*
>   old men and women
>   (a) (CONJ. a (starý) (muž. CO) (žena.CO))
>   (b) (CONJ. a ((starý) muž. CO) ((starý. ELID) žena. CO))

This exception makes it technically possible to work with rooted trees, rather than with networks of more dimensions.

4.4.3 FURTHER SPECIFIC DIFFERENCES

New attributes for the existing nodes are being established, carrying information that might be interesting for the use of the tagged corpus for further research, be it a research aiming at an enrichment of the tectogrammatical description, as e.g. in 1., or a research of how language is used in communication, as in 2. The following issues belong here:

1. In order to capture lexical collocations as wholes the component parts of a collocation get a positive value of a newly introduced attribute PHRi, where i is the serial number of this collocation (a "phraseme" or idiom) in the sentence.

2. Special attributes COREF, CORNUM and CORSNT are introduced (for the time being, only to nouns and pronouns) to capture at least some basic aspects of (esp. textual) coreferential relations.

The values of these attributes can be characterized as follows: in COREF, the lemma of the antecedent is inserted; the attribute CORNUM contains the serial number of the antecedent if it occurs in the same sentence, or else, the value is NA (non-applicable); the attribute CORSNT obtains one of the following two values: PREV (if the antecedent occurs in the previous sentences), or else NA.

In cases of grammatical coreference (such as with the "subjects" of infinitives as complements of the so-called verbs of control), the attribute COREF of the "restored" subject gets the lemma of the "controller" as its value; the attribute CORNUM then gets the serial number of the controller as its value and CORSNT gets the value NA, cf. (8):

(8) *Rodiče radili Jirkovi nechodit tam*
     parents adviced George not-to-go there

In the TGTS of (8), there will be a node added as an Actor of the verb *nechodit*, with *Cor* as its lexical value, and with *Jirka* in its COREF, 3 in its CORNUM and NA in its CORSNT.

3. With "restored" nodes standing for elements deleted in the surface structure of the sentence but present in its underlying structure the attribute DEL gets the value ELID, if the "restored" element stands alone, cf. e.g. the TGTS (7b) above, or else ELEX ("expounded" deletion), see the TGTS (9') for (9), if the interpretation is "(very old men) and (very old women)," i.e. with a single added node for the deleted restrictive adjunct "old" marked as ELEX rather than adding also the node(s) dependent on it.

(9)   *velmi staří muži a ženy*
       very old men and women
(9') (CONJ.a (((velmi) starý) muž. CO) ((starý. ELEX) žena. CO).

4. Parenthetical items in the sentence without a specific syntactic relation to one of its elements get the functor PAR (see (10)), while a parenthetical item which exhibits a dependency relation to some element of the sentence obtains a regular functor (see (11), where CRIT stands for the functor of Criterion and "já" is the lemma for "I').

(10) *Jirka myslím.PAR přijde pozdě*
      George I-think will-come late

(11) Jirka (podle mne) je talentovaný pianista
      George according to-me is talented pianist
(11') (Jirka. ACT) (já. CRIT) být ((talentovaný. RSTR) pianista. PAT)

5. A special functor PREC is introduced to denote the syntactic function of those elements of the sentence (with the analytic function of a particle) that as a rule stand at the beginning of the sentence, have a more or less discoursive function of cohesion but do not connect clauses into complex sentences; there belong the particles *tedy*, *tudíž* "thus", *tj.* "i.e.," *totiž* "as a matter of fact," etc. (e.g. *He was ill. Thus he couldn't come there.*)

6. Direct speech is distinguished by an index DSP ("direct speech") attached to the root of the TGTS of the sentence enclosed in quotation marks; if more than a single sentence is in quotation marks, an index DSPP ("part of direct speech") is attached to the root of the TGTS of the first and of the last sentence of such a direct speech.

7. Quoted word(s), if occurring in quotation marks (be they single or double) in the surface shape of the sentence, get the index QUOT, unless they constitute a sentence of its own; e.g. while the noun *pleasure* in *They call it "pleasure"* gets "QUOT", the verb *come* in *He told her: "Come back soon"* gets the index DSP indicating direct speech.

5. CONCLUDING REMARKS

5.1 ISSUES FOR FURTHER DISCUSSION

A complete tectogrammatical tagging of a large corpus is, of course, a very demanding task and it is no wonder then that the specifications we are now working with cannot cover all subtle oppositions that should be distinguished in the representation of the meaning of the sentence. However, we have found our task very stimulating and leading to new insights concerning issues some of which either (i) are technically complex and could not yet been entirely integrated into our apparatus (as e.g. a fully automatic handling of PP attachment and other cases of morpho-syntactic ambiguity), or (ii) have not yet been analyzed in any existing grammar or monograph of Czech. Let us briefly mention here some of the open questions that are still waiting for a monographic inquiry; some of them concern the theoretical framework, some are connected only with the decisions concerning tagging and its ambiguities.

5.1.1 ISSUES CONCERNING TYPES OF VALENCY SLOTS

The issues concerning valency belong to the crucial ones when completing the tagging scenario. This is true both of the determination of valency frames for verbs as well as those of nouns.

Some of the functors seem to cover more than one type of syntactic relations and thus might be more subtly differentiated; this concerns e.g. the Locative (cf. the difference between *zranil se v lese* "he injured himself in the forest" and *zranil se na ruce* "he injured himself on his hand", the latter being in some sense closer to an inner participant (argument). However, the question remains of how to classify the Locatives *v kuchyni* "in the kitchen", *jednání uvnitř koalice* "discussions within the coalition." Similar problems concern the modification of Means (cf. the difference between *psát rukou* "to write with hand", *na stroji* "on the typewriter," *tužkou* "with a pencil" and *pohnout rukou* "to move one's hand").

Another such question concerns the relation between the functor Dir-3 and the so-called Intent (e.g. *šla nakoupit* "she went shopping"). A further question of this kind is that of the difference between e.g. *pojmenovat nějak* "to give some name" and *pojmenovat po kom* "to name (something, somebody) after somebody"; the latter example certainly is not just an instance of the functor Manner.

In the valency frames of nouns, we work with the modifications of Restrictive (adjunct) and Identity. It is then an open question how to distinguish among such examples as *pan N.* "Mister N.", *poslanec N.* "the deputy N.", *termín sloveso* "the term verb". The following criterion might be applied: with two adjacent (congruent, or non-declined) nouns the second noun functions as an Identity modifier if (a) it is non-declined (e.g. *parníkem* [Instr.] *Hradčany* [Nom.] "with the steamer Hradčany") or (b) it can be put (without a change of meaning) into a genitive case (e.g. *pojem subjekt/u* "the notion (of) subject-Nom. /Gen. "). In all other cases the first noun would then be classified as a Restrictive adjunct. However, even with this rule some intermediate cases remain: e.g. in the combinations of first name – family name, the family name may also be in genitive (esp. if the first name has a shape of a nickname: *Jan Novák*, but *Honzík Novák/* Nom. Sg. or *Nováků*/Gen. Pl.).

5.1.2 TOPIC-FOCUS ARTICULATION

One of the "burning issues" in the TFA annotation is to make more precise the notion of contrastive topic. It is also necessary to make sure whether for a given language a distinction between contrastive and non-contrastive (parts of) focus is grammatically determined, and to pay much more attention to the study of the systemic ordering of kinds of dependents ("canonical order"). The boundary line between the syntactic function of focus sensitive particles (rhematizers, focalizers) and those of other subclasses of Attitude adverbials has to be systematically studied; up to now we distinguish between RHEM (rhematizer), ETHD (ethical dative), INTF (intensifier), and ATT (attitudinal adjunct). The primary (prototypical) and secondary (marked) positions of overt focalizers (for a most recent treatment, see Hajičová, Partee and Sgall 1998) should be taken into account. It also should be considered whether some of these functors should not be reclassified as grammatemes (in accordance with an older proposal by P. Sgall).

5.1.3 COORDINATION CONSTRUCTIONS AND DELETIONS

It should be further investigated under which conditions a coordination construction is to be understood as a coordination of sentences (clauses) or of their parts (up to now we handle such examples as *Sedlák a Bureš objevili virus L.* "S. and B. discovered the virus L" as a narrow coordination, although such a sentence does not exclude that each of the persons discovered the virus separately).

Also other cases of deletions are still open for discussion. Up to now, we do not generally restore the governing verb of a whole sentence the deletion of which is registered in the analytic trees by means of an extra node labeled as ExD. In those cases where perhaps also some of the dependents of the restored node should be restored, we are not yet capable to specify under which conditions this restoration should take place (to avoid repeating what does not belong to the deleted position).

5.1.4 ISSUES OF THE LEXICON AND WORD FORMATION

The present tagging scenario does not work with a composition of lexical meaning (degrees of hyponyms, etc.) from its parts or features, and we are aware that lexical semantics is a domain to be investigated. In the subdomain of word formation, up to now we have only worked with some of the most productive affixes and their roles (the verbal prefix of negation, some postverbal nouns and adjectives, postadjectival adverbs, possessive adjectives and pronouns). The boundary lines of some of these groups (and of many other) have not been drawn with full adequacy. For instance, the intransitive verbs derived by the "reflexive" particle *se*, such as *šířit se* "expand" are treated as specific lexical units; their relationship to the base forms is only to be found in the analytic trees; however, it is necessary to look for criteria distinguishing the set of such verbs.

5.1.5 COREFERENCE IN DISCOURSE

It has been mentioned above that only the elementary cases of textual anaphora are recorded. It will be necessary to look for a more complete application of the considerations of our previous research (Hajičová 1993), i.e. to work more systematically especially with the degrees of salience of the items contained in the stock of information shared by the speaker and (according to the speaker's assumptions) the hearer(s).

5.1.6 GRAPHIC SYMBOLS

Our treatment of dashes, quotes and quoted words, direct speech, and so on, as well as of the difference between a full stop and a semicolon as marking sentence boundaries of different strengths, or of the boundaries between paragraphs, is only preliminary. It has to be studied to which degree and in which ways the corresponding graphic symbols (or the prosodie phenomena they represent) contribute to the underlying structure of sentences (which also characterizes some aspects of the sentence as occupying certain positions in the discourse pattern).

5.2 CONCLUSION

If compared to the prevailing present-day trends in parsing and annotation, the present scenario of PDT is promising in going deeper in the sense of including much of semantically relevant phenomena. The aim of tagging under this approach is not only to check the grammatical structure of sentences (and their well-formedness), making choice of the reading to be preferred, but also to provide an adequate input for the semantico-pragmatic interpretation of sentences and of their specification in what concerns their embedding in context.

It will of course take some time before the part of PDT equipped with tectogrammatical tags is large enough to be of actual relevance either for practical applications or for further studies. The expected application of statistically based methods should lead to a more general and efficient shape of the procedure, but even then the tagging will contain many errors of most different kinds. However, we believe that the resource offered by the Prague Dependency Treebank will be soon useful for authors of future monographic inquiries into Czech grammatical and textual phenomena and their relationships to those of other languages: the rich empirical material gathered and analyzed in PDT, certainly makes a more systematic insight into the studied issues possible, and the related studies will in turn help us to remove the individual errors and to amend the procedures. In this way a means for a principled way of testing the descriptive framework of FGD can be gained.

We are aware that many questions remain open, and some of them have been sketched above. These and many other puzzles are i. a. connected with the freedom of language (the speakers being free to decide for any deviation of the norm they only can think of) and make it necessary to look for descriptive methods adequate to account not only for the norm, but also for most different deviations (cf. Sgall 2002).[1]

1   The research reported on in this paper (a preliminary form of which with the title "Dependency-Based Underlying-Structure Tagging of a Very Large Czech Corpus", was published in T. A. L. 2000) has been carried out within the project supported by the Czech Grant Agency 405-96-K214 and by the Czech Ministry of Education LN 00A 063.

WHAT WE HAVE LEARNED FROM COMPLEX ANNOTATION OF TOPIC-FOCUS ARTICULATION IN A LARGE CZECH CORPUS

[Qu'est-ce que nous avons appris de l'annotation complexe en articulation en thème – rhème dans un grand corpus du tchèque]

Abstract (En): After a short summary of the theory of Topic-Focus Articulation (TFA) the present contribution documents on several examples illustrating the annotation of the basic features of TFA on a large corpus (the Prague Dependency Treebank) that corpus annotation brings an additional value to the corpus if the following two conditions are being met: (i) the annotation scheme is based on a sound linguistic theory, and (ii) the annotation scenario is carefully (i.e. systematically and consistently) designed. Such an annotation is important not only for the surface shape of the sentence but even more for the underlying sentence structure: it may elucidate phenomena hidden on the surface but unavoidable for the representation of the meaning and functioning of the sentence.

Résumé (Fr): Après un bref résumé de la théorie de Topic-Focus Articulation (TFA), la présente étude démontre, à l'aide de plusieurs exemples illustrant l'annotation de principaux traits de TFA sur un large corpus (the Prague Dependency Treebank), que l'annotation du corpus apporte une valeur ajoutée au corpus, si deux conditions sont réunies: (i) le schéma de l'annotation est basé sur une théorie linguistique solide, (ii) le procédé d'annotation est établi avec soin (c'est-à-dire de façon systématique et cohérente). Une telle annotation est importante non seulement pour la structure de surface de la phrase mais encore davantage pour la structure phrastique sous-jacente, car elle est susceptible de mettre en évidence les phénomènes cachés au niveau de la structure de surface, mais incontournables lors de la représentation du sens et du fonctionnement de la phrase.

1. MOTIVATION

Corpus annotation may bring an additional value to the corpus if the following two conditions are being met: (i) the annotation scheme is based on a sound linguistic theory, and (ii) the annotation scenario is carefully (i.e. systematically and consistently) designed. The usefulness of annotated data for further linguistic research is well supported by the existence of annotated corpora of various languages: let us quote as examples the Penn Treebank for English (Marcus et al., 1993; 1994), the PropBank and Penn Discourse Treebank developed also for English by the teams at the University of Pennsylvania, the Tiger Treebank for German (Brants et al., 2002), or the Prague Dependency Treebank for Czech (Hajič, 1998; Hajič et al., 2006).

Corpus annotation is not a self-contained task. It offers a most useful support for natural language processing, it is an irreplaceable resource of linguistic information for the build-up of grammars, and, most importantly, it provides an invaluable test for linguistic theories standing behind the annotation schemes. One of the important features is that it is possible to take into account in corpus annotation not only the surface shape of the sentence but even more importantly the underlying sentence structure: such an annotation may elucidate phenomena hidden on the surface but unavoidable for the representation of the meaning and functioning of the sentence.

In the present contribution, we first give (in Sect. 2) a brief overview of the underlying theory of Topic Focus Articulation we subscribe to (abbreviated in the sequel as TFA) and we outline (in Sect. 3) how this theory is reflected in the Czech corpus annotation of the Prague Dependency Treebank (PDT). In Sect. 4 two linguistic hypotheses are presented to illustrate how theoretical hypotheses can be tested on language corpora. Some lessons learned in the course of our TFA annotation are given in Sect. 5 concerning (i) contrastive topic, (ii) focalizers and their scope, and (iii) some notes on the relationships of passivization, TFA and the use of indefinite article in English. Sect. 6 summarizes our experience.

2. LINGUISTIC THEORY AND CORPUS ANNOTATION

2.1 UNDERLYING THEORY OF TFA IN A NUTSHELL

Issues connected with the articulation of sentence with regard to their communicative rather than surface syntactic structure (functions such as subject, object, predicate) had been brought into the foreground of linguistic studies in Prague since Vilém Mathesius' first papers on the topic (e.g. Mathesius, 1929; 1939); as the Czech term he used (*aktuální členění větné*) was not directly translatable into English, Jan Firbas – on the advice of Josef Vachek (as acknowledged in Firbas, 1992, p. xii) and apparently inspired by Mathesius' use of the German term *Satzperspektive* in his fundamental paper from 1929 – coined the term *functional sentence perspective* (FSP); German researchers in this field often speak about *Thema-Rhema Gliederung* and the prominent British linguist M.A.K. Halliday introduces the term *information subsystem* (Halliday, 1967; 1967–68) or *information structure* (reflecting the given-new strategy) distinguishing it from *thematic structure*; the former term has been re-invented and is generally used nowadays by several modern linguists.

The above-mentioned terminological differences often refer to some notional distinctions: the dichotomy reflected in the name of our theory, namely *Topic-Focus Articulation* (TFA) is not a mere "translation" or "rephrasing" of the terms used in FSP but indicates certain differences in the starting points:

(i) Firbas (1964) specifies the *theme* as the element (or elements) carrying the lowest degree of communicative dynamism within the sentence. This specification implies that every sentence *contains* an item with the lowest degree of communicative dynamism (CD), and thus would exclude the existence of sentences without a theme (so-called topicless sentences). It must be added that Firbas (1992) modifies his definition of theme by saying that in the absence of theme, the lowest degree of CD is carried by the first element of non-theme (in this reformulation he refers to Sgall's objection against Firbas' original definition of theme made at a FSP conference in Sofia in 1976).

(ii) Accepting Firbas' assumption that every item in the sentence carries a certain degree of CD, should not mean, however, that the notion of a bipartition (the focus of a sentence conveys an information *ABOUT* its topic) can be abandoned; an important argument for the necessity of a recognition of such a bipartition is the analysis of negation (see Hajičová, 1972; 1973; 1984).

(iii) The so-called *factors* of linear arrangement, prosody, semantics and contexts as discussed by Firbas and his followers are not just four "factors" of FSP but they fundamentally differ in their nature: the first two (word order and prosody) belong to the means of expression of information structure and the other two (semantics and context) to its functional layers.

(iv) Most importantly, TFA is understood as a structure belonging to the *underlying, deep structure* of sentences (tectogrammatics, literal meaning) because the TFA structure is semantically relevant.

In the theory of TFA, the underlying relation between topic and focus is based on the relation of "aboutness": the topic is understood as a specification of "what we are talking about" and the focus as "what we are saying about topic". In other words, the speaker communicates something (the Focus of the sentence) about something (the Topic of the sentence); this relation can be schematically captured as:

F(T): the Focus holds about the Topic

and in case of negation:

~F(T): (in the prototypical case) the Focus does not hold about the Topic

The pragmatic background of this opposition is the cognitive dichotomy of *given* (*old*) versus *new*, but the two oppositions are not identical as can be illustrated by examples (1) and (2):

(1) John and Mary entered the dining-room. They first went to the window...
(2) Mary called Jim a Republican. Then he insulted HER.
(2') Mary called Jim a Republican. Then he INSULTED her.

In the second sentence in (1), "the window" refers by no doubt to the window of the dining-room mentioned in the first sentence, thus to the cognitively "given" or "old" information, but this sentence is "about" John and Mary and it says about them that what they did, was to go to the window (rather than to the table, to the other door, etc., or just to look around in astonishment...). In the second sentence in (2) as well as in (2'), both "he" and "her" are cognitively "given," the pronouns refer to John and Mary, respectively, but only (2') is "about" John and Mary and says that the relation between them was an insult (thus somehow implying that calling somebody a Republican is not, or need not be an insult), while the second sentence in (2) is about Jim's insult saying that this insult was directed against Mary (thus implying that calling somebody a Republican is understood as an insult). The difference in the TFA of the second sentences in (2) and (2') is indicated, in spoken language, by the position of the intonation center, denoted here by capitals.

2.2 SEMANTIC RELEVANCE OF TFA

Related to the attempt of the TFA proponents at an explicit description of the dichotomy of topic and focus and thus of its integration into a formal description of language as early as at the beginning of the 1960's, was the consideration which level of language description TFA belongs to. Since then it is commonly accepted in the linguistic literature on semantic aspects of sentence structure that TFA is semantically relevant, even if truth conditions are taken into account. We will not recapitulate the discussions of these issues here, but we want to recall them by re-quoting some of the examples hinting at the semantic relevance of TFA as they appeared in some writings: from Chomsky's observations not at the time fully reflected in his model, through Lakoff's sentences that had led him to formulate an alternative model of transformational grammar, so-called generative semantics, with different semantic representations for his (a) and (b), to Rooth's very influential dissertation (esp. in the circles of semanticists, but, fortunately also among linguists of different streams); to document that these observations were duly documented and analyzed by the theory of TFA, we also quote three of the many examples adduced by Sgall and his colleagues.

(3) (a) Everybody in this room knows at least two LANGUAGES.
     (b) At least two languages are known by everybody in this ROOM.
         (Chomsky, 1957; 1965)
(4) (a) Many men read few BOOKS.
     (b) Few books are read by many MEN. (Lakoff, 1971)

(5) (a) I only introduced BILL to Sue.
    (b) I only introduced Bill to SUE. (Rooth, 1985)
(6) (a) Londoners are mostly at BRIGHTON.
    (b) At Brighton, there are mostly LONDONERS. (Sgall, 1967)
(7) (a) I work on my dissertation on SUNDAYS.
    (b) On Sundays, I work on my DISSERTATION.
(8) (a) English is spoken in the SHETLANDS.
    (b) In the Shetlands, ENGLISH is spoken. (Sgall et al., 1986)

As can be seen from the above mentioned examples, the means of expression of TFA are multifarious and should be distinguished from the uniform semantic function (this is the main reason why we do not agree with the subsumption of the function of the dichotomy and the means of its expression under "four" factors as if they were of the same notional category). Let us mention here, again very briefly, four such means:

(i) Surface order of words, a most visible means esp. in languages that do not have a grammatically fixed word order. In the first writings, esp. from the tranformationalist circle, the authors assumed that it is the order of quantifiers that is responsible for the semantic differences (see (3) and (4) above, for examples taken from English), or perhaps the difference between active and passive constructions (but compare the possible Czech translation of (3) and (4), in which no passivization is necessary to make the change in the order). However, as illustrated by (7) and (8), the presence of a quantifying expression is not crucial.

(ii) In spoken language, the most important means of expressing the difference in TFA is the sentence prosody including the placement of the intonation center; in our more recent work with spoken language corpora, the F0 characteristics of the curve was attested as to be a marker of a "contrastive topic" (Veselá et al., 2003). Halliday (1967) adduces a brilliant example of the importance of the placement of the intonation center, pointing out the necessity to pronounce the warnings at the bottom of an elevator in London underground stations (9)(a) with the (normal) placement of the intonation center at the end and comparing it with the inadequacy of (9)(b) with its funny interpretation "you should carry a dog." The greater was our surprise to see that in the newly opened modern underground stations in London at the time of the centenery celebrations there was (9)(c), which evoked the same funny intepretations as Halliday's (9)(b). The intention of the authors of this change was – perhaps in addition to make the instruction shorter and thus more urgent – to read the instruction with the non-normal position of the intonation center at the beginning of the sentence, as in (9)(d).

(9) (a) Dogs must be CARRIED.
    (b) DOGS must be carried. (Halliday, 1967)
    (c) Carry DOGS. (a warning in London underground, around 2000)
    (d) CARRY dogs.

(iii) Another possible means for expressing TFA are specific syntactic constructions such as the *it*-clefts (in contrast to *wh*-clefts) in English, cf. (10)(a); in Czech, the
sentence – unless we do want to make it more emphatic, with a subjective order and
the placement of the intonation center on the subject in the front position – can be
translated as (10)(b), with the same TFA.

(10) (a) It was JOHN who talked to few girls about many problems.
      (b) S málo děvčaty mluvil o mnoha problémech HONZA.

(iv) A specific device is morphemic means indicating which element of the sentence is its topic or focus, such as the particles *ga* and *wa* in Japanese and similar morphemic means used in some other languages such as Yukaghir, Tagalog etc.

3. THE REFLECTION OF THE TFA THEORY IN CORPUS ANNOTATION

The Prague Dependency Treebank (PDT, see Hajič et al., 2006; Mikulová et al., 2006)
is an annotated (electronic) collection of Czech texts with a mark-up on three layers:
(i) morphemic, (ii) surface shape, and (iii) underlying (tectogrammatical) incl. underlying dependency relations such as Actor, Patient, Addressee, Temporal, Local, Manner, etc. and values concerning TFA. The current version (annotated on all three layers
of annotation) contains 3 168 documents with 49 442 sentences and 833 357 occurrences of forms. In addition to these three layers, the current annotation also covers
some basic relations of textual coreference and fundamental discourse relations.

Each node of the dependency tree representing the sentence on the tectogrammatical (underlying) level is assigned one of the three possible values of a special TFA
attribute, namely t for a contextually bound non-contrastive node, c for a contextually
bound contrastive node and f for a contextually non-bound node. These values serve
then as a basis for the bipartion of the sentence into Topic and Focus; an algorithm of
such a bipartition was formulated and tested on the whole PDT collection (see below).

4. ANNOTATED CORPUS USED FOR TESTING OF LINGUISTIC HYPOTHESES

As an illustration of what possibilities a consistent and systematic annotation of a text
corpus offers for linguistic theory, we present in our contribution two examples.

Hypothesis A1:

The global division of the sentence into its TOPIC (what the sentence is about) and
its FOCUS (what is said about the topic) can be made on the basis of contextual boundness.

Some first formulations of the steps of a possible algorithm for a (global) division of a sentence into its Topic and Focus based on this hypothesis are given in Sgall (1979; see also Sgall et al., 1986: 216f). The original algorithm was later implemented and then tested on the whole of PDT and the results were reported in Hajičová, Havelka and Veselá (2005).

The basic steps of the algorithm are as follows:

(a) if the main verb carries f, it belongs to Focus (F); else, it belongs to Topic;

(b) all the nodes directly dependent on the main verb and carrying t belong to Topic, together with all nodes depending on them;

(c) all the nodes directly dependent on the main verb and carrying f belong to Focus, together with all nodes depending on them;

(d) if the main verb carries t and all nodes directly depending on the main verb carry also t, then follow the rightmost edge leading from the main verb to the first node(s) on this path carrying the value f; this/these node(s) and all the nodes depending on it/them belong to Focus.

The results of the implementation are quite encouraging and they allow for some interesting observations: in 85.7% the verb belongs to Focus; in 8.58% the verb belongs to Topic but there always was a node (or nodes) depending directly on the verb that was contextually non-bound and thus belongs to Focus; only in 4.41% of sentences the Focus was more deeply embedded (i.e. depends on some contextually-bound node). The algorithm failed in 1.2% cases when its application has led to an ambiguous partition and in 0.11% cases where no Focus was identified. Looking at these figures, we see another interesting result of the implementation of the algorithm and its application on the annotated corpus: in 95% of the cases the hypothesis (present also in the FSP theory, see Firbas on the transitional character of the verb) that in Czech the boundary between Topic and Focus is in the prototypical case signalled by the position of the verb was confirmed.

To validate the results of the automatic procedure in comparison with "human" annotation, a subset of the corpus (with the TFA assignment hidden) was selected and human annotators were asked to mark, on the basis of their native speakers' judgements, what is the sentence "about," which part of the sentence is its Topic and which is its Focus. These "human" assignments were then compared with the results of the automatic procedure (Zikánová et al., 2007; Zikánová and Týnovský, 2009). When evaluating the results, the main observation was that the correspondence supports the algorithm; the most frequent differences, if any, concerned the difference in the assignment of the verb to topic or to focus. This confirms the transitional character of the verb in Czech.

The results then can be summarized as follows: in Czech, the boundary between Topic and Focus can be determined in principle on the basis of the consideration of the status of the main predicate and its direct dependents. The TFA annotation leads to satisfactory results in cases of rather complicated "real" sentences in the corpus. Certain modifications of the annotation procedure are necessary, but the material gathered and analyzed in this way may be further used for the study of several aspects of discourse patterning (Hajičová, in press).

Hypothesis A2:

In the focus part of the sentence the complementations of the verb (be they arguments or adjuncts, in the sense of underlying, tectogrammatical dependency relations) follow a certain canonical order (not necessarily the same for all languages).

Before the A2 hypothesis was formulated, a series of psycholinguistic experiments (with speakers of Czech, German and English) was carried out to establish a tentative ordering. However, the PDT offers a richer and more consistent material for its testing as the underlying dependency relations within the sentence are annotated and the appurtenance of the elements into Focus can be determined by the implemented TFA algorithm (see *A1* above). This information can be used to compare the order of the complementations in the actual sentence with the assumed order according to the scale of systemic ordering and to propose some more subtle formulation of the hypothesis or its modification, as documented by the studies of Rysová (2011a; 2011b).

5. LESSONS LEARNED

In addition to the two examples given in the previous Section, the manual annotation itself and the annotated corpus material have provided some other interesting observations and suggestions.

5.1 CONTRASTIVE TOPIC

The original formulation of the TFA theory worked with the notion of contextual boundness, which served as the basis for the recognition of the Topic-Focus dichotomy. However, thanks to a more consistent work with the empirical material during the corpus annotation, an observation was made that in some sentences a part of the Topic can be distinguished that actually expresses a contrast, though different from the contrast expressed – by default – in the Focus. (Focus is understood by most researchers as a choice of alternatives thus actually involving a contrast to the non-selected alternatives.) This contrastive (part of the) Topic can be distinguished from the other part(s) of the Topic by two features: by some specific intonation contour (see above about F0) and by the use of a long form of pronoun in the topic position in Czech, see (11), with the intonation center marked by capitals.

(11) Milena nás seznámila se svým BRATREM. *Jeho* jsme pozvali do PRAHY a do *Brna* jsme jeli s NÍ.
      Milena – us – acquainted – with – her – BROTHER. *Him* – (we)Aux – invited – to PRAGUE – and – to – *Brno* – (we) went – with – HER.

In (11), *jeho* is the long form of Acc.sing. of the pronoun "on" (he), the short form of this pronoun being *ho* as in (12).

(12) Pozvali jsme ho do PRAHY.
      (we) invited – Aux. – him – to – PRAGUE

This observation (see Koktová, 1999) has led us to introduce the notion of a contrastive topic into the TFA theory and in accordance with it to introduce a third value of the TFA attribute in the annotation scheme of PDT, namely the value *c* (Hajičová et al., 2007).

5.2 FOCALIZERS AND THEIR SCOPE

Firbas (1957) observed a rhematizing function of the adverb *even*; in his later paper (Firbas, 1959) he speaks about a class of intensifying elements. The relation between some specific class of sentence elements to TFA was also mentioned by Sgall (1967) in connection with examples with quantifiers (such as *mostly*). Daneš (1985) distinguishes in this connection direct restrictors (*jen* "only"), indirect (*vyjma* "except for") and contextualizers (*také* "also", *a přece* "and still"). In all these writings, an observation is made that there is a class of sentence elements that is closely related to the indication of the focus of the sentence.

Connected to this, is the relation between the semantic scope of negation and topic/focus articulation; let us mention here already Vachek (1947), the analysis of the negative particle *niet* in Dutch (Kraak, 1966), the analysis of the German *nicht* (Zemb, 1968) and our systematic attention paid to the relation between TFA and the semantic scope of negation with the relevant consequences for the relation of presupposition in Hajičová (1973; 1975) and our comparison of the scope of negation with the function of focalizers in Hajičová (1995).

Firbas (1959: 53) characterizes his intensifying elements as follows: "intensifying elements [...] are, as it were, superimposed on the sentence structure, considerably *changing* its FSP by rhematizing (frequently even turning into rheme proper) the element to which they are made to refer". Our position is different: the focalizer (prototypically, by its word-order position and also with regard to the placement of the intonation center) just *indicates* which element(s) of the sentence are its focus (but see below); the TFA of the sentence is a part of the underlying structure of the sentence (its meaning), the position of the focalizer and the prosody of the sentence are the outer forms (expression) of this function and as such do not change the function.

Interesting examples are also those sentences that contain two focalizers, which need not even be in separate clauses, cf. (13) in English and its Czech counterpart in (13'), and also (14) with negation and a focalizer.

(13) (Preceding context: Who has sent just a postcard even to John?) MARY has sent just a postcard even to him.

(13') (Kdo poslal i Honzovi jenom pohlednici?) I jemu poslala jen pohlednici MARIE.

(14) Jen dobré srdce bezmocným nepomůže.
Only good heart the-helpless-Dat will-not-help.

Sentences (13) and (14) document that the class called "focalizers" need not be only indicators of focus. In Hajičová, Partee and Sgall (1998, Sect. 6.3), the sentences quoted here as (15) and (16) are given used in the contexts (again, the placement of the intonation center is indicated by capitals): *Who criticized even MOTHER TERESA as a tool of the capitalists?* and *Is there a film only JIM liked?*, respectively.

(15) JOHN criticized even Mother Teresa as a tool of the capitalists.

(16) Only Jim liked AMADEUS.

These observations, first, have served as a further argument for the introduction of the notion of contrastive topic (see the use of the long form of the Czech pronoun *jemu* in (13')) and to the suggestions to differentiate between a global focus (*JOHN, AMADEUS* in (15) and (16), respectively) and a focus of a focalizer (*Mother Teresa, Jim* of focalizers *even* and *only* in the same sentences). At the same time, the analysis of the large PDT corpus has indicated that the class of focalizers is bigger than originally (and usually) assumed and that it contains such Czech particles that can be translated into English as *also, alone, as well, at least, even, especially, either, exactly, in addition, in particular, just, merely, only, let alone, likewise, so much as, solely, still/much less, purely, too* etc.

To summarize our observations presented in Sect. 5.2, there is a special class of particles that have a specific position in the TFA of the sentence; these particles have some common features with negation. The so-called focalizer can occur also in the topic of the sentence and there can be more than a single focalizer in a sentence. It is therefore necessary to distinguish between the focus of the whole sentence and the focus of a focalizer. The scope of a focalizer has important consequences for the semantic interpretation of the sentence.

5.3 PASSIVIZATION, TFA AND INDEFINITE ARTICLE IN ENGLISH

A quite self-evident basic hypothesis says that in English passivization is one of the possibilities how to "topicalize" Patient (Object). A natural, though rather simplified implication is that such a topicalized Patient can be used with an indefinite article only in specific cases.

For the purpose to check under which conditions such an implication holds, we have used another Praguian corpus, namely the parallel corpus of English and Czech called Prague Czech-English Dependency Treebank. This corpus consists of 49 208 sentences with the total number of 54 304 predicates (roughly: clauses). In the corpus, there are 194 cases which seemingly contradict the above mentioned assumption, i.e. in which a subject of a passive sentence is accompanied by an indefinite article.

Looking at these cases in more detail (Hajičová et al., 2011), most frequent constructions are those with General Actor, i.e. an Actor that is not expressed in the surface shape of the sentences. The surface subject has the function of the Patient. The placement of an indefinite expression at the front position (even though it is the focus of the sentence) is due to the grammatically fixed E. word-order. In the Czech counterparts, the Patient is placed at the final position, in the normal focus position. These cases are exemplified here by sentences in (17) and (18) and the sentence elements in question are printed in italics.

(17) (Preceding context: Soviet companies would face fewer obstacles for exports and could even invest their hard currency abroad. Foreigners would receive greater incentives to invest in the U.S.S.R.)
Alongside the current non-convertible ruble, *a second currency* would be introduced that could be freely exchanged for dollars and other Western currencies.

(17') Cz. Zároveň se současným nekonvertibilním rublem bude zavedena *druhá měna*, která by mohla být volně směnitelná za dolary a další západní měny.

(18) (Preceding context: He notes that industry executives have until now worried that they would face a severe shortage of programs once consumers begin replacing their TV sets with HDTVs. Japanese electronic giants, such as [...], have focused almost entirely on HDTV hardware, and virtually ignored software or programs shot in high-definition.)
And *only a handful of small U.S. companies* are engaged in high-definition software development.

(18') Cz. A vývojem softwaru pro vysoké rozlišení se zabývá *jen hrstka malých amerických společností*.

A second group of cases can be characterized by the use of the indefinite article in the meaning "one of the," cf. (19).

(19) *A seat on the Chicago Board of Trade* was sold for $390 000, unchanged from the previous sale Oct. 13. (The following context: Seats currently are quoted at $ 361 000 bid, $395 000 asked. The record price for a full membership on the exchange is $550 000, set Aug. 31, 1987.)

(19') Cz.: *Členství v Chicagské obchodní radě* bylo prodáno za 390 000 dolarů, což je o 5 000 dolarů méně než při posledním prodeji minulý čtvrtek.

Exceptionally, but still, there occurred cases which can be interpreted as a contrast in the topic part, cf. (20).

(20) (Preceding context: DOT System. The "Designated Order Turnaround" System was launched by the New York Stock Exchange in March 1976, to offer automatic, high-speed order processing.) *A faster version*, the SuperDot, was launched in 1984 .

(20') Cz. Rychlejší verze SuperDot byla spuštěna v roce 1984.

It is a matter of course that a more systematic investigation of the mentioned issue is necessary; it will be also of interest to look at these structures in a spoken corpus of English to see whether a "fronted" Patient into the subject position accompanied by an indefinite article in English is marked by some specific features of the intonation contour that would indicate its appurtenance to Focus or to a contrastive part of the Topic.

6. SUMMARY

Every linguistic theory needs testing and evaluation; annotated text and spoken corpora are suitable (and hitherto unsurpassed) tools for that purpose. The results are invaluable: in our contribution we have tried to document that a consistent and systematic testing brings new findings, and these findings then may lead to additions or modifications of the theory.

ACKNOWLEDGEMENT

The work on the final version of this contribution was supported by the grant of the Czech Grant Agency GAČR P406/12/0658.

4. BEYOND THE SENTENCE BOUNDARY

FOREWORD

The analysis of the topic-focus articulation (TFA) of the sentence has led, naturally enough, to a study of issues related to a broader context, that is of phenomena of the domain of discourse (text). On the one hand, TFA has to be considered as a structuring that is semantically relevant, that is, a structuring that has an impact on the meaning of the sentence alone and belongs to the systems of individual languages rather than to the domain of cognition, on the other hand, the structure of the sentence as a component part of a whole text plays an important role in this whole and TFA reflects the cognitively-based "given" – "new" strategy. This ‚Janus face" character of the TFA phenomenon has led to our inquiry whether it is possible to combine the "dynamic," communication based view of language and discourse with the description of (underlying) sentence syntax duly respecting the TFA aspect, in other words, how to combine the "dynamic" (communication based) view of language and discourse (and textual co-reference) with the description of (underlying) sentence syntax. To this aim, we (Hajičová and Vrbová, 1982) introduced the notion of the stock of knowledge as a hierarchized structure assumed by the speaker to be shared by him and the hearer (a more detailed treatment can be found in Hajičová, 1993, 1997, 2003a, 2003b) and we proposed some heuristics guiding the development of the activation degrees. This scale has to be reflected in a description of the semantico-pragmatic layer of the discourse.

In the present Part, we reproduce two papers relating to the above issues. The earlier one *Focussing – A Meeting Point of Linguistics and Artificial Intelligence* (1987) presents the original version of the heuristics and applies the "rules" to a piece of text created for the purpose. The paper also reacts to the use of the term "focus" in writings oriented towards the domain of artificial intelligence and compares the notion referred to by this term with the notion of topic in the TFA theory. In the second, more recent paper *Contextual Boundness and Discourse Patterns Revisited* (2013) we formulate the hypothesis more precisely stating that a finite mechanism exists that enables the addressee to identify the referents on the basis of a partial ordering of the elements in the stock of knowledge shared by the speaker and the addressee (according to the speaker's assumption), based on the degrees of activation (salience) of referents. The proposed heuristics are applied to a piece of real (literary) text discussing certain implications of the proposed analysis and some related problems, and briefly sketching a possibility of how to test the proposed approach to text analysis on a large annotated corpus of texts.

In that paper, the stepwise application of the "rules" is displayed in the form of a table with numerical values of the assigned activation degrees; in order to make the illustrative example more convincing, we add here a visualization that corresponds to the table but makes the dynamic development of the discourse more transparent. We are grateful to Mgr. Barbora Hladká both for this visualisation and for her checking the formulation of the "rules".

FOCUSSING – A MEETING POINT OF LINGUISTICS AND ARTIFICIAL INTELLIGENCE

1. INTRODUCTION

The present paper is aimed to show – on the example of one particular issue – the fruitfulness of a close cooperation of linguists and AI specialists in their effort to capture the procedural aspects of human understanding.[1]

2. FOCUSSING IN LINGUISTICS AND IN ARTIFICIAL INTELLIGENCE

2.1 INFORMAL SPECIFICATIONS

During the recent 10 years we have witnessed a curious situation: not only that *single term* has been used for two *different* notions (which is a common situation even within a single field of science), but it has been used exactly for two *opposite* notions. This is the case of the term *focus:* introduced into linguistics by Halliday (1967) and by Chomsky (1971), and employed since then by linguists of most different breedings (cf. its systematic treatment in the framework of functional generative description, e.g. in Sgall, Hajičová and Benešová, 1973, and a formal definition in Sgall, 1979), it was soon frequently used in the writings closely connected with the research in the domain of AI (cf. e.g. Grosz, 1977; Sidner, 1979); the latter use is said to stem from the notion of "focussing of attention" present in the works on (cognitive) psychology.

---

1   Sections 2 and 3 of this paper are a modified version of my contribution to Festschrift for Jacob Mey (Hajičová, 1986).

To be able to refer to the two readings of a single term, I use in the sequel transparently indexed labels *focus*$_L$ for the former (linguistic) understanding and *focus*$_{AI}$ for the AI interpretation. For the purpose of our discussion that follows, *focus*$_{AI}$ can be informally specified as that part of the (meaning of the) sentence that conveys some (irrecoverable) information predicating something about "the given," recoverable, contextually bound part (i.e. of the *topic* of the sentence, distinguishing thus a dichotomy of topic and focus).[2] Taking (1) as a part of discourse consisting of (a) and (b) in this order, then focus$_L$ of (b) is *had been crying nearly all the day.*[3] In terms of the AI-oriented research, *focus*$_{AI}$ of (b) refers to the baby, since the baby is one of the items "just introduced" (namely, by (a)) and the utterer of (b) focusses his/her attention on it. In terms of linguistic analysis, however, the expression referring to the baby in (b), namely the pronoun *it,* belongs to the topic rather than to the focus$_L$ of (b).

(1) (a) The mother picked up the baby.
(b) It had been crying nearly all the day.

2.2 ACTIVATION

The connecting ties between focus$_L$ and focus$_{AI}$ immediately emerge, if one takes into account a dynamic character of the development of the discourse: at the initial point of a discourse, the interlocutors share a certain "stock of knowledge," part of which is activated by the situational context. During the discourse, the stock of knowledge the speaker assumes to share with the hearer(s) changes according to what is in the center of attention at the given time-point, what is most salient or activated (foregrounded) in the memories, what has been just said. The speaker chooses, in a smooth discourse, only those items to be used in the topic of the sentence which he supposes to be among the most salient in the stock of knowledge of the hearer; this enables the hearer to identify relatively easily the objects referred to by the parts of the topic of the sentence.

Thus, after "the baby" has been foregrounded by uttering (1)(a) (*the baby* constitutes (a part of) the focus$_L$ of (1)(a)), the image of the object in the interlocutors' memory identified by the expression *the baby* becomes highly activated in the stock of knowledge shared by the speaker and by the hearer; in the sentence that follows the expression identifying this object belongs to the focus$_{AI}$ (of attention), while referred to by the topic of the sentence, even by means of a pronominal form (viz *it* in (1)(b)).

However, an item is activated also after its mentioning in the topic part of the sentence, see (1)(b') as another possible continuation of (1)(a):

---

2   It should be noted that even in linguistics there is not a uniform use of this term; for a short survey, see Hajičová (1983).

3   In all our examples throughout this paper we work with a single reading of the quoted sentences. It should be emphasized, however, that most sentences allow for an ambiguity in the assignment of topic and focus which corresponds to Chomsky's notion of the range of permissible focus.

(1) (b') She had been ironing all the afternoon.

When uttering (1)(b'), the speaker assumes "the mother" to belong to the items activated above a threshold making it possible to refer to it by a pronoun in the topic part of the next utterance; this activation has been achieved by mentioning the mother in the immediately preceding sentence.

While a non-activated item can be referred to only in the focus$_L$ part of the sentence, an activated item can be referred to in the topic *as well as* in the focus$_L$ part of the sentence (marginal cases concerning embedded items are left aside in this paper). In the latter case, such an item is referred to by a definite NP or an anaphoric pronoun and carries as a rule the intonation center of the sentence; see the sequence of (2)(a) through (c):

(2) (a) John and Mary met at the railway station.
   (b) She greated him.
   (c) and only then he greeted HER.

In (2)(c), *her* used in the focus$_L$ of the sentence refers to Mary, whose image in the stock of knowledge assumed by the speaker to be shared by the hearer is activated to such an extent that the speaker can use a pronominal form; also John's image in this stock of knowledge is activated so as to make a pronominal reference possible; in our (linguistic) terms, the sentence (2)(c) is structured in such a way as to say something *about* John (*John* is in the topic part), viz. to assert that it was HER who was greeted by him.

2.3 THE CHANGES OF ACTIVATION

An interesting question that arises in this connection is to what extent the changes of the degrees of activation (salience) depend on the topic-focus$_L$ articulation of the individual sentences.

(a) It is rather obvious that the items referred to by the parts of the focus$_L$ of the immediately preceding sentence are the most activated ones at every time-point of the discourse.

(b) If an item is referred to in the topic part of the sentence, then at least two issues are to be taken into consideration;

(i) A pronominal reference seems to "strengthen" the activation of the item referred to to a lesser degree than a reference with a full (definite) NP.

(ii) The activation of the items referred to in the topic part of the sentence seems to "fade away" less quickly than that of the items referred to in the focus$_L$ part of the sentence.

(c) If the degree of activation of an item x is being changed (lowered, or raised), then also the degree of activation of the items associated with the object referred to by x is being changed in the respective direction. It should be taken into consideration, however, that frequently a mentioning of a particular object brings into the foreground only a fraction of a set of objects that has been activated earlier. Also other scales or hierarchies should be considered: thus, there is a hierarchy of more or less immediate associative relationships, or that of prominence with regard to the individual sentences and their positions in the text (e.g. sentences metatextually opening a narration or one of its portions, headings, etc., are more prominent than other elements of the text, in that the objects which the former introduce retain their activation to a higher degree than objects introduced in the latter parts), etc.

(d) If an item of the stock of shared knowledge is neither referred to in the given utterance, nor included among the associated objects, then its activation lowers down; as mentioned in (b)(ii) above, the drop in activation is quicker if the item was referred to in the focus$_L$ of the preceding sentence and slower if it was referred to in the topic part of the previous sentence.

(e) There are some specific expressions in particular languages that "give prominence" to the items they precede in that they raise their activation more than otherwise would be the case. This holds e.g. about the English phrases *as for...* or *concerning ...* : they function as "thematizers" (a term suggested by G. D. Rinnan, pers. comm.) and introduce a topic that was not expected, i.e. the sentence recalls an object that is being mentioned only after an occurrence of several intervening sentences. [4]

3. FOCUS$_{AI}$ AND DEGREES OF ACTIVATION

An interesting convergence between the linguistic and the Al-oriented treatment of the dynamic aspects of discourse can be illustrated by the recent study of McKeown (1985). At least three points of agreement are worth mentioning:

In her discussion of a more differentiated approach to focus$_{AI}$, McKeown works with three graded notions: (a) the immediate focus of a sentence (current focus, CF); (b) the (partially ordered) potential focus list (PFL), including the elements of the sentence that are potential candidates for a change of focus; (c) a focus stack (a stack of past immediate foci).

If we look at these notions from the point of view of the approach to the hierarchy of activation of the stock of shared knowledge sketched in Sect. 2.3 above, then:

(a) at a certain time-point t_n at which the sentence S_n is being uttered, the CF of S_n is that element from the activated part of the stock of shared knowledge that has been chosen by the utterer of S_n as its topic proper;[5]

---

4   For a tentative formulation of rules corresponding to the points (a) through (e), see Hajičová and Vrbová (1982) and here in Sect. 4.

5   The term *topic proper* is used for the communicatively least dynamic element of S_n; for the notion of *communicative dynamism* – i.e. the "deep word order," represented at the level of the meaning of the sentence – and the notion of *systemic ordering*, the basic ordering of the participants (cases, or theta-roles) which is given by the granular of each particular language, see Sgall el al. (1973; 1986).

(b) the PFL after the utterance of S_n includes those items of the stock of shared knowledge that belong to the most activated layer of the stock; we doubt that it might be sufficient to work only with the elements of S_n as the possible candidates for a change of focus$_{AI}$ in S_{n+1}, since the latter also can be chosen from elements other than those included in S_n if they are activated to a sufficient degree for such a choice, cf. Garrod and Sanford's (1982) test examples quoted here as (3)(a) through (c).

(3) (a) The engineer repaired the TV set.
　　(b) It has been out of order for two weeks.
　　(c) The engineer/He took only five minutes to repair it.

(c) the focus stack at the time-point t+1 (i.e. when uttering S_{n+1}) contains the foci$_{AI}$ of S_n, S_{n-1}... S_1, i.e. the topics proper of S_n, S_{n-1},..., S_1.

3.2 When specifying the legal focus$_{AI}$ moves, McKeown (1985, 66f) imposes the following order of preferences:

(A) 1. change focus$_{AI}$ to member of previous PFL if possible;
　　2. maintain focus if possible;[6]
　　3. return to topic (used in its non-terminological sense, EH), of the previous discussion; more precisely, choose the CF from the focus stack.

Confronting again this hierarchy of the choices of the speaker with what we said above about the degrees of activation, one arrives at an extensive coincidence, too:

(L) 1. the highest degree of activation is found with those items that are referred to explicitly in the previous sentence; the absolutely highest degree is assigned to those items that are identified by the focus$_L$ of the immediately preceding sentence;
　　2. the next-to-the highest degree of activation is assigned to those items that are identified by the elements of the topic of the immediately preceding sentence (i.e. included in its focus$_{AI}$);
　　3. the next lower degree of activation is assigned to those items that have been mentioned in some preceding sentence or are in some associative links with those mentioned in them.[7]

Even a perfunctory look at the sets (A) and (L) shows that the strategy offering the speaker a choice on the basis of the degrees of activation (with the items which have the highest degrees being most at hand) does not contradict in any point the one proposed by McKeown; as a matter of fact, the activation hierarchy offers a more variable choice, not damaging the coherence of discourse.

3.3 The procedure of generation as formulated by McKeown starts from the so-called default focus$_{AI}$; each predicate[8] is assigned a default focus, which is such a

---

6　McKeown's formulation of two separate steps quoted here as (A)1. and 2. seems to suggest that CF of the last sentence is not a member of PFL of the last sentence.

7　(L)3. differs from (A)3. in that the latter does not take into account the associated objects, which is explicitly admitted in McKeown (198S, p. 67).

8　If we understand well McKeown's treatment, "predicate" is used here in the sense of "rhetorical predicate" (following e.g. Grimes), so that "arguments" stand for very abstract cognitive roles such as feature and entity with

phrase that can be expressed as the surface subject of an active sentence including that predicate; the default focus$_{AI}$ can be "overridden" only by such a choice of focus$_{AI}$ that stands higher than the default focus$_{AI}$ on the hierarchy summarized here as (A)1. through 3. (in this order). In our terms, a verb is passivized only if the NP in the subject position of the passive identifies an item that is activated in the stock of shared knowledge to a (considerably) higher degree than that item identified by the NP that would be in the subject position of the active sentence. Such a strategy is in accordance with Mathesius' (1921) specification of the functions of subject in English: English uses passivization for the same purpose as the languages with the so-called free word order use the word order variation, namely to start sentence with what is the sentence about, if the latter is not the underlying subject, or Actor/Bearer.

4. FOCUSSING AND DISCOURSE STRUCTURE

4.1 DISCOURSE AND SENTENCE

4.1.1 In contemporary linguistics, discourse structure is often studied with a specific attention paid to the coherence of a text, especially to coreference. However, it is a matter of high importance not to overlook the fact that the communicative function of natural language has its impact also on the structure of the sentence, the topic-focus articulation of which is of primary importance for text coherence. This articulation (relevant for presuppositions and for the scope of negation) and the communicative dynamism (semantically relevant in what concerns the scopes of operators and related phenomena) has to be systematically accounted for (see Sgall et al., 1973; 1986; Hajičová 1973; 1983). We have tried to sketch in Sect. 2. 3. of the present contribution how this articulation and the coherence of the discourse interact with the degrees of activation (salience) of the items in the stocks of knowledge of the speaker and of the hearer. It should be borne in mind, of course, that human communicative activity, to which discourse belongs as a specific (though prototypical) case, is determined by much more complex issues than just the knowledge of language; discourse is influenced by factual knowledge, beliefs and other attitudes, aims and psychological motives of all kinds. Therefore, discourse should be viewed as a sequence (or even a more complex collection) of utterance tokens together with their sense (which includes reference assignment to the referring expressions contained in the utterance), rather than a sequence of sentences. A formal model of discourse thus belongs more to the domain of description of the use of language than to that of language system.

4.1.2 Computational models of aspects of discourse have been often constructed in close connection with the research in the experimental domain of AI; an interesting

---

an attributive predicate. In our approach we work with participants of verbs (deep cases, theta-roles) such as Actor/Bearer, Addressee, Objective, Effect, Source, etc. (see Note 5 for the notion of systemic ordering).

integrated approach to the structure of discourse was most recently presented by Grosz and Sidner (1985). The authors assume the structure of discourse to be composed of three distinct but interacting constituents:

(i) the structure of the actual sequence of utterances in the discourse (taken as a linguistic notion); the utterances in discourse can be grouped together into segments, the indications of the boundaries between them being mainly linguistic[9]), (ii) the structure of intentions (replacing Grosz' notion of "task" as used in her previous studies), and (iii) an attentional state. The components (ii) and (iii) are supposed to pertain to nonlinguistic notions.

The attentional state, which is most pertinent to the issues discussed in the present paper, contains information on the objects, properties and intentions that are the most salient ones in the given time point. Attentional state is supposed to be an abstraction of the so-called foci of attention of the participants of the discourse; it "summarizes" the information presented in the preceding utterance tokens that is important for the processing of the given utterance token. It also supplies means how to use the pieces of information supplied by the other two components for the generation and interpretation of the utterance tokens.

4.2 "TOPIC" OF DISCOURSE

Some researchers – both in the fields of linguistics and of AI – claim that one should work with a special autonomous notion of a "discourse (text) topic" rather than with (or besides) a notion of a "sentence topic". One of the difficulties of such an approach is the fact that the notion of "discourse" itself is still somewhat unclear: How can discourse as a unit be identified? Should a discourse unit have a single topic or should each "discourse segment" (context space, etc.) have a "topic" of its own? Is there one topic per each discourse segment or should we rather work with a set of topics for one segment?

A plausible way of looking for answers to these questions offers itself if one works with the hierarchy of activation of the elements of the stock of shared knowledge, which was briefly characterized in Sect. 2. 3. above. The activation of individual elements of this stock changes at each time point of the discourse. In a preliminary way, we can assign numerical values to the degrees of activation (see Hajičová and Vrbová, 1982; the "rules" are reproduced in the present paper from Sgall, Hajičová and Panevová, 1986, p. 263) and the flow of the discourse can be then represented by means of a scheme similar to that in Fig. 1; the sample text is taken over from Hajičová and Vrbová, 1981 where the sample is discussed from the point of view of the changes of activation).

---

9 The authors unduly assume that these linguistic means can be analyzed only on the discourse level rather than on the sentence level; they are not right in their claim that such questions as the influence of these (linguistic) elements on the truth conditions are irrelevant.

Tentative rules: [10]

(1) If $P(x_a)$, then $a^n \to a^n$

(2) If $NP(x_a)$ is in the focus of S, then $a^n \to a^0$

(3) If $NP_d(x_a)$ is in the topic of S, then $a^n \to a^1$

(4) If $a^n \to a^m$, then b^{m+2} obtains for every object b that is not itself referred to in (the TR of) S, but is immediately associated with an item present there

(5) If *as for* x_a, *concerning* x_a is the leftmost expression in S, then $a^n \to a^1$

(6) If x_a neither is included in S nor refers to associated objects (see Rule (4) above), then $a^n \to a^{n+1}$

Notation: x_a denotes an expression x referring to an object a; a^n denotes that this object is salient to the degree n in the stock of shared knowledge (the maximum of salience is denoted by $n = 0$). To the left (right) of the arrow we indicate the state immediately preceding (following) the utterance of a sentence S in which x occurs; $P(x_a)$ denotes that x is expressed by a weak (unstressed) anaphoric pronoun or is deleted in S (albeit present in the TR concerned); $NP_d(x_a)$ denotes that x is a definite NP (including such expressions as *one of the...*).

The sample of text:

(for ease of further reference the clauses are assigned serial numbers; the capital letters denote the intonation centre of each clause)

(1) The school garden was full of CHILDREN.

(2) (a) They talked NOISILY,
    (b) but the teachers didn't REPROVE them.
    (c) because they were so EXCITED.

(3) Outside PARENTS were waiting.

(4) (a) One of them, a father, stood in front of a MICROPHONE,
    (b) as if he were prepared to TALK.

(5) (a) The puils got CALM.
    (b) and their teachers lined them UP.

(6) Both pupils and teachers were in a festive MOOD.

(7) The teachers were SERIOUS.

(8) In fact, all ADULTS in the garden were serious.

(9) They were dressed in evening DRESS.

(10) (a) As for the pupils, they had school UNIFORMS.
     (b) neatly washed and PRESSED.

(12) (a) One of the parents approached the biggest BOY
     (b) and ASKED him:

---

10 The numerical values assigned to the individual items of the stock of knowledge are only tentative and we are fully aware that in a more definite proposal one should work with a wider scale and a more subtle differentiation on it.

(13) "Is it allowed to sit down on the GROUND?"

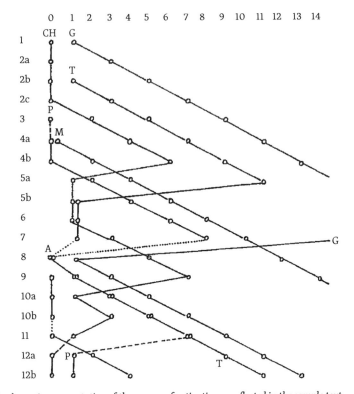

Figure 1 A schematic representation of the process of activation as reflected in the sample text.
Abbreviations: CH – children, F – father, P – parents, T – teachers, A – adults, M – microphone, G – garden,
D – dress

The lines follow the changes of the activation of the objects mentioned in the text (decreasing from the left to right); no distinction in the shape of the lines is made between a mentioning of the same object by the same lexical unit (*children – children*) and that by different lexical units (*children – pupils; dress – uniform*); a dotted line connects two mentioned objects between which there is some kind of an associative relation (uniform – collar; teachers, parents – adults) and an interrupted line connects nodes representing two objects standing in the relation of "one of the..." (parents – a father; pupils – a boy). In this figure, for the sake of simplicity, we take into account only those objects that are actually mentioned in the sentences and leave out all those that stand in some associative links to the mentioned ones (thus the "history" of activation represented in Fig. 1 does not reflect point (c) from Sect. 2.3. above; i.e. the applications of Rule (4)).

Paying due regard to the changes of the activation of the elements of the stock of shared knowledge during the discourse may give us a sound basis for finding out the character of the scale (hierarchy) between the case when an item is marginally (once) mentioned in the discourse and the case in which just one item is foregrounded throughout the whole discourse, consisting of a single segment;[11] only in the latter case it would appear as fully appropriate to speak about the given discourse as having a single "topic". If the scale is found to be smooth, continuous without significant or typical groupings of some kind, then it would be possible to state that only the scale itself can be established (and analyzed, e.g. statistically). On the other hand, if it is found that there are certain prototypical configurations on the scale, which occur rather frequently, others being just marginal, then these configurations may be used as points of departure for the specifications of "the set of the topics of a segment of discourse," "... of a sequence of segments," etc., or of similar (or other) concepts. Our example[12] seems to suggest that a spectrum on the diagram can be singled out within which certain items remain foregrounded; if the activation of these items fades away, it does not fade too far and for a long time (e.g. teachers between the utterance of (2b) and their reactivation in (5b) as contrasted to the garden between (1) and (8), and then fading away again). There are, of course, other items that temporarily get into the foreground (microphone in (4a), the garden in (1) and (8)), but their activation fades away rather quickly.

The fact that the patterning of a discourse is much more varied than the structure of a sentence, can also be illustrated by the fact that the "topic" of the sample quoted above alternatively can be seen in something like "school festival," i.e. an event that is not explicitly mentioned in the discourse and thus cannot be identified in the text itself. Human understanding of the discourse presumably proceeds from the notions anchored in the expressions of the text (such as students, teachers, parents, festive mood of dressing, in our example) to some broader and more general notions (such as school festival). Parallel to that, one may assume that the explicit mentioning is provided for the nodes lower in the frame (script, scenario, plot...) with "superordinated" nodes being derived from these lower levels; in such a case, the frame (script, scenario, plot...) of a school festival is invoked by filling in its (obligatory) slots for participants of the festival, their manner of dressing, its place, etc. through their activation in the stock of knowledge. Thus it can be claimed that there are "topics" of text segments which are expressed more immediately in the utterances of each segment, and "topics" of the discourse, without such a relatively direct relationship to linguistic expressions. However, it would probably be easy to find cases where the "topic" of a segment has a less immediate relationship to the linguistic expression than the "topic(s)" of the whole discourse. Much more of empirical investigations is necessary, before anything more certain can be stated on the regularities of discourse patterning, and it seems that the changes in the hierarchy of activation should be taken into account in such studies.

---

11 In between, there may be cases of smaller or larger sets of items foregrounded for shorter or longer segments, or repeatedly, etc.

12 We assume here that our sample represents a whole discourse, although the sample consists just in the opening utterances of a text.

4.3 DISCOURSE SEGMENTS

A segmentation of the discourse (which itself still includes many open questions[13]) may be viewed from a similar angle. Trying to factor out segments for our sample on the basis of changes of activation, one can (with certain hesitations and provisions) draw the following dividing lines:

(A) (1) through (2) – children (pupils) are foregrounded;
(B) (3) through (4) – in (3) parents are foregrounded accompanied by a subsequent fading away of children;
(C) (5) through (7) – in (5b) children are reactivated and teachers come to the fore-ground, too, with parents fading away;
(D) (6) through (9) – from (6) on, children are fading away, teachers stay in the fore-ground and parents are reactivated;
(E) (9) through (11) – in (9) the dressing comes into the foreground, with other items slowly fading away;
(F) from (12) on, "dressing" fades away.

The boundary between the above segments has been drawn at the point when the activation of (a) certain item(s) fades away in several subsequent utterances while (a) new item(s) is/are foregrounded. It would be interesting to compare the segmentation achieved in this way with those based on the considerations mentioned by Grosz and Sidner (1985).

5. CONCLUDING REMARKS

The objective of our discussion in Sect. 4 was to show that the notion of the degrees of the activation of the items of the stock of shared knowledge together with the rep-resentation of the dynamic development of the discourse by means of the changes of these degrees offers a fruitful basis of the study of the interplay of factors important for such notions as "discourse topics" and "discourse segments". It should be stressed that the notion of a topic of a sentence has been relatively well established, referring to one of the parts of the representation of the meaning of the sentence (see Sgall et al. 1973; 1986). On the other hand, when speaking about "topic" of (segments of the) discourse, one rather has in mind items of the stock of knowledge the organization of which is not strictly regulated by rules or principles similar to those of grammar; the relationships of the items of the stock of knowledge to linguistic expressions in

13   Grosz and Sidner (1985) quote some papers that try to bring evidence for the segmentation to be possible; how-ever, it has not yet been found our e.g. what *criteria* can be used to distinguish between two discourses following each other and two parts (segments) of a single (entire) discourse, etc.

the given utterances are less immediate and less perspicuous. The notions concerning "discourse topics" can be reliably established and fruitfully discussed only if they are anchored in a systematic analysis of the interplay between linguistic structuring of utterances and psychological factors determining the pattern of the discourse.

We wanted to show that this issue is a good evidence for the necessity of a close cooperation of linguists, psychologists, specialists in AI and computer scientists, to be able to use effectively the results achieved in these domains for speeding up the investigation of a given issue.

CONTEXTUAL BOUNDNESS
AND DISCOURSE PATTERNS REVISITED

ABSTRACT

Two issues relevant to discourse description and analysis are discussed, namely which property of the sentence structure reflects its discourse anchoring, and how to combine the "dynamic" (communication based) view of language and discourse with the description of (underlying) sentence syntax. To this aim, our approach to the information structure of the sentence (of its topic-focus articulation, TFA) is briefly summarized, introducing then the notion of the hierarchy of activation of the elements of the stock of knowledge assumed by the speaker to be shared by him and the hearer and proposing some heuristics guiding the development of the activation degrees. These heuristics are applied to a piece of text discussing certain implications of the proposed analysis and some related problems, and briefly sketching a possibility of how to test the proposed approach to text analysis on a large annotated corpus of texts.

1. MOTIVATION

One way to look at discourse is to view it as a sequence of utterances (rather than just sentences) with their referential indices (Jakobsonian's shifters) and information structure (topic-focus articulation, TFA in the sequel) fully determined. Our long-time study of the topic-focus articulation of the sentence has led us to the conviction that this aspect of the sentence structure is a good "bridge" towards a study of (at least one aspect of) the dynamic development of discourse. This, of course, is not a new idea: to our knowledge, its first comprehensive treatment, though clad in psychological rather than linguistic considerations, was given by Weil (1844). Weil writes (p. 11): "Words are the signs of ideas; to treat of the order of words is, then, in a measure, to treat of the order of ideas" (quoted from the 1887 English translation, reprinted in Weil, 1978). Weil recognized two types of the "movement of ideas," namely *marche parallèle* and *progression*:

> If the initial notion is related to the united notion of the preceding sentence, the march of the two sentences is to some extent parallel; if it is related to the goal of the sentence which precedes, there is a progression in the march of the discourse (p. 41).

(It should not be overlooked that Weil also noticed a possibility of a reverse order called by him "pathetic": "When the imagination is vividly impressed, or when the sensibilities of the soul are deeply stirred, the speaker enters into the matter of his discourse at the goal", p. 45.)

In more modern terms, one can say that two adjacent utterances may either be linked by their topics, or the topic (theme) of one utterance may be linked to the focus (rheme) of the preceding one (see the two basic types of thematic progressions in Daneš, 1974).

In the present contribution, we summarize our approach to two issues relevant in this context, namely what in the sentence structure reflects its discourse anchoring, and how to combine the "dynamic" (communication based) view of language and discourse with the description of (underlying) sentence syntax. To this aim, we briefly summarize in section 2.1 our approach to the information structure of the sentence (of its topic-focus articulation, TFA), then introduce the notion of the hierarchy of activation of the elements of the stock of knowledge assumed by the speaker to be shared by him/her and the hearer (section 2.2). Following this, some heuristics guiding the development of the activation degrees are proposed in section 3 and then applied to a piece of text in section 4. Certain implications of the proposed analysis and related problems are presented in section 5. In section 6 we give a brief outline of the possibility of how to test the proposed approach to text analysis on a large annotated corpus of texts.

2. TOPIC-FOCUS ARTICULATION AND THE HIERARCHY OF ACTIVATION OF THE ELEMENTS OF SHARED KNOWLEDGE

2.1 TOPIC-FOCUS ARTICULATION OF SENTENCES

Topic-focus articulation reflects the cognitively based "given"/"new" strategy but differing from it in that TFA belongs to the systems of individual languages rather than to the domain of cognition. Therefore, we subscribe to the claim that the description of TFA is an integral part of the representation of the (literal) meaning of the sentence (Sgall et al.,1986), that is, that TFA is semantically relevant. The semantic relevance of TFA can be understood on the basis of the relation of "aboutness" – a declarative sentence asserts that its Focus holds about its Topic: $F(T)$, with the negative counterpart $\sim F(T)$. A formal treatment along these lines can be found in Peregrin (1994, 1996); see also Partee's tripartite structures in Hajičová et al. (1998).

In the representation of the meaning of the sentence the primary opposition for the description of TFA is the distinction of contextually bound (*cb*) and non-bound (*nb*) items. The distinction of contextual boundness should not be understood in a straightforward etymological way: an *nb* element may be "known" in a cognitive sense (from the context or on the basis of background knowledge) but structured as non-bound, "new", in Focus; see example (1) contrasted with (2). In the relevant sentences of both examples the capitals denote the intonation center, if the sentences are read aloud.[1]

(1) She had separated from her first boyfriend with no great pain. With the second it was worse... She LOVED him, and he was...
(Kundera p. 102)
(2) From the moment she ran into Josef at the Paris airport, she's been thinking of nothing but HIM... In the bar, he was older and more interesting than the others, funny and seductive, and he paid attention only to HER.
(Kundera p. 98)

Both in (1) and (2), the pronouns refer to cognitively "known" persons, that is, known from the previous context; however, only in (1) the sentences are structured in such a way that these elements are contextually bound (i.e. "spoken about"), while in (2) "him" and "her" are structured as contextually non-bound – they belong to the focus of the given sentences, as documented by placing the pitch on them if the segment is read aloud; this interpretation is strengthened by the fact that both pronouns are introduced by a focusing particle (*nothing but* in the first sentence and *only* in the second).

There are two reasons to distinguish the opposition of contextual boundness as a primary (primitive) one and to derive the Topic/Focus bipartition from it: i) the Topic/Focus distinction exhibits – from a certain viewpoint – some recursive properties which are best described by the *cb/nb* distinction; and ii) Topic/Focus bipartition cannot be drawn on the basis of an articulation of the sentence into constituents, but requires a more subtle treatment (for arguments, see section 4).

The bipartition of the sentence into topic and focus (and the scopes of the focusing operators) can be derived from the distribution of contextual boundness with the individual nodes of the structural (dependency based) tree and from the underlying order of the nodes of the tree.

In the prototypical case, the head verb of the sentence and its immediate dependents (arguments and adjuncts) constitute the Topic of the sentence if they are contextually bound, whereas the Focus consists of the contextually non-bound items in such structural positions (and of the items syntactically subordinated to them). Also the semantically relevant scopes of focus sensitive operators such as *only*, *even*, etc. can be characterized in this way.

---

1   The examples in section 3 are taken from Milan Kundera's book *Ignorance* (translated from the French original by Linda Asher, published by Harper/Collins Publishers, New York, 2002); the figures refer to the pages from which the sentences are extracted.

The Topic and Focus (reflecting the aboutness relation) can then be specified by the following set of the rules determining the appurtenance of a lexical occurrence to the Topic (T) or to the Focus (F) of the sentence (see Sgall, 1979–1980: 180; Sgall et al., 1986: 216ff):[2]

(a) the main verb (V) and any of its direct dependents belong to F if they carry index *nb*;

(b) every item *k* that does not depend directly on V and is subordinated to an element of F different from V, belongs to F (where "subordinated to" is defined as the irreflexive transitive closure of "depend on");

(c) if V and all items *k* directly depending on V are *cb*, then it is necessary to specify the rightmost *k'* node of the *cb* nodes dependent on V and ask whether some of nodes *l* dependent on *k'* are *nb*; if so, these *nb* nodes and all their dependents belong to F; if not so, then this step is repeated until an *nb* node depending (immediately or not) on a *cb* node directly dependent on V is found. This node and all its dependent nodes are then specified as F.

(d) every item not belonging to F according to a) to c) belongs to T.

The situations captured by the rules are schematically exemplified in application of these rules in Figure 1(a) through (c) and are illustrated in Figure 2 by a simplified representation of the first sentence in example (1), repeated here for convenience as example (3); the capitalized symbols are self-explanatory (RSTR stands for "restrictive attribute") and denote the kinds of dependency relations between the governing and dependent nodes:

(3) (Preceding context: Irena had two boyfriends and separated from both of them).
She had separated from her first boyfriend with no great pain.

The topic of the sentence (3) is the *cb* verb and its *cb* dependents with their subtrees, that is, *she had separated from her first boyfriend*; the focus is the *nb* part of the upper subtree and its subtree(s) *with no great pain*. As for the restrictive attribute "first", there are two interpretations possible: if the whole context is taken into account (see the continuation in (1), where the second boyfriend is mentioned apparently in contrast to the first one), "first" can be understood as a contrastive *cb* element in the topic. Alternatively, in terms of recursive properties of TFA, "first" can be understood as an *nb* element, that is as the "local focus" of the subtree "first boyfriend". In both interpretations, "first" would be an element of the topic part of the sentence.

In this way, the information structure of the sentence can be described as one of the aspects of underlying syntax, characterized by the opposition of contextual boundness and the left-to-right order of the nodes.

---

2   The application of this original definition of Focus was later complemented by the notion of proxy focus (Hajičová et al., 1998).

2.2 THE HIERARCHY OF ACTIVATION OF THE ELEMENTS OF SHARED KNOWLEDGE

The research question we have asked then is whether it is possible to combine the "dynamic" (communication based) view of language and discourse with the description of (underlying) sentence syntax, the TFA aspect of which has already been described above in section 2.1. Or, in other words, how to combine the "dynamic" (communication based) view of language and discourse (and textual co-reference) with the description of (underlying) sentence syntax.

To this aim, we (Hajičová and Vrbová, 1982) introduced a more detailed treatment (see especially Hajičová, 1993, 1997, 2003a, 2003b): the notion of the stock of knowledge assumed by the speaker to be shared by him and the hearer. This stock of shared knowledge, of course, is not an undifferentiated collection, but a hierarchized structure based on the different degrees of salience (activation) of its elements. This scale has to be reflected in a description of the semantico-pragmatic layer of the discourse. In this sense our approach can be viewed as pointing to a useful enrichment of the

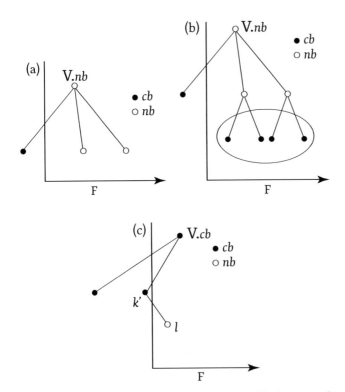

Figure 1   Schematic representations of situations captured by the Topic and Focus rules.

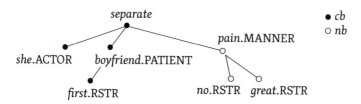

Figure 2 *Simplified representation of the first sentence in example (1).*

existing theories of discourse representation (see also Krahmer, 1998; Krahmer and Theune, 1999; Kruijff-Korbayová, 1998).[3]

(SOME) HEURISTICS GUIDING THE DEVELOPMENT OF THE ACTIVATION DEGREES

The underlying hypothesis for our analysis of discourse structure was formulated as follows:

Hypothesis: A finite mechanism exists that enables the addressee to identify the referents on the basis of a partial ordering of the elements in the stock of knowledge shared by the speaker and the addressees (according to the speaker's assumption), based on the degrees of activation (salience) of referents.

The following three basic heuristics (a) through (c) based on the position of the items in question in the topic or in the focus of the sentence (see previous section), on the means of expression (noun, pronoun) and on the previous state of the activation, can be formulated to determine the degrees of salience of the elements of the stock of shared knowledge:

(a) In the flow of communication, a discourse referent enters the discourse, in the prototypical case, first as contextually non-bound, thus getting a high degree of salience. A further occurrence of the referent is contextually bound, the item still has a relatively high degree of salience, but lower than an element referred to in the focus (as *nb*) in the given sentence: see example (4).

(4) The night before her mother left, Irena introduced her to her companion, Gustaf, a Swede. The three of them had dinner in a restaurant, and the mother, who spoke not a word of French, managed valiantly with English. Gustaf was delighted: with his mistress, Irena, he spoke only French, and he was tired of that language, which he considered pretentious and not very practical. (Kundera p. 22)

---

3   There have been several other studies devoted to hierarchization and scalarity in discourse; see for example, Ariel (1988, 1990), Barzilay and Lapata (2008), Chafe (1976), Givon (1983), Gundel (2011), Gundel et al. (1993), Lambrecht (1994), Prince (1981), to name just a few. For a more detailed analysis of these approaches and for a comparison of them with our approach, see Hajičová (2012).

In the first sentence of this paragraph, "Gustaf, a Swede" is introduced for the first time; he is re-mentioned simply as "Gustaf" in the topic part of the third sentence (the sentence is "about" him) and in the following sentences, as a relatively salient element with no competitor in reference, he is referred to just by a pronoun "he". We should say in this connection that the stock of knowledge of the speaker/hearer contains also some permanently salient referents such as *here, now, Europe, Shakespeare,* etc., which can stand in the topic part of the sentence without having been mentioned in the previous co-text.

(b) If an item is not referred to in the given sentence, the degree of salience is lowered; the fading is slower with a referent that had in the previous co-text occurred as contextually bound; this heuristic is based on the assumption that a *cb* item has been "standing in the foreground" for some time (as a rule, it was introduced in the focus, then used as contextually bound, maybe even several times) and thus its salience is reinforced; it disappears from the set of the highly activated elements of the stock of shared knowledge at a slower pace than an item which has been introduced in the focus but then dropped out, not re-mentioned (see Chafe's (1994) question of how long a referent, once having acquired a "given" status, will retain it).

If the referent has faded too far away it has to be re-introduced in the focus of the sentence: see example (5).

(5) In 1921 Arnold Schoenberg declares that because of him German music will continue to dominate the world for the next hundred years. Twelve years later he is forced to ... After the war ... he is still convinced ... He faults Igor Stravinskij for paying too much attention to his contemporaries ...
[two pages later]
As I said, he was living in the very lofted spheres of mind, ... The only great adversary worthy of him, the sublime rival whom he battled with verve and severity, was Igor Stravinskij.
(Kundera pp. 144, 146)

(c) If the difference in the degree of salience of two or more items is very small, then the identification of reference can be done only on the basis of inferencing. In the segment of example (6), both Milada and Irena are highly salient items and can be referred to by the pronoun *she*; the assumed concrete reference assignment is indicated by M for Milena and I for Irena.

(6) Milada had been a colleague of Martin's working at the same institute. Irena had recognized her [M] when she [M] first appeared at the door of the room, but only now, each of them with a wine glass in hand, is she [I] able to talk to her [M]. She [I] looks at her [M]: Milada still has the same shape face ...
(Kundera p. 39)

The mentioned three basic heuristics served as a basis for our formulation of several rules for the assignment of the degrees of salience, which we have applied to numerous text segments to check how the determination of these degrees may help reference assignment.

The following basic rules determining the degrees of salience (in a preliminary formulation and taking into account only nominal referents) have been designed, with $dg_i(r)$ indicating the salience degree of the referent r after the i-th sentence S_i of a document is uttered:

(i)   if r is expressed by a weak pronoun (or zero, i.e. deleted in the surface shape) in a sentence, it retains its salience degree after this sentence is uttered: $dg_i(r) \rightarrow dg_{i-1}(r)$;

(ii) if r is expressed by a noun (group) carrying nb, then $dg_i(r) = 0$;

(iii) if r is expressed by a noun (group) carrying cb, then $dg_i(r) = 1$;

(iv) $dg_i(q) \rightarrow dg_i(r) +2$ obtains for every referent q that is not itself referred to in S_i, but is immediately associated with an item present here;

(v)   if r neither is included in S_i, nor refers to an associated object, and has been mentioned in the focus of the preceding sentence, then $dg_i(r) \rightarrow dg_{i-1}(r) +2$;

(vi) if r neither is included in S, nor refers to an associated object, and has been mentioned in the topic of the preceding sentence, then $dg_i(r) \rightarrow dg_{i-1}(r) +1$.

Since the only fixed point is that of maximal salience, our rules technically determine the degree of salience reduction (indicating 0 as the maximal salience). Whenever an entity has a salience distinctly higher than all competing entities which can be referred to by the given expression, this expression may be used as giving the addressee a sufficiently clear indication of the reference specification. It should be emphasized that what matters is the relation higher/lower degree, rather than the absolute numerical value; also the difference of 1 is too small to be relevant (see (c) above).

4. ANALYSIS OF A PIECE OF TEXT

One of the analyzed texts illustrating the development of salience degrees during a discourse, as far as determined by such rules, was a sample of literary text (of about 60 sentences) taken from the English translation of Josef Škvorecký's Czech book *Scherzo capriccioso* (published in 1984 by Sixty-Eight Publishers, Toronto; translated by Paul Wilson as *Dvorak in Love*, published by Lester and Orpen Dennys Ltd, Toronto, 1986; the segment analyzed here is on pp. 251–253). The episode depicts the author's imagination of the inspiration for Dvořák's opera *Rusalka* (Water Nymph). This analysis (Hajičová, 2003b) can be used also for a cross-linguistic comparison, namely that of the English translation and the Czech original text. Therefore, we have applied the same rules to assign the salience degrees to the same referents in the Czech original text, and the result was rather convincing: the development of activation in both texts followed the same lines, with the exception of three points: (i) the sentence boundaries differ (e.g.

Eng. 53 and 54 is in Cz. "merged" into a single sentence); (ii) the grammatically fixed English word order forced the translator to use a different formulation, in order to preserve the TFA of the original Czech sentences (in order to place "two figures" in 1 in the position of focus in Eng., a pronominal subject "they" referring to the children had to be inserted, while in Cz. the object "two figures" was placed into focus just by a change of word order; a similar structural change was necessary in 35); and (iii) a possible case of a translator's mistake (sent. 34). In this context, one can go back to Weil (1844), who remarks: "... in translating from one language to another, if it is not possible to imitate at the same time the syntax of the original and the order of the words, retain the order of the words and disregard the grammatical relations" (p. 26 of the Eng. translation).

The relevant (slightly shortened) part of the text is in Appendix. Table 1 shows the assigning numerical values of the reduction of salience to noun/pronoun tokens (or "zero", see later) referring to seven selected "objects" (or better to say: mental images of objects): Dvořák's daughter Magda (M), her lover Kovarik (K), the lady (L), referred to also as *Rusalka (water lily)*), the black man (A), referred to also as *banjo, baritone voice*), the buggy (B, also *horses, figures*), the rowboat (R), and Dvořák (D). In the assignment of salience degrees in Table 1 we do not take into account the rule (iv) for associated items (thus e.g. *banquet* in sentence 12 is associated with L and A); however, we understand the expressions *straw hat, a pair of white shoes*, and *a crumpled white pile* in 13 through 15 to be in such a close association with L that we take them to directly refer to her and assign the activation degrees accordingly. The same holds true for such a more or less direct reference as is the case of *banjo, baritone voice* which we subsume under A. It should be added that we have in mind underlying representations of the sentences in which elements deleted in the surface shape of the sentence are reconstructed, so that we assign a value to the "zero" in 9 (as if there were the pronoun *they* referring to M and K), in 17, 21, 32 and 33 (as if there were the pronoun *she* referring to the Lady), in 25 and 45 (as if there were the pronoun *he* referring to Kovarik), in 54 (as if there were the pronoun *she* referring to M and in 57 and 58 (as if there were the pronoun *he* referring to Dvořák).

Table 1 Salience degrees

After sentence No. #	Salience degree of						
	M	K	L	A	B	R	D
1	1	1	0	0	–	–	–
2	1	1	2	2	–	–	–
3	1	1	4	4	–	–	–
4	2	1	1	1	2	–	–
5	3	2	2	2	0	–	–
6	4	3	1	3	0	–	–
7	5	4	2	1	2	–	–
8	1	1	3	2	4	–	–

After sentence No. #	Salience degree of						
	M	K	L	A	B	R	D
9	1	1	4	3	6	–	–
10	2	2	1	4	8	–	–
11	1	0	2	5	10	–	–
12	0	1	3	6	12	–	–
13	2	1	0	7	14	–	–
14	3	2	0	8	16	–	–
15	4	3	0	9	18	–	–
16	5	4	1	10	20	–	–
17	6	5	1	11	22	–	–
18	7	6	1	12	24	–	–
19	8	7	1	0	26	–	–
20	9	8	1	2	28	–	–
21	10	9	1	4	30	–	–
22	11	10	1	6	32	–	–
23	12	11	1	8	34	–	–
24	13	1	2	10	36	–	–
25	14	1	3	12	38	–	–
26	1	1	4	14	40	–	–
27	1	2	5	16	42	–	–
28	2	3	0	18	44	–	–
29	3	1	1	20	46	–	–
30	4	2	1	22	48	–	–
31	5	3	1	24	50	–	–
32	6	4	1	26	52	–	–
33	7	5	1	28	54	–	–
34	8	1	1	30	56	–	–
35	1	1	2	0	58	–	–
36	2	2	3	1	60	–	–
37	3	3	1	3	62	–	–
38	4	4	1	5	64	–	–
39	1	1	2	7	66	–	–
40	2	1	3	9	68	0	–
41	3	2	4	11	70	1	0
42	4	3	5	13	72	2	0
43	5	4	6	15	74	3	0
44	6	1	7	17	76	4	2

After sentence No. #	Salience degree of						
	M	K	L	A	B	R	D
45	7	1	1	19	78	5	4
46	8	2	2	0	80	6	1
47	9	3	3	2	82	7	1
48	10	4	4	4	84	8	1
49	11	1	5	6	86	9	2
50	12	1	6	8	88	10	3
51	13	2	1	10	90	11	4
52	14	3	2	12	92	12	5
53	1	4	3	14	94	13	6
54	1	5	4	16	96	14	7
55	2	6	5	18	98	15	0
56	3	7	6	20	100	16	1
57	4	8	7	22	102	17	1
58	5	9	8	24	104	18	1

The rows represent the state of the activation of the selected items after the sentence pertaining to the serial number on the left has been uttered. The numbers in the columns denote the degree of activation; a dash stands for the case that the given referent has not yet entered the scene. We would like to emphasize again that the numerical values are of no substantial importance; what is relevant is the relative degree, with zero being the highest, one being higher than two, etc.

5. DISCUSSION OF IMPLICATIONS OF THE ANALYSIS AND RELATED PROBLEMS

As we have suggested in our previous papers, such an analysis of discourse makes it possible to throw some light on several issues of discourse structure:

(a) Certain patterning can be readily observed: for example, a more or less regular change of groupings of items at the "top of the stock" if the discourse fluently passes from one group of items talked about to another group, or a cluster of items staying on the top with other items just entering the stage and leaving it very quickly.

(b) The proposed representation of the flow of discourse offers one way of segmenting the discourse more or less distinctly into smaller units according to which items are the most activated ones in these stretches. In our sample, the segmenting can be illustrated as follows: the first segment is characterized by the items Magda, Kovarik, and partly also the lady; in the next segment, from sentence 13, the lady dominates the top of the stock, up to sentence 23 through 25; from this point, Magda and Kovarik "return" to the stage, and in the last segment, from sentence 41, the Master appears on the scene.

(c) An interesting issue for further investigation is that of the identification of possible thresholds (i.e. the placement of vertical lines in the flow charts): thus one can investigate whether and under which conditions such a threshold adds to other prerequisites for the possibility/impossibility of pronominal reference, for the use of a full definite noun phrase (NP) in topic, for the necessity to use stronger means for a reintroduction of some already mentioned item, and for the necessity of such a re-introduction to occur in the focus. The presence of "competitors," of course, is highly relevant for such investigations.

(d) Last but not least, the proposed representation of the flow of discourse can serve as a basis for the identification of "topics" of the discourse. It is often disputable to determine "the" topic of a given discourse; however, the discourse topic(s) occur (or at least the items associated with these topic(s), whatever the notion of association may be understood to stand for) most probably among the items staying longer (or more frequently) among the most activated items, that is, at the top of the stock. A look at Table 1 confirms what apparently the author wanted the reader to understand: the episode is about Rusalka, that is, the lady; her activation does not go beyond the degree 7, while all other items cross this point at least once.

Let us turn now in more detail to the relationships between the choice of co-refer-ring expressions (weak pronoun, noun, noun group with simple or complex adjuncts) and the degrees of salience, as illustrated by our sample text. In the first sentence of our segment, the pronoun *they* refers to Dvořák's small daughter Magda and to his guest Kovarik, who take a walk in the surroundings of Dvořák's house in Iowa (during his stay in the US). The following observations can be made:

(i)   A weak (or zero) pronoun refers to a highly salient item (see sentences 9, 11, 34); this pronoun expresses a contextually bound item; the use of a strong (long) pro-noun is limited to cases when the reference is made to a contextually non-bound item (in the focus of the sentence) or to a contrastive item in the topic (expressed by an (optional) phrasal stress; in the latest version of our analysis of the TFA, this item is marked by a special superscript in the underlying representation of the sentence; see Hajičová et al., 1998).

(ii) If two items are close to each other in their degrees of salience, the use of a weak pronoun is limited to cases (a) with relevant grammatical oppositions (gender, number) and (b) with a clear pragmatic basis for inferencing (see e.g. "they" in 2 and "them" in 4).

(iii) Otherwise, the co-reference to one of the competitors is to be made clear by the use of a noun (see "the beauty" in 16), or even of a noun group with simple or complex adjuncts (see "the girl across the river" in 30).

(iv) Such stronger means have to be used also if the salience has faded away (see "the man," "Kovarik," and "the child" in 19, 24, 26, respectively); if the salience goes beyond a certain threshold of comprehensiveness, the item needs to be reintro-duced by a reference in Focus. In our sample, this is illustrated by the different kinds of means referring to the black man: its activation has dropped significantly and thus in 19, 35 and 46 the reference to him is made by a referring expression in Focus.

This example should make it possible for the reader to check (at least in certain aspects) the general function of the procedure we use, as well as the degree of its empirical adequacy in the points it covers. We are aware of the still tentative character of our analysis, which may and should be enriched in several respects (not to cover only noun groups, but to account for possible episodic text segments, for oral speech with the sentence prosody, etc.).

6. PERSPECTIVES: INTEGRATED ANNOTATION OF TEXT CORPORA

In spite of the fact that the mechanism proposed above has been tested on a couple of texts, both from Czech and English and even in Bulgarian and Malayan, a much broader range of texts analyzed as for all the three aspects, namely the underlying sentences structure, the assignment of topic-focus articulation and the co-reference relations would be necessary for a deeper evaluation of the analysis. Manual annotation is a very time-consuming and costly task; an opportunity to work with larger data is now offered by the existence of computationally available annotated text corpora.

For Czech, we are now working on a project based on the data available in the Prague Dependency Treebank (PDT; Hajič et al., 2006; Mikulová et al., 2006). PDT is a corpus of Czech texts comprising 3 165 documents (mainly of a journalistic genre) annotated on three levels: (a) morphemic (with detailed part-of-speech tags and rich information on morphological categories), (b) surface shape ("analytical", in the form of dependency-based tree structures with relations labeled by superficial syntactic functions such as Subject, Object, Adverbial, Attribute, etc.), and (c) underlying dependency-based syntactic level (so-called tectogrammatical) with dependency tree structures labeled by functions such as Actor, Patient, Addressee, etc. and including also information on the TFA of sentences. In addition, two kinds of information are being added in the latest version of PDT, namely annotation of discourse relations (Mladová et al., 2008) based on the analysis of discourse connectors (inspired by the Pennsylvania Discourse Treebank; see Miltasaki et al., 2008; Prasad et al., 2008a, 2008b) and information on grammatical and on textual intra- and extra-sentential co-reference relations.

Thanks to such a richly annotated corpus, we basically have at our disposal all the information we need for an application of our rules to activation assignment: the underlying sentence representation with restored (superficial) deletions as well as with part-of-speech information, the Topic-Focus assignment (via the TFA attribute with values contextually-bound and contextually non-bound) and co-referential chains for nominal and pronominal realization of referential expressions. The activation algorithm has already been implemented and applied to (selected but full) documents, the "activation" diagrams have been visualized and the task now is to test the hypotheses our approach is based on and the possibilities the approach offers for text analysis and generation, as indicated in points (a) through (d) in the Discussion section.

CONCLUSION

We are aware that, along with the rules based on the heuristics characterized above, there are other factors that have to be investigated, which are important for different kinds of discourses. This concerns various aspects of the discourse situation, of domain knowledge, of specific textual patterns (with episodes, poetic effects, and so on). We are convinced that factors of these and further kinds can be studied on the basis of the salience degrees, which are typical for basic discourse situations. In any case, we are convinced that it is useful for a theory of discourse semantics to reflect the degrees of salience. This makes it possible to distinguish the reference potential of referring expressions and thus the connectedness of the discourse. Also, application domains such as text segmentation (in accordance with topics of individual segments), or advanced information retrieval (specifying texts in which a given topic is actually treated, rather than being just occasionally mentioned) may take advantage of this approach.

ACKNOWLEDGEMENTS

I would like to thank my colleague Barbora Hladká for her invaluable comments on the draft of the article as well as for her work on the visualization of the schemes.

FUNDING

Some parts of this contribution are based on previous articles: Hajičová (2003a, 2003b, 2012). The work on the present article was supported by the projects of the Grant Agency of the Czech Republic P406/12/0658 and has been using language resources developed and/or stored and/or distributed by the LINDAT-Clarin project of the Ministry of Education of the Czech Republic (project LM2010013).

APPENDIX 1

(1) Across the river they could now see a fire with two figures beside it.
(2) When they moved closer,
(3) they could make out two white horses against the background of the dark bushes.
(4) Then he recognized them.
(5) The pale blue buggy.
(6) Two hours ago, the beauty from Chicago had sat on the seat,
(7) while the black man in livery had gone into Kapino's for beer.
(8) They stopped...
(9) and looked across the river.
(10) The young lady in the white dress was biting into a chicken leg.
(11) He looked at Magda.
(12) The child's eyes, wide in amazement, stared across the river at this fairytale banquet.
(13) He looked at the straw hat.
(14) Yes, beside it in the grass a pair of white shoes had been casually tossed
(15) and beside them lay a crumpled white pile.
(16) The beauty stood up
(17) and threw the half-eaten leg into the fire.
(18) She stretched,
(19) She said something to the man...
(20) She lifted up her skirts
(21) and, stepping gingerly through the grass,
(22) she began walking upstream.
(23) her head became a coolly glowing torch.
(24) Intoxicated, Kovarik stepped forward
(25) and silently followed the beautiful phantom's pilgrimage.
(26) The child padded silently behind him.
(27) The child whispered.
(28) "She's a Rusalka! A water nymph!"
(29) He caught his breath.
(30) The girl across the river unlaced her bodice
(31) and ... she had lifted the skirt over her head,
(32) slipped out of it
(33) and stood there in nothing but white knee-length knickers...
(34) He couldn't take his eyes off her.
(35) From downstream they could hear a banjo playing.
(36) A pleasant baritone voice sang: "..."
(37) The girl let her hands drop...
(38) Cautiously, she stepped into the water.
(39) On their side of the river, ..., something creaked.

(40) Looking towards the sound, he could barely distinguish the outline of a small rowboat

(41) and, in it, someone's dark silhouette.

(42) The moonlight fell on the head, the white whiskers, the hair in disarray.

(43) The Master!

(44) He looked quickly across the stream

(45) and saw the Rusalka up to her waist in the water. "Borne like a vapour..."

(46) The Master's head turned in profile towards the velvet baritone.

(47) He doesn't see;

(48) he only hears,

(49) he thought.

(50) He himself saw.

(51) The Rusalka was slowly lowering herself into the water, ...

(52) Finally, all that remained on the water was a burning water lily.

(53) Suddenly the child saw too

(54) and shrieked,

(55) "Papa!"

(56) The Master started,

(57) looked around

(58) and then saw.

APPENDIX 2

In the original paper *Contextual Boundness and Discourse Patterns Revisited* the dynamics of the assignment of the degrees of salience was represented (for technical reasons set by the journal publisher) by means of numerical values (see above, p. 179). In order to make the characterization of the flow of activation more transparent, I attach here a visualization (prepared by Barbora Hladká) of the changes of the degrees of activation as assigned by our algorithm. Figs. 1 to 3 reflect the activation changes assigned to the discourse entities Kovarik (K), the Lady (Rusalka, L) and Dvorak (D), respectively. Fig. 4 is a summarizing representation of the flow of activation of five entities present in the story: Magda (M), Kovarik (K), the Lady (L), the black man (B) and Dvorak (D). This summarizing representation makes clear especially the following points: (i) it indicates where the boundary between discourse segments in the story can be drawn, namely (a) the first segment, up to the sentence 13 is characterized by the presence of Magda, Kovarik and the Lady on the scene, (b) in the segment between the sentences 13 and 24 the Lady dominates the top of the stock, (c) from 25 through 41 Kovarik and Magda return on the stage and (d) after 41 till the end Dvorak is the dominating entity; and (ii) it makes it clear what the story is about (the "topic"of the discourse, the Lady); the activation of this entity never goes beyond the degree 7, which is not true about any other item.

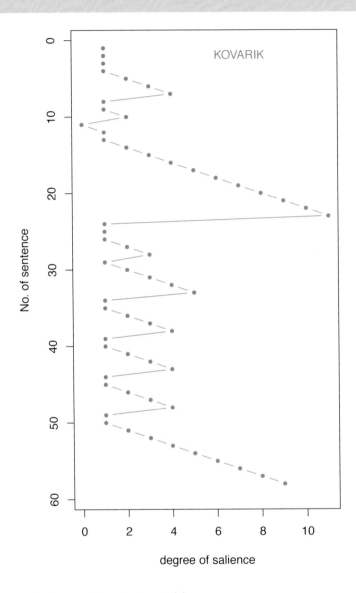

Figure 1 Activation changes of the entity Kovarik (K)

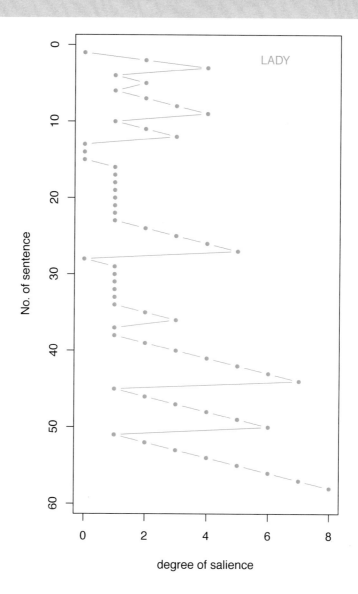

Figure 2 Activation changes of the entity Lady (Rusalka, L)

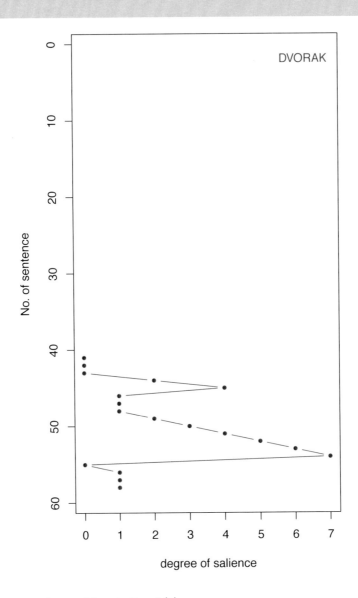

Figure 3 Activation changes of the entity Dvorak (D)

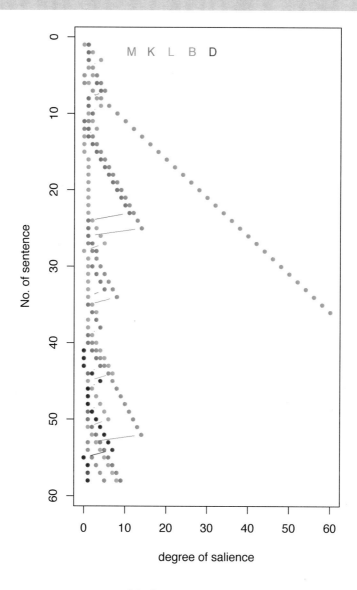

Figure 4 Summarizing representation of the flow of activation of the entities Magda, Kovarik, Lady, Black man and Dvorak

5. COMPARISON WITH OTHER APPROACHES

FOREWORD

The study of what is now generally called information structure of the sentence was originally a matter of European linguistics; the first studies were mostly psychologically oriented and were published in the latter half of the 19th century (mostly concentrated in the German geographic area though one should not forget H. Weil's 1844 study based on the "order of ideas" and on comparison of ancient and modern languages). This tradition was continued – though very critically – in the first half of the twentieth century especially by Vilém Mathesius, one of the founding members of the Prague Linguistic Circle and, after him and mostly in agreement with him, by other European scholars. With the introduction of formal description of language, the first attempt to formulate and incorporate a formal account of information structure into a systematic language description was undoubtedly the Praguian theory of Topic-Focus Articulation (see esp. Sgall 1967). In the present Part, we include contributions in which we try to compare this approach with other, later treatments.

This concerns first of all Chomskyan transformational generative grammar, where the first mentioning of the term *topic* (in the sense used by M. A. K. Halliday and covered in most European approaches by the term theme) can be found in Chomsky's Syntactic Structures (1957) and then again in Aspects of the Theory of Syntax (1965). These were mostly mentions in footnotes; a more systematic treatment of this aspect of sentence structure is included in Chomsky's paper Deep Structure, Surface Structure and Semantic Interpretation (1968) and it is this treatment that is critically analyzed in our Czech contribution from 1972 translated here as *Functional Sentence Perspective and the Latest Developments in Transformational Grammar*. Our hypothesis of the underlying order of sentence elements as reflecting the communicative dynamism is then compared with some assumptions of the later stage of Chomskyan approach, the Government and Binding theory in the 1986 paper *A Note on the Order of Constituents in Relation to the Principles of GB Theory*. Another important contribution to the development of formal description that paid attention to the information structure was the formulation of the theory of optimality. As pointed out in our 2001 paper *Possibilities and Limits of Optimality Theory in Topic-Focus Articulation*, one of the criteria for the assignment of an optimal structure was related to the information structure of the sentence. The final paper in this Part, *The Position of TFA (Information Structure) in a Dependency Based Description of Language* (2007), had a twofold aim: it was supposed to summarize the basics of the TFA theory and to explore which of the formal frameworks, phrase-structure based or dependency based, is best suited for the representation of the information structure. Both these points are discussed on the background of the Meaning-Text model as proposed by I. Mel'chuk.

FUNCTIONAL SENTENCE PERSPECTIVE AND THE LATEST DEVELOPMENTS IN TRANSFORMATIONAL GRAMMAR[1]

In the past few years the discussion among proponents of transformational methodology is becoming more and more concerned with the topics that are included in our country under the general term *functional sentence perspective or topic-focus articulation* (TFA in the sequel).[2] These questions are crucial in the current debate, which is evident from the fact that they are used as the main arguments in support of either of the conceptions of transformational generative grammar, represented on the one hand by Noam Chomsky, Ray Jackendoff and others (the so-called extended standard theory) and on the other by George Lakoff, James D. McCawley, and partly Paul Postal and John Ross (so-called generative semantics), just to name the most prominent figures. In the present paper we try to illustrate both of these approaches by a few simple examples (Sect. 1 and 2), to demonstrate that there is a third way (which is already well-known in this country) to approach questions connected to TFA in the generative description of the language (Sect. 3), and in conclusion to at least indicate a few further issues, that are closely related to this topic (Sect. 4).

1.1 The concept of the transformational description of language, which first appeared in the United States, is often used to show that the character of the language being described to a considerable extent influences the choice of the apparatus used to describe it. The American research has so far spent little time on questions connected

---

1 Translated by Masha Volynsky. – This article was prepared in 1971 (as an extended version of the lecture at the Circle of modern philologists, cf. the abstract in *Jazykovědné aktuality* 8, 1971, no. 3/4, pp. 30–32) for the journal Časopis pro moderní filologii (ČMF); it appeared concurrently with the works of L. Uhlířová (SaS 33, 1972, 37–43) and P. Sgall (SaS 33, 1972, 160–164), which were published in SaS on similar topics. When this article could not be published due to the closing of ČMF, some of the parts that would otherwise have significantly overlapped with the above mentioned articles had to be shortened in preparation for its publication in SaS; in order to maintain our line of argument, though, we could only make minor changes.

2 Cf. Daneš, ed. (1974) and Tyl, ed. (1970).

to word order and particularly the question of how far do variations in the word order influence the meaning of the sentence; this makes it evident how much this research was itself influenced by the language described – English – which has a grammatical-ized word order. In English transformational grammar this tendency is particularly reflected by Chomsky's definition of syntactical concepts such as subject and object: these concepts are defined as functions of nominal groups given, basically, by the or-der of these phrases in the underlying phrase marker. So, the subject is the nominal group to the left of the verb and the object is the nominal group that comes after the verb in the deep structure. A more in-depth analysis of the significance of the rela-tions between the nominal groups and the verb, though, led C. J. Fillmore[3] to exclude the syntactical concepts like subject and object from the deep structure and to define the various verb modifications (actants in Tesnière's terminology, "cases" in Fillmore's terminology) as units on the same layer. In his conception, the subject does not ap-pear as a partner of the whole predicate phrase; instead, the actor (agentive) acts on the same levels as the "objective," "dative", "instrumental" etc. To support his theory Fillmore provides sentences such as (1) and (2) as examples, where the relationship between phrases *the door* and the verb *open* is always the same, even though the phrase *the door* stands in different syntactical positions; on the other hand, different phrases take the position of the subject (*I* in example (1), *the door* in example (2)), and their syntactic relation to the verb is not identical (Fillmore here distinguishes between the agentive and the objective).

(1) I open the door.
(2) The door opens.

Compared to Chomsky's strict order of the nominal groups (with regard to the verb), which can be interpreted as syntactical functions, Fillmore proposes an unor-dered sequence of verb modifications, whose function is defined as a "case", or as a sequence of symbols, whose order remains without an interpretation. In the following section, we want to show that this negative approach to the question of the order of the elements in deep structure is not completely adequate and that one has to take into account the ordering of elements in deep structure with regard to its semantic relevance.

1.2 The necessity to capture the distinction between sentences in semantic struc-ture, which we describe in our terminology as being distinguished only by its TFA, has brought Chomsky to such concepts as presupposition and focus.[4] He provides a

---

3   See esp. Fillmore (1968). C. J. Fillmore develops his theory further in other writings, e.g. in Fillmore (1970); cf. also papers cited here in fn. 26.
4   See Chomsky (1971). Although Chomsky (1965) uses the terms Topic and Comment in two footnotes (p. 221, p. 224), he does not pay so much attention to them and defines them inaptly on the basis of grammatical relati-onships in the surface structure. From his later definition of focus it is clear that he was influenced by M.A.K. Halliday (cf. e.g. unpublished work by Halliday (1967a), and Halliday (1967-68, pp. 199-244)). Lakoff (1969) also points out their concurring opinions.

number of arguments against the possibility of defining presupposition and focus of a sentence on the basis of its deep structure, and suggests to instead define focus on the basis of the intonation centre of the sentence, in other words, based on the surface structure, specifically its phonetic interpretation.

There is, though, a certain inconsistency in Chomsky's formulations; they suggest that there is only one phrase in every sentence, which could be taken as the focus (whether when identifying the focus in the deep or surface structure). Chomsky writes that "the focus is determined [...] as *the* (highlighted by E.H.) phrase containing the intonation center" (p. 200). Yet the examples he presents show that this cannot be the case. Chomsky himself then talks about the *range of permissible focus.*[5]

(3) It wasn't an ex-convict with a red SHIRT that he was warned to look out for.
    (a) He was warned to look out for an AUTOMOBILE salesman.
    (b) He was warned to look out for an ex-convict wearing DUNGAREES.
    (c) He was warned to look out for an ex-convict with a CARNATION.
    (d) He was warned to look out for an ex-convict with a red TIE.

In example (3) the bearer of the intonation centre is the word SHIRT; but as the possible continuations (a) through (d) show, the focus can be either the phrase *an ex-convict with a red shirt* (a), or *with a red shirt* (b), or *a red shirt* (c), or *shirt* (d). All of these phrases contain the same intonation centre – the word SHIRT. So it is important to distinguish between the permissible range of focus and the selection of a specific focus from that range.

To counter Chomsky's definition, we can also point out that even by designating the focus in the surface structure there would still be a problem if one wants to define the focus as a phrase. For sentence (4), it is certainly possible to consider the part of the sentence *with Bill about money* as the focus though it would be difficult to call it a phrase; if we use Chomsky's method of natural responses to identify the focus, then certainly it is possible to consider sentence (5) to be such a natural response. We would probably reach the same conclusion using the question test.[6]

(4) The question is not whether I should argue with Bill about MONEY.
(5) It is whether I should argue with the director about a free ticket.

2. The proponents of the second of the current trends of transformational grammar, the so-called *generative semantics* – above all G. Lakoff – believe, disputing Chomsky's "extended standard theory", in the hypothesis about transformations as operations, which cannot change the meaning of the derived structures. They thus suggest to capture all the relevant distinctions in a highly abstract underlying structure. In addition

---

5   In examples, we mark the word that is the carrier of the intonation centre in the sentence by capital letters.
6   For a detailed description of Chomsky's focus and presupposition see Sgall and Hajičová (1971) and Sgall op.cit. here in fn. 1. G. Lakoff also discusses Chomsky's conception, op. cit. in fn. 4.

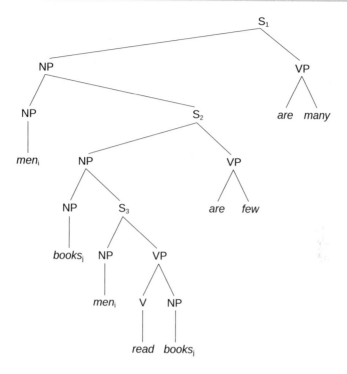

Figure 1

to transformations Lakoff defines the so-called *global rules, global constraints,* which ensure that two sentences are not derived with different meanings.[7] As an illustration we can use examples (6a) and (7a). If we were to capture the difference between these sentences and at the same time retain the hypothesis that transformations do not alter the meaning, the given sentences need to be derived from two different deep structures. We need to ask ourselves here, where to look for this difference: as examples (6a–c) and (7a–c) indicate the distinction between active and passive constructions is not relevant.[8]

(6) (a) Many men read few books.
    (b) Many are the men who read few books.
    (c) There are many men who read few books.

---

7   See esp. Lakoff (1970) and Lakoff, op. cit. in fn. 4 and other writings quoted there.
8   As it was shown by V. Mathesius (1924), the difference between the active and the passive is secondary and serves for the purpose of information structure. There are a number of examples of a significant semantic difference between sentences with word-order variation; it seems, though, that their common feature is the presence of two different quantifiers in the sentence or a possible co-occurrence of quantifiers and negation. Cf. examples given by P. Sgall (1967; 1970), which show that it often does not even have to be a clear quantification: *Na Moravě žijí Češi – Češi žijí na Moravě* [lit. In Moravia live Czechs – Czechs live in Moravia]; *Zdes' kurit' – Kurit' zdes', Kushajt'e za stolom – Za stolom kushajt'e* [lit. Eat at the table – At the table you should eat]. Also cf. Sgall's paper quoted in fn. 1.

(7) (a) Few books are read by many men.
    (b) Few are the books that many men read.
    (c) There are few books that many men read.

Lakoff[9] considers possibilities (a), (b) and (c) to be synonymous and suggests capturing the syntactical differences between (6) and (7) on the basis of different positions of the quantifiers in the hierarchy of the underlying structures for both of the two sentences (Fig. 1 for sentences (6a–c) and Fig. 2 for sentences (7a–c)). Lakoff introduces the global rules in order to prevent the possibility of deriving from a single deep structure two sentences which are not synonymous. The rule is defined as a set of conditions, which the derivation has to fulfil, in order to get a grammatically correct sentence. (The conditions relate to the relationships between the order of quantifiers in the surface phrase marker and which quantifier "commands"[10] the other in the deep and surface structure.)

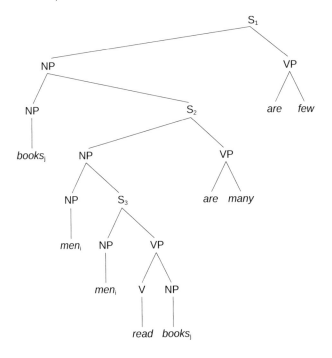

Figure 2

---

9   See esp. Lakoff (1965) and the formulation of global rules in Lakoff (1970).

10 We use the term *command* as introduced by Langacker (1969): The node A commands the node B if (1) neither A or B mutually dominate each other, and (2) the node S (i.e. the node for the sentence), which is the closest dominating node for the node A, at the same time dominates the node B. So, e.g., in Fig. 1 the quantifier *many* commands the quantifier *few* (node S1 most closely dominates the quantifier *many*, and also dominates the quantifier *few*) and not the other way round (node S2, which most closely dominant over the quantifier *few*, is not dominant over the quantifier *many*). In Fig. 2 the situation is the opposite: the quantifier *few* commands the quantifier *many* (node S1 dominates both the quantifiers *few* and *many*).

According to Lakoff, this limitation is valid not only for the active and passive constructions with two quantifiers, but also in the case of different order of verb modifications:

(8) John talked to few girls about many problems.
(9) John talked about many problems to few girls.

Based on Lakoff's reflections leading to the definition of global rules, we can see the importance of the order of quantifiers in the surface structure of the sentence, specifically the order of nominal groups modified by quantifiers. The sentences above and the following examples with negation also show that the given syntactic differences undeniably have something in common with the scope of the quantifiers (operators) as used by logicians. This is clear from examples (10) and (12) below:

(10) Many arrows didn't hit the target.
(11) Not many arrows hit the target.
(12) The target wasn't hit by many arrows.

The sentence (10) can be paraphrased as "About many arrows it is not true that they hit the target," while the paraphrase of (11) and (12) is "It is not true that many arrows hit the target".

In sentences (11) and (12) the scope of the negation includes also the quantified nominal groups *many arrows*; in sentence (10), this nominal group is outside the scope of negation. For the above three examples Lakoff suggests two underlying phrase markers in such a way that would show that sentence (10) is distinct in its meaning from sentences (11) and (12), which are synonymous.[11] Moreover, the global rule (which is applicable both for quantifiers and negation) makes sure that sentences that are not synonymous are not derived from a single phrase marker.

To counter Lakoff's approach it can be also pointed out[12] that an introduction of highly abstract underlying structures – which Lakoff based on the hypothesis that only the deep structure is significant for semantic interpretation – carries with it a number of transformational rules, with which these deep structures, considerably removed from the syntactical, as well as semantic (according to Dokulil and Daneš)[13] sentence structure have to be transfered to the surface structure. These rules are not otherwise syntactically motivated. As a result, the global rules have to be overly general and broad, and so the systems which utilise them are no longer linguistically interesting.

3. From the comments made above, it is clear that Lakoff's approach is not really appropriate. The hypothesis that transformations do not change the meaning is so

---

11   Lakoff's analysis is actually a response to Jackendoff's proposal to take into account the order of elements in the surface structure in a semantic interpretation (see e.g. Jackendoff 1969). Jackendoff's proposal is supported by Chomsky with additional arguments in Chomsky (1971) and (1972).

12   Cf. Chomsky (1972, p. 192).

13   See Daneš and Dokulil (1958). More recently see esp. Daneš (1968).

interesting[14], though, that it is certainly worth it to look for a place where the TFA of a sentence can fit in. As has been shown, the phenomena mentioned can be described, under certain conditions, within transformational grammar,[15] given the assumption that it is possible to empirically capture the informational structure with the help of Firbas' hierarchy of communicative dynamism.[16] The focus would then be considered to be one of the parts of the semantic representation (deep structure), which contains a lexical unit with the highest level of communicative dynamism. The semantic representation would then, beside others, capture the gradation of communicative dynamism (such as the arrangement of elements of semantic representation from left to right) and the differences between the different types of verb modification (as a part of complex symbols, if we use the phrase structure grammar terminology, or as part of the value of nodes or edges on the basis of e.g. dependency grammar).

This approach allows us to explain certain previously unclear phenomena in an interesting way. Fillmore (1970), for example, provides a number of quadruples of sentences, which display certain previously unexplained distinctions; as, for example, in the following:

(13) (a) An oak developed out of every acorn.
  (b) Every acorn developed into an oak.
  (c) Every oak developed out of an acorn.
  (d) An acorn developed into every oak.

While it is possible to consider sentence (13b) as a paraphrase of sentence (13a), we cannot say the same about the relationship between sentences (13d) and (13c), even though formally they are similar counterparts: the verb *develop out of* is replaced by the verb *develop into* and the object nominal phrase becomes the subject and vice versa. If we take a closer look at these sentences, though, we see that while in the first pair the object phrase in sentence (a) is modified by the pronoun *every* (which is a general quantifier), in the second pair the object phrase is modified by an indefinite article in sentence (c). We can consider the verb pair *develop out of* - *develop into* (similar to *make out of* - *make into* etc.) as the inverse alternative of the same verb; the choice of one or the other alternative depends (similarly to the choice of active or passive verb form in English) primarily on the communication relevance of the verb modification in the given communicative situation. It is possible to show that the primary form is the form *develop out of*. The inverse alternative *develop into* (just as the passive) allows the con-

---

14   This issue has been recently analysed with interesting and convincing arguments in Hall-Partee (1971).
15   See esp. P. Sgall's writings quoted in fn. 1 and 8 and Sgall (1972c).
16   Firbas (1964) defines the concept of communicative dynamism as "the extent to which the sentence element contributes to the development of the communication, to which it 'pushes the communication forward', as it were" (p. 270). In his conception of information structure, it is not merely a topic-focus dichotomy (or in other terminology theme-rheme), but a whole scale, which is primarily conditioned by the semantic structure of the sentence. Secondarily, though, this distribution of degrees is changed in cases of a marked contextual dependence ‚ i.e. when a unit that has a higher degree of communicative dynamism was mentioned in the preceding context.

textually bound verb modification (*every acorn* in sentence (a) and *an acorn* in sentence (c)), as communicatively the least contextually bound element, to stand at the beginning of the sentence, even when originally it is not the subject. Nothing prevents the pronoun *every* to move in this way: We can consider this pronoun to be a member of certain types of quantifiers (just as *all, the* and so on), which can modify contextually dependent elements (cf. the acceptability of sentence (b)). The use of the indefinite article in itself signals that the element it modifies is not contextually bound. But if the contextual boundness of the element is already emphasised by e.g. the use of the passive form of the verb, then the sentence is usually evaluated as unacceptable since the subject is the nominal group with the indefinite article, if this phrase is not the carrier of the intonation centre of the sentence (i.e. the focus). The use of an indefinite article in the thematic part of the sentence is limited to a specific usage of the indefinite article, as for example in its generic meaning (*A lion growls. Lions growl.*[17]) or its meaning "one of the" (*A box is empty. = One of the boxes is empty.*[18]), or at the beginning of the text (discourse). Using these considerations we can also explain Fillmore's evaluation of sentence (13d) as unacceptable and sentence (13a) as acceptable.[19] The indefinite article in sentence (13a) certainly signals contextual non-boundness of the nominal group in the subject (so obviously, in fact, that it is not necessary to underline it with a stress on this phrase), so the phrase *an oak* is the focus (with indefinite meaning, and contextually non-bound). Such an explanation is not acceptable for sentence (13d); there, the nominal group with the indefinite article is at the beginning of the sentence, where the inverse alternative of the verb (*develop into*) is used similarly to the passive. It is therefore in a strong thematic position, in which the indefinite article can modify the nominal phrase only in the specific meanings mentioned above – the meaning of the sentence (13d) does not reflect this usage of the indefinite article.[20]

4. The points discussed above are connected to a number of other issues, such as e.g. the question of syntactical function of the quantifiers and negation (cf. above in Sect. 2 the analysis of ex. (10) through (12)) or the question of different understandings of the concept of presupposition, which is very common in current linguistics research.

The term and notion of *presupposition* was taken from logic. The British philosopher Sir Peter Frederick Strawson provides the most in-depth explanation the concept.[21] He describes a difference between two logical relations – the relation of implication and the relation of presupposition. An example of the former notion is the following pair of sentences.

---

17   Cf. Dahl (1969, p. 32).
18   Cf. Chafe (1970, p. 213).
19   Nowhere does Fillmore mention what intonation and emphasis relations he expects in these sentences. Which is why in the possible explanation above, we consider such a situation that would certainly be least striking (unmarked) for a native speaker.
20   For explanation see Sgall (1972b), where the author also discusses other related issues.
21   Strawson (1952).

(14) Tom is a younger son.

(15) Tom has a brother.

Statement (15) is entailed by statement (14) in the sense that the truth value of statement (15) is a necessary condition for sentence (14) to be true – only if Tom has a brother can he be a younger son.

(16) All John's children are asleep.

(17) John has children.

In the above pair, statement (16) presupposes statement (17) in the sense that the truth value of statement (17) is a condition of truthfulness or falsehood (i.e. meaning-fulness) of statement 16) – only if John has children can statement (16) or its negation be true.

We believe that the term *presupposition* is used in linguistic writings for at least three kinds of phenomena.[22] The first type concerns Chomsky's understanding of pre-supposition; in the TFA terminology it is roughly identical with the term "theme" or the "topic of the sentence" in the sense of what is being talked about. A question arises whether it is possible to say, based on the study of the character of the presuppositions of the pair of sentences such as (18) and (19) (which differ in that in sentence (18) the scale of communicative dynamism is in agreement with the semantic structure of the sentence and in sentence (19) that is not the case), that the second of the two examples is connected with more specific presuppositions, or that the number of pre-suppositions in this case is increasing.[23]

(18) John writes poetry.

(19) Poetry is written by John.

We suppose that sentence (19) can be connected to a specific presupposition (*Some-body*) *writes poetry*, while sentence (18) does not have any similar specific presupposi-tion (e.g. *John writes (something)*).

The second type of presuppositions, in a certain sense also connected with TFA, can be called *referential presuppositions*. James D. McCawley[24] explores the relationship

---

22   Cf. also Sgall and Hajičová (1970) and Hajičová (1972). Many authors who use the term *presuppositions* are aware of these distinctions and try to differentiate their conception by classifying presuppositions into different types. Ö. Dahl differentiates between existential and factual presupposition and presupposition of given selective attributes (cf. Dahl 1970); E. L. Keenan (1971) distinguishes logical and pragmatic presuppositions (Keenan 1971). A systematic classification of phenomena in this sphere based on the logical relations between so-called logical forms (basically abstract semantic representations) and logical forms and natural language sentences is covered in Lakoff and Railton (1970). However, it is not always possible to draw a clear borderline; a telling example is Lakoff's discussion about Chomsky's focus (op. cit. in fn. 4) where the author, without even being aware of it, uses the term *presuppose* twice in one sentence, both times with a different meaning – first in the sense of Chomsky's presupposition and once to mean what we call here *referential presuppositions*.

23   Cf. Kiefer (1970).

24   McCawley (1970b).

between proposition in logic and the representation of the meaning of a sentence and comes to the conclusion (p. 173) that it is necessary to distinguish between two levels of the semantic representation: one, which determines the properties the speaker assumes to characterise the notions included in what he or she is saying, and second, which shapes the utterance itself (in an indicative sentence), i.e. the meaning of the utterance. According to McCawley, nominal groups, which themselves represent variables inserted into their own propositions, have the first function, similar to the function of presupposition (even though the author does not use this term): so, e.g. sentence (20) would be represented by the tree in Fig. 3.

(20) The man killed the woman.

The negation (*The man didn't kill the woman*), McCawley claims, only contradicts the proposition proper.

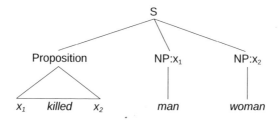

Figure 3

In his conception of information structure Dahl follows McCawley's analysis: according to him, the theme of the sentence usually contains one or more "descriptions of nominal groups" (NP: x_i), while proposition is usually in the focus.[25]

This approach to the notion of presupposition is primarily concerned with the syntactical structure of the sentence; Fillmore's conception of presuppositions[26] is somewhat analogous to this approach in the domain of lexical meanings. Fillmore draws a clear distinction between the meaning of the word and its presuppositions. So, for example, if the speaker utters a command (21), he or she supposes, among other things, that the door is closed, that the recipient can follow this command (is in the same room etc.), and so on. These presuppositions (of the verb *open*) will remain untouched, according to Fillmore, even in the case when the sentence is negated: it is possible to

---

25   See Ö. Dahl, op. cit. in fn. 17. Dahl works within an approach close to generative semantics and proposes to capture the information structure already in the base component of generative transformational grammar, specifying the topic of the sentence as that part of the linear semantic representation that is to the left of the main symbol of implication (in his definition every predication is basically an implication; so, for example, he interprets the sentence *Lions growl* as *If X is a lion, then x growls*). This work so far provides only a brief outline of the general approach demonstrated on examples of a certain type (cleft sentences, existential sentences, sentences with an emphasis). The approach itself is interesting and useful, there can be some reservations, though, about the individual points of the elaboration and the interpretation of the individual examples or phenomena (cf. Firbas and Pala 1971 and Růžička 1970).

26   Cf. op. cit. in fn. 3 and numerous other writings of the same author, such as e.g. Fillmore (1968; 1969; 1970).

utter the command (22) with the same assumptions. The meaning proper of the verb is affected in the case of negation.

(21) Open the door.
(22) Don't open the door.

Under the same type the presuppositions there can be included also those connected to modifications of different classes of verbs. P. and C. Kiparski[27] classify verbs into *factive* and *non-factive* according to whether the modification of these verbs (expressed by a dependent clause, an infinitive construction or participial structure) expresses a true reality. With factive verbs, their modifications express a true reality and act as presuppositions: If the sentence (23a) is true, sentence (23c), which is its presupposition, is also true. When negated (example (23b)), the presupposition, i.e. sentence (23c), is not affected.

(23) (a) I regret that it is raining.
     (b) I don't regret that it is raining.
     (c) It is raining.

The situation is different with non-factive verbs: If sentence (24a) is contradicted, then what is expressed with the verb modification, i.e. sentence (24c), is also contradicted. Sentence (24c) then is not a presupposition of sentence (24a), but it is a part of the assertion of this sentence.

(24) (a) It is true that John is ill.
     (b) It is not true that John is ill.
     (c) John is ill.

Kartunnen[28] explores these relations in more detail and comes up with a more detailed classification of verbs based on which assumptions about truth or falsity of what is being expressed by the verb modification (whether in a positive statement or in a negation of the given verb) it is connected. J. L. Morgan[29] looks at the more complex compound sentences and comes up with the necessity to differentiate in which context the verb is used: He distinguishes a group of so-called "world-creating verbs" (e.g. *to dream*), whose presuppositions are valid for everything that is within the "reach" of these verbs (reach is understood as roughly all the sentences that directly or indirectly depend on the given verb). So, for example, the verb *realize* is a factive verb and its presupposition is that the modification expresses a true reality (sentence (25b) assumes the truth of the sentence (25a)).

27 P. and C. Kiparski (1970).
28 Karttunen (1970; 1971c). For the distinction between factive and non-factive verbs compare also the latest articles by I. Poldauf (Poldauf, 1972a; 1972b).
29 Morgan (1969). For a discussion on mutual combination and cancellation of presuppositions of this type cf. also Lakoff (in prep.).

(25) (a) Harry was the thief.
　　　(b) I realized that Harry was the thief.
　　　(c) I dreamed I realized that Harry was the thief.

The issues of selectional restrictions also fall into the same domain. Chomsky introduced selectional restrictions as syntactical features of lexical units, in which two lexical units must agree (e.g. verb with the substantive). McCawley rejects this view and adds that it is not a matter of syntactical distinction, but of semantic features.[30] He also suggests to treat these features as presuppositions and to distinguish them from the meaning of the sentence itself: This would explain why sentences (26) and (27) are not paraphrases of each other, since sentence (26) simply states that a certain person hurt herself, while sentence (27) also makes clear that this person was a woman. The "female" feature is one of the presuppositions of sentence (26) while it belongs to the meaning of sentence (27).[31]

(26) My neighbour hurt herself.
(27) My neighbour is a woman and has suffered an injury.

Similarly to the way we have discussed the meaning and the presuppositions of a lexical morpheme, it is also possible to talk about presuppositions of grammatical morphemes, e.g. morphemes of verb tenses. This concerns Chomsky's and McCawley's interpretation[32] of the use of the present perfect in English in sentences like (28) and their explanation why the perfect cannot be used in sentence (29).

(28) Princeton has been visited by Einstein.
(29) *Einstein has visited Princeton.

Chomsky's original interpretation was that the surface subject of the sentence has to refer to something that still exists. From McCawley's analysis and other examples he provides, it becomes clear that this is not the case of a presupposition connected with the surface subject, but, in fact, with the topic of the sentence. (When the same sentences are uttered with a different intonation in a way that the original focus is thematised, then the presupposition concerns what is in the predicate: Sentence (29) would be, given this formulation, grammatically correct if the intonation centre was on the word *Einstein*).

If we were to summarise this brief overview,[33] we could say that the common features of the different types of presuppositions are (a) that there is a distinction be-

---

30　He agrees on this with Fodor and Katz, who introduce selectional features in the semantic component of language.
31　Kuroda (1969) and Dahl (op. cit. in fn. 22) tend to agree with this opinion.
32　See Chomsky (1971) and McCawley (1971).
33　We approached here only one problem – questions of how the concept of presupposition is understood by different authors. Another important issue, which we do not have space to discuss here, is the incorporation of presuppositions of different types into the description of language.

tween what is being asserted by the use of the given expression and what is being presupposed, and (b) the relation between the given statement and negation is used as a test (i.e. operational definition). The presupposition, unlike the meaning, is not affected by negation. The meaning, on the other hand, is denied by the negation of the sentence. Yet examples like (30) and its negation (31) show that there are indeed cases that belong to a third kind: Some part of the sentence is not even denied by negation (i.e. it is not the meaning), but neither does it remain valid (i.e. it is not the presupposition).[34] Under negation we are then concerned with the possibility of what was true in the affirmative sentence: It is not possible to say about sentence (31) that it implies whether someone came or did not come, the arrival could have happened but did not necessarily happen. Yet if the dependent clause (example (32)) takes the position of the topic, then the event expressed by this dependent clause is evidently not affected by the negation, since it is assumed that it has actually happened (as in the affirmative sentence).

(30) He was happy that they came. [*Byl nadšen tím, že přijeli.*]
(31) He was not happy that they came. [*Nebyl nadšen tím, že přijeli.*]
(32) The fact that they came did not make him happy. [*Tím, že přijeli, nebyl nadšen.*]

One of the possible explanations can be found in the TFA aspect and its capturing in the semantic representation, as we outlined in Section 3. In sentence (32) the verb of the dependent clause is in the topic of the sentence and as such it is "presupposed," that is unaffected by negation. In (31), the dependent clause is in the focus of the statement and under negation, there remains only the possibility of what was true in the affirmative sentence.[35] However, it is necessary to look more closely at what other factors are significant here – if, for example, the situation is different according to different levels of condensations.[36] In the closest connection, apparently, this kind of element is not affected by negation (the argument it expresses is a "referential" type of presupposition), while in a more loosely structured statement (as e.g. in some types of dependent clauses) it is a type of potential mode of meaning.

Examples (31) and (32) once again show that the topic of a statement behaves differently than its focus and that the position of the sentence element in the topic or in the focus has a semantic relevance. Other evidence supporting the claim that informa-

---

34 For the necessity to distinguish next to meaning proper and presuppositions also a third basic type of semantic phenomena (which we called *allegation*) cf. Hajičová (1971).

35 This documents that issues of language negation and its semantic scope have to explored in close connection with information structure (TFA); this approach is applied in Czechoslovak linguistics in many classical works on negation. To mention just some of the most recent of them, these issues are discussed in Vachek (1939, 1974); cf. also Daneš 1954 and Křížková (1968; 1969) about negation in Slavonic languages. For a detailed overview of these opinions and a comparison with the transformationalist perspective cf. Hajičová 1972b, chapters 5 and 6).

36 For the term "condensations" cf. e.g. Vachek (1955, pp. 63–77; 1961, p. 9f). In literature, the term "depredication" or "nominalisation" is sometimes used to show the differences between a statement with different syntactical tightness (independent clause – dependent clause – nominal clause).

tion structure is connected with the meaning, are the examples provided by Lakoff[37] as interesting, but not yet explained distinctions. Thus e.g. the sentence (35), derived by a coordination of sentences (33) and (34), can be interpreted as "each one of them saw some explosion, but each one could have seen a different one," while a similar coordination of passive constructions (36) and (37) can be paraphrased only as "both saw the same explosion" (38).

(33) John saw an explosion.
(34) Max saw an explosion.
(35) John and Max saw an explosion.
(36) An explosion was seen by John.
(37) An explosion was seen by Max.
(38) An explosion was seen by John and Max.[38]

If we accept the above evaluation of the function of the passive construction and the necessity of interpreting the nominal group expanded by an indefinite article in the position of the topic of the sentence as contextually bound (e.g. in the sense "one of the"), then the explanation of the difference in the meaning of sentences (35) and (38) is clear enough.

5. We believe that given the emphasis placed on questions connected with TFA in the current transformationalist discussions – to whose position and explanation (although from a different perspective) Czechoslovak linguists have contributed significantly – these issues are today critical to a great number of aspects of further development of linguistic theory. It is then most welcome that these issues are being considered by various theories of language description. It will certainly be useful to follow these developments and compare and critically evaluate the results. This will probably also lead to a better insight into such problems as comparison and evaluation of different types of grammars (phrasal and dependency, transformational and stratificational etc.); based on the current state of knowledge, we can say that in the given field there appear, above all, new arguments supporting dependency grammar as the basic component of generative description, possibly even for the generative (i.e. stratificational) approach to semantics as opposed to the interpretive one. In both cases it would mean a convergence of transformational grammar with earlier as well as more recent findings of European linguistics.

---

37 Lakoff (1970).
38 For an interpretation of these sentences the placement of intonation centre is important (cf. fn. 5). I. Poldauf has brought it my attention that if we pronounce the sentence (38) with the intonation pitch on the word *explosion*, then it is possible to interpret this sentence in the same way as the sentence (35). This favours our hypothesis that this is not a question of a semantic distinction of the given word order (or the use of a passive construction), but of information structure of the sentence (if the word *explosion* in example (38) is the carrier of the intonation centre, then it becomes the focus of the statement).

A NOTE ON THE ORDER OF CONSTITUENTS IN RELATION TO THE PRINCIPLES OF GB THEORY

1. The order of major constituents seems still to lie beyond the main concerns of most generative grammarians, though in a certain sense this issue played a most important role in the split of the transformational grammar in the late sixties into interpretative and generative semantics (cf. Chomsky 1968, Lakoff 1969) and though also in the most recent development of Chomskyan government-binding theory (GB) it cannot be left out without mentioning (cf. Chomsky 1982: 8, 27 f, 31, 34, 39, 93ff, 121, 128, 133, to quote only the most relevant places). The present note is intended to propose a possible account of the collection of empirical phenomena closely related to the order of constituents within the rule system and the subsystems of principles as advocated recently by the GB. Not being an expert in GB (the obstacles being given not only by geographical distance, but mainly by the linguistic background), I cannot give any theory internal arguments and I do not want to make any claims of contributing to the theory as such. However, having the privilege to be a disciple of Petr Sgall, who was the first to introduce a systematic account of these issues into a formal description of language without depriving it of their empirical complexity and semantic far-reachedness (cf. e.g. Sgall 1967), I feel obliged to examine the feasibility of conciliating his insights with other prominent generative theories.

    2. Taking for granted for the purpose of our present discussion that

(i) universal grammar consists of interacting subsystems, which, from one point of view, are the various components of *the rule system of grammar*, and, from another, *the subsystems of "principles"* (Chomsky 1982: 5),

(ii) the components of the rule system are the base, a transformational component (transforming D-structures into S-structures), a LF-component (deriving logical forms from S-structures) and a PF-component (transforming S-structures into phonetic forms of sentences),

our task can be formulated as follows:

(1) to summarize first the hypotheses that we feel to be relevant for the order of constituents;

(2) to propose at which level of the general scheme of the rule system the order of constituents should be assigned;

(3) to look for a possible "division of labour" between the rule system and the subsystems of principles to account in an adequate way for the issues connected with the order of constituents.[1]

3. A long-term empirical investigation by linguists of most different orientation in general and Sgall's efforts to arrive at a systematic account of the issues under discussion within a specific framework of generative description of language (functional generative description, FGD) in particular have led to the following substantial assumptions (see Sgall, Hajičová and Panevová, in press, esp. Chapter 3):

(a) There is an intrinsic (basic) ordering of the types of complementations of verbs (arguments in a broader sense of the term, or ϑ-roles, see below) given by the grammar of a particular language, which is observed in the unmarked cases, i.e. in case the given complementations convey contextually non-bound information (they form the so-called focus of the sentence); in the sequel, we will refer to this basic ordering by the term *systemic ordering (SO)*.[2]

(b) For each sentence there is an order of its constituents that corresponds to the degrees of *communicative dynamism* (CD); as mentioned in (a), CD coincides with SO in the focus part of the sentence, while in the topic part (contextually bound items; roughly speaking, that part that renders what is the sentence about), CD is given by the degrees of salience of the constituents concerned and by other factors concerning the structure of the discourse; CD is semantically relevant (cf. the distinction in truth conditions between (1) and (2)) and in the surface shape of the sentence the same CD may be rendered by various means, cf. (3)(a) through (c) for the CD *Mary – flower – John*, which differs in its presuppositions from e.g. *John gave Mary a FLOWER* in a similar way as *One of the boys came LATE* differs from *(It was) a BOY (who) came late*. The CD in (4)(a) through (c) is again identical, differing from that of (5) and (6) in an analogous way. Here, as well as in the sequel, the capitals denote the bearer of the intonation centre.

(1) Everybody in this room speaks two LANGUAGES.
(2) Two languages are spoken by everybody in this ROOM.
(3) (a) Mary was given a flower by JOHN.
    (b) It was JOHN who gave Mary a flower.
    (c) JOHN gave Mary a flower.

---

1   A more detailed and a more general account of some of these points is presented in Hajičová and Sgall (in press).
2   The empirical research based on a contrastive study of Slavic languages, English and German has led to the following specification of SO for the main ϑ-roles in English: Actor – Addressee – Objective (Patient) – Instrument – From where – Direction – Locative (for a detailed discussion, see already Sgall et al., 1973), The position of the verb is not discussed here; for the purposes of this paper, the verb can be assumed to precede its ϑ-roles under SO.

(4) (a) Last year John came to Stanford from CAMBRIDGE.
(b) Last year John came from CAMBRIDGE to Stanford.
(c) John came from CAMBRIDGE to Stanford last year.
(5) Last year John came from Cambridge to STANFORD.
(6) John came from Cambridge to Stanford last YEAR.

In addition to the difference in presuppositions it should also to be noted that these sentences differ in their potential to answer particular questions; the three sentences in (4) all can answer the question *From where did John come to Stanford last year?*, whereas (5) is rather a full (redundant) answer to *Where did come from Cambridge last year?* and (6) can answer *When did John come from Cambridge to Stanford?* (Similarly, the three sentences in (3) all can answer a question for the Actor, in contrast to *John gave Mary a FLOWER*, which answers a question for the Objective).

(c) Every sentence splits into its *topic* (conveying the contextually bound information, specifying those items that the speaker mentions to bring them into the foreground so that the hearer may identify them in his stock of knowledge to be able to modify them) and its *focus*;[3] the dichotomy of topic and focus is decisive for the assignment of the semantic scope of negation, in other words, the dichotomy is responsible for some of the presuppositions of the sentence (in the given reading).[4]

4. When we try to locate the account of the order of constituents in a specific place of the rule system and the system of principles, we must emphasize one point: Since the underlying (deep) order, which may differ from the order of constituents of the phonetic form, has its consequences for the semantic interpretation of the sentence, it follows that this order should be at the disposal of the LF-component. At the same time, as we have illustrated by (3), the phonemic component (now called by Chomsky the phonetic form component) may assign to a given order of constituents different phonetic forms (differing in the surface order of constituents, or in a combination of some of these). Thus the points in the rule system that are possible candidates for the representation of the order of constituents are the D-structure and the S-structure.

There are two alternatives:

(i) Taking into account the assumptions (a) and (b) in Sect. 3, we can say that SO should be represented in the D-structure, while CD should belong to the S-structure. Since SO is specified in terms of types of complementations of verbs, which more or less correspond to ϑ-roles, the D-structure seems to be an appropriate place for accounting for (a). D-structures are mapped to S-structures by the rule "Move-α"; perhaps this rule could be formulated in such a way that it would rearrange the constituents according to their degrees of CD; the traces left behind the shifted constituents would not then be assigned any position in the hierarchy of CD.

3   We leave aside for the purpose of this paper the embedded elements, which can belong to the topic even if contextually non-bound, and to the focus, even if contextually bound, cf. e.g. *best* and *your*, respectively in *The dress I like best was made by your mother*.

4   As for the placement of the boundary between topic and focus, most of our examples are ambiguous.

(ii) An alternative solution would be to let the base generate directly the order of constituents coinciding with the CD of the constituents of the sentence generated. When characterizing the D-structures, Chomsky (1982: 39) states that it is the representation of ϑ-roles assignment and has also the properties that follow from X-bar theory and from parameters of the base in a particular language among which he mentions also the ordering of major constituents. Under this approach, the role of the "Move-α" rule would be considerably reduced in comparison with the role this rule would play in alternative (i).

As example (4) above illustrates, the rule "Move-α" should be adjusted in order to be applicable to one or more elements of the topic (contextually bound items) to transfer them to the end of the sentence. While in (4)(a) this optional rule is not applied (CD coincides with the surface word order), in (b) it is applied to *to Stanford,* and in (c) first to *to Stanford* and then to *last year.* The moved items do not acquire additional stress, so that the intonation centre is assigned (by phonemic rules) to the item that is marked as most dynamic (i.e. occupies the rightmost position in the D-structure). It is an open question whether with this approach also the three variants of (4) can be handled by rules deriving S-structures from D-structures.

5. If we accept the position (ii), taking D-structures as the direct representation of CD, it remains to examine the assumptions (a) to (c) from the viewpoint of the interplay of principles rules, and lexical conditioning.

It seems possible to add to the theory the following subsystem of principles:

(a) The basic (unmarked) ordering of ϑ-roles (SO) can be determined by lexical means, in a way similar to what Chomsky calls "projection principle": in the lexical entries of the base component not only the ϑ-roles possible (optional) and necessary (obligatory) as complementations of the given lexical item are specified, but also their SO. If the hypothesis that SO is identical for different "frames" (subcategorization properties of different lexical items as for their ϑ-roles) concerning the same word class is found to be plausible for the given language, then the "frames" can contain just the numerical values which can be assigned to ϑ-roles according to their position under SO. This approach has been formally elaborated in Hajičová and Sgall (1980) and Plátek, Sgall and Sgall (1984); in the latter paper a framework is presented that covers also the main features of the interplay of the ϑ-roles assignment and the syntactic relations of coordination and apposition.

(b) A second principle can state that whenever a D-structure contains two items A and B, where SO (A, B), but CD (B, A), then B is contextually bound, i.e. belongs to the topic (here X(Y, Z) is read "Y precedes Z under X").

Recalling our examples from Sect. 3, *John* in (3)(a) through (c) is assigned the ϑ-role Actor, *Mary* is assigned the role Addressee; in the SO of English Actor precedes Addressee, while in the CD in (3)(a) through (c) Addressee precedes Actor. Thus, the sentences say something about the Addressee as (a part of) the topic; *Mary* is a contextually bound element of the sentence referring to a person who belongs (at the time point of utterance of the sentence) to the activated part of the knowledge shared by the speaker and by the hearer.[5]

(c) In a similar vein, on the basis of SO and CD one can specify what is the topic and what is the focus of the given D-structure; for the tectogrammatical (underlying) representations as defined in the functional generative description (oriented rooted trees) this was done by Sgall (1979). The corresponding principle can be so formulated that at least one element of the subset consisting of the verb[6] and the constituents assigned the 9-roles determined by the verb according to (A) – including the optional adverbials of all kinds – is contextually non-bound; the contextually non-bound elements of the mentioned set constitute the focus of the sentence (together with the embedded items belonging to them). Thus every sentence contains a focus, whereas the presence of a topic is optional, the thetic judgements being the prototypical cases of topicless D-structures.

6. The importance of the inclusion of a description of such phenomena as listed above into general linguistic theory can be now illustrated more explicitly, e.g. on the difference in meaning of (7)(a) and (7)(b), capitals again denoting the intonation centre.

(7) (a) Staff is allowed behind this COUNTER.
    (b) STAFF is allowed behind this counter.

In (7)(a) one speaks about the staff, or, perhaps more probably, about the rights of the staff, and states that (one of) the right(s) is to be behind the particular counter; more technically speaking, *staff*, and, on a preferred reading also the verb belong to the topic, whereas the adverbial constitutes the focus.[7] In contrast, (7)(b) speaks about that particular counter (topic) and states that the persons who are allowed to step there are the staff. Note that the two sentences differ (at least on their preferred readings) in the truth conditions: If I am a member of the staff, I should be behind the counter (rather than somewhere else), if I receive and accept the message expressed by (7)(a), which is not the case with (7)(b).

As for the 9-roles in both (a) and (b), *staff* is assigned the role of Objective, *behind the counter* the role of Location (it is not decisive for our point whether there is no Actor role assigned, or whether the role of a General Actor is assumed to be present). In the SO of English, Objective precedes Locative; (7)(a) and (b) differ in their CD, which in (a) is in accordance with SO, while in (b) the CD is Locative – Objective. Thus for (7)(b), there is only one reading, namely that having the Locative and the verb as contextually

5   For the notion of the stock of shared knowledge and the hierarchy of activation of its elements, see Hajičová and Vrbová (1992) and more recently Sgall et al. (in press).

6   Auxiliary verbs as well as prepositions and conjunctions are assigned no 9-roles and no positions under SO or CD.

7   There is also a topicless D-structure underlying (7)(a), which is rather marginal, since staff, as a definite NP in the subject position, not carrying the intonation centre, is understood, with a high preference, as contextually bound ("given").

bound. In (7)(a), the Locative is the last (most dynamic) item of the D-structure and thus is contextually non-bound according to the principle (C) (i.e. under the natural assumption that there must be at least one non-bound item, if the sentence is to bring some "new" information); the Objective is contextually bound, and so is the verb, in one of the two D-structures; such an ambiguity of the appurtenance of the verb to the topic or to the focus is a common phenomenon.

POSSIBILITIES AND LIMITS OF OPTIMALITY IN TOPIC-FOCUS ARTICULATION

1. INTRODUCTION

Optimality theory (OT, Prince and Smolensky 1993) has attracted serious attention among linguists of different theoretical streams and of different linguistic interests, ranging from phonology and morphology (in the earlier stages of its elaboration) through syntax (see e.g. several papers in Barbosa et al. 1998, Legendre, Grimshaw and Vikner eds., in press), up to semantics (see e.g. Hendriks and de Hoop, forthcoming, de Hoop and de Swart 1999, and the papers from the conference on OT and semantics in Utrecht, January 2000, which are to be published in a special issue of the Journal of Semantics). The purpose of the present contribution is to examine how the OT framework, based on ranking of constraints, can be used for the description of the information structure of the sentence. We examine and evaluate *two alternatives* of an incorporation into the OT scenario of the empirical and theoretical findings on *topic-focus articulation* (TFA, see Sgall et al. 1973, 1986, Hajičová et al, 1998) of the sentence in general, and for *Czech* in particular. In conclusion, we attempt to summarize in which points the OT framework and the TFA approach may contribute to each other.

2. "CLASSICAL" OT APPROACH TO INFORMATION STRUCTURE

A first attempt at a systematic analysis of the information structure of the sentence using the framework of OT can be found in Choi (1996), whose theoretical framework is the Lexical-Functional Grammar of Bresnan (Bresnan 1978). She uses as her empirical material German and Korean. Choi works with a canonical order (unmarked, contextually neutral order) of the functional roles (cf. the Praguian notion of systemic ordering in Sgall et al. 1986, and the related notions of "functional hierarchy" of grammatical categories of Bresnan and others, of *accessibility hierarchy* of Keenan and Comrie, or the *hierarchy of thematic roles* with Kiparsky, Bresnan and others) and attempts to capture the relation between the information structure and the word order. In her treatment of information structure she follows E. Vallduví (1992), who works with two parts of the so-called *ground*: namely *link* (Choi's *topic*) and *tail*, which can be compared with the Praguian distinction of topic proper and the rest of topic. In addition, Choi distinguishes two kinds of focus: contrastive and completive (presentational). Her evaluation procedure is based on two features: [NEW] (new information) and [PROM] (prominence, contrast) and with the combination of two values for each of them, see Figure 1.

	+Prom	**−Prom**
−New	topic	tail
+New	contrastive focus	completive focus

Figure 1

Choi illustrates her distinction between contrastive and completive focus by the following German examples (capitals denote the position of the main pitch accent):

(1) *(Was ist passiert?) Ich glaube, daß Hans dem Schüler das BUCH gegeben hat.*
(2) *(Was hat Hans dem Schiller gegeben? die Zeitung?) Ich glaube, daß Hans das BUCH dem Schüler gegeben hat (nicht die ZEITUNG).*

In both (1) and (2), *das Buch* is assigned the feature +New, but in (1) there is a completive focus, which has the feature -Prom and in (2) the focus is contrastive, with the feature +Prom.

Choi claims that in German embedded clauses, the difference of the two kinds of focus is decisive for the grammaticality of the sentences: while a contrastive focus is placed in the second position in an embedded object ("content") clause (see (3)(a) and (b)), it is not so with a completive focus (according to her opinion, (4) is ungrammatical).[1]

(3) (a) *Ich glaube, daß Hans das BUCH dem Mann gegeben hat, nicht die ZEITUNG.*
    (b) *Ich glaube, daß Hans nur das BUCH dem Mann gegeben hat.*
(4) *(Was ist passiert?) *Ich glaube, daß Hans das BUCH dem Mann gegeben hat.*

It remains an open question (not touched by Choi at all) whether the two kind of focus are distinguished by the character of the pitch accent on the focussed element.

---

1   It is an open question whether the word order of (3)(a) and (3)(b) corresponds to the intuition of all or most German native speakers.

Choi's formulation of the corresponding constraints is based on her assumption that the elements of the ground in German can be scrambled, though topic is moved more easily than the tail, and that only contrastive focus can be moved. The two constraints can then be formulated as follows:

NEW: an element with the feature -New must precede the element with the feature +New

PROM: an element with the feature +Prom must precede the element with the feature -Prom

Another group of constraints concerns the canonical order mentioned above:

CN1: The sentence element with the function of Subject (SUBJ) must be structurally more prominent than other elements (non-SUBJ)

CN2: All elements with the exception of SUBJ must be ordered according to the functional hierarchy, which is specified as follows (the sign < means "before"):

indirect object < direct object < adverbial

The whole procedure of generation based on the OT scenario can be illustrated on one of the German examples given above:

Let us assume that the input of GEN (i.e. the functional structure of the embedded clause to be generated) consists of the predicate *geben* and its arguments *Hans* (SUBJ), *der Schüler* (Indirect Object) and *das Buch* (Direct Object), that the whole content clause is in the focus and that the focus is completive (i.e. all its elements have the features +New and -Prom). The module GEN generates the candidates given in (5):

(5)	PROM	CN1	NEW	CN2
==> Hans dem Schüler das Buch				
Hans das Buch dem Schüler				*
dem Schüler Hans das Buch		*		
das Buch Hans dem Schüler		*		*
dem Schüler das Buch Hans		**		
das Buch dem Schüler Hans		**		*

The constraints are ordered from the strongest (PROM) to the weakest (CN2) and asterisks indicate whether they are violated (two asterisks mean that they are violated twice: e.g. in the fifth and the sixth lines, the subject Hans "jumped" over both indirect object and direct object, in contrast to the third and fourth line, where the subject "jumped" only over the indirect object and the direct object, respectively). The arrow indicates which candidate is chosen as the optimal one.

In this case, the optimal candidate fulfils all the constraints; it is possible to imagine a case where no candidate fulfils all the constraints but where a candidate exists which violates a weaker constraint than other members of the candidate set; this candidate will be supposed to be the "best" candidate. This situation may be illustrated by example (2) above, with a contrastive focus; the corresponding input to GEN is in (6):

(6) *Hans* (–New, +Prom), *dem Schüler* (–New, –Prom), *das Buch* (+New, +Prom)

If we add a prosodic constraint determining that "high pitch accent" can be placed only on the element with +New, the evaluation procedure would then choose the second line as the optimal output even though it violates two constraints: the order of the indirect and the direct object is reversed and the element with the feature –New (*Schüler*) does not precede the element with the feature +New (*Buch*). These two features, however, are weaker than other features that are violated by the other candidates, see the evaluation scheme in (7).

(7)

	PROM	CN1	NEW	CN2
Hans dem Schüler das BUCH	*			
=> Hans das BUCH dem Schüler			*	*
dem Schüler Hans das BUCH	**	*		
das BUCH Hans dem Schüler		*	**	*
dem Schüler das BUCH Hans	**	**	*	
das BUCH dem Schüler Hans	*	**	**	*

3. BASIC ASSUMPTIONS OF THE THEORY OF TFA

In our attempt at an application of OT to the description of the topic-focus articulation of Czech sentences the following basic assumptions of the TFA theory (as developed in the Functional Generative Description, FGD, see Sgall, Hajičová and Benešová 1973; Sgall, Hajičová and Panevová 1986; most recently, Hajičová, Partee and Sgall 1998) are observed:

(i) The TFA of a sentence is a semantically relevant language phenomenon, and as such should be represented on the underlying structure of the sentence (its tectogrammatical representation, TR, in terms of FGD);

(ii) one of the important oppositions of TFA is the underlying order of the elements of the sentence structure (their communicative dynamism, CD);

(iii) the CD of the elements in the focus part of the sentence obeys the so-called systemic ordering (i.e. a canonical ordering of the complementations of the head word, see Hajičová and Sgall 1987, Sgall et al. 1995);

(iv) the main pitch accent is on the last element of the focus (i.e. the element with the highest degree of CD);

(v) the topic or some part of it may be of a contrastive character (in case of choice from a set of alternatives within topic); the contrastive (part of) topic is less dynamic than the rest of the topic, and typically carries a contrastive accent (different from the main pitch accent).

4. ALTERNATIVE I

We have considered two alternatives for the description of TFA within the OT scenario; they differ in the specification of the input to GEN.

In Alternative I, the input to GEN are "underspecified tectogrammatical representations" (called quasi-TR's in the sequel), which can be characterized as follows:

(i)   the syntactic structure is represented in terms of the dependency relations;

(ii) the TFA is indicated by markers for the elements in the topic (T) and in the focus (F);

(iii) the elements of the quasi-TR's are ordered according to the unmarked ("canonical") order, called systemic ordering (SO).

The output of GEN is a candidate set consisting in permutations of the words of the sentence (with the respective dependency relations); the evaluation module evaluates these candidates according to several (rather simplified, for the purpose of our discussion) constraints, namely:

A. main pitch accent should be placed on the last element of focus according to SO;

B. the order in focus should obey the SO and the focus should be continuous, i.e. not interrupted by elements of topic;

C. a secondary pitch accent should be optionally carried by the element in contrastive topic, i.e. the first element of topic.

The result of the evaluation procedure are sentences with TR's obeying the SO in the focus part but with variants of communicative dynamism (underlying word order) in the topic part.

Alternative I can be illustrated by the following Czech example. Let us assume that the input to GEN (i.e. the quasi-TR of the sentence to be generated) consists in the predicate *přinesl* ("brought") and its dependents *Jirka* (Actor, "George"), *babičce* (Addressee, "to-grandmother"), and *kytku* (Objective, "flower-Accusative"). The only element of the focus is the Objective, all other elements are in the topic. This input is schematically represented in (8):

(8) *přinesl*.T   *Jirka*.Act.T   *babičce*.Addr.T   *kytku*.Obj.F
    "brought"   "George"   "to-grandmother"   "flower"

Notation: T denotes an element of Topic, F: an element of focus. Act, Addr and Obj are the tectogrammatical dependency relations of Actor, Addressee and Objective, respectively.

The module of GEN generates the candidates given in (9). We give first in (a) an illustration of a simplified set of candidates for the case if the placement of the intonation centre is ignored, adding then in (b) a sample of an enriched candidate set with the distinction of the placement of the main pitch accent (intonation centre, denoted by capitals), and, finally, an example of few candidates from a still larger candidate set with the distinction of the contrastive topic (denoted by underlining):

(9) (a)

Jirka.Act.T	*přinesl.T*	*babičce.Addr.T*	*kytku.Obj.F*
Jirka.Act.T	*babičce.Addr.T*	*přinesl.T*	*kytku.Obj.F*
Jirka.Act.T	*babičce.Addr.T*	*kytku.Obj.F*	*přinesl.T*
přinesl.T	*babičce.Addr.T*	*Jirka.Act.T*	*kytku.Obj.F*
přinesl.T	*babičce.Addr.T*	*kytku.Obj.F*	*Jirka.Act.T*

etc.

(b)

Jirka.Act.T	*přinesl.T*	*babičce.Addr.T*	*KYTKU.Obj.F*
Jirka.Act.T	*přinesl.T*	*BABIČCE.Addr.T*	*kytku.Obj.F*
JIRKA.Act.T	*přinesl.T*	*babičce.Addr.T*	*kytku.Obj.F*

etc.

(c)

<u>*Jirka*</u>.Act.T	*přinesl.T*	*babičce.Addr.T*	*KYTKU.Obj.F*
<u>*Jirka*</u>.Act.T	*přinesl.T*	*BABIČCE.Addr.T*	*kytku.Obj.F*

etc.

The evaluation procedure, applying the above quoted constraints on the full set of candidates exemplified by (9)(c), with A. being the strongest and C. the weakest, gives the result given in (10) (the selected structures are marked by an arrow, the assumed bearer of the contrastive topic is underlined):

(10)

					A	B	C
==>	<u>Jirka</u>.T	*přinesl.T*	babičce.T	KYTKU.F			
==>	<u>Jirka</u>.T	*přinesl.T*	babičce.T	KYTKU.F[2]			
	<u>Jirka</u>.T	*přinesl.T*	BABIČCE.T	kytku.F	*		
	přinesl.T	<u>babičce</u>.T	Jirka.T	KYTKU.F		*	
==>	<u>babičce</u>.T	Jirka.T	*přinesl.T*	KYTKU.F			

etc.

As can be seen, the optimal candidates are structures with different tectogrammatical (underlying) representations (differing in the order in the topic part of the sentence). This is an undesirable result: since the underlying word order (CD) is semantically relevant (as is nowadays commonly acknowledged), an additional procedure would be needed to select a particular pair <TR, S>, i.e. assigning to each surface structure the corresponding underlying representation (TR).

---

2   Constraint C is not violated because no element of topic is contrastive.

5. ALTERNATIVE II

Therefore, we have proposed Alternative II, where the input structures for GEN are fully specified (rather than quasi-TR's, as those in Sect. 4) with points (i') and (ii') equal to (i) and (ii) for Alternative I, and with additional specifications (iii') through (v'):

(i')   the syntactic structure is represented in terms of the dependency relations;
(ii') the topic-focus articulation is indicated by markers for the elements in the topic (T) and in the focus (F);
(iii') the elements of the TR's are ordered according to the underlying order of sentence elements (CD);
(iv') the contrastive topic is marked (C);
(v')   the structures are (optionally) marked for the feature of emotiveness.

The output of GEN is a reference set similar as in Alternative I (see (9)(c) above) and the following, more specific constraints (though again rather simplified) can be formulated (thanks to the enrichment of the input structures):

A. The main stress (intonation centre, main pitch accent) is carried by the element of the sentence carrying the highest degree of CD.
B. Surface order of elements is in concordance with the underlying order (CD).
C. The finite verb immediately follows the first complementation of the given verb.
D. The so-called phrase accent (rise) is only on the contrastive element of the topic.
E. If the sentence has the feature E(motive), the focus is in the first position of the sentence (cf. Section 6 below for some comments on this feature).
F. The focus proper (i.e. the element of the sentence carrying the highest degree of CD) is at the end of the sentence.
G. The contrastive element of the topic is at the beginning of the sentence.

The following tentative hierarchy of constraints can be assumed for Czech:
A, E, D, G < C, F < B

The output of the evaluation procedure then consists of all sentences corresponding to the particular TR specified in the input to GEN. The evaluation procedure based on this hierarchy of constraints can be illustrated as follows:

Let us assume that the input to GEN (i.e. the TR of the sentence to be generated) consists of the predicate *číst* ("read") and its dependents *Jarda* (Actor), *Lidce* (Addressee, "to-Lidka"), and *pohádku* (Objective, "tale-Accusative"). The elements of the focus are the verb and the Objective, the Actor is in the position of the contrastive topic and the Addressee is the other element of topic. This input is schematically represented in (11):

(11) Jarda.Act.C.1   Lidce.Addr.T.2   čte.F.3   pohádku.Obj.F.4
         "Jarda"   "Lidka"   "read"   "tale"

Notation: T denotes a non-contrastive element of Topic, C: a contrastive element of topic, F: an element of focus, and numbers indicate the position of the given element in the underlying word order (CD). Act, Addr and Obj are the tectogrammatical dependency relations of Actor, Addressee and Objective, respectively.

The module of GEN generates the candidates exemplified in (12) (instead of dependency relations we give the surface shapes of the sentence elements: *Jarda-Nom.*, *Lidce-Dat.*, *čte*-3rd Pers.Sing.Pres., *pohádku*-Acc; capitals denote the intonation centre (IC)):

(12) (a) (i) *Jarda*.C.1   *Lidce*.T.2   *čte*.F.3   *pohádku*.F.4
              Jarda.C.1   *Lidce*.T.2   *pohádku*.F.4   *čte*.F.3
              Jarda.C.1   *čte*.F.3   *Lidce*.T.2   *pohádku*.F.4
              Jarda.C.1   *čte*.F.3   *pohádku*.F.4   *Lidce*.T.2
              Jarda.C.1   *pohádku*.F.4   *Lidce*.T.2   *čte*.F.3
              Jarda.C.1   *pohádku*.F.4   *čte*.F.3   *Lidce*.T.2
    (ii) *Lidce*.T.2   *Jarda*.C.1   *čte*.F.3   *pohádku*.F.4
          Lidce.T.2   *Jarda*.C.1   *pohádku*.F.4   *čte*.F.3
          etc.
    (iii) *čte*.F.3   *Jarda*.C.1   *Lidce*.T.2   *pohádku*.F.4
          čte.F.3   *Jarda*.C.1   *pohádku*.F.4   *Lidce*.T.2
          etc., up to
    (iv) ...
          pohádku.F.4   *čte*.F.3   *Lidce*.T.2   *Jarda*.C.1
    (b)   *Jarda*.C.1   *Lidce*.T.2   *čte*.F.3   *POHÁDKU*.F.4
          Jarda.C.1   *Lidce*.T.2   *pohádku*.F.4   *ČTE*.F.3
          Jarda.C.1   *čte*.F.3   *Lidce*.T.2   *POHÁDKU*.F.4
          etc.
    (c)   *Jarda*.C.1   *Lidce*.T.2   *ČTE*.F.3   *pohádku*.F.4
          Jarda.C.1   *Lidce*.T.2   *POHÁDKU*.F.4   *čte*.F.3
          Jarda.C.1   *čte*.F.3   *LIDCE*.T.2   *pohádku*.F.4
          etc.
    (d)   *Jarda*.C.1   *LIDCE*.T.2   *čte*.F.3   *pohádku*.F.4
          etc.
    (e)   *JARDA*.C.1   *Lidce*.T.2   *čte*.F.3   *pohádku*.F.4
          etc.

The candidates in the set exemplified in (12)(a) differ in the order of element, those in (b) through (e) both in the order and in the assignment of the IC to one of their elements. These sets are followed by groups of 24 permuted members each (with 2, 3 and 4 IC's), with one to four contrastive phrasal stresses (CP), then with one IC and one CP, with two and three IC's and one CP, then with 2 IC's and 2 CP's, with 1 IC and 2 and 3 CP's.

The result of the evaluation procedure is illustrated in (13) on the subset of candidates that meet the four strongest constraints, namely A, E, D and G. (We leave out of consideration the other six-member subsets, since the constraints B and G are violated in all of them and in some of them also C and/or D are/is violated, so that none candidate is "better" than the best one of the set below.)

(13)

				A	E	D	G	C	F	B
Jarda.C.1 Lidce.T.2	čte.F.3	POHÁDKU.F.4		*						
Jarda.C.1 Lidce.T.2	POHÁDKU.F.4	čte.F.3			*	*	*			
=> Jarda.C.1 čte.F.3	Lidce.T.2	POHÁDKU.F.4						*		
Jarda.C.1 čte.F.3	POHÁDKU.F.4	Lidce.T.2					*	*		
Jarda.C.1 POHÁDKU.F.4	Lidce.T.2	čte.F.3			*	*	*			
Jarda.C.1 POHÁDKU.F.4	čte.F.3	Lidce.T.2				*	*	*		

The optimal output is the third line, i.e. the sentence *"Jarda čte Lidce POHÁDKU"* (lit.: Jarda reads to-Lidka fairy-tale).[3]

6. OPEN QUESTIONS

As emphasized above, the constraints are formulated in a rather simplified way and do not cover the whole richness of the TFA phenomena. Let us mention here some of the open questions connected with our tentative formulations:

(a) *Constraint C:* its formulation allows only for cases when the verb can be placed before another part of T; possibilities of the verb following some part of F are left out of consideration. If the latter cases are taken into account, then C should have a larger "weight": this is to say that both the first and the third lines of (13) should be marked as "optimal outputs," which would lead, however, to an otherwise unwanted effect of free variation (see below, Sect.7).

(b) *Constraint D:* according to some views, the contrastive phrase accent (rise) is – at least in allegro speech – optional; for a more systematic discussion of the contrastive parts of T and the possibilities of the positions of the so-called focus sensitive particles, see Hajičová, Partee and Sgall (1998).

(c) *Constraint E:* this constraint is based on the introduction of a feature E (motive) in the input to GEN (see V. Mathesius' notion of "subjective order"). In the formulation of this constraint, we do not take into account the placement of Focus Proper in positions other than at the very beginning and the very end of the sentence (such as in *Skoro vždycky jezdí TÁTA do Prahy.* "Almost always (there) goes FATHER to Prague."). In a similar vein, we leave open the questions whether a contrastive element of the topic can be in another position than at the very beginning of the sentence (see constraint G). It is also necessary to consider under which conditions the input to GEN can and should be enriched by features that are not directly se-

---

3   To account for a subjective order (see constraint E above), namely "JARDA čte Lidce pohádku." only the weak constraints F and B are disobeyed; other permutations are (duly) excluded by the stronger constraint G.

mantically relevant but are important for the speaker's choice of expressions (the same question arises with stylistic features).

(d) *Constraint F*: our restricted formulation of the constraint E together with the constraint F, as well as C, (unduly) excludes e.g. the Cz. sentence *KENNEDYHO včera zabili* ("KENNEDY yesterday they-assassinated") in the context "What happened?", in which both the verb and the name belong to focus.

7. DISCUSSION

One of the disputed issues for Optimality Theory is the so-called free variation of two (or even more) forms with the same "degree" of optimality. Some of the supporters of OT try to avoid free variation as far as possible and they claim that it is always possible to make "the" best choice. We believe that as a working hypothesis, the effort to avoid free variation is very fruitful and leads to a subtle and deep inquiry into the conditions under which this or that shape of the sentence in the language under investigation is preferred. For instance, the above mentioned ordering of constraints B and C (C before B) for Czech selects the sentence with the verb in the second position as the optimal variant and thus refuses a sentence with the verb on the boundary between T and F if this boundary is not immediately before or immediately after the second element. It is still an open question, however, whether the constraints B and C should not have the same strength, i.e. both placed at the rightmost end of the evaluation table. At the same time, it should be checked, whether the "third" position of the verb (which, in fact, is prototypical after a clitic), is not preferred, whenever the two items preceding the verb are contrastive parts of the topic. If this is so, then the constraint C may be split into two constraints: C1, for cases when one or more elements of the topic are contrastive and thus (all) carry the marker of a contrastive topic, and C2, for the general case (= the original C):

C1. The finite verb immediately follows those of its complementations that have the feature of a contrastive element of the topic (C).

C2. The finite verb immediately follows the first complementation of the given verb.

With the split of C into C1 and C2, the order C1 before C2 and B (with both B and C2 having the same strength), and with a corresponding modification of the constraint G (to account for more than one element in the contrastive topic) the evaluation procedure for the input of GEN as in (11) (repeated here for convenience) with one element as a contrastive topic and as in (14) with two elements of the topic being contrastive would result in the choices marked by an arrow in (11') and (14'), respectively:

(11) *Jarda*.Act.C.1   *Lidce*.Addr.T.2   *čte*.F.3   *pohádku*.Obj.F.4
    "Jarda"   "Lidka"   "read"   "tale"

(11')

				F	C1	C2	B
=> Jarda.C.1	Lidce.T.2	čte.F.3	POHÁDKU.F.4		*		
Jarda.C.1	Lidce.T.2	POHÁDKU.F.4	čte.F.3	*		*	*
=> Jarda.C.1	čte.F.3	Lidce.T.2	POHÁDKU.F.4				*
Jarda.C.1	čte.F.3	POHÁDKU.F.4	Lidce.T.2	*			*
Jarda.C.1	POHÁDKU.F.4	Lidce.T.2	čte.F.3	*		*	*
Jarda.C.1	POHÁDKU.F.4	čte.F.3	Lidce.T.2	*		*	*

(14) Jarda.Act.C.1 Lidce.Addr.C.2 čte.F.3 pohádku.Obj.F.4
    "Jarda"   "Lidka"   "read"   "tale"

(14')

				F	C1	C2	B
=> Jarda.C.1	Lidce.C.2	čte.F.3	POHÁDKU.F.4	*			
Jarda.C.1	Lidce.C.2	POHÁDKU.F.4	čte.F.3	*	*		
Jarda.C.1	čte.F.3	Lidce.C.2	POHÁDKU.F.4				
Jarda.C.1	čte.F.3	POHÁDKU.F.4	Lidce.T.2		*	*	
Jarda.C.1	POHÁDKU.F.4	Lidce.C.2	čte.F.3		*	*	*
Jarda.C.1	POHÁDKU.F.4	čte.F.3	Lidce.C.2		*	*	*

With the flexibility of the surface order of sentence elements in Czech, we thus doubt that free variation can be excluded from language description altogether.

We have seen that the candidate sets are very large (and would be much larger if the OT scenario were applied to the whole set of language means corresponding to underlying, tectogrammatical features). OT is not conceived of as a component part of a model of the activity of a speaker or hearer; the constraints are understood as abstract components of a system specifying the set of sentences of the given language. We can observe here a tendency known e.g. from the development of Chomskyan (and other) models: a large number of generative rules is substituted by a more universally formulated apparatus of principles and parameters (or, later, of the theory of minimalism). The idea is to replace the necessity of formulating many generative rules (with the problems of their ordering etc.) by a set of constraints formulated in a non-procedural, declarative way. It is believed that in such a way, the relation between the initial (underlying) structures and the surface means of expression can be described in a more economic and transparent way.

It remains an open question, of course, if the manysidedness and richness of this relation can be described by a hierarchy of constraints as defined by OT: it would be necessary to examine whether also such means as case endings, prepositions and other auxiliary words can be treated in the same way (first attempts in this direction can be found in the contributions in Barbosa et al. eds. 1998 and in Legendre, Grimshaw and Vikner eds. in press). One of the claims of OT is that the constraints are universal, while their ranking is language specific. Our simple example, however, suggests that this hypothesis might be too strong; even in their simplified versions, some of the constraints necessary for the description of a single language are rather specific; their inclusion into the "universal" constraint set makes the set too large and the description uneconomic.

8. SUMMARY

We have tried to indicate, in a rather preliminary and tentative way (not covering such important issues as e.g. the placement of adjectives before the governing nouns even if the former are more dynamic than the latter, the placement of clitics, non-projective constructions, zero-pronoun and pronominalization etc.) that OT offers certain possibilities how to describe and analyze also those aspects of sentence structure that are closely connected with the communicative function of language. We believe that the results of the inquiries into topic-focus articulation presented in the Praguian writings on that issue offer some insights that might be useful for the formulation of constraints within OT: there belongs a specification of the canonical order in the terms of systemic ordering, which can be defined for a rich range of arguments and adjuncts, an account of the placement of the verb (in topic or in focus), the recognition of the focus possibly consisting of several elements (i.e. of more than a single constituent) and a reflection of the semantic relevance of TFA giving the possibility to generate the elements of the sentence *in situ*.

THE POSITION OF TFA (INFORMATION STRUCTURE) IN A DEPENDENCY BASED DESCRIPTION OF LANGUAGE

ABSTRACT

Information structure of the sentence (its topic-focus articulation, TFA in the sequel), though disguised under different terms and slightly different interpretations, belongs nowadays among the most frequently discussed issues of the sentence structure and its semantic and communicative function (Section 2). Based on our long-term study of these issues influenced heavily by the Prague School approach to functional linguistics and, first of all, by Petr Sgall's pioneering insights into the semantic relevance of TFA, we present an answer to three basic questions: (1) on which layer of linguistic description the basic features of TFA are to be represented (Section 3), (2) which basic oppositions are to be captured (Section 4), and (3) which formal description of language structure is best suited for such a representation (Section 5). In passing, we compare our standpoints to those embodied in other models, paying a special attention to Igor Meľčuk's Meaning Text Theory. In the concluding section (Section 6), we briefly sketch how a carefully--designed linguistically-based annotation of a corpus may serve as a testbed for a linguistic theory.

1. INTRODUCTION

In the Introduction to his book on Communicative Organization in Natural Language (Meľčuk 2001, CONL in the sequel), Igor Meľčuk formulates six questions the answers to which substantiate why the book was written and what it is (and, deliberately, is not) about. The first of these questions concerns why "his hands are trembling" whenever he sits and works on the book. His uncertainty stems from the fact that "so many brilliant linguists have written and are still writing so many works on the extremely difficult subject" (CONL, p. 1).

However, the autor still finds a good excuse for writing CONL: he considers the communicative organization of sentence "strictly from the perspective of constructing actual sentences from a representation of their meanings within a particular framework: the Meaning-Text Theory" (CONL, p. 2). He notes that this viewpoint has not been explored before (at least not systematically enough).

I share the view that information structure is nowadays a hot topic in linguistics and that for the past forty years much has been published on this issue. Among those writings, many explore TFA from the point of view of the framework I subscribe to, namely the Functional Generative Description (FGD). Therefore, the reasons why I have chosen the information structure of the sentence as the central topic of my invited talk, are a bit different from those Igor Mel'čuk considers. One of the aims of the present paper is to offer starting points for a comparison of different theories.

As some of the fundamental points of the Meaning Text Theory (MTT) and FGD are close to each other (for a comparison, see e.g. Žabokrtský 2005), I was curious to see whether and in which points the two theories differ in the understanding and description of TFA. For this purpose, I will briefly summarize the arguments for our treatment of TFA as a semantically relevant phenomenon which is to be captured at the underlying (tectogrammatical, in our terms) level having the form of dependency tree structures and illustrate on a couple of hypotheses formulated within our theory how a carefully-designed linguistically-based annotation of a corpus may serve as a testbed for linguistic theories.

2. SOME HISTORICAL MILESTONES

The writings on what we refer to as TFA and what is more generally (and recently) covered by the term information structure date back centuries ago; the issue is treated under different terms and there is not always possible to find a one-to-one mapping between them; also, they receive a slightly different interpretation. However, they share the underlying idea: a description of the structure reflecting the functioning of language in communication, which is different from the subject-verb-object structure (described in any formalism). One of the oldest and most stimulative, at least for its time, is Weil's (1844) comparison of the means expressing information structure in languages of different types. Of great interest is his proposal to distinguish two types of "progressions" of sentences in a discourse, in relation to which part of a given sentence serves as a starting point for the subsequent one. Sentences may follow each other in a parallel mode, i.e. they share their starting points (marche parallèle), or in a sequential mode, i.e. the starting point of a given sentence follows up the second (final) part of the preceding sentence (progression). In more modern terms, one can say that in the parallel mode, the sentences share their themes (topics), in the sequential mode the theme (topic) of one sentence relates to the rheme (focus) of the preceding sentence. (It should be noted that more than one hundred years later, a similar, though a more subtle approach was developed by Daneš 1970 in his paper on thematic progressions.)

It is not our intention here to present a historical survey; let us only mention that though the first hints for a systematic treatment of these issues within structural linguistics were given by Prague scholars in the second quarter of the last century (initiated by Vilém Mathesius and later continued by Jan Firbas), one should not forget that the topic was, so to say, hanging in the air, receiving the attention esp. in German linguistics (for a more detailed discussion, see Sgall et al., 1973, 1980 and 1986).

With the entrance of formal linguistics on the scene, it is not surprising that the first suggestions for an inclusion of TFA into an integrated formal description of language came from Prague; Sgall's Functional Generative Description (Sgall 1964; 1967a) working with a tectogrammatical (underlying, deep) level of sentence structure incorporated the TFA opposition into the description of this level (Sgall 1967b).

It should be noted that the examples serving as arguments during the split of generative transformational grammar into interpretative and generative semantics reflected the difference in TFA (actually, on both sides of the dispute, though not recognized as such; see e.g. Chomsky 1971 and Lakoff 1971a, to name just the main figures). A "breakthrough" on that side of Atlantic was Mats Rooth's doctoral dissertation on association with focus (Rooth 1985), in which the author (referring i.a. to Jackendoff 1972) quite convincingly argues for the "semantic effect of focus" in the sentence offering the explanation of this effect in terms of a domain of quantification (p. 197); his starting arguments were restricted to the presence in the sentence of the so-called focusing particles such as *only*, *even*, but he extended his proposal also to the so-called adverbs of quantification (*often*, *always*) and cases such as cleft constructions in English.

The interest was aroused, and after Barbara Partee's (who was one of Mats Rooth's supervisors) involvement in the discussion of the semantic consequences of different TFA structures (see e.g. Partee 1991) the TFA issues took up an important position in the discussions of formal semanticists (for a Czech contribution to that discussion see Peregrin 1994; 1996), but not only within that domain (quite noticeable is the interest in the TFA issues in German linguistics).

One of the crucial contributions of the above mentioned discussions was the due respect to the reflection of the differences in TFA in the prosodic shape of the sentences (which view, actually, has been present in the Praguian studies of TFA). Let us mention here only Jackendoff's (1972) introduction of the difference in A and B prosodic contour and Rooth's (1985) consistent regard to the placement of the intonation pitch in his example sentences.

3. WHERE TO REPRESENT TFA

3.1 SEMANTIC RELEVANCE OF TFA

To give an answer to the question posed in the title of this section, let us start with some examples (maybe notoriously known). The capitals denote the intonation centre, the names in brackets indicate the source of the examples.

(1) (a) Everybody in this room knows at least two LANGUAGES.
    (b) At least two languages are known by everybody in this ROOM.
    (Chomsky 1957; 1965)
(2) (a) Many men read few BOOKS.
    (b) Few books are read by many MEN. (Lakoff 1971a)
(3) (a) Londoners are mostly at BRIGHTON.
    (b) At Brighton, there are mostly LONDONERS. (Sgall 1967b)
(4) (a) I only introduced BILL to Sue.
    (b) I only introduced Bill to SUE. (Rooth 1985)
(5) (a) I work on my dissertation on SUNDAYS.
    (b) On Sundays, I work on my DISSERTATION.
(6) (a) English is spoken in the SHETLANDS.
    (b) In the Shetlands, ENGLISH is spoken. (Sgall et al. 1986)
(7) (a) Dogs must be CARRIED.
    (b) DOGS must be carried. (Halliday 1967)
    (c) Carry DOGS. (A warning in London underground, around 2000)
    (d) CARRY dogs.

It is not difficult to understand that the pairs of sentences under each number differ not only in their outer shapes or in their contextual appropriateness, but also in their meanings, even in their truth conditions. This difference may be attributed to the presence of quantifiers and their order (with an explicit quantification in (1) and (2) and a more or less explicit in (3) and (4)), but from (5) on, such an explanation is not possible. Also, an exclusive reference to the surface order of the sentence elements would not be correct, as illustrated by (4) and (7).

A more adequate explanation is that based on the relation of *aboutness*: the speaker communicates something (the Focus of the sentence) about something (the Topic of the sentence), i.e. F(T), the Focus holds about the Topic. In case of negative sentences, the Focus does not hold about the Topic: ~F(T).

A supportive argument for the semantic relevance of TFA can be traced in the discussions on the kinds of entailments starting with the fundamental contributions of Strawson. Strawson (1952, esp. p. 173ff.) distinguishes a formal logical relation of entailment and a formal logical relation of presupposition; this distinction – with certain simplifications – can be illustrated by (8) and (9):

(8) *All John's children are asleep.*
(9) *John has children.*

If John's children were not asleep, the sentence (8) would be false; however, if John did not have children, the sentence as well as its negation would not be false but meaningless. Thus (9) is a presupposition of (8) and as such it is not touched by the negation of (8).

Returning to the relation of aboutness, we can say that (8) is about John's children, and for (8) to be meaningful, there must be an entity John's children the speaker can refer to.[1]

The close connection between the notion of presupposition and TFA can be documented by a more detailed inspection of the notion of presupposition, exemplified here by sentences (10) and (11).

(10) *The King of France is (not) bald.*
(11) *The exhibition was (not) visited by the King of France.*

It follows from the above mentioned discussions on presuppositions that Strawson's (1964) ex. (10) is about the King of France and the King's existence (referential availability) is presupposed, it is entailed also by its negative counterpart; otherwise (10) would have no truth value, it would be meaningless. On the other hand, there is no such presupposition for (11): the affirmative sentence is true if the King of France was among the visitors of the exhibition, while its negative counterpart is true if the King of France was not among the visitors. The truth/falsity of (11) does not depend on the referential availability of the entity "King of France". This specific kind of entailment was introduced in Hajičová (1972) and was called allegation: an allegation is an assertion A entailed by an assertion carried by a sentence S, with which the negative counterpart of S entails neither A nor its negation (see also Hajičová 1984; 1993, and the discussion by Partee 1996). Concerning the use of a definite noun group in English one can say that it often triggers a presupposition if it occurs in Topic (see sentence (10)), but only an allegation if it belongs to Focus (see sentence (11)).

These considerations have led us to the attempt at a more systematic analysis of the relations between affirmative and negative sentences (Hajičová 1972, 1984, 1993). The scope of negation can be specified, in the prototypical case, as constituted by the Focus, so that the meaning of a negative declarative sentence can be interpreted as its Focus (F) not holding of it, i.e. ~F(T). In this way it is possible to understand the semantic difference present in (10) and (11).

In a secondary case, the assertion holds about a negative Topic: F(~T), see (12) on the reading when answering the question "Why didn't he come?"

(12) *He did not come because he was afraid.*

Here again, the scope of negation is dependent on TFA: it is restricted to the Topic part of the sentence. The assertion entailed (on this reading) by the *because*-clause in Focus is not touched by negation.[2]

---

1   This need not mean that the entity the sentence is "about" should exist in the real world, but it should be referentially available (cf. the discussion of the notion of referential vs. existential presuppositions in Hajičová 1976, 55–58, reflected also in Sgall et al. 1986).
2   On another possible reading of (12), e.g. if the sentence is followed by *but because he was on his leave of absence*, his being afraid is neither entailed nor negated, i.e. the assertion belongs to the allegations of the sentence, i.e. he might have come for some other reason. The negation concerns Focus, schematically: ~F(T).

3.2 WHICH LAYER OF LINGUISTIC DESCRIPTION DOES TFA BELONG TO?

The analysis summarized in Sect. 3.1 points out very clearly that TFA undoubtedly is a semantically relevant aspect of the sentence and as such should be represented at a level of an integrated language description capturing the meaning of the sentence (whatever interpretation we assign to the notion of "meaning"). For the formal description of language we subscribe to, namely the Functional Generative Description, this is the underlying, *tectogrammatical* layer; the tectogrammatical representations of sentences (TRs) are specified as dependency tree structures, with the verb (of the main clause) as the root of the tree. While the labels of the nodes of the tree are counterparts to the autosemantic words of the sentence, counterparts of function words as well as of grammatical morphemes are just indices of the nodes and the edges of the tree: the morphological values of number, tense, modalities, and so on, are specified by indices of the labels of the nodes. For each node of the TR it is specified whether it is contextually bound or non-bound (see Sect. 4.1 below). The edges of the tree are labeled by underlying syntactic relations (such as Actor/Bearer, Addressee, Patient, Origin, Effect, several Local and Temporal relations, etc.). In the corresponding surface shapes of the sentences, there are several means (the extent of their exploitation is different in different languages) rendering the TFA distinctions: the word order, the placement of the intonation center and the intonation contours, specific syntactic constructions (such as clefting in English), or specific morphemic means (such as the particle *wa* in Japanese).

A similar question can be posed as for the MTT approach: as a multilayered description of language, this theory postulates a series of layers of representation, the "highest" (or deepest) of which, *SemR*, is declared to be the meaning, specifying the meaning of a set of synonymous sentences. The concept of meaning is thus based on the concept of same meaning; however, as Mel'čuk (1988, pp. 14, 25ff, 52) claims, a certain degree of approximation in the semantic representation is necessary, if linguistically interesting results are to be obtained. Mel'čuk (2001, pp. 25ff.) develops this idea further: Two utterances are called "more or less synonymous" if they "mean roughly the same," i.e. "they must express (almost) the same set of semantic units organized in the same configurations" (CONL, p. 14). This relation is distinguished from the notion of strict (full) synonymy: "two utterances are called strictly (fully) synonymous if a native speaker cannot find any semantic distinction whatsoever between them, including what can be referred to as 'communicative nuances'" (ibid).[3]

---

3   Kahane (2003) summarizes this idea as follows: "During the process of sentence construction ... lexical and syntactic choices carried out by the Speaker very often lead to the modification of ... the initial semantic representation, making it more precise and specific. ... The initial semantic representation is taken to be rather approximate... The meaning can become more precise – or less precise..." In FGD, we distinguish between strict synonymy and quasi-synonymy; with the latter, the difference in truth-conditions is relevant only in specific contexts and citations.

SemR has as its central component SemS, i.e. a representation of propositional, or situational meaning of a family of more or less synonymous sentences, the other three components being Semantic Communicative Structure (SemCommS), the Rhetorical Structure (RhetS), and the Referential Structure (RefS) (Meľčuk 2001, p. 4).

The particularity of the theory, however, is the postulation of an intermediate deep-syntactic level, DSyntR, between the semantic (SemR) and the surface syntactic representation (SSyntR). Thus the module called semantics comprises two layers or representation, SemR and DSyntR. The latter layer is aimed at representing the lexico-grammatical organization of a concrete sentence; its central component is the deep syntactic structure, the other three components being DSynt-Communicative Structure (different from the SemCommS, see below), the DSynt-Anaphoric Structure and DSynt-Prosodic Structure. Formally, the DSyntS is an unordered dependency tree the nodes of which are labeled with full lexical units of the language and the arcs are labeled with symbols for deep syntactic relations (such as I, II through VI and attributive relation ATTR; coordination is also understood as one of the dependency relations).[4]

It is not the objective of the present paper to discuss the overall organization of the MTT model. Therefore, we restrict ourselves to saying that we do not consider a two-layer semantic module the MTT approach postulates to be necessary unless one of them is proclaimed as a layer of language system and the other as a (partial) reflection of the content of the sentence. We consider the main boundary line to separate linguistic meaning from the basically extra-linguistic content. Since the SemR of MTT is described as to include also the representation of the communicative (information) structure, we constrain ourselves to the issues relevant for this representation.

4. WHICH BASIC OPPOSITIONS ARE TO BE CAPTURED?

4.1 CONTEXTUAL BOUNDNESS AS THE BASIC OPPOSITION

In the approach of the Functional Generative Description to TFA, the underlying structure is represented as containing the attribute of contextual boundness: for every autosemantic lexical item in the sentence (i.e. for every node of its tectogrammatical representation) it is specified whether it is (a) contextually bound (cb), an item presented by the speaker as referring to an entity assumed to be easily accessible by the hearer(s), i.e. more or less predictable, readily available to the hearers in their memory, or (b) contextually non-bound (nb), an item presented as not directly available in the given context, cognitively "new". While the characteristics "given" and "new" refer only to the cognitive background of the distinction of contextual boundness, the

---

4   In FGD, coordination is not considered to be a dependency relation; rather, it is understood as a third dimension of the structure, making the resulting representation of the sentence a network of three orderings, rather than a two-dimensional tree.

distinction itself is an opposition understood as a grammatically patterned feature, rather than in the literal sense of the term. This point is illustrated by (13): both Tom and his friends are "given" by the preceding context (indicated here by the preceding sentence in the brackets), but they are structured as non-bound (which is reflected in the surface shape of the sentence by the position of the intonation center).

(13) (Tom entered together with his friends.) *My mother recognized only HIM, but no one from his COMPANY.*

In the prototypical case, the head verb of the sentence and its immediate dependents (arguments and adjuncts) constitute the Topic of the sentence if they are contextually bound, whereas the Focus consists of the contextually non-bound items in such structural positions (and of the items syntactically subordinated to them). Also the semantically relevant scopes of focus sensitive operators such as *only, even,* etc. can be characterized in this way.

The bipartition of the sentence into the Topic and Focus (reflecting the aboutness relation) can then be specified by the following set of the rules determining the appurtenance of a lexical occurrence to the Topic (T) or to the Focus (F) of the sentence (see Sgall 1979; Sgall et al. 1986, pp. 216ff)

(a) the main verb (V) and any of its direct dependents belong to F iff they carry index nb;

(b) every item k_i that does not depend directly on V and is subordinated to an element of F different from V, belongs to F (where "subordinated to" is defined as the irreflexive transitive closure of "depend on");

(c) iff V and all items k_j directly depending on it carry index cb, then those items k_j to which some items l_m carrying nb are subordinated are called "proxy foci" and the items l_m together with all items subordinated to one of them belong to F, where $1 \le j, m$;

(d) every item not belonging to F according to (a) – (c) belongs to T.

There are two reasons why to distinguish the opposition of contextual boundness as a primary (primitive) one and to derive the Topic-Focus bipartition from it: (i) the Topic/Focus distinction exhibits – from a certain viewpoint – some recursive properties which are best described by the cb/nb distinction, and (ii) Topic/Focus bipartition cannot be drawn on the basis of an articulation of the sentence into constituents but requires a more subtle treatment (for arguments, see Sect. 5 below).[5]

The semantico-pragmatic interpretation of sentences (for which the TRs represent suitable input) may then include an application of Tripartite Structures (Operator –

---

5   It is a matter of course that the distinctions made have to be checked by means of some operational tests or criteria. Several such test have already been discussed in literature the remarkable point being that they all more or less return very similar results. Not going into detail on this point, we just refer to the question test (Sgall et al. 1986), the test by means of an acceptable negative continuation (response) (Chomsky's 1971 "natural response," Posner's 1972 "Kommentieren" test) and tests based on the scope of negation or other focus sensitive operators (e.g. Hajičová, Partee and Sgall 1998).

Restrictor – Nuclear Scope), as outlined by B. H. Partee in Hajičová et al. (1998). Let us briefly recall some of the characteristic sentences discussed there (with their relevant TRs) and specify (in a maximally simplified notation) which parts of their individual readings belong to the Operator (O), Restrictor (R) and Nuclear Scope (N) of the corresponding tripartite structures. We assume that in the interpretation of a declarative sentence, O corresponds to negation or to its positive counterpart (the assertive modality) or to some other operators such as focusing particles, R corresponds to Topic (T), and N to Focus (F).

(14) *John only sits by the TELEVISION.*
(14') O *only,* R *John,* N *sits by the TELEVISION.*
(14") O *only,* R *John sits,* N *by the TELEVISION.*

In (14), the particle occupies its prototypical position in the TR, so that the focus of the particle is identical with the F of the sentence on either reading, i.e. with the verb included in F in (14'), and in T in (14"). If a focusing particle occupies a secondary position, rather than that of the main operator, we use the ASSERT operator (introduced by Jacobs 1984) in the interpretation. If the operator is included in T, its own focus (which differs from the sentence F in such marked cases) does not cross the boundary between the T and the F of the sentences, see (15):

(15) *(What did even PAUL realize?) Even Paul realized that Jim only admired MARY.*
(15') O ASSERT, R *(O even,* R *realized,* N *Paul),* N *(O only,* R *Jim admired,* N *Mary)*

Let us just note that in the cases in which T or F is complex, as illustrated by (15), it is the opposition of contextual boundness that is responsible for the difference: while contextually bound items then belong to the local (partial) R, the non-bound ones belong to the corresponding N.

4.2 COMMUNICATIVE OPPOSITIONS IN SEMCOMM OF MTT

In MTT, the main structure of semantic representation, the semantic structure (SemS) is supposed to be formally a connected directed graph, with nodes (semantemes) corresponding to disambiguated lexicographic word senses of the language in question. The arcs are labeled with numbers specifying predicate-argument relations.

The communicative organization of sentences is represented on the level of meaning by the Semantic-Communicative Structure (SemComm).[6]

---

6   It should be appreciated that Mel'čuk emphasizes the involvement of meaning in his approach; however, he is not precise when he ascribes (CONL, p. 22) to Lambrecht's book (1994) an exceptional status in drawing a systematic distinction between semantico-pragmatic (in MTT terms: communicative) categories and their formal expression in sentences, see our discussion and references in Sect. 2 above.

This structure is supposed to organize the meaning of the sentence into a message "from the viewpoint of its transmission by the Speaker and its reception by the Addressee" (CONL, p. 23); this is done by (i) specification of the division of the SemS of the sentence into (possibly overlapping) parts, called communicative areas, and by (ii) specification of a dominant node of each communicative area marked by one of a set of mutually exclusive values (one of the communicative oppositions, Comm-oppositions). Eight Comm-oppositions are distinguished (CONL, p. 49, with a more detailed specification on pp. 74ff): (i) thematicity (rheme vs. theme vs. specifier), (ii) givenness (given vs. new vs. irrelevant), (iii) focalization (focalized vs. neutral), (iv) perspective (foregrounded vs. backgrounded vs. neutral), (v) emphasis (emphasized – neutral), (vi) presupposedness (presupposed vs. non-presupposed (= asserted or neither), (vii) unitariness (unitary vs. articulated), (viii) locutionality (signaled vs. performed vs. communicated). These SemComm categories can combine with each other within one SemS and may be obligatory ((i) and (ii)) or optional (the rest). In addition, they are assumed to form a hierarchy (indicated in the list by the order in which they are listed); Mel'čuk (CONL, p. 74) admits that the hierarchy is not strict and that he is unable to sufficiently motivate the order of all the oppositions, which therefore is more or less arbitrary.

On the level of DSyntR, the communicative structure of the sentence (its DSynt-Communicative Structure) is to a great extent determined by its Sem-CommS (pp. 64ff) though due to lexical or grammatical constraints of the language involved, it can require restructuring of the Sem-Comm-data: this is illustrated by a comparison of the Russian sentence *Iz-za ego ot'ezda my polnost'ju pomenjali nashi plany* (literal E. translation: *Because of his departure, we completely changed our plans*). with its assumed analysis on the semantic level and the deep-syntactic level. While on the semantic level, Sem-theme of the SemR is "he left" and the "cause" semanteme is a part of the semantic rheme, there is no easy way in Russian to express causation verbally as a separate lexeme; therefore the preposition *iz-za* is to be used, which, on the deep syntactic level, is supposed to be a part of DSynt-Theme. This argumentation necessarily leads to a question how deep the deep syntactic representation is if it depends so much on the means available in a given language. This point, however, is not crucial for our present discussion since the representation of the fundamental aspects of TFA (or communicative structure, in MTT terms) are present at the SemR in any case.

What is more pertinent to our discussion where TFA or communicative structure are to be represented, are issues related to the scopes of quantifiers and negation. As Kahane (2003) notes, the scope of quantifiers is not directly encoded in standard MTT semantic representations; Mel'čuk (CONL, pp. 358–360) in his discussion on the scope of *only* (the ambiguity of the written sentence *Word-final position only admits voiceless consonants*) considers that a specification of this must be indicated in both the SemS and the SemCommS. In SemS, this is to be done by the choice of arguments of the semanteme *only* (*only voiceless* vs. *only consonants*) and the consequent different assignment of "rhematic focus" (*voiceless* vs. *voiceless consonants*). As for DSyntR, it is the

DSynt-Prosodic Structure which marks the lexical expression as for its accent (*voiceless* vs. *consonants*).[7]

4.3 CONTEXTUAL BOUNDNESS AS A BASIS FOR MORE SUBTLE DISTINCTIONS

At the first sight, it may seem that the MTT account offers more possibilities to cover a larger display of subtle distinctions than the FGD approach. The question thus arises whether the effort to propose as economic description of the relevant phenomena as possible does not cost too much in terms of adequacy and coverage.

We claim that this is not the case with FGD. From the eight oppositions listed above, (ii), (vii) and (viii) lie beyond the linguistic structuring of meaning and pertain to the cognitive layer, rather than to the structure of sentences. The opposition of givenness (ii) can be understood as a cognitive background of the opposition of *cb/nb*. It is not clear whether the opposition of emphasis ((v) in the list) is semantically relevant and should be as such captured by the representation of (linguistic) meaning. The same holds of the opposition of perspective (listed as (iv) and obtaining the values of foregrounded vs. backgrounded vs. neutral): it is characterized as that piece of information that has, from the viewpoint of the speaker, a special or reduced psychological prominence, or is in the central or peripheral part of the situation. Contrary to Mel'čuk (CONL, p. 202), we take it as a relevant feature where the "peripherality" comes from: it is important to examine whether it is based on some internal semantic considerations, or from discourse organization, or from another source; only in the first case, it should be considered as relevant for the representation of meaning, and accounted for as such.

We thus remain with oppositions (i), (iii), and (vi). The opposition (i) directly relates to the bipartition of the sentence into Topic and Focus derived on the basis of *cb/nb* nodes of the representation (see Sgall's rules given above); in our discussion of presupposition and allegation in Sect. 3.1 we have also indicated how the opposition of "presuposedness" ((vi) in the list) relates to TFA. Focalization ((iii) in the list) covers, in our opinion, several phenomena: it maybe be characterized as a "narrow focus": usually understood as a Focus consisting in a single node (plus attribute), which may be exemplified by a case of the prototypical position of a focus sensitive particle. Alternatively, it relates to a contrastive node in the Topic part of the sentence (a focusing particle can occur also in the Topic part and it may indicate a "local focus," see the analysis of (15) above).

---

7   Mel'čuk does not mention other possibilities of the scope of *only* in his example: if the context after the given sentence is "... It does not indicate all positions relevant for the given structure" the theme would include only *word-final position* and the rest of the sentence would be the rheme. It would be interesting to see how this interpretation would be captured in the Sem-CommS differently from the case when the scope of *only* includes just *voiceless consonants*.

The recognition of a primary distinction of contextual boundness, on the other hand, offers a possibility to represent other distinctions related to TFA and referred to in present-day linguistic writings. First of all, it allows for an account of the possible recursivity of TFA, exemplified first of all in sentences which contain embedded (dependent) clauses. The dependent clause D functions as a sentence part of the clause containing the word on which D depends, so that the whole structure has a recursive character; one of the questions discussed is whether the T-F articulation should be understood as recursive, too. Several situations obtain: (i) one of the clauses may be understood as the F of the whole sentence, though each of the clauses displays a T-F articulation of its own ("local" topics and foci: *(the) market, unused possibilities*, and *saturated, transmission*, respectively), as in (16); (ii) in a general case the boundary between T and F may lie within one of the clauses (as in (17)). (The examples marked by PDT are taken from the Prague Dependency Treebank, see Sect. 6 below.)

(16) *Zatímco trh s rozhlasovým signálem už je nasycen, nevyužité možnosti stále má televize zejména při regionálním a lokálním vysílání. (PDT)*
Lit. While (the) market with radio signal already is saturated, unused possibilities still has television-Nom. especially with regional and local transmisson.

(17) *Na základě návrhu zákona, který vláda projednala na své poslední schůzi, se budou daně snižovat až o 10 procent. (PDT)*
Lit. On the basis of the propsal of the law, which the government has approved on its latest meeting, the taxes will be lowered up to ten percent.

Also the notion of *verum* focus can be captured by means of *cb/nb* distinction, with the yes-no modality constituting the whole Focus (see (18)).

(18) *(Have you attended the last meeting?) No, I did not attend the last meeting.*

The approach based on the *cb/nb* opposition makes it possible to account for the TFA of coordinated structures, in which each of the clauses connected in a coordinative construction, i.e. in a compound sentence, exhibits a Topic/Focus articulation of its own. In (19), the Topic of the first clause is *je bez něho* (it is without him), the Focus being *nemyslitelná* (unthinkable), while in the second clause, the Topic is *zároveň má samozřejmě v sobě* (it has at the same time in itself) and the Focus is *spoustu nejrozmanitějších nebezpečí* (many multifarious dangers).

(19) *Je bez něho nemyslitelná, ale zároveň má samozřejmě v sobě spoustu nejrozmanitějších nebezpečí. (PDT)*
Lit.: it-is without him unthinkable but at-the-same-time it-has in itself many multifarious dangers.

An interesting issue is that of contrast in Focus. There are different kinds of contrast: a "neutral" one as in (20) or (21), a correction as in (22), or the case called by V. Mathesius the second instance (as in (23)).[8]

(20) *(Preceding context: Kde se mluví česky?) Česky se mluví v ČESKU.*
(Where is Czech spoken?) Czech is spoken in CZECHIA.

(21) *(Preceding context: Mluví se česky v Česku nebo na Slovensku?)*
Česky se mluví v ČESKU.
(Is Czech spoken in Czechia or in Slovakia?) Czech is spoken in CZECHIA.

(22) *(Preceding context: Mluví se česky ve Slovinsku nebo na Slovensku?)*
Česky se mluví v ČESKU.
(Is Czech spoken in Slovenia or in Slovakia?) Czech is spoken in CZECHIA.

(23) *(Preceding context: Na Slovensku se mluví česky.)*
(In Slovakia one speaks Czech)
  a) *(Ne.) Česky se mluví v ČESKU*
    (No.) Czech is spoken in CZECHIA.
  b) *(Ne.) Na Slovensku se mluví SLOVENSKY.*
    (No.) In Slovakia one speaks SLOVAK.
  c) *V ČESKU se mluví česky.*
    In CZECHIA one speaks Czech.

It can be said (in agreement with Rooth 1985) that by default, every Focus involves a choice of alternatives, so that the "contrast" present in (20) or (21) is just what underlies Focus. However, even in the topic part of the sentence one may see a choice of alternatives if some element of Topic is contrastive (and marked as such, cf. Hajičová, Partee and Sgall, 1998). A typical example, known from Lakoff (1971b) and the older discussions (with *he* bearing a rising contrastive stress in both examples; *her* is stressed with the typical sentence final falling pitch contour in (a); in (b) the intonation centre is on *insulted*) is in (24) and (24'):

(24) (She called him a Republican.) *Then he insulted HER.*
(24') (She called him a Republican.) *Then he INSULTED her.*

5. WHICH TYPE OF FORMAL DESCRIPTION

In early discussions on the integration of the topic-focus articulation into a formal description of grammar, the proponents intended to specify this aspect of the structure of the sentence in terms of the type of formal description they subscribed to. Within

---

8 Since the same sentence (with a narrow focus) can be used in any of the contexts of (19)–(22), we assign this sentence the same TR in the different uses.

the framework of generative transformational grammar, Chomsky (1971, p. 205) defined focus as "a phrase containing the intonation center," i.e. in terms of constituency (phrase-structure) based description (see also Jackendoff 1972, p. 237). Such a description served as a basis also for several studies on the relationship between syntax and semantics (e.g. Schmerling 1976; Selkirk 1984; 1985): the boundaries between topic and focus or some more subtle divisions were always supposed to coincide with the boundaries of phrases. Sgall and his followers (see already Sgall 1967b) work within a framework of dependency grammar and define the boundary between the two parts on the basis of syntactic dependency, of the opposition of contextual boundness and of the left-to-right order of nodes. The boundary between Topic and Focus can then be characterized as intersecting an edge between a governor and its dependent (the latter may be a single node or a subtree), with the provision that whatever is to the right of the given dependent in the tectogrammatical dependency tree, belongs to the Focus, the rest to the Topic (see Sgall's definition above in Sect. 4.1). A similar strategy can be traced in MTT: formally, the CommS is encoded by spotting out some areas of the semantic (dependency) graph and labeling each of them with a communicative marker. A dominant node of each area (of theme or rheme), which is characterized as the node that summarizes the semantic content of the area, is marked by underlining (Polguère 1990).

However, the definition of Focus (and of presupposition, in Chomskyan terms) as a phrase is untenable since it is not always possible to assign the focus value to a part of the sentence that constitutes a phrase. This claim is supported by examples as those adduced by Hajičová and Sgall (1975): in the given context, the Focus of the sentence is *for a week to Sicily*, which would hardly be specified as a constituent under the standard understanding of this notion. These examples, however, bring no difficulties for a dependency-based description.

(25) *John went for a week to Sicily.* (He didn't go only for a weekend to his parents.)

It was convincingly argued by Steedman (1991; 1996; 2000) that it is advisable to postulate a common structure for accounting both for the syntactic structure of the sentence as well as for its information structure. For that purpose, he proposes a modification of categorial grammar, the so-called combinatory categorial grammar. A syntactic description of a sentence ambiguous as for its information structure should be flexible enough to make it possible to draw the division line between Topic and Focus also in other places that those delimiting phrases; in Steedman (1996, p. 5), the author claims that his "theory works by treating strings like *Chapman says he will give*, *give a policeman*, and *a policemen a flower* as grammatical constituents" and thus defining "a constituent" in a way that is different from the "conventional linguistic wisdom". In other words, Steedman proposes to work with non-standard constituents, as can be illustrated by (26) with the assumed intonation center at the last element of the sentence: the division of (26) into Topic and Focus is ambiguous because the verb may belong either to the topic or to the focus part of the sentence.

(26) *Fred ate the BEANS.*

The representation of such an ambiguity in a dependency framework like that of the Praguian Functional Generative Description causes no difficulty. In case the root of the tree (the verb) is *cb*, then it depends on the *cb/nb* feature of its dependents whether *Fred ate* or just *ate* are the elements of the Topic (answering the question *What did Fred eat?*, or *Who did eat what?*, respectively). If the verb is *nb*, then again two divisions are possible: either the whole sentence is the Focus (*What happened?*), or the verb and the object are the elements of the Focus (*What did Fred do?*). In the underlying tree structure, the *cb* nodes depend on the verb from the left, the *nb* nodes from the right. A division line between Topic and Focus is then drawn as characterized above.

In (26), we assumed the (normal) placement of the intonation center on the object *beans*. However, as also discussed by Steedman, the sentence may have different intonation patterns, and this may reduce its ambiguity: if the intonation center is on *Fred*, then *Fred* is the sentence Focus and the rest is the Topic (*Who ate the beans?*). If the intonation center is on the verb, then only the verb is the Focus the rest being the Topic (*What did Fred do with the beans?*). This again can be easily captured in the dependency representation of the meaning of the sentence by the assignment of the primary opposition of *cb/nb* nodes.

6. ANNOTATED CORPORA AS TESTBEDS FOR LINGUISTIC THEORY

Any modern linguistic theory has to be formulated in a way that it can be tested by some objective means; one of the ways how to test a theory is to use it as a basis for a consistent annotation of large language resources, i.e. of text corpora. Annotation may concern not only the surface and morphemic shape of sentences, but also (and first of all) the underlying sentence structure, which elucidates phenomena hidden on the surface although unavoidable for the representation of the meaning and functioning of the sentence, for modeling its comprehension and for studying its semantico-pragmatic interpretation.

Without going into any detail, we illustrate here on the example of the Prague Dependency Treebank (PDT, see e.g. Hajič 1998), based on the framework of the Functional Generative Description (FGD), how such a testing may be done.

PDT is an annotated collection of Czech texts, randomly chosen from the Czech National Corpus (CNK), with a mark-up on three layers: (a) morphemic, (b) surface shape "analytical", and (c) underlying (tectogrammatical). The current version (publicly available on address http://ufal.mff.cuni.cz/pdt2.0), annotated on all three layers, contains 3 168 documents (text segments mainly from journalistic style) comprising 49 442 sentences and 833 357 occurrences of word forms (including punctuation marks).

On the tectogrammatical level, which is our main concern in the present paper, every node of the tectogrammatical representation (TGTS, a dependency tree) is assigned a label consisting of: the *lexical value* of the word, of its *"(morphological) grammatemes"* (i.e. the values of morphological categories), of its *"functors"* (with a more subtle differentiation of syntactic relations by means of *"syntactic grammatemes"* (e.g. "in", "at", "on", "under"), and the TFA attribute of containing values for *contextual boundness*. In addition, some basic intersentential links are also added. It should be noted that TGTSs may contain nodes not present in the morphemic form of the sentence in case of surface deletions; TGTSs differ from the theoretically adequate TRs in that coordinating conjunctions are represented as head nodes of the coordinated structures, which makes it possible for the TGTSs to constitute two-dimensional trees.

Every node of the TGTS is assigned one of the three values of the attribute specifying TFA: *t* for a contextually bound non-contrastive node, *c* for a contextually bound contrastive node, *f* for a contextually non-bound node.

A very simplified (preferred, given by the context) TGTS of the sentence (27) is in Fig 1.

(27) *Nenadálou finanční krizi podnikatelka řešila jiným způsobem. (PDT)*
     Lit.: (The) sudden financial crisis-Accus. (the) entrepreneur-Nom. solved by other means. (context: the enterpreneur had to solve several problems before)

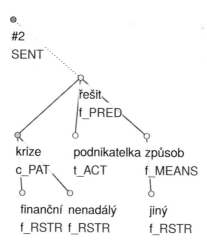

Figure 1 The preferred TGTS of sentence (27).

One of the hypotheses of the TFA account in TFG was the following:

Hypothesis: The division of the sentence into its T and F can be derived from the contextual boundness of the individual lexical items contained in the sentence (see above, Sect. 4.1).

An application of the rules in Sect. 4.1 gives the following result:

Topic: *Nenadálou finanční krizi podnikatelka* [the sudden financial crisis the enterpreneur]

Focus: *řešila jiným způsobem* [solved by other means]

The implementation of the algorithm has led to a differentiation of five basic types of Focus and it significantly supported the hypothesis that in Czech the boundary between T and F is signalized by the position of the verb in the prototypical case (the boundary between T and F: immediately before the verb in 95 % of the cases) and it has also been confirmed that the TFA annotation leads to satisfactory results even with rather complicated "real" sentences in the corpus.

Another hypothesis that has already been tested on our annotated corpus concerns the order of elements in the Focus. It is assumed that in the focus part of the sentence the complementations of the verb (be they arguments or adjuncts) follow a certain canonical order in the TRs, the so-called systemic ordering (not necessarily the same for all languages). In Czech, also the surface word order in Focus corresponds to the systemic ordering in the prototypical case.

For Czech, the following systemic ordering is postulated (see Sgall et al. 1986): Actor – Time:*since-when* – Time:*when* – Time:*how-long* – Time:*till-when* – Cause – Respect – Aim – Manner – Place – Means – Dir:*from-where* – Dir:*through-where* – Addressee – Origin – Patient – Dir:*to-where* – Effect.

Systemic ordering as a phenomenon is supposed to be universal; however, languages may differ in some specific points: the validity of the hypothesis has been tested with a series of psycholinguistic experiments (with speakers of Czech, German and English); for English most of the adjuncts follow Addressee and Patient (Sgall et al. 1995). However, PDT offers a richer and more consistent material; preliminary results have already been achieved based on (a) the specification of F according to the rules mentioned above, (b) the assumed order according to the scale of systemic ordering (functors in TGTS), and (c) the surface word order (Zikánová 2006).

7. CONCLUSION

A deeper empirical analysis of sentences (in their context) in various languages convincingly shows that the issues referred to as belonging to TFA (or communicative structure, information structure, theme-rheme or whatever terms are used) are semantically relevant. Therefore, their description should be integrated into the description of the underlying, deep syntactic (tectogrammatical) level of linguistic description. It is this level that is suitable as the input to semantico-pragmatic interpretation. The phenomena connected with TFA on other levels (word order, or also particles, clefting etc.) serve as means expressing TFA.

We have argued that the primary opposition to be distinguished is the opposition of contextual boundness, from which the bipartition of the sentence into its Topic and Focus and other related notions can be derived. Such a description offers an adequate, effective and economic way of capturing the corresponding semantically relevant distinctions. A well-suited way of testing the theoretical assumptions and hypotheses is the present-day availability of corpora annotated in a systematic and linguistically-based manner, as the experience of the Prague Dependency Treebank indicates.

ACKNOWLEDGEMENTS

The author gratefully acknowledges the most useful comments and suggestions given by Jarmila Panevová and Petr Sgall after having read the pre-final version of the manuscript. The present paper has been written under the support of the grant MSM0021620838.

APPENDIX:
A GLIMPSE BACK
AT HISTORICAL SOURCES

FOREWORD

In the Appendix, we reprint two papers documenting the early stage of the development of the research in computational linguistics carried out in Prague in two directions: the theoretical one and the one oriented towards the use of "machines".

The contribution *Some Experience with the Use of Punched-Card Machines for Linguistic Analysis* co-authored by Jarmila Panevová was originally presented in 1966 at the International Colloquium held in Prague and introduces two projects for which the use of punched-cards was crucial. One of the projects aimed at an analysis of a sample of Czech texts from a technical domain and was based on a complex linguistically-founded multilayer description of the sentence as proposed by Petr Sgall within the framework of Functional Generative Description. The other project characterized in the paper concerned an attempt to build a small English-Czech POS-tagged parallel corpus in order to study the lexical correspondences between the two languages in contexts.

The inclusion of the paper *A Functional Generative Description* by Petr Sgall and Eva Hajičová into the volume is motivated by two reasons: first, it should serve as an overall characterization of the framework that has been the starting point and the methodological basis for all the studies selected for publication in the present volume, and, second, it has a historical value in that it documents the consistency of ideas underlying the Functional Generative Description as proposed by Petr Sgall in the middle of the 1960's. For that purpose, the main emphasis is laid on Sections 1 and 3, which are reprinted here in full, and Section 5, which is only slightly abridged. The deletions concern Section 2.1.3, containing theorems and their proofs to illustrate that there exists an effective procedure enumerating all syntagms for the basic component as defined in the previous Section. Sections 6.2 and 6.3 containing the rules and meta-rules for the generation of semantic representations (called later tectogrammatical) with the order of nodes corresponding to the communicative dynamism are only briefly characterized here and illustrated by few examples. All the reductions and deletions are indicated and commented upon (in square brackets) in the relevant places.

SOME EXPERIENCE WITH THE USE OF PUNCHED-CARD MACHINES FOR LINGUISTIC ANALYSIS

After gaining the first experience with the use of punched-card machines for processing the linguistic data (e.g. in the analysis of the combinations of particular verbal categories in verbal forms and their frequency counts, the frequency of graphemes in Czech technical texts, etc.) we tackled the problems of mechanical processing systems for a more complicated task, namely the complex analysis of a larger sample of technical text from the point of view of morphology, syntax and to a certain degree of semantics as well. The analysis itself was carried out by linguists and the results were then transposed onto punched cards; in that way a collection of punched cards has been formed, which can be processed in a mechanographic way and which represents a sort of a universal collection of material, on which various different problems of Czech morphology, syntax, semantic structure of sentence, etc. can be studied; these are the points, from which each unit of the studied text was analyzed.

We mention the universal character of the use of our collection of material in the sense that we have tried to characterize each unit of the given text from various points of view so that even the mutual relations (combinations, realization of particular combinations) of the units of that text can be traced.

On the other hand our approach to the analysis of the given text, the points and criteria of it were, of course, conditioned by the overall orientation and final objectives of our work. When gathering the collection of our material, we kept the following three types of possible aims in view:

(1) the formulation of an algorithm of independent synthesis of Czech for the purpose of Machine Translation;

(2) the formulation of a certain type of Intermediate Language for the purpose of Machine Translation;

(3) the formulation of a generative model of Czech using several levels according to the proposal of P. Sgall (see Sgall, 1967a).

All these objectives should be understood to be very closely related to each other, as pure variants of one of the principal problems of linguistic structure – the problem of the relation of form and function in language. The categories, distinguished in the gathered material, were chosen with regard to the above mentioned tasks.

The result of the analysis of Czech electromechanical texts (chosen from technical books, journals, written by both Czech authors and translated from other languages) was transposed onto the punched cards – we use the ARITMA punched-card system (with cards subdivided into 90 columns which are further processed in the alpha-numerical way). The text was analyzed sentence by sentence; one punched card corresponds to one meaningful word from the text. The grammatical words (the so-called auxiliaries) were transposed onto the same card as the respective meaningful word, i.e. as a constituent of such a word, e.g. preposition + noun, conjunction + the word it adjoins, analytical forms of verbs etc. are analyzed as one unit; further on in this report we shall use the term "word" in this sense. The punched card is provided by punching the alphabetical shape of the word, then the last five letters of the word put on reversely (for morphological studies) and several indications of the position of the word in the text (i.e. the symbol of the text (book or journal), the number of the page, the serial number of the compound sentence on the page and the serial number of the word in the compound sentence). These indications enable us to trace the units easily back in the text. Thus each word of the text (in the sense specified above) has a punched card of its own.

Besides those basic data, every punched card is furthermore provided with all the data resulting from the grammatical analysis of the given word. To achieve a better survey of all the data involved, we shall now describe them as to the linguistic level they belong to.

As to morphology, the subdivision of word classes we distinguish is more subtle than the traditional nine parts of speech, since the morphological criteria are introduced into this classification more consistently, e.g. the substantivized adjectives form a special class, as in Czech *zpropitné*. Other data transposed onto the punched card are case, number, gender, the type of declension (for nouns) and person, number, tense, mood, voice, aspect and the type of conjugation (for verb). Both the graphic shape of the ending and the type of alternation were put down as well. The subdivision of declension and conjugation types is again more subtle than in Czech grammars, written for native speakers of Czech, e.g. the declension type "hrad" considered in traditional grammars as the only type for masc. inanimate with hard ending has been divided into three subtypes according to the ending of locative singular (-e: *v lese*, -u: *v proudu*, both -e and -u: *v potoku*, *v potoce*). It is evident that such an analysis presupposes a detailed elaboration of declension and conjugation types with regard to the endings alternation in Czech, so that on the basis of the assignment of a certain declension (conjugation) type, every form (forms) of a given word may be uniquely formed.

As for the adverbs and adjectives, the data required concern the degree, the characteristics of the so-called short and composed forms, etc.

The syntactic analysis resulted in assigning each word a sentence part essential-ly in compliance with the tradition of Czech dependency syntax. Further, some basic data about coordination were put down as well as an indication whether the word had a rection or whether it was itself determined by a rection of its governor. Moreover, we tried to put down at least the minimal data about the governor and its dependents: the serial number of the governor, the part of speech it belongs to and the type of modifi-cation (i.e. what parts of speech its modifiers belong to). This investigation was based on the notion of grammatical dependency, the only independent member of the sen-tence being the predicate of the main clause. The dependent clause was then handled as being equivalent to the sentence part.

We tried to put down even the basic data from the semantic structure of the sen-tence, i.e. what might be called the grammatical semantics. We were not concerned with the lexical semantics in that stage of analysis, the first attempts in this field be-ing carried out quite recently, as we shall mention further on. As for the categories of syntactic semantics, the semantic part of the sentence was distinguished, taking into account the role of the word in the structure of the utterance: the word may be the actor of the action, its goal, the action itself (predicate) or their free adjunct. Besides that, the semantic part of speech was put on (i.e. the original word class, indicating whether the goal, attribute, action, etc. is concerned); we can say that in terms of the semantic parts of speech and their relations to the morphological word classes the transformational relations can be rendered as well: e.g. *a flying plane* – "a plane which flies"; "flying" is here a verb in the terms of the semantic parts of speech; *a wooden table* means a table made of wood (formally an adjective ending is added though se-mantically we consider this form to be a noun) etc. The categories of morphological semantics differ at particular word classes – it is necessary to put down the meaning of individual formal verbal categories, e.g. Tense (on the morphological level, it may have the form of present, though on the semantic level it may obtain the meaning of historical present), Modus and Aspect, etc.

In the case of adverbials and clauses, the meanings as time, place, manner, rea-son, purpose, instrument, means, etc. are put down as well, the repertory of which was with very few changes taken over from the Syntax of Present-Day Czech by prof. Šmilauer (1969). In this respect the possibility of using our material for lexicological studies has been revealed, since in the technical text presumably a limited group of words with the meaning of time, instrument, of action etc. might occur, or eventually it is interesting to follow which words may belong to more than one group like that.

Let us now turn to the technical questions of transposing such an amount of data on one punched card. For some categories, due to the high number of elements of this category, two columns had to be reserved. To save the place, we have chosen for the most part of our analysis an alphabetic code (Aritma machines distinguish 29 differ-ent alphabetic signs in one column, while only 10 numerical signs). This way of en-coding the data was convenient for the linguist, who prepares the records for punch-ing, since a properly chosen alphabetic code can be as a rule more easily remembered than a numerical one, even though we realize that the approach is very uneconomic from the point of view of sorting. When it is possible, two categories are joined into mutually disjoining combinations and just one column is reserved for them (e.g. case and number of nouns; that means, that for nominative singular and nominative plural there are reserved distinct symbols).

Detailed characterization like that transposed onto the card provided the possibility of rich and diversified classification of the data and their combinations, and moreover it provides the possibility of mechanical counting of the frequency of investigated data. Here are some of the possibilities which suggest themselves: to examine, how often and in what sentences actor is a syntactic subject of the sentence and how often and where it represents some other sentence part. Or, it is possible to use the material for many detailed studies of some monographic problems of grammar, e.g. for the investigation in the field of causative relations to sort out (mechanically) only those cards that have to do something with the rendering of "reason", then to sort them according to some other points of view: e.g. by what means the meaning of reason is rendered (dependent clause, noun phrase etc.).

The material described here may be also used for morphological investigations: we can examine, in how many terms some endings are ambiguous (e.g. Czech -u in genitive, dative, locative etc.). The criteria of classification may be systematically arranged in order to start with the hierarchic organization of levels in language and to characterize in that way the feature in question "from the top to the bottom" – from function to form – beginning with the data from the semantic level the morphological data being the last step. This is the way we used when analyzing, sorting and tabulating our material.

The material was sorted in three stages:

(1) In the first stage the sorting was based on the data from the semantic level to obtain the syntactic data: which semantic sentence part with certain morphological semantics is rendered by which sentence part and word class (in this respect, the quantitative relation between the sentence and nominal form of rendering the determination of a certain type was examined).

(2) At the second stage not only the word category by which the meaning is rendered but also the form (case, preposition) by which it is rendered was investigated.

(3) At the third stage of the sorting, the morphological form of the word was obtained (its endings, alternation).

The sorted cards were then copied in required arrangements and the respective values added to sums or subsums automatically on the tabulating machines.

In this way 82 pages of technical text were analyzed, which represent about 22 thousand punched cards (i.e. words). We consider the first period of investigations to be finished (in 1964) and for the present time we do not continue in further analysis. The results obtained were arranged in tables and thus represent a material, which can be used by the linguists, working on monographic themes from Czech grammar. We suppose we have gained a basic account of what are the possibilities of mechanographic processing of linguistic data with the help of punched-card systems, what are the flaws of such a processing either in our preliminary project or in the possibilities of punched-card machines as such. It has turned out, for instance, that for our purposes the mere data about the word class of the governor are not sufficient (the indication about the serial number of this governor is of no use for the automatic processing by the punched-card machines) – and that we should need more information about the governor and its dependents as well. Due to the technical difficulties we encounter in our Computing Centres when processing such pretentious tasks, we came to a conclusion, that the punched-card system is not flexible enough and thus rather unsuitable for such tasks. On the other hand the punched-card machines seem to be more convenient in the case when a more simple type of sorting is concerned, e.g. alphabetic ordering of the material collected.

Similar conclusions may be drawn from our preliminary experience and results of another extensive project, aimed at the investigations of English vocabulary. This project is based on the analysis of more than 100 000 running words, for which about 286 pages of about 90 articles and 5 books from the field of electronics have been processed. The pages of the books and articles were chosen at random, the only condition (besides the prescribed field of technical interest) to be fulfilled was that the translation into Czech must exist. Each word (word in this project means everything what is between two blank spaces) was punched into one card and the following data were examined (and punched into the punched cards, as well):

(1) the so-called grammatical categories (based on a the combination of morphological and syntactic criteria; the categories in this project differ a little from the word categories mentioned above in the discussion about the Czech analysis, since the languages investigated are different as well; in this case, 33 possibilities were allowed);

(2) the Czech equivalent for the given word that would occur in the Czech translation of the text in question. These Czech equivalents were put down in the so-called basic form (e.g. infinitive, nominative singular etc.).

These data were chosen with regard to the presupposed system of MT dictionary, which will presumably be the dictionary of stems rather than the dictionary of forms. Besides those two major data, the serial number of the word in the whole collection of the material, the symbol of the text (which indicated from which particular article or book the page in question had been chosen), and the succeeding word (i.e. the immediate context) were put down on the card as well.

Originally, the chief aim of this project and also the most immediate one was to make a frequency count of the words in English technical (electronic) texts, which should provide a basis for compiling an English-to-Czech dictionary for MT. After finishing the analysis of the material to be punched, this main aim was expanded to serve not only to the practical purposes of MT but to further investigations of lexical semantics and other respects as well. Some of the main possibilities which are revealing themselves in an outline are as follows:

(1) the frequency count of English word forms as such,

(2) the frequency count of English word forms with respect to the grammatical categories they belong to,

(3) the frequency count of English word forms with respect to the corresponding Czech equivalents,

(4) any combination of previous points of views,

(5) the investigation of the number of categories that one word-form can enter (the so-called conversion in English, taken from a broader standpoint),

(6) to sort out that part of the collection, where the word category of the main word (i.e. the word investigated) combines with the category of its immediate context (punched on the card) so that it produces a (possible) syntagm; e.g. Adjective with Noun etc. This subpart of the whole material may serve some detailed monographical purposes, concerning both the terminology and the grammatical relations in English (as compared with Czech).

The material described above can also be used just as an indication, where (i.e. in which particular text and with which serial number) the word form in question occurs and thus facilitates the work of a linguist, who wants to investigate the context criteria for the translation of a given word-form.

Though the sorting in this project is mainly alphabetical (either according to the "main words" or to Czech equivalents or grammatical categories or any combination of those three data), we are not satisfied with the existing possibilities of punched-card machines we have at our disposal, since for such an extensive material the whole processing is too slow, and unfortunately not too accurate.

On the other hand, the main advantage of the punched card system (especially for lexicological or lexicographical work) is that, firstly, the punched cards are very similar to cards, generally used for such kind of work for years and linguists need not get used to a quite different technique, secondly, such punched cards, if duly arranged by the sorting machine, may serve as catalogue cards. For this purpose the so-called "interpreters" (not yet included into the ARITMA punched-card system) should be necessary so that the data on the punched card can be easily read.

We may conclude that we suppose the most efficient system for mechanization of linguistic analysis, and the most suitable for linguists, to be a combination of the punched-card system (plus the interpreter) with some type of computer, the pre-input unit of which would be a converter for converting the data from the punched cards onto the magnetic tapes. All the other processing would be then left for the computer. We are convinced that such a combination would combine the advantages of the punched cards with the rapidity and promptness of the computers.

A FUNCTIONAL GENERATIVE DESCRIPTION (BACKGROUND AND FRAMEWORK)

In the development of transformational grammar, a certain rapprochement to descriptions of the stratificational type can be traced, so that a stratificational system having the form of a generative device appears to deserve interest (Section 1). A characteristics of such a system, especially of its generative component, is given in Section 2. Since questions of semantics and of its relationship to syntax are crucial for the choice of the form of the system, we discuss (in Section 3) some problems connected with the distinction between linguistic meaning and cognitive (ontological) content, and illustrate them on the domain of tense and time reference (3.1) and of the verb with its participants (3.2). The transductive components of the description are briefly exemplified in Section 4, and our remarks in Section 5 concern problems connected with the so-called topic-comment articulation and its position in the description as a whole. In Section 6 we then present an outline of the generative component of the description taking into account TCA (6.1), and a list of meta-rules that determine the functioning of the whole system (6.2 and 6.3).

1. THEORETICAL BACKGROUND

1.1 As has been already pointed out (cf. Lamb, 1967, Hajičová and Sgall, 1968), the transformational theory has been developing in many respects towards the stratificational type of linguistic description. The standard theory of TG (dating since 1964) is characterized, in this sense, by (i) transferring the recursive properties from the transformational component to the base; (ii) taking into account the relationship between content and expression (in Hjelmslevian terms) in that a specific level of semantic interpretations is assumed and distinction between deep structure and surface structure is viewed as related to that of content and expression in a specific sense. If the stratificational type of description is defined as working with a sequence of levels ordered from content to expression, then the introduction of generative semantics[1] in TG completes its transition to the stratificational type. Furthermore, there are also some less relevant points in which TG seems to come closer to systems of the stratificational type out of which the possibility to use the dependency syntax can be mentioned here; cf. Katz's use of terms as "head" and "modifier", Fillmore's (1968b) remarks on representing "cases" by dependency diagrams, and especially Robinson's (1969) proposal of a dependency-based transformational description. This development of TG can be interpreted also as a further step in a more general process concerning the Chomskyan linguistic reasoning as departing from descriptivist traditions and approaching closer to the trends rooted not only in Cartesian linguistics but also in European structuralism.

From what has been said, it appears as useful to look for a generative formulation of a stratificational description based on dependency syntax (cf. the system proposed in Section 2), which would allow a systematic confrontation of the generative approach with the achievements of other schools of linguistic thinking.

1.2 Certainly, a generative formulation of a stratificational (or functional) description has to respect the methodological principles stated by Chomsky (enumeration of the set of sentences, assignment of structural characteristics to every sentence). However, it is necessary to reconsider what is to be regarded as the proper aim of linguistics; reflecting along these lines, we find an agreement – perhaps unexpected but not wholly accidental – between various trends: be it Hjelmslev's relationship of content and expression, Prague functional approach, or formulations as

> "To understand the ability of natural languages to serve as instrument to the communication of thoughts and ideas we must understand what it is that permits those who speak them consistently to connect the right sounds with the right meanings" (Katz, 1966, p. 100).

– cf. Chomsky, 1968b, p. 15; Lakoff, 1969, p. 117 – they show that the proper task of linguistics consists in the description (and/or explanation) of the relation between the set of the semantic representations and that of the phonetic forms of utterances. This relation (the binary relation of sign), as is well known, can be described in a constructive way as a pair of general (many-to-many) mappings (with a description of the stratificational type, these mappings correspond to the transductive parts of the generative and recognition procedures). However, to provide for the transductive procedures, an explicit specification of the both mentioned sets is necessary. There are

---

1   See Lakoff and Ross (1967); for tentative remarks to this effect, cf. Sgall (1964b). As was noted in Sgall (1968), what matters is whether the properties of an interpretive semantic component ensure the existence of its inverse device; if so, the question whether generative or interpretive semantics is to be used, is rather a technical (or, in Bierwisch's, 1969, terms a terminological) problem. Certainly, in this case, the transductive rules – be it transformations or rules of another type – cannot be semantically relevant, so that notions connected with the topic-comment articulation (which is semantically relevant in the general case, cf. Sgall, 1967b) must be accounted for by the semantic representations. It is well known that this articulation is based on a hierarchical scale. Therefore, in the system described in Section 2 here, we take the order of nodes (relation W) in a semantic representation of a sentence, roughly speaking, as reflecting this scale; for a discussion cf. Sections 5 and 6.

principal difficulties in a specification of the set of semantic representations; without a systematic cooperation with other sciences linguistics cannot meet the two basic requirements of Chomsky.

The first of them, the enumeration of the set of semantic representations, belongs to fundamental aims of the study of the structure of thought, but it cannot be plainly considered a prerequisite for the proper linguistic task. It is possible to define the general mappings for a set that can be conceived as including the set of semantic representations as its subset. This would in a sense mean that language is treated as a code (cf. McCawley, 1968) rather than a set of sentences, or that its description is "based on the notion of a transducer rather than that of a generator" (see Kay, 1970).

The second requirement, concerning the assignment of structural descriptions, is connected with a similar problem. The questions involved here were discussed in Sgall (1968), with results close to the views quoted above. In the present paper (Section 3) we try to tackle these problems with respect to the distinction between cognitive content and linguistic meaning, which is essential for the European trends of structural linguistics.

2. THE FRAMEWORK

2.1 The proposed description of language has a basic (generative) component – specifying the set of propositions, i.e. of tectogrammatical (semantic) representations of sentences – and several transductive components. Each of the components is weakly equivalent to a context-free grammar (i.e. a context-free grammar can be formulated the terminal language of which is identical with the output language of the given component); but the language described need not be context-free, for the input and output languages of the transductive components (if they are defined in an adequate way) correspond only to the syntax (tactics) of the individual levels, the set of sentence representations on a level being only a subset of the corresponding input language (cf. Sgall et al., 1969, p. 43, and – for an elementary survey of the framework – Sgall, 1967a).

In formulating the basic component we follow the way chosen in Sgall (1967b, § 8) defining first the component as such, and then the proposition as an element meeting some restrictions conditioned by the first definition. As an intermediate notion we define the syntagm (a representation of a phrase). As for effective procedures for generation and recognition of propositions, see 2.1.3.

2.1.1 *Definition 1:* The *basic component* of the description is a sequence (A, A_0, U, P, G, N, Z) where

A is a finite set of symbols (interpreted as the vocabulary of the tectogrammatical level, cf. 2.1.2);

A_0 is a subset of A (interpreted as the set of word forms with which the production of a proposition can begin, and which are the possible heads of phrases);

U is a covering of A, i.e. a set of subsets of A, such that for every $v_i \in A$ there is a $u_i \in U$, where $v_i \in u_i$. U is interpreted as the set of those sets of lexical units which are relevant for the structure of propositions;

P is a binary relation on U (interpreted as a set of expansion rules; in the terminology of dependency syntax $P(x, y)$ is read "an element of x depends – in some proposition – on an element of y"), where for any u_i, u_j such that $P(u_i, u_j)$:

a) if $u_j \cap A_0 \neq 0$, then $u_i \subset A_0$;

b) if $P(u_k, u_h)$, then either $u_i \cap u_k$ or $u_j \cap u_h$ is empty, or else $u_i = u_k$ and also $u_j = u_h$;

as for the interpretation, (a) such words as *just, only, very*, which do not belong to A_0, are not expanded by words of other syntactic groups; (b) there is only one rule for each pair of word forms (if two lexical semantemes can be joined in two different phrases, then these are differentiated at least by one of the grammatemes, e.g. by that corresponding to the type of the syntactic dependency, cf. 2.1.2);

G is a function from A into 2^A, i.e. into the set of all subsets of A (where $G(v_i)$ is interpreted as the set of word forms incompatible with v_i, cf. Definition 2);

N is a subset of 2^P where for every $n_i \in N$, and for every p_j, p_k (elements of P, taken as a set of pairs), if $p_j \in n_i$ and $p_k \in n_i$, where $p_j = (u_e, u_f)$ and $p_k = (u_g, u_h)$, then $u_f = u_h$; the elements of N are interpreted as sets of rules concerning each a certain type of the so called "necessary expansion," e.g. with verbs which are only transitive;

Z is a mapping from the Cartesian product $2^A \times P$ into P meeting certain specific conditions, cf. Definition 4 (this mapping concerns – as for the given interpretation a type of conditionally obligatory expansion);

Note: As for the phenomena that were treated in the previous versions by the set Q (obligatory word order) and by the mapping Z^2 (Ivić's, 1964, non-omissible determiner), we assume now that they can be accounted for by the transductive components.

Definition 2: A *syntagm* F (interpreted as a representation of a phrase on the tectogrammatical level) is defined as a sequence (M, D, W, T), where

M is an abstract finite set (of nodes);

D is a binary relation on M such that the graph (M, D) is a directed rooted tree, that is a connected graph fulfilling the following conditions: there is exactly one m_r in M such that $D(m_r, m_j)$ holds for no m_j (m_r is called the root of the tree); for every m_i in M distinct from m_r there is exactly one m_j such that $D(m_i, m_j)$; $D(m_i, m_j)$ can be read as "m_i depends on m_j" and interpreted as the relation of "immediate" dependency;

W is a relation of strict ordering on M that meets the condition of projectivity, cf. e.g. Hays (1961), Marcus (1965); $W(m_i, m_j)$ is read as "m_i precedes m_j" and interpreted as the (deep) word order relation;

T is a mapping of M into A (a labelling of the graph) such that the conditions (c) to (e) are fulfilled.

Note: in the sequel we write (for any $m_i \in M$) only v_i for $T(m_i)$, g_i for $G(v_i)$, and u_i for an element of U such that $v_i \in u_i$. The symbol $\subset$ denotes the strict inclusion; the binary relations are understood as sets of pairs.

c) if $D(m_i, m_j)$, then there is such a (single, cf. condition (b) on P in Definition 1) pair u_i, u_j that $P(u_i, u_j)$;

d) if $W(m_i, m_h)$ and there is a $m_j \in M$ such that $D(m_i, m_j)$ and $D(m_h, m_j)$, then $v_h \notin g_i$;

e) if m_r is the root of the tree (M, D), then $T(m_r) \in A_0$

Definition 3. Two syntagms F and F' are equivalent (i.e., in the interpretation, they correspond to a single phrase), iff there is a one-to-one mapping f from M onto M' such that for every $mi \in M\ T(m_i) = T'(f(m_i))$, and for every $m_j \in M\ D(m_i, m_j)$ iff $D'(f(m_i), f(m_j))$, and $W(m_i, m_j)$ iff $W'(f(m_i), f(m_j))$. – Here and in the sequel "iff" is used instead of "if and only if".

Definition 4: A *proposition* is a syntagm F where the conditions (f) to (h) are met:

f) if m_r is the root of the tree (M, D), then for any u_r there is no u_j such that $P(u_r, u_j)$;

g) if, for any $m_i \in M$, there is a $u_j \in U$ and a $n_k \in N$ such that $(u_j, u_i) \in n_k$, then there is some $m_h \in M$, such that $D(m_h, m_i)$ and $(u_h, u_i) \in n_k$;

h) if, for any $m_i, m_j \in M$ and $D(m_i, m_j)$ and $Z(u_g (u_i, u_j)) = p_k$ (where $v_j \in u_g$ and $p_k \in P$), then there is a m_h such that $D(m_h, m_j)$ and $(u_h, u_j) = p_k$;

As for the interpretation, (f) ensures that the labelled tree represents a sentence, not only a nonsentential syntagm (constituent phrase); (g) ensures that no necessary expansion is missing; (h) accounts for conditionally obligatory expansions of the type of Fillmore's *break* ((Agentive) Instrument).

2.1.2 We suppose, of course, that the set A consists of complex elements, though this is not reflected by the tentative formulation of the basic component given above. Without attempting to give a formal account here, we assume that a v_i can be regarded as a sequence of several semantemes: one or more lexical semantemes, several morphological ones (grammatemes), and a single syntactic semanteme. We cannot go here into details as for the complicated questions of internal structure of the lexical semantemes, which should be accounted for (cf. now Bierwisch,1969); the sequence of morphological grammatemes could be specified as an element of the Cartesian product of some "categories" as Tense, Mood, Aspect, Number, Comparison, where the subset of categories underlying the product is determined by the "semantic word class" of the lexical semanteme(s) (cf. Sgall et al., 1969, p. 25). The syntactic semanteme corresponds to the type of dependency and could be formalized equivalently as the label of the edge connecting the given node with the node on which it depends.

The structure of the set A conditions also the structuring of other sets, especially that of U and G. As for the latter, for a v_i the element of $G(v_i)$ should be specified in part with the aid of its syntactic semantemes, to get e.g. v_i -Agentive $\in G(v_j$ -Agentive) for any v_i, v_j containing this semanteme, and similarly with other types of dependency that cannot occur twice as depending on a single verbal node (cf. condition (d) in Definition 2). We do not attempt here to solve such semantic questions as the characteristics of anomalous sentences (for which the internal structure of lexical semantemes and a procedure more or less similar to Katz's projection rules seems to be necessary).

2.1.3 [shortened: presents theorems and lemmas to show that there is an effective procedure enumerating all syntagms for a given compient.]

So it is possible to state that the basic component of the system assigns different derivations to different propositions, and that the single derivation belonging to a proposition is determined uniquely by the proposition itself.

In a more illustrative way the derivation of a proposition can be regarded as a passing from the leftmost to the new node of the whole proposition in a diagram representing a dependency graph (cf. Fig. 1), where a step – corresponding to a pair (F^c, F^d) – is marked by a full arrow (connecting the supporting and the new nodes of F^d) preceded by a sequence of dotted arrows (connecting the new node of F^c with the supporting node of F^d); if the supporting node of F^d is identical with the new node of F^c (cf. Theorem 2), this sequence is empty.

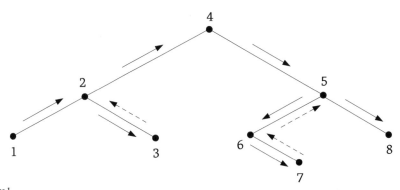

Figure 1

Note: In Fig. 1 and 2 the nodes are numbered in the order corresponding to the steps in which they are reached for the first time in the course of the passing.

2.2 The transduction of a proposition to the next lower (phenogrammatical) level can be regarded as a similar passing along the tree, but this time the passing begins at the root of the tree and then proceeds according to the following rules (cf. Sgall, 1966a):

	next rule if the answer is	
	YES	NO
(aa) Is the given node incident to a free (i.e. yet unmarked) edge?	(ab)	(ac)
(ab) Mark the leftmost free edge and go along it to the other node incident to it!	(aa)	
(ac) Is the given node the root of the tree?	Stop	(ad)
(ad) Pass upwards to the next governing node!	(aa)	

The above rules (illustrated by Fig. 2) could easily be formulated more explicitly by the means of the relations D and W as defined in 2.1.1.

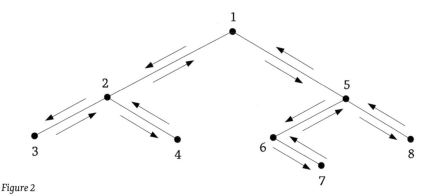

Figure 2

Furthermore, when applying (aa), the label of the given node is modified according to tables accounting for the correspondence between the symbols of the two levels. The main of the modifications is carried out at the first application of (aa) to the given node; the information concerning the lastly processed node (i.e. the immediately governing one) is used in this step, see Table 1 for an example.

With this approach, the conditions may be provided for that are widely referred to in traditional linguistics (for a full elaboration large and deep empirical investigations are, of course, necessary): the (phenogrammatical) shape of a word-form (including its auxiliary words) is most frequently conditioned by factors belonging to one of the following four groups, if stylistic factors are left out of consideration:

i.   semantics and word class of the given word,
ii. its type of dependency (its syntactic "function"),
iii. semantics and the syntactic function of some words depending on it,
iv. the (phenogrammatical) shape of the immediately governing word.

Supposing that in the moment, when the modification is carried out, the information concerning the given node and also the lastly processed one is accessible, we are able to provide for (iv) – and also for (i) and (ii) – by the step characterized as the first application of (aa). At all subsequent applications of (aa) the conditions of type (iii) are provided for.

2.3 From a formal point of view, the procedure of transduction can be conceived of as a general mapping of the set of propositions defined in 2.1 into a set of similar labelled rooted trees (labelled with phenogrammatical symbols). This general mapping could be compared to the transformational component of Chomskian descriptions. However, we want to ensure the transductive components to be weakly equivalent to context-free grammars (cf. 2.0); for the time being, we have not found any other way than that using notions from the automata theory and confronting the set of projective rooted trees with input and output languages of certain types of automata (cf. Pospíšil, 1966). These languages can be regarded as linearizations of the set of trees, and it is possible, of course, to find procedures corresponding to those of 2.1 and 2.2 and concerning these linearizations instead of the graphs. However, when linearizing these graphs, we have essentially two possibilities: either the relation W (Tesnière's linear order) or the relation D (Tesnière's structural order) can be taken as the basis of the linearization (the other relation being represented by parentheses, operators or similar means). If we want to begin the transduction with the root of the tree, we have to work with a linearization of the latter type. In Sgall et al. (1969) a linearization of the former type was chosen for the basic component (with an additional provision for the so-called closeness of the dependency relation), and thus it was necessary to conceive the transductive component as a pair of pushdown transducers the first of which is needed mainly for the change of the W-based linearization to the P-based one.

3. CONTENT VS. MEANING

3.0 Two different tendencies can be traced in the study of semantics. Under the influence of logical semantics, the transformationalists mostly try to analyze the cognitive (ontological) content of utterances, using in some way or another the predicate calculus as a starting point. The aim of this approach is to give – in the form of a semantic interpretation or of a generative semantics – an explicit account of such properties of the content of utterances as their analyticity, contradictoriness, semantic anomaly, and of such relations between the interpretations of two sentences as compatibility, implication, etc.

On the other hand, linguists working within the tradition of European structuralism do not attempt at a description of cognitive content, which is independent of individual languages, but at an account of the structure of linguistic meaning, the elements of which are understood as "points of intersection" of conceptual contents (as a reflection of reality) and of the organizing principle of the grammar of the individual language (cf. Dokulil and Daneš, 1958, p. 240).

To illustrate this distinction, let us take for instance the German preposition *mit*: in a transformational grammar it would be treated as a result of different transformations, i.e. as a surface structure representation of different deep structure – or semantic – objects (e.g. of Fillmore's Instrument, of phrasal conjunction in *der Vater mit seinem Kind*, of a commitative adjunct in *eine Zigarette mit Filter*); from the structuralist point of view, there is only a single meaning of *mit*, as was argued by Coseriu (1970).

We consider it useful to avoid both extreme standpoints in these questions. Linguistic meaning is not identical with the cognitive content and if it is to be studied by linguistic means, structural features of individual languages must be taken into account. However, we do not accept fully the implications of the structuralist approach, which – if formulated acutely – would exclude ambiguity of surface forms (if every morpheme has a single "general meaning," cf. Jakobson's (1936) treatment of cases or Hjelmslev's (1943) account of lexical meaning), or even their synonymy: if there are two different morphemes, then the content is shaped in two different ways by the linguistic structure and there is no common meaning; e.g. between *John likes music* and *Music pleases John* there is (according to Daneš, 1968, p. 61) such a difference, for the former sentence has a semantic pattern "bearer of attitude-attitude-object of attitude", whereas the latter has a pattern "source-effecting-recipient of effection"; with this approach it is possible to find a distinction of meaning e.g. between *The jury is coming in* and *The jury are coming in,* not to speak about cases where the synonymy is perhaps even more evident. Considering the comments Daneš gives on the pair *He lived usefully* and *He lived a useful life* (p. 60/61), we see that even here he hesitates to recognize the synonymy; he says that "from the viewpoint of the language-specific semantic structure, there is a difference ..., as the grammatical structure ... necessarily has a back-effect on the presentation ... of the communicated cognitive content. But ... the said back-effect of the grammatical sentence pattern is a seeming one only, and its real effect is merely a stylistic one." Perhaps even such unclear (or contradictory) statements testify the necessity to reckon with cases of synonymy on the given level and to provide criteria and a theoretical framework for their treatment.

It should be noted that the unclearness of such statements (which could be, of course, found with other linguists, too, and to a greater extent) reflects the complexity of the problems involved. We cannot attempt here to formulate (not even tentatively) a general standpoint, but it might be useful to examine some issues illustrating different domains of grammar to see how borderlines between linguistic meaning and cognitive content could be characterized. In Section 3.1 we try to investigate in this regard the meaning of tenses, in Section 3.2 questions concerning the semantic interpretation of the syntactic relations between a verb and its complements.

3.1 In a semantic analysis of tense and time reference, there are two possibilities: either the "time of the clause" or the tense of its head verb is taken as the starting point. The former approach (that of McCawley, 1971, Wunderlich, 1969, and others) leads to such assumptions as the following two:

(1) If the clause contains an adverb as *yesterday,* it is this adverb that identifies the time reference of the clause, and the tense of the verb is to be regarded as a surface element, similar to those of concord in number, etc. (if we understand correctly Wunderlich's and McCawley's conclusions).

(2) The tense of the verb refers to the "time of the clause" in a way that is rather like the way in which personal pronouns refer to what they stand for (McCawley, 1971, p. 19).

In our opinion, there are serious difficulties connected with both these assumptions. If *yesterday* is treated as in (1), so should be probably expressions as *last year, last decade* etc[2]; but is there a semantic criterion distinguishing these expressions from those as *in the Tertiary, before the discovery of fire* etc.? Or should all expressions of this kind (even those where indefinite embeddings ought to be accounted for) be regarded as relevant for the question whether the verb of the given clause has a tense meaning or not?

---

2   But the semantic character of "vor vier Tagen", "in einer Woche," etc., is different; in "Im Sommer sagte er, daß er es in einer Woche tun kann" it is not possible to see the relation "*e* nach *s*" for *kann.*

As for (2), we can only say that a sentence as *Marseille was founded by Greeks*, or *He wrote all these books* (or, in any case, its Czech equivalent) is not odd for us, and a question which may follow can concern either the identity of some item referred to by anaphoric means, or some additional information. The latter example can give raise to the questions: *Who wrote them? What books wrote he? When did he? Why did he? How did he?* etc., but there is an essential difference between the first two and the rest of them. The former are in the given context in a sense equivalent to *Who do you speak about? What books do you mean?* etc. For the third question there is no such equivalent; a question as *What time are you speaking about?* would have a similar function only if the preceding sentence were something like *Then he wrote all these books*. Similarly, a question as *Which way do you mean?* would be in that sense equivalent to *How did he?* if the "stimulus" sentence were e.g. *He wrote all these books in that way*. – We suppose that this difference shows that verbal tense has not a pronominal character.

Certainly, questions provoked by assumptions (1), (2), as well as those concerning overlapping of time intervals identified by verbal forms, call for a deep and extensive study. These questions, however, concern, in our opinion, not the relationship between linguistic expression and linguistic meaning, but the relationship between linguistic meaning and cognitive content. Thus having in mind the difficulties involved in advancing our knowledge from the structure of expression to the domain of cognition (or of ontological structures), it might be useful to base the study of the latter domain on a relatively systematic knowledge of the structure of linguistic meaning. Therefore we have chosen the latter of the two approaches mentioned at the beginning of 3.1, i.e. we take the tense of the verb and not conceptual time relationships as the starting point. The results of our analysis were presented in Hajičová, Panevová and Sgall (1970).

Thanks to these results we can give an explicit definition of the traditional terms "basic" and "relative tense" (as they are used e.g. in Czech grammars), which can be understood as "deictic" (referring to the point of speech), and "anaphoric" (referring to the point of event of a clause in the given proposition). There are at least two possibilities (which have not been kept apart clearly in traditional grammars)[3]:

((a)) An occurrence of a verbal form V_i renders a basic tense iff $R_i = S$; otherwise the tense rendered is a relative tense.

((b)) An occurrence of a verbal form renders a basic tense iff the corresponding node V_i is not reported by any verb[4]; otherwise, a relative tense is rendered.

Our theorems[5] show what advantage the latter definition has: if the condition of ((b)) holds, then for the given V_i, $R_i = S$ by Theorem 1, so that to decide whether a certain

---

3   In the sequel, we use the symbols introduced in Hajičová, Panevová and Sgall (1970), esp. V_i for a verbal node of a dependency tree, E_i for the point of event of V_i, R_i for the point of reference of V_i, S for the point of speech.

4   A verb V_i is reported by V_j iff there is a V_k in the given dependency tree such that the following conditions hold:
     (i) V_k depends on V_j and is the head of a "content" clause (indirect speech in the broader sense including the clauses of perception)
     (ii) V_i is governed by V_k (where "is governed by" is the transitive closure of "depends")

5   In this section we refer to Theorems 1 and 2 of the paper by Hajičová, Panevová, and Sgall (1970), not to those in

occurrence of a verbal form renders a basic tense or not, we have only to consider its position in the sentence (to see whether it is included in a reported clause or not). But with ((a)) we have also to consider the grammatemes of tense of all verbs reporting V_i, before we can state whether its tense is basic or not. (And even this would not do, for with a sentence including an adverb from a certain class, as e.g. "He told me he would go to Australia in 1984" the time point E_i can be analyzed as being after S – at least with regard to the cognitive content – even if none of the conditions for V_i given in Theorem 2 were fulfilled). Furthermore: when not (z), but one of the other conditions of Theorem 2 is fulfilled, we know – having considered the grammatemes of tenses – whether E_i is anterior or posterior to S, i.e., whether the event belongs to the past or to the future, but even according to ((a)) we cannot say that a basic tense is rendered by V_i, so that we must distinguish between a case when the verb renders a basic tense and that when the verb determines that the given event is past, present or future. (This means that it is preferable not to say that in a sentence as "I am told he came" the reported verb renders a basic tense (here the past), but to say that it renders a relative tense – here: anteriority to a present event.)

The best way to account for the mentioned distinction appears to consist in regarding ((b)) as the definition of the two types of tense, to disregard ((a)) – or to choose another term for that distinction, if it appears useful – and to consider a new formulation ((c)) – corresponding to Theorem 2 – as valid:

((c)) The event is determined as past, present or future by the verb token identifying it if neither this verb token nor any verb reporting it renders anteriority to its point of reference, or none of these verb tokens renders posteriority to its point of reference.

3.2 There are two main approaches to the questions of semantic relationship between a verb and its participants. The first of them, elaborated especially by Tesnière, regards the subject of an intransitive verb as in a sense equivalent with the subject of an active transitive verb, i.e. it identifies the first "actant" (participant) of a verb having two arguments with the single argument of intransitive verbs; it is assumed that there exists an ordering of the participants relevant for the grammatical and semantic structure of sentence. The other, represented by Fillmore, and at least in a certain respect also by Halliday (1967), works with distinct participants (cases) as relevant for the semantic interpretation, so that the single participant of an intransitive verb is not determined solely as the first, but as an Objective, Dative, etc.

In the approach adopted in Sgall (1967b) and in Sgall et al. (1969), these relationships were provided for on the tectogrammatical level of the description by the means of functors (i.e. syntactic semantemes, cf. here 2.1.2), among which actor, goal and free modification are relevant for the issue under discussion, and of "suffixes" (grammatemes). With this approach, in accordance with Tesnière, the actor (which more or less

---

Section 2 of the present paper. In this section we refer to Theorems 1 and 2 of the paper by Hajičová, Panevová, and Sgall (1970), not to those in Section 2 of the present paper.

corresponds to Fillmore's agentive, but it is not constrained to animate nouns only) is identified with the first "actant" of the intransitive verb.

We are not concerned here with arguments about the relative merits of either of these treatments; we want only to show (in Section 6) that a device of the type given in Section 2 can provide for the relations of the given kind (cf. Sgall, 1972d, where this was shown for the examples from Russian discussed by Zimmermann, 1967).

Let us add some remarks concerning the questions of linguistic meaning and cognitive content. The main difficulties connected with Tesnière's approach are probably those related with converse and symmetric predicates. The relationship between *A precedes E* and *B follows A*, or that between *A married B* and *B married A* has not been provided for in any description of this type. In Fillmore's approach, this type of relationship could be, perhaps, accounted for by an equivalence relation on the set of semantic representations (cf. McCawley, 1968, p. 168), if, in each example *A* and *B* correspond to two different cases (with a verb as *marry*, evidently, this difference between cases should be connected with the difference of sex). However, at least with action verbs corresponding to converse predicates there is a distinction that should be reflected at the level of linguistic meaning, viz. the distinction illustrated by Fillmore (1970), p. 13, where he speaks about the buying/selling transaction viewed "from one of the participants' point of view"; it remains yet unclear (cf. Sgall 1972b) what is the relation of such a distinction to the topic-comment articulation. Anyway, Fillmore's examples with *viciously, willingly* have to be taken into account, but as they stand, it is difficult to say whether they illustrate limited classes of lexical elements or open classes including recursive embeddings, etc.; cf. what has been said about (1) in Section 3.1. We assume that here also the relationship between linguistic meaning and linguistic content is involved, which can be described explicitly only after a relatively systematic knowledge of the relationship between linguistic expression and meaning is achieved.

4. TRANSDUCTIVE COMPONENTS

4.1 Some general properties of the transductive components of our system were characterized in Section 2.2 and 2.3. Let us add here that there are, in the present form of the system, two levels where the sentence is represented by a dependency graph (the levels of tectogrammatics and phenogrammatics), and then three levels where the sentence is represented as a sequence (the levels of morphemics, phonemics, and phonetics). To illustrate the first two transductive components, we present here a sample of rules for the Czech language in the form of Table 1.

[Note: Only the first part of Table 1 is reproduced here in full, in order to illustrate the shape of the Table. The second part is abridged and only three out of the original 11 examples of rules are reproduced.]

Tectogrammatical input	Condition (governing node)	Phenogrammatical output
V-temp$_i$	V-temp$_i$	N_V-subscr
V-temp$_i$ $\begin{cases} \text{result} \\ \text{mod}_k \end{cases}$	0	$\begin{cases} V\text{-subscr} \\ V\text{-pass-subscr} \end{cases}$
V-temp$_i$	0	$\begin{cases} N_V\text{-subscr} \\ V\text{-subscr} \\ V\text{-pass-subscr} \end{cases}$

Table 1 Part 1

Note: *The choice of the passive form is limited to a subset of verbs that should be characterized by a special index. This condition – belonging to the type (i) in Section 2.2 – can be included easily into the corresponding lines of the Table.*

Phenogrammatical input	Condition (governing node)	Morphemic output	English counterpart
V-temp$_{11}$	0	když, v době, kdy, ... + V	When she lived in Prague, she attended your lecture
NV-temp$_{11}$	0	při+N_V-loc	on his arrival
V-temp$_{12}$	V-Future	potom až-co + V-subscr	He will come after he has finished

Table 1 Part 2

Abbreviations used in Table 1:

V – verb; N_V – verbal noun; loc, gen – morphemic case forms of the respective noun; temp$_i$ – a grammateme of adverbial modification with one of the temporal meanings; mod$_k$ – modality other than indicative; subscr – the sequence of subscripts (or grammatemes attached by hyphens) identical with that in the first column; F – optional (in our case the rules concerns the Czech verbal noun odchod [departure] only); 0 – there is no relevant condition of the type (iv) in 2.2

This table has two parts, the first of which contains some examples concerning the transduction from the tectogrammatical to phenogrammatical level (especially the choice between finite in active and passive and between verbal noun). The second part of Table 1 illustrates in a similar way the transduction from the phenogrammatical to the morphemic level; here the examples are taken from the set of grammatemes characterizing some types of adverbial modification (complement), namely those with a temporal meaning. The first column of each table contains the relevant parts of the complex symbol in the input. In the second column the conditions in terms of some features of the governing node label are stated, under which the given input symbol is transduced; it is assumed that the governing word has already been transduced on the lower level, cf. Section 2.2. The third column contains the relevant parts of the complex symbol at the output (in the usual graphemic shape, as for prepositions and conjunctions). In the second part of Table 1, an additional fourth column is attached, giving some examples in English translation to illustrate the distinctions that are accounted for by the different kinds of "temp$_i$" grammatemes for Czech. The examples are taken from Panevová (1969).

[4.2 deleted]

4.3 In addition to the modifications of transduced symbols characterized in 2.2, 4.1, and 4.2 there are also modifications of some other types, which need to be accounted for in a special way (this is in accordance with the fact that each of these modifications is limited either to a highly restricted class of grammatical constructions or to a stylistically marked class of phenomena). This applies to changes in the order of symbols, in the orientation of the dependency relation, and to deletions (cf. Sgall et al., 1969, pp. 61–62). Since there are strong restrictions concerning these phenomena (including the recoverability of the deletions), it may be assumed that the transducers used can meet not only the conditions of pushdown automata, but even of a more restricted class.

5. TOPIC – COMMENT ARTICULATION

We suppose that a definitive form of integrated linguistic descriptions cannot be stated unless the phenomena of the topic-comment articulation of a sentence be analyzed in a systematic way. The difficulties encountered by the transformational approach in connection with sentences such as *Many books are read by few men, Not many arrows hit the target*, etc. can be solved without transformations changing the meaning, and also without global constraints, if the scale of communicative dynamism in the sense of Firbas is accounted for by means of an ordering of the elements of the semantic representation of a sentence (for a detailed elaboration, see Sgall, Hajičová, and Benešová, in prep.).

With this approach e.g. passivization would be described as such, apart from the word-order relation. (Let us note that in many languages the order of participants with respect to the verb is not connected with passivization in the way known from English, and that it is a peculiarity of English that, if the "deep subject" belongs to the comment, then the sentence regularly is converted to its passive form so that the order topic-comment is maintained; see Mathesius, 1929; 1942).

This approach could account also for such well-known examples as *Two languages are known by everybody in this room*, etc., which were discussed in Sgall (1969)[6]. The order of quantifiers, which is semantically relevant in the general case, would be given explicitly in the semantic (tectogrammatical) representations[7].

---

6   Cf. Sgall (1967) and Firbas (1971), and the writings quoted there.
7   Many new insights and a proposal of some features of a framework accounting for phenomena of this kind were given by Seuren (1969).

As was shown by Firbas and others, the semantic structure of a sentence often determines one variant of the topic-comment articulation of this sentence as the unmarked, while other variants are conditioned by certain types of the preceding context (e.g. the order *Mouton published many linguistic monographs* is unmarked, whereas in a context where linguistic monographs were mentioned already, the corresponding NP can be chosen as the topic, which yields the marked variant *Many linguistic monographs were published by M.*)[8]. In modern terms, we can say that the unmarked variant is connected with no specific[9] presuppositions, whereas with each of the marked variants (if intonation is taken into account, these are numerous even in non-Slavic languages) additional presupposition may be implied.

Let us illustrate this on an example concerning the semantic structure of questions. A *wh*-question can be treated as questioning the value of a variable and presupposing the truth value of the predication as given. On the other hand, a *yes-no* question does not imply such a presupposition and questions the truth value of the predication. It has been shown[10] that at least in some languages there are also *yes-no* questions corresponding to English examples as *Is it John who likes apples?*, which clearly imply a presupposition concerning the truth-value of the predication; but here the presupposition is determined not by the grammatical form of the question (it is a *yes-no* question) but by the marked character of its topic-comment articulation. (This marked character is reflected by a marked variant of the word-order, of the intonation, or by specific grammatical means; it would be of interest to examine from this point of view e.g. the placement of the particle *li*, of the sentence stress, and of the word-order in questions in Russian).

Certainly, the relation of the topic to the other elements of a sentence does not equal to the relation between different elements of the comment. It would be possible to take structures as *He told me about John that S* (where John must be mentioned in S) as a starting point[11] and to conceive the performative matrix sentence as e.g. *I declare to you about NP that S* (where *NP* with an identical referential index is contained in S).

---

8   Cf. Section 6 for an account of the unmarked order (where the hierarchy of CD is in accordance with the systemic ordering of participants) as opposed to the marked one (involving topicalization).

9   There are at least three different types of presuppositions:
     a) determined by an element in a lexical meaning (and studied esp. by Fillmore),
     b) determined by a (sub)component in the sentence structure (and discussed by McCawley 1969a), and
     c) determined by the topic-comment articulation.
     Of course, also a non-marked variant of this articulation can contain presuppositions of the types (a) – if it contains e.g. a verb as *blame*, – or (b) in cases as *The man killed* (or ... *kissed?*) *the woman*.

10   By P. S. Peters, who gave this classification of questions in his Prague lecture "How can Transformations be Constrained?," May 1970.

11   This means that in the tectogrammatical representation or deep structure a verb of speaking (verba dicendi, cognitandi, sentiendi) has two different "cases" instead of a single Objective:
     V + about NP-Objective$_1$ + that S-Objective$_2$ (see Sgall, 1969, p. 236); perhaps also the problem pointed out by Postal (1969, p. 415, Section (D)) might be solved in such a way. Let us note that in some languages the (superficial) construction *say (think, hear...) about N$_i$ that S* (including N$_i$) is more usual than it is in English; an optional (or obligatory, with some verbs?) transformation deleting *about N$_i$* would be, of course, necessary.

5.1 To account for the phenomena of topic/comment articulation (TCA) in the framework of a functional generative description two more classes of linguistic phenomena should be incorporated into the description[12], namely:

(i) the distinction between contextually bound and non-bound elements, which is identical or at least very close to Chomsky's distinction between presupposition and focus;

(ii) a systematic ordering of the units that depend on a single governor (cf. Section 5 above about the unmarked order, and Sgall, Hajičová, and Benešová, in prep., § 3.6); with a verbal governor, these units are more or less identical with Tesnière actants and circonstants, Halliday's participants and circumstances, or Fillmore's cases; as a rather simplified illustration we use here the tentative ordering actor, locative, dative, objective, instrument, condition, cause[13].

The inclusion of these phenomena into the description is based on the assumption that in the actual left-to-right ordering of the lexical units of a proposition or semantic representation (SR), i.e. in their hierarchy of CD, the verb is preceded by it contextually bound participants and followed by the non-bound, the ordering of the bound participants being conditioned by various factors; we assume that here all permutations are possible, while with the non-bound participants this ordering is identical to the systemic ordering characterized in (ii) above. We are aware that such an assumption is rather strong, since some of the participants (or at least of free modifications or circumstances) may, perhaps, even if non-bound, occupy various positions in the hierarchy of CD. For the time being, we assume that the free participants (free modifications, adverbials) behave, in this respect, in the same way as the "intentional" participants (case values).

In our treatment of participants we follow, in the main, their classification suggested by Fillmore, though some further modifications of his case theory will probably be in place (cf. Sgall, 1972b); e.g. we agree with Fillmore in regarding locative as a participant with the verb *stay*, while with the verb *hit* the corresponding participant is classified here as objective.

We assume that some of the participants function only as "intentional" ones, e.g. agentive, objective, others having either the function of an intentional participant, or of a free participant (according to the verb; e.g. locative is a free participant with *study*, *play*, *see* etc., but an "intentional" participant with *stay*, *find oneself*, *dwell*). To illustrate (to a certain extent) also the types of units functioning primarily as free participants, we add condition and cause to the participants discussed by Fillmore. Our approach

---

12 Cf. the definition and theorems in Section 2 above. – Instead of the formalism of the theory of graphs we use in the sequel the (more illustrative) form of dependency diagrams and we speak in terms of "passing" along the edges of such a tree diagram from one node to another; the placement of the nodes in the vertical dimension of the diagram corresponds to the transitive closure of the dependency relation D; the linear order of nodes represented by the horizontal dimension corresponds to the relation W, interpreted as the hierarchy of CD. – For empirical reasoning and motivating remarks on the proposed treatment, cf. Sgall, Hajičová, and Benešová (in prep.), esp. Part II and Ch. 7.

13 It is still an open question whether the systemic order of e.g. instrument and objective is the same for different languages, or for all English constructions.

also provides for the possibility of embedding sentences into the position of participants[14].

The nodes of the tree, or more precisely the lexical parts of their labels, are generated from the left to the right, i.e. we do not proceed from a symbol for the sentence through symbols for phrase categories to symbols for lexical units, as is the case of a phrase-structure grammar (using phrase-markers), but we insert the lexical units in the course of the derivation of the sentence accordingly to the hierarchy of CD[15]; in contrast to the generative procedure suggested by our Theorems 1 and 2 (and illustrated in Fig. 1 in Sec. 2.1.3), here even the lexical labelling of a node standing to the left of its governing node always takes place before the lexical labelling of this governing node.

We assume the framework to be complemented in three respects:

a) each occurrence of a lexical unit in the SR belongs not only to a class u_i (in our example in Fig. 3 this class, interpreted as the syntactic characteristics of the word token, is substituted only by a subscript of the participant), but also either to the class of contextually bound or to that of non-bound units, which is indicated in our example by the presence (or absence) of the superscript b for "bound"; [Note. Fig 3 is omitted and the example referred to here is reproduced in the note below.]

b) the set P (a binary relation on $\{u_i\}$ for $1 \le i \le N$, interpreted as expansion rules, corresponding to the pairs of labels of possible edges of the dependency tree) is partially ordered, as will be illustrated for the purpose of the present discussion by the list of rules and their ordered groupings, added to this paragraph (where $N = 17$);

c) the functioning of the whole system is determined by meta-rules, i.e. traffic rules restricting the possibility of applications of the rules (elements of P)[16]; the meta-rules are given in § 6.2. and 6.3 below in the form of an informal algorithmical procedure[17].

[Note. For the sake of brevity the list of rules and their groupings mentioned in point (b) above are omitted here as their characterization given in this point is sufficient for their understanding. Sections 6.2 and 6.3 are not reprinted here in full but the procedure is characterized briefly by the introductory paragraphs 6.2 and 6.3 from the original version and by some examples.]

6.2 The meta-rules are given here in the form of a procedure (list of instructions) where after every instruction one or more possible next steps are indicated. If there is more than one continuation in the *yes*- or *no*-column, this means a free (indetermin-

---

14 This means that the element of the set U that contains the symbol V must comprise the subscript denoting the types of participants, too, i.e. such symbols as $V_{a, ag}$, $V_{a, obj}$, etc. are used in a more detailed elaboration of the description.

15 Cf. now Paducheva (1969, esp. the conclusion of her paper), as to the necessity of combining the syntactic and lexical derivations.

16 It can be shown (cf. Goralčíková's paper in this volume) that even with these meta-rules the output language of the generative component (i.e. the set of all SR's) is a context-free language.

17 This procedure may be considerably simplified if the position of a verb in relation to its participants (in the scale of CD) is not specified by the left-to-right order, cf. Section 6.3 below.

istic) choice. If the given instruction has the form of a question, the continuation in case of negative answer is given in the *no*-column. If negation is attached, a new node labelled Neg is to be established below the given node (to its left or to its right, according to the instruction; for an empirical support for such treatment cf. Hajičová, 1973) and we return immediately back to the given node, which has a verbal label. If the instruction orders the adding of the superscript b or of a lexical unit, this means a step in establishing (specifying) the label of the given node.[18] However, this specification is in fact necessary only with the main verb; to make the SR's more illustrative, the superscript b is added also to dependent nodes.

List of meta-rules [examples]

Instruction	Next step	
	Yes	No
(A) Establish a node and add a subscript u_i (for the first word of the sentence)	(B)	–
(B) Is the given u_i a verbal subscript?	(C), (D), (E)	(F)
(C) Add the superscript b!	(D), (E)	–
(D) Attach negation to the left!	(E)	–
(E) Add a lexical unit (consistent with the given u_i)!	(J)	–
(F) Add the superscript b!	(E)	–

[Note. To illustrate the functioning of the meta-rules, a list of steps is added (in the order of the application of the meta-rules) corresponding to the derivation of the SR of the sentence *People killed animals with arrows, because they did not know guns*; all the nodes representing the lexical items included in the main clause were assigned the superscript b (thus belonging to the topic of the sentence) while the dependent *because*-clause was supposed to be the focus (comment) of the sentence. The subscripts of the participants are assigned as follows: *People*$_{ag}$ *killed animals*$_{dat}$ *with arrows*$_{instr,}$ *because they*$_{ag}$ *did not know*$_{cause}$ *guns*$_{obj}$.]

6.3 The sequence of meta-rules can be considerably reduced if only the order of participants is defined (i.e. in the dependency tree a linear ordering W is defined for the immediate descendants of a single node only, as in a phrase-marker, and not for

---

18 The "identification" is not a simple matter here, since the labels are established, according to the meta-rules, in two or three stages:
a) the subscript corresponding to the given u_i,
b) the superscript b,
c) the lexical unit (rendered here schematically by the graphemic shape of the word);
d) furthermore, if $u_j \cap u_i \neq 0$, a rule of the form (u_k, u_j) can be applied on u_i, but the subscript has to be replaced then by the subscript corresponding to $u_i \cap u_j$. This means that in an elaborated description the set V should be formulated not only as a covering, but as a partition of A.

all nodes in the tree). Only on some lower level the placement of the verb (in the word order) is specified.

[Note. The functioning of the reduced meta-rules is illustrated then by a list of steps (in order of the application of the meta-rules) corresponding to the derivation of the SR of the sentence quoted above. It is also remarked that this approach is accompanied by several advantages connected with the transductive components, though it might be perhaps considered a disadvantage if, in this case, the generation of an SR of a sentence did not proceed strictly according to the hierarchy of CD (from the left to the right), the head verb being chosen before its participants (and, in general, the governing word before those depending on it). It is then possible to combine the left-to-right generation with the simpler variant of transductive components, if a transductive procedure for trees (not for their linearizations) is chosen.]

ABSTRAKT

Der vorliegende Band umfasst eine Sammlung ausgewählter Beiträge, die im Laufe meines professionellen Werdegangs veröffentlicht wurden. Die Beiträge gründen auf dem theoretischen Rahmenwerk der Funktionalen Generativen Beschreibung (FGB), wie sie in den frühen sechziger Jahren von Petr Sgall entworfen und seither von Sgall und seinen Schülern weiterentwickelt wurde. Dieses Rahmenwerk entstand als Alternative zu Chomskys ursprünglichem Konzept der generativen Transformationsgrammatik und kann in gewisser Weise als Vorläufer verschiedener alternativer Rahmenwerke, in denen die semantische Ebene Berücksichtigung findet und den Ausgangspunkt des generativen Prozesses bildet, verstanden werden. Die FGB ist tief in der Struktur- und Funktionslehre der Prager Linguistischen Schule und dem Konzept der Sprachbeschreibung von der Funktion zur Form verwurzelt, was sich in ihrem mehrstufigen Modell niederschlägt, das in angemessener Weise die kommunikative Funktion von Sprache berücksichtigt und zwischen (sprachlicher) Bedeutung und (außersprachlichem) Inhalt unterscheidet.

Die thematische Bandbreite der vorliegenden Sammlung reicht von Themen wie der Verb-Argument-Struktur über die Informationsstruktur des Satzes durch Erfassung seiner Tiefenstruktur in einem annotierten Korpus bis zu Themen, die über die Satzstruktur hinausgehen. Abschließend wird der Ausgangspunkt des vertretenen Ansatzes mit anderen Konzepten verglichen.

In seiner Gliederung erfasst der Band (bis auf den Schlussteil) in gewisser Weise die zeitliche Entwicklung meiner Forschungsarbeit, die in den späten sechziger und frühen siebziger Jahren mit Studien zum Kern der syntaktischen Tiefenstruktur (Teil 1, "Underlying Syntactic Structure" (Die syntaktische Tiefenstruktur)) ihren Anfang nahm. Einen großen Stellenwert stellen außerdem Untersuchungen zur Valenz dar, da die hier vertretene Theorie der Funktionalen Generativen Beschreibung auf der Beschreibung der Dependenzsyntax sowohl auf Ebene der Tiefenstruktur (tektogrammatische Ebene) als auch auf Ebene der Oberflächenstruktur beruht. Das Aufkommen der sogenannten "Kasusgrammatik" von Charles Fillmore gab Anlass zu einem detaillierten Vergleich zwischen der Lehre der FGB und dem Ansatz von Fillmore. Mit der Problematik der Valenz, insbesondere in Bezug auf die Syntax des Tschechischen, beschäftigte sich im Rahmen der FGB vor allem Jarmila Panevová (siehe Panevová 1974, 1978, 1980, Panevová und Sgall 1976, und Hajičová und Paneová 1984 Vergleich von Valenzrahmen nach der Definition der FGB-Theorie am Beispiel ausgewählter tschechischer und englischer Verben). Die in dieser Sammlung enthaltenen Studien befassen sich darüber hinaus mit einigen spezifischen Aspekten des Fillmoreschen Verfahrens, namentlich mit seiner Definition des ersten Arguments (*Agentiv* oder *Actor-Bearer*?), die eng mit der Notwendigkeit oder Redundanz der Einführung von "sich kreuzenden Klammern" als spezifischem formalen Mittel verbunden ist (siehe Hajičová 1981, in diesem Band nicht erfasst). Im Allgemeinen beschäftigen sich die Beiträge mit dem Stellenwert der Fillmoreschen Kasus im Rahmen einer umfassenden Sprachbeschreibung: Ausgehend von der Unterscheidung zwischen der Ebene der (linguistischen) Bedeutung und der Ebene des (kognitiven) Inhalts werden (in *Remarks on the Meaning of Cases* (*Bemerkungen zur Bedeutung der Kasus*)) Gründe für eine Differenzierung zwischen formalen Mitteln wie morphologischen Kasus und Präpositionen in Präpositionalgruppen, Valenzstellen in Bezug auf ihre (linguistische) Bedeutung und ontologischen Kategorien dargelegt. In Abhandlungen zur syntaktischen Informationsstruktur, die in Teil 2 dieser Sammlung enthalten sind, wird näher auf Valenzstellen und ihre Anordnung in der Tiefenstruktur des Satzes eingegangen.

In Teil 2, das den Titel "Topic-Focus Articulation and Related Issues" ("Topik-Fokus-Gliederung und verwandte Themen") trägt, liegt das Augenmerk auf den Aspekten der Sprache, die nicht durch den Prädikat-Argument-Kern in der Tiefenstruktur erfasst werden können, aber durch ihre semantische Relevanz trotzdem zu ihm gehören, insbesondere auf der Topik-Fokus-Gliederung (Informationsstruktur des Satzes) und verwandten Themen wie Negation oder Präsupposition. Die Unterscheidung zwischen der formalen und "topikalen" Gliederung des Satzes geht auf Vilém Mathesius und seine bahnbrechenden Studien zurück (1907; 1939), in denen er die psychologisch orientierten Arbeiten von H. Weil (1844) sowie den Linguisten um die *Zeitschrift für Völkerpsychologie* (z.B. Georg von Gabelentz, Hermann Paul, Philip Wegener) kritisiert und ihnen entgegenhält, dass die Begriffe, die sie unter den Namen psychologisches Subjekt und psychologisches Prädikat behandeln, sich eher auf die faktische Situation, welche die Aussage reflektiert, als auf die seelische Verfassung des Sprechers beziehen. In der tschechischen Linguistik entstanden auf Grundlage der revolutionären Studien von Mathesius zwei eng verwandte Ansätze, die sich jedoch in manchen grundlegenden Aspekten unterscheiden: die sogenannte *funktionale Satzperspektive* (mit Verweis auf ihren Begründer auch Brünner Schule genannt, Jan Firbas gilt als Vertreter der Masaryk-Universität in Brünn) und die Theorie der *Topik-Fokus-Gliederung* (auch Prager Theorie genannt, mit Verweis auf Petr Sgall und seine Mitarbeiter, die als Vertreter der Prager Karluniversität gelten). Um den Bezug zwischen Mathesius' ursprünglichen Gedanken und den zwei genannten "Schulen" deutlich zu machen, beginnt Teil 2 des vorliegenden Bandes mit der Studie *Vilém Mathesius and functional sentence perspective, and beyond* (*Vilém Mathesius, die funktionale Satzperspektive und darüber hinaus*), die anlässlich des 100. Jubiläums des Lehrstuhls für Anglistik der Prager Karlsuniversität entstand und im Jahr 2012 veröffentlicht wurde.

Eines der grundlegenden Probleme bei der Untersuchung und Beschreibung der Topik-Fokus-Gliederung (TFG) unter dem Aspekt der Beziehung zwischen Form und Funktion ist ihre Stellung innerhalb des Sprachsystems. Studien zur semantischen Relevanz der Gliederung in Bezug auf die Negation stellen ein wichtiges Argument für ihre Einbindung in die Beschreibung der Tiefenstruktur des Satzes, d.h. der Ebene der (linguistischen) Bedeutung, dar. Die semantische Relevanz der TFG für die Interpretation einer Negation wird systematisch im Beitrag *Negation and Topic vs. Comment* (*Negation und Topik vs. Comment*) (1973) behandelt, der auf Beobachtungen von Zemb (1968) für das Deutsche und Kraak (1966) für das Niederländische verweist. Die detaillierte Analyse der Negation, insbesondere die Frage "was in einem Negationssatz negiert wird", führte zu tieferen Untersuchungen zur Notion der Präsupposition und zur Definition eines dritten Glieds, der sogenannten Allegation. Der Begriff wurde 1971 in einem Beitrag auf der Computerlinguistik-Konferenz COLING in Debrecen eingeführt (siehe Hajičová 1971) und anschließend in mehreren weiteren Studien (Hajičová 1974, 1975, 1984) auf den Prüfstand gestellt, die ausführlichste Studie bildet der Beitrag *On Presuppostion and Allegation* (*Zu Präsupposition und Allegation*), der in diesem Teil des Bandes enthalten ist.

Wie im ersten Beitrag dieses Teils erläutert wird, gründet die hier vertretene Herangehensweise an die TFG auf einer strikten Differenzierung zwischen der semantisch relevanten Funktion der TFG und den Formen, durch die sie sich manifestiert. Diese Formen können morphologischer, syntaktischer oder prosodischer Natur sein. Prosodische Mittel der TFG stehen im Zentrum der Studie *Questions on Sentence Prosody Linguists Have Always Wanted To Ask* (*Fragen zur Satzprosodie, die Linguisten schon immer stellen wollten*); behandelt werden insbesondere das Problem der Bestimmung der Position des Intonationszentrums in englischen Sätzen sowie die Frage nach der Möglichkeit, die Grenze zwischen Topik und Fokus prosodisch zu kennzeichnen, oder einen Gegensatz im Topik-Teil des Satzes auszudrücken, letzteres wird auch an Beispielen aus dem Deutschen illustriert.

Doch Topik und Fokus, und insbesondere die verschiedenen Stufen des sog. "communicative dynamism", welcher als Skala von den kommunikativ am wenigsten wichtigen Teilen zu den kommunikativ wichtigsten Teilen des Satzes verstanden wird, schlagen sich auch in der Anordnung der Satzglieder nieder, und das sowohl in der Oberflächenstruktur des Satzes als auch in seiner Tiefenstruktur. Argumente für eine nötige Unterscheidung zwischen den beiden Schichten werden in dem 1995 veröffentlichten Beitrag *Surface and Underlying Word Order* (*Wortstellung in der Oberflächen- und Tiefenstruktur*) zusammengefasst. Für die These einer in der Tiefenstruktur enthaltenen Reihenfolge von Valenzstellen im Fokus-Teil des Satzes, die von psycholinguistischen Experimenten gestützt wird, spricht sich die 1998 veröffentlichte Studie mit dem Titel *The Ordering of Valency Slots from the Communicative Point of View* (*Die Anordnung von Valenzstellen aus kommunikativer Sicht*) aus.

In Zusammenhang mit den Untersuchungen zu den prosodischen Mitteln der TFG kam die Frage auf, ob die binäre Unterscheidung zwischen Topik und Fokus ausreicht oder eine feinere Differenzierung vonnöten ist. In der TFG-Theorie wird bislang von einer binären Aboutness-Beziehung (der "Fokus" sagt etwas über das "Topik" aus) und der oben erwähnten Skala des "communicative dynamism" (Wortstellung in der Tiefenstruktur) ausgegangen. Dennoch existieren Ansätze zur Informationsstruktur des Satzes, die im Rahmen eines Satzes mehr als ein Topik und ein Fokus unterscheiden; einen Grund, der gegen eine solche Differenzierung spricht und in der Studie *How Many Topics and Foci?* (*Wie viele Topiks und Fokusse?*) (2000) behandelt wird, stellt das Beispiel der sogenannten Rhematisierungspartikel (Fokalisierer, Fokalisierungspartikel) dar. Die Ergebnisse vorgenommener Untersuchungen zu den Rhematisierungspartikeln deuten an, dass eine enge Beziehung zwischen dem (semantischen) Skopus dieser Partikel und dem Skopus von Negationspartikeln besteht. Die genannten Untersuchungen gründen auf einem tschechischen Beitrag (Hajičová 1995) und einer Monografie, die in Zusammenarbeit mit Barbara Partee und Petr Sgall (Hajičová et al. 1998) entstand; erneut aufgegriffen wurde die Problematik im Jahr 2010 in der Studie *Rhematizers Revisited* (*Erneut zu den Rhematisierungspartikeln*), die Teil des vorliegenden Bandes ist.

In Folge der Erweiterung der empirischen Daten, auf welche die linguistische Analyse zugreifen kann, sowie der Möglichkeit, die Gültigkeit der theoretischen Ergebnisse anhand von umfangreichem linguistischen Material, das uns heute dank des technischen Fortschritts in Form von großen elektronischen (computergestützten) Textkorpora zur Verfügung steht, zu verifizieren, entstand ein Schema der Korpusannotation, das die behandelten Themen abdeckt und so als geeignetes Testbed für die entwickelte Theorie dienen kann. Erste Bemühungen, dieses Vorhaben für die tschechische Sprache umzusetzen, gehen in die neunziger Jahre des vergangenen Jahrhunderts zurück (siehe Hajič 1998). Die Bemühungen manifestierten sich in der Entwicklung eines mehrstufigen linguistischen Annotationsschemas auf Grundlage der theoretischen Prämissen der Funktionalen Generativen Beschreibung, das auf Teile des Tschechischen Nationalkorpus appliziert wurde. Das annotierte Korpus erhielt den Namen Prague Dependency Treebank (PDT). In Teil 3 des vorliegenden Bandes mit dem Titel "Theoretical Description Reflected in Corpus Annotation" ("Theoretische Deskription in der Korpusannotation") sind der Thematik zwei Beiträge gewidmet. Der erste Beitrag (*Theoretical Description of Language as a Basis of Corpus Annotation: The case of Prague Dependency Treebank* (*Theoretische Sprachbeschreibung als Grundlage der Korpusannotation: Das Beispiel der Prague Dependency Treebank*)) beinhaltet eine umfassende Beschreibung, wie die Grundsätze der FGB in der PDT angewendet werden. Der zweite Beitrag (*What We Have Learned from Complex Annotation of Topic-Focus Articulation in a Large Czech Corpus* (*Was wir aus der komplexen Annotierung der Topik-Fokus-Gliederung in einem umfangreichen tschechischen Korpus gelernt haben*)) befasst sich mit mehreren Hypothesen und Annahmen im Rahmen der Untersuchung der Topik-Fokus-Gliederung (detaillierter wird das Thema in den in Teil 2 des vorliegenden Bandes enthaltenen Studien behandelt). Die Studien zeigen, wie sich mit Hilfe von annotierten Korpora Hypothesen prüfen lassen, in welchen Punkten die Theorie durch das empirische Material gestützt wird und in welchen Punkten und wie sie modifiziert werden kann. Es versteht sich dabei von selbst, dass das Annotationsschema der PDT kein festgefahrenes Modell darstellt, sondern stetigen Revisionen und Anpassungen unterliegt, die in aktualisierten Versionen der PDT berücksichtigt werden (zum aktuellsten Stand, siehe Bejček et al. 2013).

Fragen, die sich auf den weiteren Kontext beziehen, werden in zwei Beiträgen in Teil 4 dieses Bandes, der den Titel "Beyond the Sentence Border ("Jenseits der Satzgrenze") trägt, behandelt. Die TFG ist einerseits als Strukturierungsmittel zu verstehen, das Einfluss auf die Bedeutung eines Satzes hat und vielmehr dem individuellen Sprachsystem als der Kognition zuzuordnen ist, andererseits spielt die Satzstruktur als integraler Bestandteil eines Textes eine wichtige Rolle im Text als Ganzes, wobei die TFG eine kognitivbasierte "gegebene" – "neue" Strategie darstellt. Der doppeldeutige Charakter der TFG gab Anlass zu Untersuchungen, ob es möglich ist, das "dynamische", kommunikationsbasierte Konzept von Sprache und Diskurs mit der Beschreibung der Satzsyntax (ihrer Tiefenstruktur) nach den Grundsätzen der TFG zu verbinden bzw., wie das "dynamische" (kommunikationsbasierte) Konzept von Sprache und Diskurs (und textueller Koreferenz) mit der Beschreibung der Satzsyntax (ihrer Tiefenstruktur) verbunden werden kann. Zu diesem Zweck wurde der Begriff des Wissensvorrats (Hajičová und Vrbová, 1982) als hierarchisierte Struktur, die der Sprecher als geteiltes Wissen beim Rezipienten voraussetzt, eingeführt (detailliertere Untersuchungen siehe Hajičová, 1993, 1997, 2003a, 2003b), außerdem wurde eine Heuristik zur Entwicklung der Aktivierungsgrade erstellt. Die erarbeitete Skala ist im Rahmen der Beschreibung der semantisch-pragmatischen Diskursebene darzulegen.

In den vorliegenden Band wurden zwei Studien aufgenommen, die sich mit den oben erwähnten Themen befassen. Die früher datierte Studie *Focussing - A Meeting Point of Linguistics and Artificial Intelligence* (*Fokussierung - An der Schnittstelle zwischen Linguistik und Künstlicher Intelligenz*) (1987) stellt die ursprüngliche Version der entwickelten Heuristik dar und appliziert die gegebenen "Regeln" auf einen zu diesem Zweck erstellten Text. Die Studie nimmt außerdem Bezug auf die Verwendung des Begriffs "Fokus," so wie er in Abhandlungen aus dem Bereich der Künstlichen Intelligenz verwendet wird, und vergleicht die Notion des Begriffs mit der Notion des Topiks in der TFG-Theorie. In der zweiten, neueren Studie *Contextual Boundness and Discourse Patterns Revisited* (*Erneut zur Kontextuellen Gebundenheit und den Diskursmustern*) (2013) wird die präziser formulierte Hypothese aufgestellt, dass es einen finiten Mechanismus gibt, der es dem Rezipienten ermöglicht, Denotate auf Grundlage einer partiellen Gliederung von Elementen des gemeinsamen Wissensvorrats von Sprecher und Rezipienten zu identifizieren (wie vom Sprecher vorausgesetzt), und dass dieser auf dem Grad der Aktivierung (Salienz) von Denotaten beruht. Die aufgestellte Heuristik wird dabei auf einen realen (literarischen) Text appliziert. Gleichzeitig behandelt die Studie bestimmte Implikationen der vorgeschlagenen Analyse sowie damit zusammenhängende Probleme. In Kürze wird zudem skizziert, wie es möglich wäre, den vorgeschlagenen Ansatz zur Textanalyse anhand von Texten aus einem großen annotierten Textkorpus zu testen. Die schrittweise Anwendung der "Regeln" wird in der Studie in Form einer Tabelle dargestellt, deren numerische Werte den zugewiesenen Aktivierungsgraden entsprechen. Um die Stichhaltigkeit des illustrativen Beispiels zu erhöhen, wird die Visualisierung der Tabelle durch eine transparentere Darstellung der dynamischen Entwicklung des Diskurses ergänzt.

In den in Teil 5 enthaltenen Studien wird die vertretene Herangehensweise an die Informationsstruktur des Satzes mit den Verfahren anderer linguistischer Theorien, wie Chomskys Transformationsgrammatik, der sogenannten Optimalitätstheorie oder Meltschuks Meaning-Text-Modell verglichen. Die Ursprünge der Forschung zu dem, was heute allgemein als Informationsstruktur des Satzes bekannt ist, liegen in der europäischen Sprachwissenschaft. Mit der Einführung der formalen Sprachbeschreibung stellt die Prager Theorie der Topik-Fokus-Gliederung zweifelsohne den ersten Versuch dar, eine formale Darstellung der Informationsstruktur zu entwickeln und sie in die systematische Sprachbeschreibung einzubinden (siehe v.a. Sgall 1967). Die in diesem Teil veröffentlichten Studien versuchen außerdem diese Herangehensweise mit anderen, älteren Verfahren zu vergleichen.

Der Vergleich bezieht sich in erster Linie auf Chomskys generative Transformationsgrammatik, denn erstmals erwähnt wurde der Begriff des *Topiks* (im Sinne der Verwendung bei M.A.K. Halliday, unter der Bezeichnung *Thema* in den meisten europäischen Ansätzen beschrieben) in Chomskys Werk *Syntactic Structures* (Syntaktische Strukturen) (1957) sowie dem späteren Titel *Aspects of the Theory of Syntax* (Aspekte der Syntaxtheorie) (1965). Zumeist wurde der Begriff dabei in Fußnoten erwähnt. Eine systematischere Abhandlung dieses Aspekts der Satzstruktur ist in Chomskys Studie *Deep Structure, Surface Structure and Semantic Interpretation* (Tiefenstruktur, Oberflächenstruktur und semantische Interpretation) (1968) enthalten. In einem tschechischen Beitrag aus dem Jahr 1972 (übersetzt als *Functional Sentence Perspective and the Latest Development in Transformational Grammar* (Funktionale Satzperspektive und die neuesten Entwicklungen im Bereich der Transformationsgrammatik)) wird diese Abhandlung einer kritischen Analyse unterzogen. In der 1986 erschienen Studie *A Note on the Order of Constituents in Relation to the Principles of GB Theory* (Bemerkungen zur Konstituentenordnung mit Bezug auf die Grundsätze der GB-Theorie) wird die vertretene Hypothese über die Existenz einer Tiefenwortstellung der Satzelemente als Ausdruck des "communicative dynamism" mit Annahmen aus dem späteren Entwicklungsstand des Chomskyschen Ansatzes, der Government and Binding Theory (Rektions- und Bindungstheorie) verglichen. Einen weiteren wichtigen Beitrag zur Entwicklung der formalen Sprachbeschreibung unter Berücksichtigung der Informationsstruktur des Satzes leistete die Optimalitätstheorie. Wie im Beitrag *Possibilities and Limits of Optimality Theory in Topic-Focus Articulation* (Möglichkeiten und Grenzen der Optimalitätstheorie in der Topik-Fokus Gliederung) gezeigt wird, bezog sich eines der Kriterien zur Bestimmung der optimalen Struktur auf die Informationsstruktur des Satzes. Der letzte Beitrag in diesem Teil mit dem Titel *The Position of TFA (Information Structure) in a Dependency Based Description of Language* (Die Stellung der TFG (Informationsstruktur) in der dependenzbasierten Sprachbeschreibung) verfolgt ein doppeltes Ziel: In erster Linie fasst er die Grundlagen der TFG-Theorie zusammen und untersucht, welches der beiden formalen Rahmenwerke, das phrasenstrukturbasierte oder das dependenzbasierte, besser für die Darstellung der Informationsstruktur geeignet ist. Beide Punkte werden dabei vor dem Hintergrund des Meaning-Text-Modells von I. Meltschuk erörtert.

Zwei Beiträge im Anhang dieses Bandes dokumentieren die Anfänge der Forschung im Bereich der Computerlinguistik in Prag. Diese entwickelte zwei Strömungen: eine theorieorientierte und eine auf den Gebrauch von "Maschinen" orientierte. Der Beitrag *Some Experience with Punched-Card Machines for Linguistic Analysis* (*Einige Erfahrungen aus der Anwendung von Lochkartenmaschinen in der linguistischen Analyse*), deren Co-Autorin Jarmila Panevová ist, wurde erstmals 1966 auf dem Internationalen Colloquium in Prag vorgestellt und präsentiert zwei Projekte, für die der Gebrauch von Lochkarten entscheidend war. Ziel des einen Projektes war die Analyse einer Auswahl von tschechischen Texten aus dem Bereich der Technik auf Grundlage einer komplexen linguistisch fundierten, mehrstufigen Beschreibung der Satzstruktur, wie sie von Petr Sgall im Rahmen der Funktionalen Generativen Beschreibung vorgeschlagen wurde. Das zweite Projekt stellte den Versuch dar, ein kleines englisch-tschechisches Parallelkorpus mit POS-Tagging zur Untersuchung der lexikalischen Korrespondenz beider Sprachen im Kontext zu erstellen.

Neu aufgenommen wurde die Studie *A Functional Generative Description* (*Funktionale Generative Beschreibung*) von Petr Sgall und Eva Hajičová, die eine umfassende Darstellung des Rahmenwerks, das den Ausgangspunkt und die methodologische Grundlage der in diesem Band enthaltenen Studien bildet, bietet und von der Beständigkeit der Grundgedanken der Funktionalen Generativen Beschreibung, wie sie Mitte der sechziger Jahre von Petr Sgall entworfen wurde, zeugt. Aus diesem Grund liegt das Hauptaugenmerk auf den Kapiteln 1 und 3, die hier im Volltext erscheinen, und Kapitel 5, das nur leicht gekürzt wurde. Ausgelassen wurde Kapitel 2.1.3, das Theoreme unter Beweis stellt, um die Existenz eines effektiven Verfahrens zu illustrieren, das alle Syntagmen für die Basiskomponente auflistet, wie im vorangehenden Kapitel definiert. Die Kapitel 6.2 und 6.3, welche Regeln und Meta-Regeln zur Generierung semantischer Repräsentationen (später tektogrammatisch genannt) mit einer dem "communicative dynamism" entsprechenden Anordnung von Knotenpunkten enthalten, werden hier nur kurz erläutert und an einigen Beispielen illustriert. Alle Kürzungen und Auslassungen sind gekennzeichnet und werden an einschlägigen Stellen im Text (in eckigen Klammern) kommentiert.

ABSTRACT

The present volume is a collection of selected papers published during my professional career. The theoretical framework I subscribe to is the Functional Generative Description (FGD) as proposed by Petr Sgall in the early sixties and developed further by him and his pupils since then. This framework was conceived of as an alternative to the original Chomskyan transformational generative grammar and in a way can be characterized as a predecessor of those alternative frameworks that take into account semantics and start the generative process from that level. The FGD is deeply rooted in the structural and functional tenets of the Prague School Linguistics in its conception of language description proceeding from function to form, which is reflected in a multilevel design of the framework, in a duly respect paid to the communicative function of language, and in the recognition of the distinction between (linguistic) meaning and (extralinguistic) content.

Thematically, the present volume covers issues ranging from the verb-argument structure of the sentence and its information structure through the capturing of the underlying structure in an annotated corpus to issues going beyond the sentence structure, adding finally some contributions comparing the point of departure of the treatment proposed in our papers with other approaches.

In a way, the structure of the volume (except for the last Part) follows the development of our research interests in time, starting, in the late sixties and early seventies, with the study of the core of the underlying sentence structure (Part 1, "Underlying Syntactic Structure"). Since the theoretical framework of the Functional Generative Description (FGD) we subscribe to is based on dependency syntax both at the deep, underlying layer (called tectogrammatical) and on the surface syntactic layer, a crucial role is played by the study of valency. The introduction of "case grammar" by Charles Fillmore was a stimulus for a detailed comparison of the tenets of the FGD with Fillmorean approach. Within FGD, the attention to the issues of valency, esp. with regard to Czech syntax, was paid especially by Jarmila Panevová (see Panevová 1974, 1978, 1980, Panevová and Sgall 1976, and Hajičová and Paneová 1984 comparing valency frames as postulated by the FGD theory of a selected set of Czech and English verbs). Our own concerns were some specific aspects of Fillmorean approach, namely his specification of the first argument (*Agentive or Actor-Bearer?*), which is closely related to the necessity or redundancy of the introduction of a specific formal device of "crossed brackets" (see Hajičová 1981, not included in this volume). In a more general vein, we examined the status of Fillmorean cases in the overal description of language: distinguishing the layer of (linguistic) meaning and a layer of (cognitive) content, we argue (in *Remarks on the Meaning of Cases*) that a distinction is to be made between the formal means such as morphological case and prepositions in prepositional groups, the valency slots in terms of (linguistic) meaning and the ontological categories. We come back to the study of valency slots with regard to their ordering in the underlying structure in the study of information structure, included in Part 2 of this volume.

In Part 2, called "Topic-Focus Articulation and Related Issues," the attention is focused on those aspects of language that are not covered by the underlying predicate-argument core but still belong to it as they are semantically relevant, namely the topic-focus articulation (information structure of the sentence) and related issues such as negation and presupposition The distinction between the formal and the "topical" articulation of the sentence dates back to Vilém Mathesius and his pioneering contributions (1907; 1939), in which he criticized the psychologically oriented studies by H. Weil (1844) and by linguists around the *Zeitschrift für Völker psychologie* (e.g. Georg von Gabelentz, Hermann Paul, Philip Wegener), claiming that the issues they discussed under the term psychological subject and psychological predicate relate to the factual situation the utterance reflects rather than to the state of mind. In Czech linguistics, Mathesius' pioneering writings on these issues gave rise to two approaches, closely related though different in some important aspects, namely the so-called *functional sentence perspective* (sometimes referred to as Brno School as the originator of that approach, Jan Firbas, was affiliated to Masaryk University in Brno) and the theory of *topic-focus articulation* (sometimes referred to as the Prague theory because it was developed by Petr Sgall and his collaborators affiliated to Charles University in Prague). In order to make the relationships between Mathesius' original thoughts and the two mentioned "schools" explicit, we start Part 2 of the present volume by the study *Vilém Mathesius and functional sentence perspective, and beyond* written at the occasion of the centenary of English Studies at Charles University and published in 2012.

One of the crucial issues in the study and description of topic-focus articulation (TFA) from the point of view of the relation of form and function is its position within the language system. An important argument in favour of its inclusion in the description of the underlying level of the structure sentence, the level of (linguistic) meaning, was the study of the semantic relevance of this articulation with regard to negation. The semantic relevance of TFA for the interpretation of negation is systematically analyzed in our paper *Negation and Topic vs. Comment* (1973) referring back to the observations of Zemb (1968) for German and Kraak (1966) for Dutch. A detailed analysis of negation, namely the question "what is negated in a negative sentence" has led to a deeper study of the notion of presupposition and to the specification of a third kind of entailment, called allegation, first introduced in my contribution delivered at the conference on computational linguistics COLING in Debrecen in 1971 (see Hajičová

1971) and then put under scrutiny in several other studies (Hajičová 1974, 1975, 1984), out of which the most comprehensive is the paper *On Presupposition and Allegation* included in this Part.

As mentioned in the first paper in this Part, one of the tenets of our approach to TFA is a strict differentiation between the semantically relevant function of TFA and the forms of its expression, which may be of morphological, syntactic or prosodic nature. Prosodic means of TFA are in the focus of the paper *Questions on Sentence Prosody Linguists Have Always Wanted To Ask;* discussed there are the issues concerning mainly the position of the intonation centre in English sentences, a possible prosodic indication of the boundary between topic and focus and also issues connected with a possibility to mark contrast in the topic part of the sentence, which is illustrated also on examples taken from writings on German.

Another means of expression of topic and focus, and especially the degrees of communicative dynamism understood as a scale from the communicatively least important to the most important items in the sentence is the ordering of sentence elements, both in the surface shape of the sentence and in its underlying structure. The arguments for the necessity to distinguish these two orders are summarized in the 1995 paper *Surface and Underlying Word Order*, while the postulation of an underlying order of valency slots in the focus part of the sentence supported by psycholinguistic experiments is argued for in the 1998 paper *The Ordering of Valency Slots from a Communicative Point of View*.

Related to the investigation of the prosodic means of expressing TFA was the question whether it is enough to work with a binary distinction between topic and focus, or whether a more subtle differentiation is neccessary. In the theory of TFA, we work with a binary relation of aboutness (the "focus" says someting about the "topic") and with a scale of communicative dynamism (underlying word order) as specified above. However, there are approaches to the information structure of the sentence that work with a differentiation of more than a single topic or a single focus in a sentence; one of our arguments against such a differentiation in the paper *How Many Topics / Foci?* (2000) was based on examples containing so-called rhematizers (focalizers, focussing particles). Our study of these particles indicates a close relationship between the specification of the (semantic) scope of these particles and that of negation and dates back to our Czech paper (Hajičová 1995) and to the monograph co-authored by Barbara Partee and Petr Sgall (Hajičová et al. 1998); we returned to these issues in 2010 in the paper *Rhematizers Revisited*, included in this volume.

The possibilities to expand the empirical basis of linguistic analysis and to validate the consistence of the theoretical findings on large language material offered by the technical availability of large electronic (computerized) corpora of texts have quite naturally led to the design of a scheme of corpus annotation which would cover the issues studied and thus serve as a good test-bed for the formulated theory.. For Czech, the efforts to this purpose started about the end of the nineties of the last century (see Hajič 1998) by the formulation of a multi-level linguistic annotation scheme based on the theoretical tenets of the Functional Generative Grammar, which was applied to a part of the Czech National Corpus; the annotated collection is called the Prague Dependency Treebank (PDT). Part 3 of the present volume called "Theoretical Description Reflected in Corpus Annotation " includes two papers related to these efforts. The first of them (*Theoretical Description of Language as a Basis of Corpus Annotation: The case of Prague Dependency Treebank*) brings an overall description of the reflection of the FGD principles in the PDT. In the second (*What We Have Learned from Complex Annotation of Topic-Focus Articulation in a Large Czech Corpus*) attention is focused on several hypotheses and assumptions we work with in the domain of topic-focus articulation (discussed in some detail in the papers in Part 2 of this volume). We document there the possibilities the annotated corpus offers for the testing of hypotheses, in which points the theoretical frame is supported by the material and in which points and in which way it can be modified. It goes without saying that the PDT annotation scheme is not a frozen scenario and it undergoes revisions and modifications, which are then realized in upgraded versions of PDT (for the most actual state, see Bejček et al. 2013).

Issues related to a broader context are discussed in two papers included in Part 4 called "Beyond the Sentence Boundary". On the one hand, TFA has to be considered as a structuring that has an impact on the meaning of the sentence alone and belongs to the systems of individual languages rather than to the domain of cognition, on the other hand, the structure of the sentence as a component part of a whole text plays an important role in this whole and TFA reflects the cognitively-based "given" – "new" strategy. This "Janus face" character of the TFA phenomenon has led to our inquiry whether it is possible to combine the "dynamic," communication based view of language and discourse with the description of (underlying) sentence syntax duly respecting the TFA, in other words, how to combine the "dynamic" (communication based) view of language and discourse (and textual co-reference) with the description of (underlying) sentence syntax. To this aim, we (Hajičová and Vrbová, 1982) introduced the notion of the stock of knowledge as a hierarchized structure assumed by the speaker to be shared by him and the hearer (a more detailed treatment can be found in Hajičová, 1993, 1997, 2003a, 2003b) and we proposed some heuristics guiding the development of the activation degrees. This scale has to be reflected in a description of the semantico-pragmatic layer of the discourse.

In the present volume, we reproduce two papers relating to the above issues. The earlier one *Focussing – A Meeting Point of Linguistics and Artificial Intelligence* (1987) presents the original version of the heuristics and applies the "rules" to a piece of text created for the purpose. The paper also reacts to the use of the term "focus" in writings oriented towards the domain of artificial intelligence and compares the notion referred to by this term with the notion of topic in the TFA theory. In the second, more recent paper *Contextual Boundness and Discourse Patterns Revisited* (2013) we formulate the hypothesis more precisely stating that a finite mechanism exists that enables the addressee to identify the referents on the basis of a partial ordering of the elements in the stock of knowledge shared by the speaker and the addressee (according to the speaker's assumption), based on the degrees of activation (salience) of referents. The proposed heuristics are applied to a piece of real (literary) text discussing certain implications of the proposed analysis and some related problems, and briefly sketching a possibility of how to test the proposed approach to text analysis on a large annotated corpus of texts. In that paper, the stepwise application of the "rules" is displayed in the form of a table with numerical values of the assigned activation degrees; in order to make the illustrative example more convincing, we add here a visualization that corresponds to the table but makes the dynamic development of the discourse more transparent.

Papers included in Part 5 compare our approach to the information structure of the sentence with the treatments within some other linguistic theories such as Chomskyan transformational grammar, the so-called optimality theory and Mel'chuk's Meaning-Text model. The study of what is now generally called information structure of the sentence was originally a matter of European linguistics; with the introduction of formal description of language, the first attempt to formulate and incorporate a formal account of information structure into a systematic language description was undoubtedly the Praguian theory of Topic-Focus Articulation (see esp. Sgall 1967). Contributions reprinted in this Part attempt to compare this approach with other, later treatments.

This concerns first of all Chomskyan transformational generative grammar, where the first mentioning of the term *topic* (in the sense used by M.A.K. Halliday and covered in most European approaches by the term *theme*) can be found in Chomsky's Syntactic Structures (1957) and then again in Aspects of the Theory of Syntax (1965). These were mostly mentions in footnotes; a more systematic treatment of this aspect of sentence structure is included in Chomsky's paper Deep Structure, Surface Structure and Semantic Interpretation (1968) and it is this treatment that is critically analyzed in our Czech contribution from 1972 (translated here as *Functional Sentence Perspective and the Latest Developments in Transformational Grammar*). Our hypothesis of underlying order of sentence elements as reflecting the communicative dynamism is then compared with some assumptions of the later stage of Chomskyan approach, the Government and Binding theory in the 1986 paper *A Note on the Order of Constituents in Relation to the Principles of GB Theory*. Another important contribution to the development of formal description that paid attention to the information structure was the formulation of the theory of optimality. As pointed out in our paper *Possibilities and Limits of Optimality Theory in Topic-Focus Articulation*, one of the criteria for the assignment of an optimal structure was related to the information structure of the sentence. The final paper in this Section, *The Position of TFA (Information Structure) in a Dependency Based Description of Language*, had a twofold aim: it was supposed to summarize the basics of the TFA theory and to explore which of the formal frameworks, phrase-structure based or dependency based, is best suited for the representation of the information structure. Both these points are discussed on the background of the Meaning-Text model as proposed by I. Mel'chuk.

The two papers in the Appendix document the early stage of the development of the research in computational linguistics carried out in Prague in two directions: the theoretical one and the one oriented towards the use of "machines". The contribution

Some Experience with the Use of Punched-Card Machines for Linguistic Analysis co-authored by Jarmila Panevová was originally presented in 1966 at the International Colloquium held in Prague and introduces two projects for which the use of punched-cards was crucial. One of the projects aimed at an analysis of a sample of Czech texts from a technical domain and was based on a complex linguistically-founded multilayer description of the sentence as proposed by Petr Sgall within the framework of Functional Generative Description. The other project characterized in the paper concerned an attempt to build a small English – Czech POS-tagged parallel corpus in order to study the lexical correspondences between the two languages in contexts.

The inclusion of the paper *A Functional Generative Description* by Petr Sgall and Eva Hajičová into the volume serves as an overall characterization of the framework that has been the starting point and the methodological basis for all the studies selected for publication in the present volume and documents the consistency of ideas underlying the Functional Generative Description as proposed by Petr Sgall in the middle of the 1960's. For that purpose, the main emphasis is laid on Sections 1 and 3, which are reprinted here in full, and Section 5, which is only slightly abridged. The deletions concern Section 2.1.3, containing theorems and their proofs to illustrate that there exists an effective procedure enumerating all syntagms for the basic component as defined in the previous Section. Sections 6.2 and 6.3 containing the rules and meta-rules for the generation of semantic representations (called later tectogrammatical) with the order of nodes corresponding to the communicative dynamism are only briefly characterized here and illustrated by few examples. All the reductions and deletions are indicated and commented upon (in square brackets) in the relevant places.

BIBLIOGRAPHY

The papers collected in this volume come from a long period of time and are reprinted from various original resources that used different ways of bibliographical reference: some being included in the texts themselves, some in the footnotes, some had separate lists of references at the end of the paper. We have decided to collect the references in a single list, which has made it also possible to update the information on the particular entry as much as possible. We have preserved, however, in this Bibliography the original dates of reference as made in our papers in the brackets after the name(s) of the author(s); in case the dates differed in different papers, we put all the dates in a single bracket and separate them by slashes. Thus, e.g. Chomsky, N. (1968/1971): *Deep Structure, Surface structure and Semantic Interpretation* means that this paper is referred to in one study included in our volume as Chomsky (1968), and in the other as Chomsky (1971).

Anderson, J. (1971). *The Grammar of Case. Towards a Localistic Theory.* Cambridge, UK: Cambridge University Press.

Ariel, M. (1988). "Referring and Accessibility." *Journal of Linguistics* 24: 65–87.

——. (1990). *Accessing Noun-Phrase Antecedents.* London: Routledge.

Bach, E. (1968). "Nouns and Noun Phrases." In E. Bach, and R. T. Harms (eds.) 1968, 91–122.

——. (1980). *In Defense of Passive, Linguistics and Philosophy* 3: 297–341.

Bach, E., and R. T. Harms (eds.) (1968). *Universals in Linguistic Theory.* New York: Holt, Rinehart and Winston, Inc.

Bald, W. E. (1971). "The Scope of Negation and Copula Sentences in English," *Journal of English Linguistics* 5: 1–28.

Barbosa, P., D. Fox, P. Hagstrom, et al. (eds.) (1998). *Is the Best Good Enough? Optimality and Competition in Syntax. Cambridge, MA:* The MIT Press.

Bartels, C. (1995/1996). "Acoustic Correlates of 'Second Occurrence' Focus: Toward an Experimental Investigation." In H. Kamp, and B. H. Partee (eds.), 11–30.

Barzilay, E., and M. Lapata, (2008). "Modeling local coherence: An Entity-based Approach." *Computational Linguistics* 34: 1–34.

De Beaugrande, R.-A., and W. Dressler (1981). *Introduction to Text Linguistics.* London: Longman.

Bejček, E., E. Hajičová, J. Hajič, et al. (2013). *Prague Dependency Treebank 3.0.* Data/software, Prague: Univerzita Karlova, MFF, ÚFAL, http://ufal.mff.cuni.cz/pdt3.0/, Dec 2013.

Bémová, A. (1979). "Syntaktické vlastnosti prefigovaných sloves [Syntactic properties of verbs with prefixes]." In *Explizite Beschreibung der Sprache und automatische Textbearbeitung* 5: 69–164. Prague.

Bémová, A., Buráňová, E., Hajič, J., et al. (1997). *Anotace na analytické rovině: návod pro anotátory [Annotations on the analytic level: instructions for the annotators].* Technical Report ÚFAL TR-1997-03. Prague: Univerzita Karlova. Translated into English and available on the web site http: //ufal. mff. cuni. cz.

Bierwisch, M. (1969). "On Certain Problems of Semantic Representations." *Foundations of Language* 5, 153–184.

Bierwisch, M., and K. Heidoplh (eds.) (1970). *Progress in Linguistics*. Haag: Mouton.

Birner, B. J., and G. Ward (1998). *Information status and noncanonical word order in English*. Amsterdam – Philadelphia: John Benjamins.

Bolinger, D. L. (1952). "Linear Modification." *PMLA* 62: 1117–1144.

——. (1972). "Accent is Predictable (If You're a Mind Reader)." *Language* 48: 633–644.

——. (1977). "Transitivity and Spaciality: The Passive of Prepositional Verbs." In: *Linguistics at the Cross-roads*, edited by A. Makkai, V. B Makkai, and L. Heilmann, 57–78, Padova, Italy: Liviana Editrice; Lake Bluff, Ill.: Jupiter Press.

——. (1976). "Gradience in Entailment." *Language Sciences* 41: 1–13.

——. (1978a). "Yes-No Questions are not Alternative Questions." In H. Hiż (ed.) 1978, 87–105.

——. (1978b). "Asking More than One Thing at a Time." In Hiż H. (ed.) 1978, 107–150.

——. (1983). "Two Views of Accent." *Journal of Linguistics* 21: 79–123.

Bosch, P., and R. van der Sandt (eds.) (1994). "Focus and Natural Language Processing." *IBM Working Paper* 7, Heidelberg: IBM Deutschland.

Brants, S., S. Dipper, S. Hansen, W. Lezius, et al. (2002). "The TIGER treebank." In E. Hinrichs, and K. Simov (eds.) *Proceedings of the First Workshop on Treebanks and Linguistic Theories (TLT 2002)*. Sozopol.

Bresnan, J. (1978). "A realistic transformational grammar." In M. Halle, J. Bresnan, and G. A. Miller (eds.) 1978, 1–59.

Carlson, L. (1983). *Dialogue games*. Dordrecht – Boston – London: Reidel.

Chafe, W. (1970). *Meaning and the structure of language*, Chicago and London: The University of Chicago Press.

——. (1976). "Givenness, contrastiveness, definiteness, subjects, topics, and point of view." In Li C. N. (ed.) 1976, 25–55.

——. (1994). *Discourse, Consciousness, and Time: The Flow and Displacement of Conscious Experience in Speaking and Writing*. Chicago, IL – London: The University of Chicago Press.

Chamonikolasová, J. (2007). *Intonation in English and Czech Dialogues*. Brno: Masarykova Univerzita.

——. (2010). Communicative perspectives in the seory of FSP, *Linguistica Pragensia* 20 (2): 86–93.

——. (forthcoming). *Approaches to the information structure of language*. Frankfurt am Main: Peter Lang Verlag.

Choi H.-W. (1996). *Optimizing structure in context: Scrambling and information structure*. PhD Thesis, Stanford.

Chomsky, N. (1957). *Syntactic Structures*. The Hague: Mouton.

——. (1965). *Aspects of the Theory of Syntax*. Cambridge, Mass.: The MIT Press.

Chomsky, N. (1968/1971). "Deep structure, surface structure and semantic interpretation." In Steinberg, and Jakobovits (eds.), 1971, 183–216. Reprinted in N. Chomsky: *Studies on semantics in generative grammar*, 120–202. The Hague – Paris: Mouton 1972.

——. (1968b). *Language and Mind*. New York: Harcourt Brace Jovanovich, Inc.

——. (1972). Some Empirical Issues in the Theory of Transformational Grammar. In *Studies on Semantics in Generative Grammar*, The Hague-Paris: Mouton, 120–202.

——. (1981). *Lectures on Government and Binding*. Dordrecht: Foris. [Quoted from the 2nd edition,1982.]

Cinque, G. (1993). "A null theory of phrase and compound stress." *Linguistic Inquiry* 24: 239–297.

Cooper, D. E. (1974). *Presupposition*. The Hague: Mouton.

Coseriu, E. (1970). "Semantik, innere Sprachform und Tiefenstruktur." *Folia linguistica* 4: 53–63.

Cresswell, N. J. (1978). "Review of Kempson 1975." *Linguistics and Philosophy* 2: 437–446.

Dahl, Ö. (1969). *"Topic and Comment: A Study in Russian and General Transformational Grammar."* Acta Universitatis Gothoburgensis (Slavica Gothoburgensia 4). Stockholm: Almqvist & Wiksell.

——. (1970). *"Some Presuppositions about Presuppositions."* Mimeo.

Daneš, F. (1954). "Příspěvek k rozboru významové výstavby výpovědi [A contribution to the analysis of the semantic structure of the sentence]." *Studie a práce lingvistické* I. Prague, 265–274.

——. (1957). *Intonace a věta ve spisovné češtině*. [Intonation and the sentence in Standard Czech]. Prague: Academia.

——. (1968). "Some Thoughts on the Semantic Structure of the Sentence." *Lingua* 21: 55–69.

——. (1970). "Zur linguistischen Analyse der Textstruktur." *Folia linguistica* 4: 72–78.

——. (1974). "Functional Sentence Perspective and the organization of the text." In Daneš, F. (ed.) 1974, 106–128.

——. (ed.) (1974). *Papers on FSP*. Prague: Academia.

——. (1985). *Věta a text*. [Sentence and text]. Prague: Academia.

Derr, M. A., and K. R. McKeown (1984). "Using Focus to Generate Complex and Simple Sentences." In *Proceedings of COLING 84*. Stanford, 319–326.

Dokulil, M., F. Daneš (1958). "K tzv. významové a mluvnické stavbě věty [On the so-called semantic and grammatical structure of the sentence]." In *O vědeckém poznání soudobých jazyků*, 231–246. Prague: Nakladatelství Československé akademie věd.

Dušková, L., et al. (1988/ 2006). *Mluvnice současné angličtiny na pozadí češtiny* [A grammar of contemporary English against the background of Czech]. Prague: Academia.

Dušková, L. (1999). *Studies in the English Language*. Prague: Karolinum

Engdahl, E., and E. Vallduví (1995). "Information packaging and grammar architecture: A constraint-based approach." In *Integrating information structure into constraint-based, and categorial approaches. DYANA* 2, edited by E. Engdahl, 39–79. Amsterdam: ESPRIT Basic Research Project 6852.

Féry, C. (1992). "Focus, topic and intonation in German." Bericht Nr. 20, Arbeitspapiere des Sonderforschungsbereich 340 Sprach-theoretische Grundlagen für die Computerlinguistik. Stuttgart University.

——. (1993). *German Intonational Patterns*. Tübingen: Niemeyer.

Féry, C., and S. Ishihara (in press). "Interpreting second occurrence focus." In *Methods in Empirical Prosody Research*, edited by D. Lenertová et al. Berlin: Mouton De Gruyter.

Fillmore, C. J. (1966). "*Toward a Modern Theory of Case.*" In *Project on Linguistic Analysis*, Report No. 13, 1–24. Columbus, Ohio.

——. *(1968/1968b). "Case for Case."* In E. Bach and T. Harms (eds.) 1968, 1–88.

——. (1968b). "Lexical entries for verbs." *Foundations of Language* 4: 373–393.

——. (1969). "Types of information." In Kiefer, F. (ed.) 1969, 109–137.

——. (1970a). "Subjects, speakers and roles." *Working Papers in Linguistics* 4: 31–63. Ohio State University. Printed in *Synthese* 21: 251–274.

——. (1970b). Verbs of judging. *Papers in Linguistics* 1: 1–117.

——. (1971). *Some Problems of Case Grammar. Mimeo.*

——. (1977). "The Case for Case Reopened." In *Kasustheorie, Klassifikation und semantische Interpretation*, edited by K. Heger, and J. Petöfi, 3–26. Hamburg: Buske.

Fillmore, C. J., and D. T. Langendoen (eds.) (1971). *Studies in Linguistic Semantics*, New York: Holt, Rinehart and Winston.

von Fintel, K. (1994). "Conditionals as Quantifier Restrictors." Ph.D. dissertation, University of Massachusetts, Amherst.

Firbas, J. (1956). "Poznámky k problematice anglického slovního pořádku z hlediska aktuálního členění větného [Notes on the problems of English word order from a functional sentence perspective viewpoint]." *Sborník prací filosofické fakulty brněnské university* A 4: 93–104.

——. (1957). "K otázce nezákladových podmětů v současné angličtině. Příspěvek k teorii aktuálního členění větného [On the question of non-thematic subjects in present-day English. A contribution to the theory of functional sentence perspective]." *Časopis pro moderní filologii* 39: 22–42, 165–173. An abbreviated and modified English version of this contribution was published in 1966 as "Non-thematic Subjects in Contemporary English." *TLP* 2: 239–256.

——. (1959). "Thoughts on the Communicative Function of the Verb in English, German and Czech." *Brno Studies in English* 1: 39–68.

——. (1964). "On Defining the Theme in Functional Sentence Perspective." *Travaux Linguistique de Prague* 1: 267–280.

——. (1971). "On the Concept of Communicative Dynamism in the Theory of Functional Sentence Perspective." *Sborník prací Filozofické fakulty brněnské univerzity* A 19: 135–144.

——. (1974). "Some Aspects of the Czechoslovak Approach to Problems of Functional Sentence Perspective." In F. Daneš (ed.) 1974, 11–37.

——. (1979). "A Functional View of 'Ordo Naturalis.'" *Brno Studies in English* 13: 29–59.

——. (1992). *Functional Sentence Perspective in Written and Spoken Communication.* Cambridge – London: Cambridge University Press.

Firbas, J., and K. Pala (1971). "Review of Dahl (1969)." *Journal of Linguistics* 72: 91–101.

von der Gabelentz, G. (1868). "Ideen zu einer vergleichenden Syntax: Wort- und Satzstellung." *Zeitschrift für Völkerpsychologie und Sprachwissenschan* 6: 376–384.

Garrod, S. C., and A. J. Sanford (1982). "The Mental Representation of Discourse in a Focussed Memory System." *Journal of Semantics* 1, 21–41.

Givon, T. (1983). "Topic Continuity in Discourse: An Introduction." In *Topic Continuity in Discourse: A Quantitative Cross-language Study*, edited by T. Givon, 1–41. Amsterdam: John Benjamins.

Goralčíková, A. (1974). "On one type of dependency grammars." *PBML* 21: 11–29. Printed also in W. Klein, and A. v. Stechow (eds.) 1973, 64–81.

Greenberg, J. (1963). "Some Universals of Grammar with Particular Reference to the Order of Meaningful Elements." In *Universals of Language*, edited by J. Greenberg, 58–90. Cambridge, Mass.: The MIT Press.

Grimshaw, J., and V. Samek-Lodovici (1998). "Optimal Subjects and Subject Universals." In P. D. Barbosa, et al. (eds.) 1998, 194–219.

Grosz, B. J. (1977). *The Representation and Use of Focus in Dialog Understanding*, Technical Note 15, SRI International, Menlo Park.

Grosz, B. J., and C. I. Sidner (1985/1986). "Attention, Intention and the Structure of Discourse." *Computational Linguistics* 12 (3): 175–204.

Gundel, J. K. (2011). "Child Language, Theory of Mind, and the Role of Procedural Markers in Identifying Referents of Nominal Expressions." In *Procedural Meaning: Problems and Perspectives*, edited by V. Escandell-Vidal, M. Leonetti, and A. Ahern, 205–231. Bradford: Emerald Group.

Gundel, J. K., N. Hedberg, and R. Zacharski (1993). "Cognitive Status and the Form of Referring Expressions in Discourse." *Language* 69: 274–307.

Gussenhoven, C. (1984). *On the Grammar and Semantics of Sentence Accents.* Dordrecht – Cinnaminson: Foris.

——. (1985a). "The intonation of 'George and Mildred': Post-nuclear generalizations." In *Intonation and discourse*, edited by C. Johns-Lewis, and Croom Helm, 77–123. London – Sydney.

——. (1985b). "Two Views of Accent: A Reply." *Journal of Linguistics* 21.

——. (1998). "On the Limits of Focus Projection in English." Manuscript.

Hajič, J. 1998). Building a Syntactically Annotated Corpus: The Prague Dependency Treebank. In *Issues of Valency and Meaning. Studies in Honour of Jarmila Panevová*, edited by E. Hajičová, 106–132. Prague: Karolinum.

Hajič, J., and B. Hladká, (1997). "Probabilistic and Rule-based Tagger of an Inflective Language – a Comparison." In: *Proceedings of the Fifth Conference on Applied Natural Language Processing*, 111–18. Washington, D. C.

Hajič, J., and B. Hladká (1998). "Czech Language Processing– POS Tagging." In *Proceedings of the First International Conference on Language Resources & Evaluation.* Granada, Spain.

Hajič, J., J. Panevová, and E. Hajičová (2006). *Prague Dependency Treebank 2.0.* CD-ROM. Linguistic Data Consortium, Philadelphia, PA, USA. LDC Catalog No. LDC2006T01 URLhttp://ufal.mff.cuni.cz/pdt2.0/.

Hajičová, E. (1971/1972a/1972). "Some Remarks on Presuppositions." *PBML* 17:11–25; printed in 1976 in *Papers in Computational Linguistics*, edited by F. Papp, and G. Szépe, 188–197. Budapest: Akadémiai Kiadó.

——. (1972b). *K funkčnímu generativnímu popisu angličtiny* [On the functional generative description of language]. Thesis, Prague: Univerzita Karlova v Praze.

——. (1972c). "Aktuální členění větné a nejnovější vývoj transformační gramatiky [Topic-focus articulation and the current development of transformational grammar]." *Slovo a slovesnost* 33: 229–239.

——. (1973). "Negation and Topic vs. Comment." *Philologica Pragensia* 16: 81–93.

——. (1974). "Meaning, Presupposition and Allegation." *Philologica Pragensia* 17: 18–25.

——. (1975). *Negace a presupozice ve významové stavbě věty* [Negation and presupposition in the semantic structure of the sentence]. Prague: Academia.

——. (1976). "Question and Answer in Linguistics and in Man-Machine Communication." *SMIL* 1: 30–46.

——. (1979). "Agentive or Actor/Bearer?" *Theoretical Linguistics* 6: 173–190.

——. (1981). "Are Crossed Brackets Necessary?" *Prague Studies in Mathematical Linguistics* 7: 199–214.

——. (1983). "Topic and Focus." *Theoretical Linguistics* 10 (2/3): 268–276.

——. (1984). "Presupposition and allegation revisited." *Journal of Pragmatics* 8: 155–167; amplified as "On presupposition and allegation." In *Contributions to functional syntax, semantics and language comprehension*, edited by P. Sgall, 99–122. Amsterdam: Benjamins; Prague: Academia.

——. (1986). "Focussing in Linguistics and in AI." In *Festschrift for Jacob Mey*, Odense: Odense University, 76–84.

——. (1989). "Negation Scope: Ambiguity or vagueness?" *Philologica Pragensia* 32: 13–18.

——. (1993). *Issues of Sentence Structure and Discourse Patterns*. Prague: Univerzita Karlova.

——. (1995). "Postavení rematizátorů v aktuálním členění věty [The status of rhematizers in the topic-focus articulation of the sentence]." *Slovo a slovesnost* 56: 241–251.

——. (1997). "Topic, Focus and Anaphora." In *16th International Congress of Linguists* (CIL 16). Abstracts of the Congress, 109, Paris.

——. (1998). "Movement Rules Revisited." In *Procesing of Dependency-based Grammars, Proceedings from the Workshop, COLING/ACL*, edited by S. Kahane, and A. Polguere, 49–57. Montreal.

——. "Dependency-Based Underlying-Structure Tagging of a Very Large Czech Corpus." *Les grammaires de dépendance. Traitement Automatique des Langues* 41: 57–8.

——. (2003a). "Contextual Boundness and Discourse Patterns." In *17th International Congress of Linguists* (CIL 17). Abstracts of the Congress, 388, Prague.

——. (2003b). "Aspects of discourse structure." In *Natural Language Processing between Linguistic Inquiry and System Engineering*, edited by W. Menzel, and C. Vertan, 47–56. Prague and Iasi.

——. (2009). "Aktuální členění věty, rematizátory a kontrastivní základ [Topic-focus articulation, rhematizers and contrastive topic]." In *Užívání a prožívání jazyka, k 90. narozeninám Františka Daneše*. 247–251. Prague: Academia.

——. (2012). On Scalarity in Information Structure. *Linguistica Pragensia* 22 (2): 60–78.

Hajičová, E., T. Hoskovec, and P. Sgall (1995). "Discourse Modelling Based on Hierarchy of Salience." *The Prague Bulletin of Mathematical Linguistics* 64: 5–24.

Hajičová, E., J. Mírovský, and K. Brankatschk (2011). "A Contrastive Look at Information Structure: A Corpus Probe." *6th Congres de la Societé Linguistique Slave*, 47–51. Aix-en-Provence: Université de Provence.

Hajičová, E., and J. Panevová (1984). "Valency (Case) Frames of Verbs." In P. Sgall (ed.) 1984, 147–188.

Hajičová, E., J. Panevová, and P. Sgall (1970). "Recursive Properties of Tense in Czech and English," *PBML* 13, 9–42; a completed and revised version printed in 1971 in *Philologica Pragensia* 14: 1–15; 57–64; reprinted in W. Klein, and A. v. Stechow (eds.), 1973, 173–235.

Hajičová, E., J. Panevová, and P. Sgall (1990). "Why Do We Use Dependency Grammar?" *Buffalo Working Papers in Linguistics*. Special issue for Paul Garvin, edited by W. Wölck, 90–93.

Hajičová, E., B. Partee, and P. Sgall, (1998). *Topic-Focus Articulation, Tripartite Structures and Semantic Content*. Dordrecht: Kluwer Academic Publishers.

Hajičová, E., and P.Sgall (1968). "Stratificational Linguistics and Prague Functionalism." *Philologica Pragensia* 11: 245–249.

——. (1975). "Topic and Focus in Transformational Grammar." *Papers in Linguistics* 8: 3–58.

——. (1985). "Towards and Automatic Identification of Topic and Focus." In *Proceedings of the 2nd Conference of the European Chapter of ACL*, Geneva. 263–267.

——. (1987). "The Ordering Principle." *Journal of Pragmatics* 11: 435–454.

——. (2004). "Degrees of Contrast and the Topic-Focus Articulation." In *Information Structure – Theoretical and Empirical Aspects, edited by* A. Steube, 1–13. Berlin – New York: Walter de Gruyter.

Hajičová, E., P. Sgall, and K. Veselá (2007). "Contextual Boundness and Contrast in the Prague Dependency Treebank." In *Language Context and Cognition: Interfaces and Interface Conditions*, edited by A. Spaeth, 231–243. Berlin – New York: Walter de Gruyter.

Hajičová, E., H. Skoumalová, and P. Sgall (1995). "An automatic procedure for topic-focus identification." *Computational Linguistics* 21: 81–94.

Hajičová, E., and J. Vrbová (1981). "On the Salience of the Elements of the Stock of Shared Knowledge." *Folia Linguistica* 15 (3–4): 291–303.

——. (1982). "On the role of the hierarchy of activation in the process of natural language understanding." In *Coling 82 – Proceedings of the Ninth International Congress of Computational Linguistics, edited* by J. Horecký, 107–113. Prague: Academia; Amsterdam: J. Benjamins.

Hall-Partee, B. (1971). "On the requirement that transformations preserve meaning." In C. J. Fillmore and D. T. Langendoen (eds.) 1971, 1–21.

Halle M., J. Bresnan, and G. A. Miller (ed.) (1978). *Linguistic theory and psychological reality*. Cambridge, Mass.: MIT Press.

Halliday, M. A. K. (1967a). *Some aspects of the thematic organization of the English clause*, Rand Corporation, Santa Monica.

——. (1967b). *Intonation and Grammar in British English*. The Hague: Mouton.

——. (1967; 1967-8). "Notes on transitivity and theme in English." *Journal of Linguistics* 3: 37–81, 199–244; 4 (1968):179–215.

——. (1970). "Language structure and language function." In *New Horizons in Linguistics*, edited by J. Lyons, 140–165. Harmondsworth, Middlessex: Penguin Books.

Halliday, M. A. K., and R. Hasan (1976). *Cohesion in English*. London: Longman.

Hausser, R. (1976). "Presuppositions in Montague Grammar." *Theoretical Linguistics* 3: 245–280.

Hays, D. G. (1961). "Grouping and dependency theories." In *Proceedings of the National Symposium on MT*, edited by H. P. Edmundson, 258–266. *Prentice-Hall* – Englewood Cliffs, N. J.

Hendriks, P., and H. de Hoop (in press). "Optimality Theory Semantics." (to appear in *Linguistics and Philosophy*).

Hintikka, J. (1978). "Answers to Questions.". In H. Hiż (ed.) 1978, 279–300.

Hiż, H. (ed.) 1978). *Questions*. Dordrecht, Holland: D. Reidel Publ. Co.

Hirschberg, J., and G. Ward (1991). "Accent and bound anaphora." *Cognitive Linguistics* 2: 101–121.

——. (1992). "The influence of pitch range, duration, amplitude and special features on the interpretation of the rise-fall-rise intonation contour in English." *Journal of Phonetics* 20: 241–251.

Hjelmslev, L. (1943). *Omkring sprogteoriens grundlaeggelse*. Copenhagen: Ejnar Munksgaard.

Hoffmannová, J. (1993). "Koherence, koheze, konexe...?" [Coherence, cohesion, connection...?]. *Slovo a slovesnost* 54 (1): 58–64.

de Hoop, H., and H. de Swart (1999). "Optimal interpretations of Discourse." Paper presented at Colloque de syntax et sémantique à Paris.

Höhle, T. N. (1982). "Explikationen für 'Normale Betonung' und 'Normale Wortstellung.'" In *Satzglieder im Deutschen*, edited by W. Abraham, 75–153. Tübingen: Gunter Narr.

——. (1991). "On reconstruction and coordination." In *Representation and Derivation in the Theory of Grammar*, edited by H. Heider, and K. Netter, 139–197. Dordrecht: Reidel.

Ivič, M. (1964). "Non-omissible determiners in Slavic languages." In *Proceedings of the 9th International Congress of Linguists*, edited by H. Lunt, 476–479. The Hague: Mouton. [Cambridge, Mass.: The MIT Press 1962].

Jackendoff, R. (1969). "An Interpretive Theory of Negation." *Foundations of Language* 1: 218–241.

——. (1971). "On Some Questionable Arguments about Quantifiers and Negation." *Language* 47: 282–297.

——. (1972). *Semantic Interpretation in Generative Grammar*, Cambridge, Mass.: MIT Press.

Jacobs, J. (1984). "Funktionale Satzperspektive und Illokutionssemantik." *Linguistische Berichte* 91: 25–58.

——. (1991). "Focus ambiguities." *Journal of Semantics* 8: 1–36.

Jacobs, R. A., and P. S. Rosenbaum (eds.) (1970). *Readings in English Transformational Grammar*, Waltham, Mass.: Ginn & Co.

Jakobson, R. (1936). "Beitrag zur allgemeinen Kasuslehre." In: *Travaux du CLP* 6: 240–281.

——. (ed.) (1961). *The Structure of Language and Its Mathematical Aspects*. Proceedings of Symposia in Applied Mathematics. Providence, R. I.: American Mathematical Society.

Jespersen, O. (1949). *A Modern English Grammar on Historical Principles. Part VII. Syntax*. Completed and edited by Niels Haislund. London: George Allen & Unwin LTD; Copenhagen: Ejnar Munksgaard.

Kahane, S. (2003). "The Meaning-Text Theory." In *Dependency and Valency. Handbook of Linguistics and Communication Science* 25: 1–2. Berlin – New York: de Gruyter.

Kamp, H., and B. H. Partee (eds.) (1995). "*Proceedings of the Workshop on* 'Context Dependence in the Analysis of Linguistic Meaning.'" University of Stuttgart Working Papers. Prague – Bad Teinach: University of Stuttgart.

Karttunen, L. (1970). "On the Semantics of Complement Sentences." In *Papers from the Sixth Regional Meeting*, 328–339. Chicago: Chicago Linguistic Society.

——. (1971a). "Implicative Verbs." *Language* 47: 340–358.

——. (1971b). "Some Observations on Factivity." *Papers in Linguistics* 4: 55–69.

——. (1978). "Syntax and Semantics of Questions" In H. Hiż (ed.) 1978, 165–210.

Karttunen, L., and S. Peters (1977). "Requiem for presupposition." In *Proceedings of the Third Annual Meeting of the Berkeley Linguistics Society*, edited by K. Whistler et al., 360–371. Berkeley.

Kay, M. (1970). *Performance Grammars*. The RAND Corporation, Report P-4391. Reprinted in Kay (2010), 149–155.

——. (2010), *Collected Papers of Martin Kay: A Half Century of Computational Linguistics*, CSLI Publications, Standford.

Keenan, E. L. (1971). "Two types of presuppositions." In C. J. Fillmore, and D. T. Langendoen (eds.) 1971, 45–52.

Keenan, E. L. (1972). "On semantically based grammar." *Linguistic Inquiry* 3: 413–461.

——. (1976). "Towards a universal definition of subject." *Linguistic Inquiry* 7: 303–333.

Keenan, E. L., and R. D. Hull (1973). "The Logical Presuppositions of Questions and Answers." In J. S. Petöfi, and D. Franck (eds.) 1973, 441–466.

Kempson, R. M. (1975). *Presupposition and the delimitation of semantics*. Cambridge, UK: Cambridge University Press.

Kempson, R. M. (1977). *Semantic Theory*. Cambridge UK: Cambridge University Press.

Kiefer, F. (ed.) (1969). *Studies in syntax and semantics*, Dordrecht: Reidel.

——. (1970). "On the problem of word order." In M. Bierwisch, and K. E. Heidolph (eds.) 1970, 127–142.

——. (1977). "Some Semantic and Pragmatic Properties of Wh-Questions and the Corresponding Answers." *SMIL* (Journal of Linguistic Calculus) 3: 42–71.

——. (1980). "Yes-No Questions as Wh-Questions." In J. R. Searle, F. Kiefer, and M. Bierwisch (eds.) 1980, 97–119.

Kiparski, P., and C. Kiparski, (1970). "Fact." In *Progress in Linguistics, edited by* M. Bierwisch, and K. E. Heidolph, 143–173. The Hague: Mouton.

Klein, W., and A. v. Stechow (eds.) (1973). *Prager Autorengruppe, Functional Generative Grammar in Prague*. Kronberg – Taunus: Scriptor Verlag GmbH.

Klima, E. S. (1964). "Negation in English." In *The Structure of Language*, edited by J. A. Fodor, and J. J. Katz (eds.), 246–323. New Jersey – Englewood Cliffs: Prentice Hall, Inc.

Koktová, E. (1986). *Sentence Adverbials in a Functional Description*. Amsterdam – Philadelphia: Benjamins.

——. (1987). "On the Scoping Properties of Negation, Focusing Particles and Sentence Adverbials." *Theoretical Linguistics* 14: 173–226.

——. (1999). *Word-Order Based Grammar*. Berlin: Mouton De Gruyter.

Kraak, A. (1966). *Negative Zinnen. Een Methodologishe Analyse*. Hilversum.

Krahmer, E. (1998). *Presupposition and Anaphora*. CSLI Lecture Notes 89. Stanford, CA.: CSLI.

Krahmer, E., and M. Theune, (1999). "Efficient Generation of Descriptions in Context." In R. Kibble, and K. van Deemter (eds.) *"Proceedings of the Workshop on the Generation of Nominal Expressions."* 11th European Summer School in Logic, Language and Information.

Krifka, M. (1991). "A Compositional Semantics for Multiple Focus Constructions." In *Proceedings of SALT I*, edited by S. Moore, and A. Wyner, 127–158. Ithaca, N.Y.: Cornell University.

——. (1995/1996). Paper Presented at the Prague Workshop "Context-Dependence in the Analysis of Linguistic Meaning." February 1995.

Kruijff-Korbayová, I. (1998). *The Dynamic Potential of Topic and Focus: A Praguian Approach to Discourse Representation Theory.* PhD. Thesis. Prague: Matematicko-fyzikální fakulta, Univerzita Karlova.

Křižková, H. (1968a). "K voprosu o tak naz. dvojnoj negacii v slavjanskich jazykách." *Slavia* 37: 21–39.

——. (1968b). "Ke vztahu tzv. záporu větného a členského ve slovanských jazycích [On the relation of the so-called sentential and constituent negation in Slavonic languages]." In *Čs. přednášky pro VI. mezinárodní sjezd slavistů v Praze*, Prague, 71–75.

——. (1969). "Zametki o meste negacii v jazykovoj strukture." In *Jedinicy raznych urovnej grammatičeskogo stroja jazyka i ich vzaimodejstvije*, Moscow, 187–205.

Kuroda, S.-Y. (1969). "Remarks on Selectional Restrictions and Presuppositions." In F. Kiefer, (ed.) 1969, 138–167.

Kuryłowicz, J. (1949). "Le problème du classement des cas." *Biulletyn polskiego tovarzystwa językoznawczego* 9: 20–43.

Lakoff, G. (1965). *Irregularity in Syntax.* Thesis. Reprinted 1970. New York: Holt, Rinehart and Winston.

——. (1969/1971a). "On Generative Semantics." In D. D. Steinberg, and L. A. Jakobovits (eds.) 1971, 232–296.

——. (1970a). "Repartee." *Foundations of Language* 6: 389–422.

——. (1970b). "Global Rules." *Language* 46: 627–639.

——. (1971b). "Presupposition and Relative Well-Formedness." In D. D. Steinberg, and L. A. Jakobovits (eds.) 1971, 329–340.

——. (in prep.1970). Linguistics and Natural Logic. *Synthese* 22: 151–271.

Lakoff, G., and P. Railton (1970). "Some Types of Presuppositions and Entailment in Natural Language." Unpublished.

Lakoff, G., and J. R. Ross (1967). *Is Deep Structure Necessary?* Mimeo. Reprinted in 1976 as "Notes from the Linguistic Underground." *Syntax and Semantics* 7, edited by J. D. McCawley, 159–164. New York: Academic Press.

Lamb, S. M. (1967). "Review of N. Chomsky, Current Issues in Linguistic Theory and Aspects of the Theory of Syntax." *American Anthropologist* 69 (3–4): 411–415.

Lambrecht, K. (1994). *Information Structure and Sentence Form: Topic, Focus and the Mental Representations of Discourse Referents.* Cambridge: Cambridge University Press.

Langacker, R. (1969). "On Pronominalization and the Chain of Command." In D. A. Reidel, and A. A. Schane (eds.) 1969, 160–186.

Langendoen, D. T. (1969). *The Study of Syntax.* New York: Holt, Rinehart and Winston.

Leech, G. N. (1969). *Towards a Semantic Description of English*, London: Longman Group Ltd.

Legendre, G. (in press): "An introduction to Optimality Theory in Syntax." In G. Legendre, J. Grimshaw, and S. Vikner (eds.) 2001, 1–25.

Legendre, G., J. Grimshaw, and S. Vikner (eds.) (2001). *Optimality-theoretic syntax. Cambridge*, MA: MIT Press.

Legendre, G., P. Smolensky, and C. Wilson (1998). "When is Less More? Faithfulness, and Minimal Links in wh-chains." In P. D. Barbosa et al., (ed.) 1998, 249–289.

Levinson, S. C. (1983). *Pragmatics.* Cambridge: Cambridge UniversityPress.

Li, C. N. (ed.) (1976). *Subject and Topic.* New York: Academic Press.

Lyons, J. (1977). *Semantics 1, 2.* Cambridge UK: Cambridge University Press.

Machová, S. (1972). *Příčina v syntaxi češtiny* [Cause in Czech syntax]. Prague: Academia.

Marcus, S. (1965b). "Sur la notion de projectivité." *Zeitschrift fuer math. Logik und Grundlagen d. Math* 11: 181–192.

Marcus, M., G. Kim, M. A. Marcinkiewicz, et al. (1994). "The Penn Treebank: Annotating Predicate Argument Structure." In *Proceedings of the Human Language Technology Workshop*. San Francisco, California: Morgan Kaufmann Publishers Inc.

Marcus, M., B. Santorini, and M.-A. Marcinkiewicz (1993). "Building a Large Annotated Corpus of English: the Penn Treebank." *Computational Linguistics* 19 (2): 313-330.

Mathesius, V. (1907). "Studie k dějinám anglického slovosledu [Studies in the history of English word-order]." Part I. *Věstník České akademie císaře Františka Josefa pro vědy, slovesnost a umění* 16: 261-265.

——. (1924). "Několik poznámek o funkci podmětu v moderní angličtině [Some remarks on the function of subject in Modern English]." *Časopis pro moderní filologii a literaturu* 10 (3-4): 244-248.

——. (1929). "Zur Satzperspektive im modernen Englisch." In *Archiv für das Studium der neueren Sprachen und Literaturen* 155: 202-210.

——. (1937). "Double Negation and Grammatical Concord." In *Mélanges de linguistique et de philologie à Jacques van Ginneken. Paris: C. Klincksieck*, 79-83.

——. (1939). "O tak zvaném aktuálním členění větném." *Slovo a slovesnost* 5: 171-174; translated in 1975 as "On Information-bearing Structure of the Sentence." *Harvard Studies in Syntax and Semantics*, edited by S. Kuno, 467-480. Cambridge, Mass.: Harvard University. Press.

——. (1941). "Základní funkce pořádku slov v češtině [The primary functions of word order in Czech]." *Slovo a slovesnost* 7: 169-180.

——. (1942). "Ze srovnávacích studií slovosledných [From comparative word order studies]." *ČMF* 29: 181-190, 302-307.

McCawley, J. D. (1968). "The Role of Semantics in a Grammar." In E. Bach and R. T. Harms (eds.), 125-169.

——. (1970a). *On the Deep Structure of Negative Clauses*. Mimeo.

——. (1970b). "Where Do Noun Phrases Come from." In R. A. Jacobs, and P. S. Rosenbaum (eds.) 1970, 166-183.

——. (1971). Tense and Time Reference in English. In C. J. Fillmore, and D. T. Langendoen (eds.) 1971, 97-113.

McKeown, K. R. (1985). *Text Generation*. Cambridge UK: Cambridge University Press.

Mel'čuk, I. A. (1988). *Dependency Syntax: Theory and Practice*. New York: State University of New York Press.

——. (2001). *Communicative Organization in Natural Language: The Semantic Communicative Structure of Sentences*. Amsterdam - Philadelphia: John Benjamins (referred to in the text as CONL).

Mikulová M., A. Bémová, J. Hajič, E. Hajičová, et al. (2006). *Annotation on the tectogrammatical level in the Prague Dependency Treebank. Annotation manual*. Tech. Report 30 ÚFAL MFF UK. Prague.

Miltsakaki, E., L. Robaldo, A. Lee, and A. Joshi (2008). "Sense Annotation in the Penn Discourse Treebank." In *Computational Linguistics and Intelligent Text Processing*, edited by A. Gelbukh, 275-286. Berlin - Heidelberg: Springer.

Mladová, L., Š. Zikánová, and E. Hajičová (2008). "From Sentence to Discourse: Building an Annotation Scheme for Discourse Based on the Prague Dependency Treebank." In *Proceedings of the 6th International Conference on Language Resources and Evaluation (LREC 2008)*, 1-7. Marrakech, Morocco: European Language Resources Association.

Morgan, J. L. (1969). On the Treatment of Presupposition in Transformational Grammar. In: *Papers from the Fifth Regional Meeting*, 167-177. Chicago: Chicago Linguistic Society.

Oh, C.-K., and D. A. Dinneen, (eds.) (1979). " Presupposition." *Syntax and Semantics* 11, New York: Academic Press.

Paducheva, E. V. (1969). "O sokraščenii sočinitel'nych grupp s povtorjajuščimisja elementami." *Naučno-techničeskaja informacija*, Serija 2: 27-34; translated in *La sémantique en U.R.S.S.* Paris 1971, 71-109.

Panevová, J. (1969). *Některé otázky závislé predikace v generativním popisu češtiny.* [Some questions of dependent predication in a generative description of Czech]. Thesis. Prague: Univerzita Karlova.

Panevová, J. (1974). "On Verbal Frames in Functional Generative Description, Part I." *The Prague Bulletin of Mathematical Linguistics* 22: 3-40; Part II, *The Prague Bulletin of Mathematical Linguistics* 23, 1975, 17-52.

Panevová J. (1978/1978a). "Inner Participants and Free Adverbials." In *Prague Studies in Mathematical Linguistics* 6: 227–254.

Panevová, J. (1980). *Formy a funkce ve stavbě* české věty [Forms and functions in the structure of Czech]. Prague: Academia.

Panevová, J., E. Benešová, and P. Sgall (1971). "Čas a modalita v češtině [Tense and modality in Czech]." *Acta Univ. Carolinae, Philologica - Monographica* 34, Prague: Univerzita Karlova.

Panevová, J., and P. Sgall, (1976). "Verbal Frames and Free Adverbials." *International Review of Slavic Linguistics* 1: 31–78.

Partee, B. H. (1971). "On the Requirement that Transformations Preserve Meaning." In C. J. Fillmore, and D. T. Langendoen (eds.) 1971, 1–21.

—. (1991). "Topic, Focus and Quantification." In *Proceedings from SALT I*, edited by S. Moore, and A. Wyner, 257–280. Ithaka, N.Y.: Cornell University.

—. (1996). "Allegation and Local Accommodation." In B. H. Partee, and P. Sgall (eds.) 1996, 65–86.

Partee, B. H., and P. Sgall (eds.) (1996). *Discourse and Meaning: Papers in Honor of Eva Hajičová*. Amsterdam – Philadelphia: Benjamins.

Paul, H. (1886). *Prinzipien der Sprachgeschichte*. 2nd ed., Freiburg im Breisgau.

Peregrin, J. (1994). "Topic-Focus Articulation as Generalized Quantification." In P. Bosch, and R. van der Sandt (eds.) 1994, 379–388.

Peregrin, J. (1996). "Topic and Focus in a Formal Framework." In B. H. Partee, and P. Sgall (eds.) 1996, 235–254.

Petkevič, V. (1987). "A New Dependency Based Specification of Underlying Representations of Sentences." *Theoretical Linguistics* 14: 143–72.

Petkevič, V. (1995). "A New Formal Specification of Underlying Representations." *Theoretical Linguistics* 21: 7–61.

Petöfi, J. S., and D. Franck (eds.) (1973). *Präsuppositionen in Philosophie und Linguistik*. Frankfurt a/M.

Pierrehumbert, J. (1980). "The Phonology and Phonetics of English Intonation." PhD. diss., Cambridge, Mass.: MIT.

Pierrehumbert, J., and J. Hirschberg, (1990). "The Meaning of Intonational Contours in the Interpretation of Discourse." In *Intentions in Communication*, edited by P. Cohen, J. Morgan, and M. Pollock, 271–312. Cambridge, Mass.: MIT Press,.

Poldauf, I. (1947). "Some Points on Negation in Colloquial English." *Příspěvky k dějinám řeči a literatury anglické* 6: 75–84.

—. (1972a). "Factive, Implicative, Evaluative Predicates." *Philologica Pragensia* 15: 63–92.

—. (1972b). "Fact and Non-Fact." *The Prague Bulletin of Mathematical Linguistics* 18: 3–14.

—. (in press/1976). "Fact, Non-Fact, and the Place of Some Other Expressions." *Prague Studies in Mathematical Linguistics* 5: 271–281.

Polguère, A. (1990). *Structuration et mise en jeu procédurale d'un modèle linguistique déclaratif dans un cadre de génération de texte*. Thèse de l'Université de Montréal.

Posner, R. (1972). *Theorie des Kommentierens*. Frankfurt am M.: Athenaeum.

Pospíšil, D. (1966). "On a Linearization of Projective W-trees." *The Prague Bulletin of Mathematical Linguistics* 6: 44–68.

Prasad, R., N. Dinesh, A. Lee, et al. (2008a/2008b). *Penn Discourse Treebank Version 2.0*. Philadelphia, PA: Linguistic Data Consortium.

Preinhaelterová, L. (1997). "Systemic Ordering of Complementations in English." *Linguistica Pragensia* 1997: 12–25.

Prince, A., and P. Smolensky, (1993). *Optimality Theory: Constraint Interaction in Generative Grammar*. RuCCs TechRep No. 2, Rutgers Univ. Center for Cognitive Science.

Prince, E (1981). "Toward a Taxonomy of Given/New Information." In *Radical Pragmatics*, edited by P. Cole, 223–254. New York: Academic Press.

Procházka O., and P. Sgall (in press/1976). "Semantic Structure of the Sentence and Predicate Logic." *Prague Studies in Mathematical Linguistics* 5: 257–270.

Putnam, H. (1961). "Some Issues in the Theory of Grammar." In R. Jakobson (ed.) 1961, 25–42.

Quirk, R. et al. (1972). *A Grammar of Contemporary English*. London; quoted from 2nd impression with corrections, 1973.

Reibel, D. A., and A. A. Schane, (ed.) (1969). *Modern Studies in English*, New Jersey.

Robinson, J. J. (1969). "Case, Category and Configuration." *Journal of Linguistics* 6: 57–80.

Rooth, M. (1985). "Association with Focus." PhD. Thesis. Amherst: University of Massachusetts.

——. (1992). "A Theory of Focus Interpretation." *Natural Language Semantics* 1: 75–116.

Ross, J. R. (1967). *Constraints on Variables in Syntax*. Thesis. Cambridge, Mass.: MIT.

——. (1970). "On Declarative Sentences." In R. A. Jacobs, and P. S. Rosenbaum (eds.) 1970, 222–272.

Růžička, R. (1970). "Review of Dahl (1969)." *Zeitschrift fuer Slawistik* 15: 733–746.

Rysová, K. (2011a). "The Unmarked Word Orded of Free Verbal Modifications in Czech (with the Main Reference to the Influence of Verbal Valency in the Utterance)." In *44th Meeting of SLE 2011, Book of Abstracts*. Logrono, 277–278.

——. (2011b). The Unmarked Word Order of Inner Participants, with the Focus on the System in Ordering of Actor and Patient." Presented at *International Conference on Dependency Linguistics* (Depling 2011) in Barcelona. Published in 2014 as "On the Word-order of Actor and Patient (in Czech). " In *Dependency Linguistics. Recent advances in linguistic theory using dependency structures*, edited by K. Gerdes, E. Hajičová, and L. Wanner, 253–271. Amsterdam: John Benjamins.

Sadock, J. M. (1969a). "Super-hypersentences." *Papers in Linguistics* 1: 1–15.

——. (1969b). "Hypersentences." *Papers in Linguistics* 1: 283–370.

Schmerling, S. (1971). "Presupposition and the Notion of Normal Stress." In *Papers from the Seventh Regional Meeting, Chicago Linguistic Society*, 242–253.

Schwarz, D. S. (1977). "On pragmatic presupposition." *Linguistics and Philosophy* 1: 247–257.

——. (1979). "Notes from the Pragmatic Wastebasket: On a Gricean Explanation of the Preferred Interpretation of Negative Sentences." *Syntax and Semantics* 10, edited by F. Heny, and H. Schnelle, 241–253. New York – San Francisco – London: Academic Press.

Searle, J. R., F. Kiefer, and M. Bierwisch (eds.) (1980). *Speech Act Theory and Pragmatics*. Dordrecht, Holland: D. Reidel Publ. Co.

Selkirk, E. (1984). *Phonology and Syntax: The Relation between Sound and Structure*. Cambridge, Mass.: The MIT Press.

——. (1995). "Sentence Prosody: Intonation, Stress and Phrasing." In *Handbook of Phonological Theory*, edited by J. A. Goldsmith, 550–569. Cambridge, Mass. – Oxford, UK: Basil Blackwell.

Seuren, P. A. M. (1967). "Negation in Dutch." *Neophilologus* 51: 327–363.

——. P. A. M. (1969). *Operators and nucleus*. Cambridge, UK: Cambridge University Press.

Sgall, P. (1964). "Zur Frage der Ebenen in Sprachsystem," In *Travaux linguistique de Prague* 1: 95–106.

——. (1964b/1966a). "Generative Bschreibung und die Ebenen des Sprachsystems." Presented at the Second International Symposium in Magdeburg, 1964; printed in 1966 as *Zeichen und System der Sprache* III, 225–239, Berlin. Reprinted in Sgall (2006), 164–181.

——. (1966a). "Ein mehrstufiges generative System." *Kybernetika* 2: 181–190.

——. (1966b). "Postavení sémantiky v generativním popisu jazyka [The status of semantics in a generative descriptiopn of language]." *Kybernetika* 2: 457–467.

——. (1967a). *Generativní popis jazyka a česká deklinace* [Generative description of language and Czech declension]. Prague: Academia; in 1966 as an English summary. *PBML* 6: 3–18; printed also in W. Klein, and A. v. Stechow (eds.) 1973, 394–408.

——. (1967/1967b). "Functional Sentence Perspective in a Generative Description of Language." *Prague Studies in Mathematical Linguistics* 2: 203–225. Reprinted (shortened) in P. Sgall 2006, 275–301.

——. (1968). "On Generation, Production and translation." Presented at 1965 New York International Conference on Computational Linguistics; published in *The Prague Bulletin of Mathematical Linguistics* 8: 3–13; reprinted in A. Klein, and v. A. Stechow (eds.) 1973, 53–64.

——. (1969). "L'ordre des mots et la sémantique." In F. Kiefer (ed.) 1969, 231–240.

——. (1970). *Zur Stellung der Thema-Rhema-Gliederung in der Sprachbeschreibung*. Presented at the Symposium on Functional Sentence Perspective, Mariánské Lázně; printed in F. Daneš (ed.) 1974, 54–74.

——. (1972a). "'Cases' in a Stratificational Description." *Prague Studies in Mathematical Linguistics* 3: 201–211.

——. (1972b). "Fillmore's Mysteries and Topic vs. Comment." *Journal of Linguistics* 8: 283–288.

Sgall, P. (1972c). "Topic, Focus, and the Ordering of Elements of Semantic Representations." *Philologica Pragensia* 15: 1–14.

——. (1973). "Kontextové zapojení a otázková metoda [Contextual boundness and the question test]." *Slovo a slovesnost* 34: 202–211.

——. (1979). "Towards a Definition of Focus and Topic." *The Prague Bulletin of Mathematical Linguistics* 31: 3–25; 32: 24–32; reprinted in *Prague Studies in Mathematical Linguistics* 7 (1981); 173–198.

——. (1980a/in press), "Case and Meaning." *Journal of Pragmatics* 4: 525–536.

——. (1980b). "A Dependency Based Specification of Topic and Focus II: Formal Account." *SMIL (Journal of Linguistic Calculus)*, 110–140.

——. (ed.) (1984). *Contributions to Functional Syntax, Semantics and Language Comprehension*. Amsterdam: Benjamins; Prague: Academia.

——. (1992). "Underlying Structure of Sentences and Its Relations to Semantics." *Wiener Slawistischer Almanach. Sonderband 33*, edited by T. Reuther, 273–82. Wien: Gesellschaft zur Förderung slawistischer Studien.

——. (1997a). "Valency and Underlying Structure. An Alternative View on Dependency." In *Recent Trends in Meaning-Text Theory*, edited by L. Wanner, 149–166. Amsterdam – Philadelphia: Benjamins.

——. (1997b). "On the Usefulness of Movement Rules." In *Actes du 16e Congrès International des Linguistes* (Paris 20–25 juillet 1997), edited by B. Caron. Oxford: Elsevier Sciences.

——. (2002). "The Freedom of Language: Its nature, its sources and its consequences." In: *Prague Linguistic Circle Papers* 4: 309–329. Amsterdam – Philadelphia: John Benjamins. Reprinted in Sgall 2006, 44–66.

——. (2006). *Language in Its Multifarious Aspects*, edited by E. Hajičová, and J. Panevová. Prague: Karolinum.

——. (2009). "Where to Look for the Fundamentals of Language." *Linguistica Pragensia* 19: 1–35.

Sgall, P., and E. Hajičová (1970). "A 'Functional' Generative Description." *The Prague Bulletin of Mathematical Linguistics* 14: 3–38; also in (1971) *Revue roumaine de linguistique* 16: 9–37.

——. (1971). "A Remark on Chomsky's Focus." *The Prague Bulletin of Mathematical Linguistics* 16: 3–12.

——. (1977). "Focus on Focus, Part I," *The Prague Bulletin of Mathematical Linguistics* 28: 5–54; (1978) Part II, *The Prague Bulletin of Mathematical Linguistics* 29: 23–41.

——. (1987). "The Ordering Principle." *Journal of Pragmatics* 11: 435–454.

Sgall P., E. Hajičová, and E. Benešová (in prep./1973). *Topic, Focus and Generative Semantics*. Kronberg - Taunus: Scriptor.

Sgall P., E. Hajičová, and E. Buráňová (in press/1980). *Aktuální členění věty v češtině* [Topic-focus articulation of the sentence in Czech]. Prague: Academia.

Sgall P., E. Hajičová, and J. Panevová (1986). *The Meaning of the Sentence in its Semantic and Pragmatic Aspects*. In J. L. Mey (ed). Dordrecht: Reidel; Prague:Academia.

Sgall P., E. Hajičová, and O. Procházka (1977). "On the Role of Linguistic Semantics." *Theoretical Linguistics* 4: 31–59.

Sgall, P., L. Nebeský, A. Goralčíková, A., and E. Hajičová (1969). *A Functional Approach to Syntax in Generative Description of Language*. New York: American Elsevier Publishing House.

Sgall, P., O. Pfeiffer, W. U. Dressler, and M. Půček (1995). "Experimental Research on Systemic Ordering." *Theoretical Linguistics* 21: 197–239.

Sidner, C. (1979). *Towards a Computational Theory of Definite Anaphora Comprehension in English Discourse*, PhD. Thesis, Cambridge, Mass.: MIT.

Skalička, V. (1950). "Poznámky k theorii pádů [Remarks on the theory of case]." *Slovo a slovesnost* 12: 134–152.

——. (1962). "Das Wesen der Morphologie und der Syntax." *AUC-Philologica 3, Slavia Pragensia* 4, 123–127.

Stalnaker, R. C. (1974). "Pragmatic presuppositions." In *Semantics and Philosophy*, edited by M. Munits, and P. Unger, 197–214. New York: New York University Press.

Stechow, von A. (1980). "Notes on Topic and Focus of Interrogatives and Indicatives." *Sonderforschungsbereich 99 Linguistik*, University of Konstanz.

Steedman, M. (1985). Dependency and Coordination in the Grammar of Dutch and English, *Language* 61: 523–568.

Steedman, M. (1991). "Structure and Intonation." *Language,* 67: 260–296.

——. (1996). *Surface Structure and Interpretation.* Cambridge, MA. – London: The MIT Press.

——. (2000). "Information Structure and the Syntax-Phonology Interface." *Linguistic Inquiry* 31: 649–689.

Steinberg, D. D., and L. A. Jakobovits (ed.) (1971). *Semantics – An interdisciplinary Reader.* Cambridge, Mass.: Cambridge University Press.

Strawson, P. (1952). *Introduction to Logical Theory,* London: Methuen.

——. (1964). "Identifying Reference and Truth Values." *Theoria* 30: 96–118. Reprinted (1971) D. D. Steinberg, and L. A. Jakobovits (eds.) 1971, 86–99.

Svoboda, A. (1968). "The Hierarchy of Communicative Units and Fields as Illustrated by English Attributive Constructions." *Brno Studies in English* 7: 49–101.

——. (1981). *Diatheme.* Brno: Masarykova univerzita.

——. (2007). *Brněnská škola funkční větné perspektivy v pojmech a příkladech* [Brno School of Functional Sentence Perspective in notions and examples]. Ostrava: Ostravská univerzita.

Šmilauer, V. (1947/1966). *Novočeská skladba* [Syntax of present-day Czech]. Prague 1947. 3rd ed. 1966.

Taglicht, J. (1984). *Message and Emphasis. On Focus and Scope in English.* London: Longman.

Tesnière, L. (1959). *Élements de syntaxe structurale,* Paris: Klinksieck.

Tichý, P. (1978). "Questions, Answers, and Logic." *American Philosophical Quarterly* 15: 27–284.

Tyl, R. (ed.) (1970). *Materiály k bibliografii prací o aktuálním členění 1900–1970.* Prague

Uhlenbeck, E. M. (1980). "Observation in semantics is not easy." In *Linguistic studies offered to Berthe Siertsema,* edited by D. J. van Alkemade, 127–135. Amsterdam: Rodopi.

Uhlířová, L. (1974). "On the Role of Statistics in the Investigation of FSP." In F. Daneš (ed.) 1974, 208–216.

——. (1987). *Knížka o slovosledu* [A book on word order]. Prague: Academia.

Uličný, O. (1973). *K pádovému systému v češtině* [On the case system of Czech]. *Slavia* 52: 347–361.

Vachek, J. (1939). "Porušování záporové shody v českých záporných větách obecné platnosti [Violation of negation concordance in negative sentences of universal validity]." *Časopis pro moderní filologii* 26: 47–52.

——. (1947). "Obecný zápor v angličtině a češtině. Příspěvky k dějinám řeči a literatury anglické [Universal negation in English and Czech. Contributions to the history of English language and literature]." *Prague Studies in English* 6: 7–72.

——. (1955). "Some Thoughts of the So-called Complex Condensation in Modern English." *Sborník prací filosofické fakulty Brněnské univerzity* 4 (A3): 63–77.

——. (1961). "Some Less Familiar Aspects of the Analytical Trends of English." *Brno Studies in English* 3: 9–74.

Vallduví, E. (1992). *The informational component.* New York: Garland.

Wegener, P. (1885). *Untersuchungen über die Grundfragen des Sprachlebens.* Halle: M. Niemeyer.

Weil, H. (1844). *De l'order des mots dans les langues anciennes comparées aux languages moderns.* Paris. Translated as *The Order of Words in the Ancient Languages Compared with That of the Modern Languages.* (1887) Boston: Ginn; re-edited (1978) Amsterdam: John Benjamins.

Verschueren, J. (1978). "Reflections on Presupposition Failure: A Contribution to an Integrated Theory of Pragmatics." *Journal of Pragmatics* 2: 107–152.

Veselá, K., N. Peterek, and E. Hajičová (2003). "Topic-Focus Articulation in PDT: Prosodic Characteristics of Contrastive Topic." *The Prague Bulletin of Mathematical Linguistics* 79–80: 5–22.

Wilson, D. (1975). *Presuppositions and non-truth-conditional semantics.* New York: Academic Press.

Wilson, D., and D. Sperber (1979). Ordered Entailments: an Alternative to Presuppositional Theories. In C. K. Oh, and D. A. Dinneen (eds.) 1979, 299–323

Zemb, J.-M. (1968). *Les structures logiques de la proposition allemande.* Paris: O.C.D.L.

Zikánová, Š. (2006). "What do the Data in PDT Say about Systemic Ordering in Czech?" *The Prague Bulletin of Mathematical Linguistics* 86: 39–46.

Zikánová, Š., and M. Týnovský (2009). "Identification of Topic and Focus in Czech: Comparative Evaluation on Prague Dependency Treebank." In *Studies in Formal Slavic Phonology, Morphology, Syntax,*

Semantics and Information Structure. Formal Description of Slavic Languages 7. Frankfurt am Main: Peter Lang, 343–353.

Zikánová, Š., M. Týnovský, and J. Havelka (2007). "Identification of Topic and Focus in Czech: Evaluation of Manual Parallel Annotations." In *The Prague Bulletin of Mathematical Linguistics* 87: 61–70.

Zimmermann, I. (1967). *Die Funktionen der Nominalphrasen im Satz.* Mimeo; presented at the Conference on transformational description, Berlin.

Zoeppritz, M. (1971). "On the Requirement that Agentives be Animate." *Beiträge zur Linguistik and Informationsverarbeitung* 21: 65–67

Zoeppritz, M. (1972). *Konkurierende Kasus.* Mimeo.

Žabokrtský, Z. (2005). "Resemblances between Meaning-Text Theory and Functional Generative Description." In *Proceedings of the 2nd International Conference of Meaning-Text Theory,* edited by J. D.